Happy Anniversary Darling
For 1993 and many more
Yours x Valerie

TRAIL OF THE OCTOPUS

TRAIL of the OCTOPUS

From Beirut to Lockerbie – Inside the DIA

Donald Goddard with Lester K Coleman

BLOOMSBURY

First published in Great Britain 1993
Bloomsbury Publishing Limited, 2 Soho Square, London W1V 5DE

Copyright © 1993 by Donald Goddard and Lester Coleman

The moral right of the authors has been asserted

A CIP catalogue record for this book
is available from the British Library

ISBN 0 7475 1562 X

Typeset by Hewer Text Composition Services, Edinburgh
Printed by Clays Limited, St Ives plc

To Natalie

—— Foreword ——

Spies are not encouraged to keep diaries, send memos or make carbon copies of reports. If they attract suspicion, 'deniability' is their only hope.

But if a spy is cut off by his own country, deniability works like a hangman's noose. With no written record to call on and no access to official files, he must rely for the most part on memory to defend himself, so that, in the end, it usually comes down to his word against his government's.

This can give rise to questions of credibility – a troublesome factor in intelligence work at the best of times. At the worst of times, it can kill. With most people disposed to give those in authority the benefit of the doubt, why should anybody believe him? If spies are trained to lie, deceive and dissemble, they may argue, how can we accept what he says without proof?

No one in modern times has suffered more from this presumption of guilt than Lester Knox Coleman III, until recently a secret agent of the United States' Defense Intelligence Agency.

His crime was to find himself in possession of information of such acute embarrassment to the American government and, to a lesser extent, the governments of Britain and Germany, that officials in Washington were unwilling to rely solely on his discretion. Though he had given them no cause to question his loyalty, the stakes were so high they felt they needed insurance, and so sought to muzzle him by means of a trumped-up criminal charge, to be suspended in exchange for his silence. This procedure had always worked well in similar cases, particularly when combined with other forms of intimidation, like death threats against the agent and his family.

But when Coleman failed to cave in as expected and instead escaped to Sweden with his wife and children, he presented his government with an awkward problem. No longer in a position to enforce his silence, and unwilling to risk a public extradition hearing in a neutral court, Washington decided instead to try to defuse the explosive potential of what he knew by destroying his character and reputation. If it could not stop him talking, it could at least try to stop people believing what he said.

In this, it was more successful, although the irony is that, if the American government had trusted its own security vetting system in the first place, the problem would probably not have arisen. Coleman would have revealed nothing of what he knew; this book would not have been written, and America would have avoided the embarrassment that is now inescapable. By misjudging its own man, Washington brought about the very situation it was most anxious to avoid.

After more than two years on the run from America's state security apparatus, the 'octopus', Coleman believes that the lives and safety of his young family now depend on 'going public', on telling his story to the only jury left that can save him.

I hope he is right.

This is the first time that a fully-fledged Western intelligence agent has come in from the field and publicly debriefed himself, right down to the nuts and bolts of his various missions. That would be interesting enough in itself, but in Coleman's case, his testimony is also sharply at variance with the official version of events leading up to the Lockerbie disaster, with official accounts of Anglo-American attempts to secure the release of Western hostages in Beirut, with the official line on Lt-Colonel Oliver North and Irangate, and, in general, with the official gloss on Western policy in the Middle East since 1985.

As this is a personal story, Coleman is naturally the primary source for it. Such documents as he does possess, and others that have come to light, not only support *his* version of events, but also reflect a paranoid determination on Washington's part to destroy him that may, in itself, be a measure of his truthfulness. Certainly no one, in or out of government, has cared to attack the substance of what he has had to say, other than with flat denials; nor have I, or has anyone else, so far identified in his story more than a few minor discrepancies of the kind that must inevitably occur in anybody's mostly unaided recollection of a complicated life, and whose absence would tend to undermine its credibility rather than reinforce it.

In any disputed account of events, the test is always, who benefits?

In this case, not Lester Coleman. Sticking to his story has made him a penniless fugitive whose life probably depends on establishing the truth.

Corroboration there has been in plenty. Besides the sources identified in the text, I should also like to thank those many others, mostly in law enforcement and government service on both sides of the Atlantic, who would not thank *me* if I broke my promise of anonymity. These are difficult times for bureaucrats still attached to the idea of accountable government.

I am also obliged to Pan Am's attorneys for *declining* to help me with my researches, thereby – I hope – denying room to those government supporters who might otherwise wish to accuse me, as they did *Time* magazine, of conspiring with the airline to pervert the course of justice.

More positively, in the matter of research, I am indebted to Katarina Shelley for her diligence and enterprise; to Carol, for making the book possible anyway, and, for his unshakable faith in the enterprise, to Mark Lucas, of Peters, Fraser & Dunlop, who had to work harder than either of us had bargained for to bring Lester Coleman in from the cold.

D.G.
August 1993

— I —

All governments lie, some more than others. To protect themselves or 'the national interest', American governments lie more than most.

The story of Washington's blackest lie in modern times began, typically, with a bureaucratic blunder. In the spring of 1988, Special Agent Micheal T. Hurley, the Drug Enforcement Administration's attaché to the American Embassy in Cyprus, was given a clear warning by an American intelligence agent that security had been breached in a 'sting' operation the DEA had mounted against Lebanese drug traffickers running heroin into the United States via Nicosia, Frankfurt and London.

Seven months later, on 21 December 1988, a bomb exploded in the cargo hold of Pan Am Flight 103 from Frankfurt to New York, killing all 259 passengers and crew. Eleven more people died on the ground as the wreckage of the Boeing 747 jumbo jet, Maid of the Seas, rained down on the Scottish border town of Lockerbie.

Among the victims were at least (two possibly five or more) American intelligence agents, who had disregarded standing orders by choosing to fly home from Beirut on an American-flag airline, and a DEA Lebanese-American courier who had previously carried out at least three controlled deliveries of heroin to Detroit as part of the 'sting'.

Those involved in this operation, along with those who had authorized, condoned or used it for other purposes, recognized at once that their neglect of the warning in May had cost 270 lives, that terrorists had slipped through the reported breach in security and converted a controlled delivery of heroin into the controlled delivery of a bomb – probably in revenge for the 290 lives lost in July when the US cruiser *Vincennes* had shot down an Iranian Airbus 'by mistake'.

The US government would lie about that catastrophic blunder, too, but the more immediate problem was the Lockerbie disaster. Like a woodlouse sensing danger, the Drug Enforcement Adminstration (DEA) rolled up in an armour-plated ball to protect its bureaucratic arse.

This worked, more or less, for two years, but the problem refused to go away. When the DEA's obduracy began to attract as many embarrassing questions as it deflected, the agency started to lie, with the grudging connivance of the intelligence community and the ungrudging assistance of the Bush administration.

It lied to the media and the public, of course, but it also lied to Congress. And the more it lied, the harder it got to keep the story straight.

For one thing, there was the problem of the intelligence agent who had warned Hurley about the 'disaster waiting to happen' months *before* the downing of Flight 103. Like most of his colleagues in the Defense Intelligence Agency (DIA), Lester Knox Coleman III had found little to admire in the work of the DEA overseas.

And for another thing, there was the problem of Pan Am and its insurers, who had commissioned their own investigation into the disaster. The more they picked up about the DEA connection, the less they felt inclined to pick up what was beginning to look like a $7-billion tab.

For those watching the situation from Washington, a recurring nightmare was that these two problems might come together like match and tinder; that Coleman would meet up with Pan Am's attorneys and tell them what he knew. Because if that happened, they might between them start a fire that would blacken the reputation, not just of the DEA, but of the United States itself. If the truth came out, it would not only undermine America's role as moral and political exemplar to the world, but inflict intolerable damage on its policy objectives in the Middle East.

The risk was simply not acceptable. The 'national interest' now required the DEA sting never to have happened, and Lester Knox Coleman III not to exist – at least as a credible witness.

It was a job for what Coleman had come to think of as 'the octopus' – America's state security apparatus.

Nothing feels right at four in the morning.

He frowned at the ceiling, trying to recall what had woken him. Careful not to disturb Mary-Claude, he slipped out of bed to look at the babies.

They were sound asleep – the seven-month-old twins, Joshua and Chad, sprawled in their crib like abandoned dolls, so quiet he bent over them suddenly to make sure they were breathing, and Sarah, curled up like a tiny blonde edition of her mother. He watched until she stirred and sighed, threatening to wake, and tiptoed away.

Still restless, he pulled on a T-shirt and shorts and went downstairs to the refrigerator. It was probably nothing – just the usual uneasiness in the final days before a mission. And worse this time, for he had been out of it for two years, since May 1988, when Control had called him home after Tony Asmar's murder in Beirut and the row with Hurley.

After a two-year lay-off, the adrenalin had naturally started to surge again at the prospect of re-entering the bloody arena of Lebanese politics, particularly as Operation Shakespeare was probably the most sensitive assignment the DIA had yet given him. Also, he was still not comfortable with the idea of using his alias on the first leg of the journey.

He had never done that before. It was a sensible precaution if the intention was not to alert the Israelis or if the general sloppiness of the DEA in Cyprus *had* set him up as a target, like Asmar, but it still bothered him. It was one thing to return to the Middle East as Lester Coleman, award-winning TV and radio newsman, and quite another to arrive without antecedents or connections as Thomas Leavy, American businessman.

And anyway, why couldn't Control just have *given* him a passport in the name of Thomas Leavy instead of getting him to apply for a real one, using his phony papers? The agency had always been good with documents.

Needing air, he opened the casement doors to the balcony. Except for a vulgar canopy of stars and the faint fuzz of phosphorescence along the beach where the waters of the Gulf lapped ashore, the night was velvet black, and so still his ears sang in the silence.

He loved this place, out of season. While waiting for a lull in the fighting in Beirut, he had decided to take the family away on holiday, renting the last in a row of beach-house condominiums at the edge of Fort Morgan National Seashore Park, a beautiful stretch of the Alabama coast, near the Florida state line. As it was only 2 May, there was no one else around, apart from a nice enough young fellow just down the street, holidaying there on his own.

He had wondered about that, too.

Disinclined to go back to bed, Coleman stretched out on the couch and reached for the file he had put together on General Michel Aoun, the Maronite Christian commander of the Lebanese Army and the country's acting President. Having persuaded Aoun to receive him and Peter Arnett in the shell-shattered ruins of the presidential palace at Baabda, he needed to be on top of every nuance in Lebanon's murderous factionalism if he was to stay on afterwards and begin to explore Aoun's constituency in the maelstrom of Beirut, the support he was getting from the Israelis, and in particular, his military alliance with Saddam Hussein against the Syrian army of occupation. Control had received reports that the Iraqi forces were getting ready to pull out, and wanted to know why.

He woke again, with a start, around seven. Somebody was hammering on the front door. It was light now, and he went through to the kitchen, which overlooked the street, to see who it was. As he looked out, a young man in a blue FBI windbreaker glanced up from below, hand on holster, and tried to hide behind a telephone pole.

Coleman pulled back from the sliding glass door, and tried to think. What now? What possible reason could there be for an early-morning visit from the FBI? Some inter-agency training gimmick to pep him up after a two-year lay-off? Some far-out psychological game, maybe to test the solidity of his cover story before the mission got started?

The hammering began again, and that made him angry. If they kept this up, they would wake the children. Whatever was going on, Control had no right to bother his family. Ignoring the commotion, he went upstairs and gently shook Mary-Claude awake. Brought up in East Beirut during the civil war, she had learned to sleep through almost anything, even artillery bombardments.

'Oh, God,' she groaned, shaking him off. 'What's the matter?'

'I don't know,' he said. 'There's somebody downstairs trying to get in.'

It was a moment before this registered. 'Oh, my God.' She sat up, wide-eyed with alarm. 'Have you called the police?'

'No, no.' He shook his head. 'I don't know what they want, but I think it's the FBI.'

'The *FBI*?' She was bewildered. He had never told her he worked for the American government, and like a good Lebanese wife she had never questioned him, but she had always known he was a spy. 'Why are they here? Have you done something wrong?'

Before he could think of anything reassuring to say, the hammering at the door began again.

— 4 —

'Oh, my God.'

'No, don't worry,' he said. 'It's a mistake. They probably came to the wrong house. I'll take care of it.'

'We have to open up, right? I mean, maybe they'll go away.'

'No.' He pulled himself together. 'Get dressed. See to the children. I'll go find out what this is all about.'

He returned to the kitchen, dragged open the sliding glass door and stepped out on the balcony. The agent he had seen before was no longer hiding behind the pole, but before Coleman could challenge him, a woman in an FBI windbreaker emerged from the car port under the house and looked up at him, also hand on holster.

'Are you Lester Knox Coleman?' she asked.

'Yes.'

'This is the FBI. We have a warrant for your arrest.'

'Oh, really?' He took a deep breath to steady himself. 'Is this a joke? What for?'

'If you'll open the door, Mr Coleman,' she said, 'we'll be glad to talk to you about it. Do you mind opening the door?'

'No, no,' he said. 'I'll be happy to open the door. Just wait a minute.'

He went inside again, fumbled with the locks and stood back, bracing himself as a third agent, older than the other two, flung open the door and grabbed him. Offering no resistance, Coleman allowed himself to be spun around, jammed up against the wall and patted down. His arms were then pulled out behind him and handcuffed together.

'You're under arrest,' announced the agent.

'Yes,' he said. 'So I see. Now would somebody mind telling me why?'

Joined at this point by his colleagues, the agent turned him around to face them.

'I'm Special Agent Lesley Behrens,' the woman said. 'I have a warrant here, issued in Chicago. You're charged with making a false statement on a passport application.'

He frowned, trying to cope with a sudden inkling of what the onset of madness might be like.

Thinking about it afterwards, in a filthy cell in Mobile City Jail, he could recall very little of what passed between them after that. They seated him on a stool at the bar. They asked him routine questions, to which he presumably responded with routine answers, but nothing registered.

Unable to withstand more than a split-second glimpse of such fathomless duplicity, all he seemed able to do was shake his head. The sudden collapse of every certainty in life was too much to grasp all at once. Each time he braced himself to consider his position, his mind simply tripped its overload switch.

It got going again when Mary-Claude appeared on the stairs with Sarah, who had started to cry. Trapped by her Lebanese upbringing between loyalty to the family and respect for authority, his wife smiled down on them uncertainly.

'Hi,' she said.

Then she saw the handcuffs, and all softness of manner disappeared.

'What is *this*?' she demanded, looking about her as though for a weapon. 'What's the problem here? What are you doing to my husband?'

'No problem,' he said easily, knowing how headstrong she could be. 'It's a mistake, that's all. Somebody's made a mistake.'

'*Mistake?*' She advanced down the stairs, Sarah clutching her hand and now crying in earnest. 'Why are you treating him like this? This is my journalist husband that I'm so proud of. What has he done?'

Mary-Claude's English – her third language, after Arabic and French – sometimes fractured under stress, but her outrage was plain enough. They all began to talk at once, except for the older agent, who gave Sarah a smile, trying to coax one from her in return.

Still passionately demanding an explanation from Special Agent Behrens, Mary-Claude suddenly noticed that in her hurry to get dressed she had left the front of her shorts undone, and stopped in mid-flight.

'I'm sorry,' she muttered, turning away to zip them up.

Her sudden embarrassment gave Agent Behrens a chance to resume command. She ordered Mary-Claude to go back to the bedroom to look for her husband's papers – all she could find – and bring them downstairs.

Mary-Claude hesitated, unable to catch Coleman's eye as Behrens was standing between them, then did as she was told, rather than risk making matters worse for him out of mere stubbornness.

He watched her go. Though still in free fall, he had already begun to doubt that Control had played any part in this. After months of painstaking preparation for a mission of obvious importance, that made no sense at all. Therefore, it had to be the DIA. No other agency, apart from his own, even *knew* of his other identity. Except the CIA, of course, which had always worked in lockstep with the DEA in Cyprus and had actually supplied him with his Thomas Leavy birth certificate in the first place.

'Oh, my God,' he said, losing his way again.

It was no use talking to Behrens and her partners. They obviously knew nothing, and he could certainly tell them nothing. It was up to Control to straighten this out. Somebody at Arlington Hall or the Pentagon had to pick up the phone and have a quiet word with the director of the FBI and that would be the end of it. Although there wasn't much time. He was due to leave in two days. If they tangled him up with all the formalities of arrest and arraignment and insisted on shipping him back to Chicago, they could blow the whole operation.

'Look,' he said, in case there was just an outside chance he could fix this himself. 'Maybe there's something I can help you with here. I mean, I can't tell you much except that something is seriously wrong and somebody is going to get into a helluva lot of trouble, but I think you might be interested in that stuff.'

He nodded toward the videotape cassette on the table, next to his file on Aoun, his passport and his wallet containing the Thomas Leavy birth certificate. He had spliced the tape together as a record of his tour of duty on secondment to the DEA in Cyprus. There was some interesting footage on Lebanese dope trafficking, some narcotic reports he had compiled, media clips on the subject, and, at the end, an audio recording of his last telephone conversation with Hurley before coming home, a conversation that not only warned him about 'the disaster waiting to happen', but clearly indicated that he worked for another government agency.

'Why don't we take that along with us?' he suggested.

'We'll take anything you want to give us,' said Behrens.

And that was interesting, too. He was getting a better grip on this now. So far, they had made no attempt to search the house, although with an arrest warrant they were legally entitled to do so, and no one had escorted Mary-Claude upstairs to make sure she didn't dispose of incriminating evidence. So what kind of charade was this anyway? They hadn't even read him his rights. Was it a DIA game after all? To see if he'd crack under pressure?

Mary-Claude reappeared on the stairs.

'I'm sorry,' she said defiantly. 'I can't find his papers. I can't find *anything*.'

He smiled at her, and nodded his approval.

'Are you *sure*?' asked Agent Behrens coldly. She advanced to the foot of the stairs. 'They're not down here. There must be something. What about his pockets? Have you looked in his pockets?'

Mary-Claude retreated a pace, afraid they would come up and search the bedroom themselves. 'All right,' she said. The twins were awake now, and screaming for attention. 'All right, I'll look again.'

'Okay.' Behrens turned back to the others. 'Take him out to the car,' she said. 'I'll be with you in a minute.'

Coleman offered no resistance as they took him by the arms. Whatever this was – a training set-up, a DEA set-up or a bureaucratic foul-up – the game had to be played to a finish. If the operation was cancelled or delayed, it wouldn't be *his* fault.

'I'll be back shortly, Mary-Claude,' he called out after her. 'Don't worry. Call the lawyer. Call Boohaker. He'll know what to do.'

Mary-Claude closed the bedroom door behind her and tried to pacify the twins, but they were hungry and cried all the harder.

'Why am I so nervous?' she asked them, getting mad. 'I am a citizen. I have my rights. This is *my* house. I don't have to give her *anything*. I must calm down and go tell her to get the hell out of here. Then I'll come back and get your bottles ready.'

She marched downstairs, pointedly ignoring Special Agent Behrens, and picked up the phone.

'Who are you calling?' Behrens asked.

'I'm not going to give you anything,' said Mary-Claude. 'And I'm not going to answer any of your questions. I'm calling my lawyer. I don't know what's right, what's wrong, and I want my lawyer's suggestion.'

'Okay.' Behrens considered her for a moment. 'Okay, don't bother. I'm going now.'

As the door closed behind her, Mary-Claude put down the phone. She could not think straight, what with the shock, the twins bawling for food and Sarah pulling at her shorts, asking 'Where did Poppy go?' In an unfamiliar house, in a country she hardly knew, thousands of miles from her family, with her husband suddenly taken away, and three babies to care for, she had never felt more lonely and frightened in her life.

She was so rattled she used the wrong measuring cup for the twins' formula and had to mix it all over again. Then, after each had finished his bottle, she paced up and down, waiting for them to settle before she called Boohaker, who was shocked to hear what had happened.

He promised to do the best he could and to call her back when he had some news.

Rather than sit around watching the telephone, she got the children dressed and put them in the car, with the idea of going to the market to buy a few things they needed. She was about to drive off when, as an afterthought, she went back into the house for Coleman's papers, in case the FBI decided to break in and get them while she was away.

By the time Mary-Claude returned from the market, about an hour later, the idea of keeping his papers from prying eyes had become an obsession. If the FBI was so eager to have them, it could only mean they would do her husband harm if the agents got hold of them. She put her now sleepy children to bed and, except for Coleman's clothes, carried everything of his she could find into the bathroom.

With no way of knowing what was harmful and what was not, she tore all his papers into shreds, including his Federal Communications Commission (FCC) broadcast engineer's licence, and chopped his ID cards into pieces, hurting her hand with the scissors. Not sure what to do next, she then made a heap of everything in the bathtub and set light to it.

Watching the smoke rise, she felt that even the war in Lebanon had been easier to live through than this. In a war, you knew that anything could happen at any time, but you also knew there was nothing you could do about it. Now, for all she knew, her husband's fate might rest with her. She wrung her hands and was still trying to decide if there was anything else she ought to do when the smoke set off the fire alarm.

'Oh, my God, what is *this*?'

She rocked back and forth in despair until she realized what she had done. Jumping up to shut off the alarm before its noise woke the children, she turned on the shower to put out the flames, and in a tearful fury flung the sodden remains into the toilet and flushed them away. Only then did she notice the marks that the fire had left in the bathtub. As she scrubbed away at them hopelessly, that seemed like the saddest thing of all somehow.

Meanwhile, Coleman was still grappling with bewilderment in the back of the car. Within days of leaving on a mission of national importance, an operation that might well affect the whole course of US strategy in the Middle East, he was riding into Mobile between two FBI agents to answer a trumped-up passport charge? It was crazy.

'You want to share the joke with us?' Behrens asked.

'No, I don't think so. It's only funny if you know the whole story.'

'Then why don't you tell us about it? You got a passport already. Why in the world would you want another one? In another name?'

'Hell, I don't know. I'm a journalist, right? Maybe I was researching a story about how easy it is to get false identification.'

'Well, now you know it's *not* that easy,' she said. 'If that's true, you should have got authorization first.'

'Yeah. And you should have read me my rights first.'

The older agent sighed. 'Okay,' he said tiredly. 'Read him his rights.'

'Fine, but why don't we all get more comfortable?'

Coleman handed them the handcuffs. For an amateur magician of his calibre, it was a simple enough escape trick. You just had to flex your wrists in a certain way as they were fastened on.

The government was not amused. Its agents put the handcuffs back on. Tighter.

'Oh, come *on*,' said Coleman. 'You know this is bullshit. What's it all about?'

— II —

The agents couldn't tell him because they didn't know but it was about the terrorist attack that destroyed Pan Am Flight 103 over Lockerbie.

Given a limited capacity for moral outrage and a steady diet of sanitized brutality in the media, people can show an alarming tolerance for atrocities that do not affect them directly. More die every day from 'ethnic cleansing' in the Balkans or from genocide in Iraq or starvation in the Horn of Africa than the 270 who died on 21 December 1988, when Flight 103 went down, but there was something so utterly desolating about that particular mass murder that almost everyone in the Western world felt they *were* affected. Just as the whole Muslim world had felt affected earlier in July when 290 pilgrims on an Iranian Airbus died in the twinkling of a SAM from the USS *Vincennes*.

Perhaps it was because the victims were so completely unprepared. It was just before Christmas – a season, if not always of goodwill, then at least of less *ill* will. A sentimental time, with people more open, more vulnerable. Traditionally, a time for families to reunite and celebrate their children and remind themselves of what life is all about – not for families to be savagely torn apart and the bodies of their children strewn across the ground.

The young people who boarded Flight 103 were in high spirits. Thirty-five of them were students of Syracuse University, looking forward to getting home for Christmas, and the mood was infectious. Even before Captain James MacQuarrie lifted the 747 off from Heathrow's runway 27L at 18.25 hours, they had a party going. The holidays had begun.

Half an hour into the flight, just north of Manchester, the Maid of the Seas levelled off at 31,000 feet, preparing to swing out over the Atlantic on the long great circle route across the ocean. Drinks were being served. Passengers moved about in the cabin, although when seated they had been advised to keep their seatbelts on because of some light turbulence. Mothers settled their babies. People eased off their shoes, making themselves more comfortable. When would dinner be served? What was the movie? Warm and enclosed against the night, no one could have known their last minutes were draining away. No one was ready.

The bomb went off in the cargo hold a few seconds before 19.03.

Everybody would have heard it. Though only a small bomb, it punched a hole in the fuselage and put out the lights. Then they would have known – just a fraction before the shock waves, the explosive decompression and an airspeed of 500 miles per hour wrenched the aircraft to pieces.

All alone in the dark, as a shrieking, roaring wind stripped the cabin bare, then they would have known, those who were still alive. Whirled out into the frozen void, lungs bursting, then they would have known.

Six miles up and falling through space, the actual stuff of nightmare, then they would have known, those still aware. It would be two to three minutes yet before the earth received them . . .

It was a terrible way to die.

The victims on the ground were even less prepared. Far below in Lockerbie, the streets were quiet, spangled with coloured lights from Christmas trees in front-room windows. Families were sitting down to an evening meal or watching television, relaxing after the day . . .

Scything out of the night sky, the wings of the aircraft, loaded with a hundred tons of fuel, exploded on impact at the end of Sherwood Crescent, cremating 11 people in an awesome orange fireball that rose slowly to a thousand feet.

Death had never been more arbitrary, nor any crime more wicked.

The truth about Flight 103 will probably never be known in all its particulars. Too many people have tampered with the evidence. Too many people have lied about it or stayed silent. Too much remains hidden behind the cloak of national security and legal privilege. Even the facts that are *not* in dispute have been used to support theories at total variance from one another, according to the degree of culpability to be concealed or the political requirements of the governments concerned.

But if the whole truth is never likely to be known, enough of it has emerged from the fog of lies and evasion to point a finger at those responsible. And there may still be other witnesses who, like Lester Coleman at the time of his arrest, have yet to realize that they hold a piece of the evidence, pinning the guilt down more precisely.

It is now widely accepted that the sequence of events leading to the Lockerbie disaster began on 3 July 1988, in the Persian Gulf. While sailing in Iranian territorial waters, the US Aegis-class cruiser *Vincennes* somehow mistook a commercial Iranian Airbus that had just taken off from Bandar Abbas airport for an Iranian F14 fighter closing in to attack and shot it down, killing all 290 passengers on board, most of them pilgrims on their way to Mecca.

Predictably, the United States government not only sought to excuse this blunder but lied to Congress about it, lied in its official investigation of the incident, and handed out a Commendation Medal to the ship's air-warfare coordinator for his 'heroic achievement'. (Although he earned nothing but notoriety for the kill, the cruiser's commander, Capt. Will Rogers III, still insists that the *Vincennes* was in international waters at the time, and that he made the proper decision. After being beached in San Diego for a decent interval, he was allowed to retire honourably in August 1991.)

The Iranians were incensed. Paying the US Navy the compliment of believing that it *knew* what it was doing, they chose to construe America's evasive response to their complaint before the UN Security Council as a cover-up for a deliberate act of aggression rather than as an attempt to hide its embarrassment. (They were already smarting from what they perceived to be America's failure to honour its secret arms-for-hostages deal.)

To reaffirm the power of Islam, and in retribution for the injury, the Ayatollah Khomeini himself is said to have ordered the destruction of not one, but four American-flag airliners. But *discreetly*. Not even the most implacable defender of an unforgiving faith could afford to provoke an open war with 'the Great Satan', particularly at a time when he was obliged to look to the West for technology and trade to rebuild an Iranian economy all but shattered by the long war with Iraq.

His minister of the interior, Ali Akbar Mohtashemi, was placed in charge of planning Iran's revenge. At a meeting in Tehran on 9 July 1988, he awarded the contract to Ahmed Jibril, a former Syrian army officer and head of the Popular Front for the Liberation of Palestine–General Command (PFLP–GC), based in Damascus. Although Jibril later denied his complicity in the bombing, he was reported to have bragged privately that the fee for the job was $10 million. (Unnamed US government sources let it be known that the CIA had traced wire transfers of the money to Jibril's secret bank accounts in Switzerland and Spain.)

Certainly, his terrorist credentials were not in dispute.

In 1970, the PFLP–GC had blown up a Swissair flight from Zurich to Tel Aviv, killing 47 passengers and crew, and had only narrowly failed to destroy an Austrian Airlines flight on the same day. The bomb malfunctioned.

Two years later, in August 1972, the pilot of an El Al flight from Rome to Tel Aviv managed to make an emergency landing after a PFLP–GC bomb exploded in the cabin at 14,000 feet, injuring several passengers. And later on, Jibril's terrorist cell in West Germany succeeded in exploding bombs aboard two American military trains.

The group was known for the sophistication of its explosive devices. Bombs designed to destroy an aircraft in flight often featured a barometric switch that could be used, with or without a timer, to detonate a charge at a predetermined altitude – and two such devices were seized by the Bundeskriminalamt (BKA), the German Federal police, on 26 October 1988, eight weeks before the fatal flight of Pan Am 103 left Frankfurt, en route to London, New York and Detroit.

Jibril had chosen Frankfurt as the target airport for several reasons. It was an important hub for American carriers, connecting with feeder airlines from all over Europe and the Middle East; the PFLP–GC's recently reinforced European section was already based in Germany, under cover of that country's sizeable Middle Eastern community, and Jibril knew he could count on the cooperation of local Islamic fundamentalists in Frankfurt, not least among the Turkish baggage-handlers employed at the airport. Their skill in evading its security system had already proved very useful in promoting Syria's heroin exports.

After several more meetings with Iranian officials in Beirut and Teheran, Jibril sent a senior lieutenant, Hafez Kassem Dalkamoni, to Germany to team up with Abdel Fattah Ghadanfar, who, since the beginning of the year, had been stockpiling arms and explosives in a Frankfurt apartment. Dalkamoni himself moved in with his wife's sister and brother-in-law, who lived in the nearby city of Neuss, where they ran a greengrocery business.

On 13 October 1988, he was joined there by Marwan Abdel Khreesat and his wife from Jordan. A television repairman by trade, Khreesat was the PFLP–GC's leading explosives expert and bomb-maker.

As Khreesat also appears to have been an undercover informant for the German or Jordanian authorities, or both, it is not known if he told the BKA about Dalkamoni, but the Mossad, Israel's security agency, and the CIA certainly did so. Documents seized by Israeli forces in a raid on a PFLP–GC camp in south Lebanon pointed clearly to a new terrorist offensive in Europe, led by Dalkamoni, and a general warning to that effect had been circulated to all European security forces by the end of September.

Acting on this intelligence, a BKA surveillance team was watching when Dalkamoni greeted Khreesat on his arrival from the airport and helped carry his bags into the Neuss apartment.

The German police were also watching when the two men went shopping for electronic components on 22 October; when Dalkamoni arrived at the apartment on 24 October with a number of foil-wrapped packages delivered from Frankfurt by Ghadanfar; while Khreesat remained indoors on 24 and 25 October assembling four (possibly five) bombs in two Toshiba radio-cassette players, two hi-fi radio tuners and a video screen, and on 26 October, when Dalkamoni and Khreesat left the apartment, as though for good, carrying their luggage.

At this, the BKA moved in, arresting both men on the street, and over the next 24 hours raided apartments and houses in five other German cities, rounding up a total of 16 terrorist suspects. Two others, one of them Mobdi Goben – another PFLP–GC bomb-builder more commonly known as 'the Professor', and the probable source of the Semtex explosive delivered to Dalkamoni by Ghadanfar – were unfortunately out of the country.

Even more unfortunate, when the Neuss apartment was searched, three (possibly four) of Khreesat's bombs were no longer there. Nor was the brown Samsonite suitcase he had brought with him from Jordan. The BKA had to be content with the bomb it found in Dalkamoni's Ford Taunus – 312 grams of Semtex-H moulded into the case of a black Toshiba Bombeat 453 radio-cassette recorder fitted with a barometric switch and time delay.

It had been assembled for just one purpose, to destroy an aircraft in flight. An urgent warning was accordingly issued to airline security chiefs throughout the world to be on the lookout for Khreesat's three (or four) missing bombs and possibly other explosive devices hidden in Toshiba radios. (Months later, in April 1989, two of Khreesat's missing bombs were found in the basement of the greengrocery business run by Dalkamoni's brother-in-law in Neuss. As if this were not embarrassment enough for the BKA, one of the bombs exploded while it was being disarmed, killing a technician. The other was then deliberately destroyed 'for safety reasons', thus denying the Lockerbie investigators possibly vital forensic evidence.)

The BKA had better luck at Ghadanfar's apartment in Frankfurt. Among lesser weapons, its search party found an anti-tank grenade launcher, mortars, hand grenades, submachine guns, rifles and another five kilos of Semtex. On the strength of this and the bomb found in the Ford Taunus, Dalkamoni and Ghadanfar were held on terrorist charges. Khreesat and the others, however, were released 'for lack of evidence' and promptly disappeared.

Still committed to Frankfurt as the best airport from which to attack an American passenger aircraft, Ahmed Jibril turned for logistical support to Libya, the PFLP–GC's principal supplier of Semtex. Dalkamoni and Mohammed Abu Talb, another key member of the European group, had already conferred at least twice with Gaddafi's agents in Malta, but they had yet to target a particular American airline.

The mechanics of getting a bomb aboard a trans-Atlantic flight were straightforward enough, given Jibril's connections in Frankfurt, but he faced a serious conflict of interest with the Syrian heroin cartel based in Lebanon. The PFLP–GC had no wish to offend Rifat Assad, brother of Syria's dictator, President Hafez Assad, and his associate, Monzer al-Kassar, who between them controlled the flow of drugs along the 'pipeline' from the Bekaa Valley to the United States via Frankfurt and London.

Al-Kassar was an arms dealer, armourer-in-chief to Palestinian extremist groups in the Middle East, including the PFLP–GC, and also, through Lt-Colonel Oliver North and former Air Force General Richard Secord, to the Contras in Nicaragua. In this latter capacity, he enjoyed the protected status of a CIA 'asset', and had intrigued his American sponsors hugely by acting as a middle man in the ransom paid by the French government in 1986 to secure the release of two French hostages held in Beirut.

Under intense pressure from the Reagan White House to do something similar to free the *American* hostages, the CIA, like the French, sought to persuade him to use his influence with Syria and the Syrian-backed terrorist factions in Lebanon, but al-Kassar was a businessman. In the business of selling *heroin* as well as arms. He would do what he could, but . . .

The CIA understood him perfectly.

So did Ahmed Jibril, who derived a large part of the PFLP–GC's funding from the profits of Syrian drug trafficking.

He knew that neither Rifat Assad, a CIA 'asset' himself, nor al-Kassar, would wish to see their drug pipeline through Frankfurt compromised by a terrorist attack that would inevitably draw attention to the gaps they had so profitably exploited in airport security. On the other hand, he also knew that they could not refuse to cooperate without seeming to lack zeal in the cause of Islam. That would seriously displease not only Iran, but the powerful, Iranian-backed Hezbollah and its allies in Lebanon, who were hell-bent on revenge for the downing of the Iranian Airbus.

Towards the end of October 1988, around the time of the BKA's raids on the PFLP–GC in Germany, Mossad agents observed Jibril and al-Kassar dining alone at a Lebanese restaurant in Paris in an attempt to resolve the dilemma.

Neither could afford to be entirely frank with the other. Jibril was unaware of just how much protection al-Kassar enjoyed from the Americans and the BKA, and al-Kassar could only guess at the strength of what was left of Jibril's underground network in Europe. Unwilling to help but unable to refuse it, al-Kassar eventually promised to use his connections to get a bomb aboard an as yet unspecified American passenger flight from Frankfurt.

But the position was more complicated even than that. Besides the revolving-door loyalties of Assad and al-Kassar, another variable in this delicate equation of interests was the octopus factor. With the CIA's permission, playing one target group off against another in the hope of crippling both was standard practice for the US Drug Enforcement Administration in Cyprus, which otherwise had no scope to manoeuvre in the charnel-house of Lebanese politics.

Although the Syrian Army's occupation of eastern Lebanon had brought the region's drug trafficking under the supervision of Rifat Assad, the Syrian presence was deeply resented by the well-armed and ferocious Lebanese clans of the Bekaa Valley who had previously run their family enclaves like independent principalities. The Jafaar clan, for one, had been shipping hash and heroin to the United States for almost half a century, since the days when Lucky Luciano held a near-monopoly on supplies from the Middle East.

With family members settled in and around Detroit as American citizens, and travelling regularly back and forth between Lebanon and the United States, the Jafaars saw no reason why they should have to pay Syrian interlopers for 'protection', even if Assad and his partner, Monzer al-Kassar, *had* proved adept at negotiating with the Colombian cartels to expand the Bekaa's interests into cocaine and other drugs.

Unable to risk its agents in a war zone split between hostile Syrians, xenophobic Islamic fundamentalists and disgruntled Lebanese drug barons, the DEA could only exploit the friction between them as a means of slowing down the export of illegal narcotics that, in value, had come to represent about 50 per cent of Lebanon's economic activity. But even here the DEA was handicapped, for the drug-smuggling route that ran from the Bekaa to Nicosia, the administrative centre for the traffic, then on to the United States via Frankfurt and London, had a political significance of often higher priority than narcotics law enforcement.

To the CIA, the Assad/al-Kassar pipeline was both a bargaining chip in seeking the release of American hostages and an important link in its Middle East intelligence-gathering network. And to the US State Department, the narcotics industry was virtually the sole means of economic support for the pro-Western Christian factions in Lebanon, without whom the whole country would collapse into the hands of Islamic extremists.

Caught between the demands of police work and these other, political considerations, and often required to share his informants and facilities with the CIA, Micheal T. Hurley, the DEA attaché in Nicosia, was obliged to confer almost daily with 'the spooks' upstairs in the embassy to see what he was free to do before sorting out the practical details with local officials of the BKA and H.M. Customs and Excise, who naturally needed to know what the Americans were up to if Frankfurt and London were involved.

Narcotics law enforcement in Cyprus tended to proceed, therefore, on the basis of ad hoc agreements between an assortment of government agents with different agendas, reflecting local priorities, and, for political reasons, was aimed more at breaking up drug distribution rings in the United States than at knocking out their suppliers in Lebanon.

Virtually all Hurley was free to do, apart from compiling narcotics intelligence reports, was to organize 'controlled deliveries' of heroin to Detroit, Houston and Los Angeles with a view to having his DEA colleagues in those cities arrest the traffickers who claimed them.

And the most reliable couriers he could find for that dangerous job were Lebanese or Lebanese-American informants who either faced 30 years in jail for dope offences if they refused to cooperate or who, like the Jafaars, hated the Bekaa Valley's Syrian overlords so much that they would do anything to get them off their backs.

These, then, were the arrangements – validated as necessary by the DEA, the CIA, the Cypriot National Police, the German BKA and H.M. Customs – that al-Kassar reluctantly made available to Ahmed Jibril.

On 5 December 1988, the US Embassy in Helsinki received a telephone warning that 'within the next two weeks' an attempt would be made to place a bomb aboard a Pan Am flight from Frankfurt to New York.

On the night of 8 December 1988, Israeli forces raided a PFLP–GC camp near Damour, Lebanon, and captured documents relating to a planned attack on a Pan Am flight out of Frankfurt later that month. This information was passed to the governments of the United States and Germany.

At around the same time and continuing until a final call on 20 December, American intelligence agents monitoring the telephones of the Iranian Embassy in Beirut heard an informant named David Lovejoy brief the Iranian chargé d'affaires about the movements of a five-man CIA/DIA team which had arrived in Lebanon to work on the release of American hostages and which planned to fly home from Frankfurt on Pan Am Flight 103 on 21 December.

On 18 December, the BKA was tipped off about a bomb plot against Pan Am 103 in the next two or three days. This information was passed to the American Embassy in Bonn, which advised the State Department, which in turn advised its other embassies of the warning. (The tip possibly originated with confederates of al-Kassar in a last-ditch attempt to divert Jibril away from Frankfurt, or at least away from Pan Am, by promoting tighter security checks and a higher police profile at the airport.)

On 20 December, the Mossad passed on a similar warning, this time relating specifically to Flight 103 next day.

At 15.12 on 21 December, airport staff began loading passenger baggage aboard the Boeing 727 that was to fly the first leg of Pan Am Flight 103 from Frankfurt to Heathrow. About an hour before its departure at 16.53, a BKA agent was said to have reported 'suspicious behaviour' in the baggage-handling area, but no action was taken.

With 128 passengers and an estimated 135 pieces of luggage,

the 727 arrived at Heathrow on time. Forty-nine passengers, most of them American, then boarded the Maid of the Seas for the trans-Atlantic leg of the flight, their bags being stowed on the port side of the forward cargo hold. A further 210 passengers with baggage, beginning their journey in London, now joined the flight, but after the State Department's warnings to embassy staffs, the aircraft was hardly more than two-thirds full when it took off at 18.25, 25 minutes late.

At 19.03, when the bomb exploded in the forward cargo hold on the port side, the 747 broke up into five main pieces that plunged down on Lockerbie, scattering bodies, baggage and wreckage over an area of 845 square miles.

It was four days before Christmas – and perhaps only a coincidence that the Iranian Airbus had been blown out of the sky by the USS *Vincennes* four days before the feast day of Id al-Adha, the high point of the Muslim year. Had Flight 103 left Heathrow on time, it would simply have vanished far out over the Atlantic, leaving little more than that coincidence to colour speculation about who and what might have been responsible.

The day after the disaster, Lester Coleman was interviewed by Tom Brokaw on the NBC network's 'Nightly News' as an expert on Middle East terrorism. Although it had yet to be shown that Flight 103 was destroyed by a bomb, the media had assumed from the start that a Palestinian terrorist group was responsible, and Coleman shared that opinion.

The Libyans probably had a role in it, he told Brokaw, because they had a large cache of Semtex explosives and about 20,000 pounds of C4, its American equivalent, supplied by CIA renegade Edmund Wilson. They also had access to electronic timers and other components, and the necessary expertise to construct a sophisticated explosive device. For some years, he said, the Libyans had acted as quartermasters for terrorist groups around the world.

Coleman went on to suggest that the Iranians had probably inspired the attack and commissioned Syrian-backed terrorists to carry it out, but that part of the interview was not aired.

If Brokaw had asked him how they had managed to get a bomb aboard Flight 103, Coleman would have had to pass, because he didn't know he knew.

— III —

Five months later, he still did not know, and probably wouldn't have cared if he had.

After being photographed and fingerprinted in the Federal courthouse in Mobile, Coleman was handed over to the US Marshals and put in a holding cell pending his arraignment before a US Magistrate that afternoon. Apart from a telephone conversation with Joseph L. Boohaker, the Lebanese-American attorney he had befriended in Birmingham, Alabama, while setting up his latest mission to Beirut, he had not been allowed to make any calls. And although he couldn't mention it to anybody, as a matter of extreme urgency, he needed to confer with Control at Arlington Hall.

Later that morning, he was visited in his cell by a pre-trial services officer for a routine interview to determine his history and circumstances. As the officer explained, his job was to verify Coleman's personal details and prepare a report that would help the court to decide on such matters as eligibility for bail.

Coleman brightened a little. If he were bailed out quickly and could recover his passport, he might yet be able to save the mission. Though under standing orders never to reveal his DIA affiliation to anyone, he could certainly tell enough of the truth about himself to satisfy the court as to his reliability and standing in the community.

It certainly proved enough to satisfy the pre-trial services officer, whose report forms part of the court record in US vs Lester Knox Coleman.

The subject is a white male who stands 5' 8" tall and weighs 175 pounds [he wrote]. He has blue eyes and brown hair, mixed with gray. He is presently wearing a beard and mustache, both of which are also graying.

Although Mr Coleman's employment history sounds quite improbable [the report went on], information he gave to the Pretrial Services Officer has proven to be true. Coleman is a freelance journalist, specializing in the Middle East, who has also worked as an undercover investigator for the Drug Enforcement Administration of the United States. NBC News Foreign Correspondent Brian Ross contacted this office on May 3, 1990, to verify Coleman's relationship with NBC News. He also indicated that Coleman has worked for other news agencies as well. Ross indicated Coleman has contributed stories regarding Middle East terrorism and drug trafficking to NBC News numerous times throughout the 1980s. They have interviewed him on air, on NBC Nightly News, as an expert in terrorism and drug production in the Middle East. Ross also verified that Coleman has testified before Senate committees on these same subjects.

Ray Tripiccio, an agent with DEA in Washington, D.C., verifies that Coleman has formerly worked in a relationship with the Drug Enforcement Administration. The only information he could give on this secret activity is that Coleman was deactivated as a contract consultant as of 6–24–88.

Coleman indicates that he is currently working on a book, and that he was attempting to make arrangements to return to the Middle East in order to do more research. (It is noted that Coleman has gone to Jefferson County Probate Court in Birmingham to have his name legally changed to Thomas Leavy. Joseph Boohaker, the subject's attorney, verifies that this was accomplished sometime in April. The present charge from Chicago apparently predates the legal name change.) Coleman states that he needed a passport in a different name because his name is known to drug traffickers in the Middle East.

The name change had allowed Coleman to take out some life insurance as Thomas Leavy in case anything happened to him while he was travelling under that name. He had no wish to leave Mary-Claude and the children destitute while she tried to claim on his existing life insurance in the name of Coleman.

'I have no indication that Mr Coleman owns any property that would be available for posting bond,' the report concluded, 'and it appears that he is presently somewhat low on funds.'

That was putting it mildly. Since being reactivated six months earlier for Operation Shakespeare, his monthly salary of $5000 had been paid into Barclays Bank, Gibraltar – scheduled as his first stop on the way to Beirut.

By the end of the interview, if it had been up to the pre-trial services officer, Coleman would probably have been released on the spot, but the Justice Department had other ideas. After his arraignment before US Magistrate William H. Steele, Coleman was consigned to the squalor of the city jail along with the pimps, pushers, muggers, drunks and assorted criminal riff-raff swept off the streets every night by the Mobile police.

For the next three days, he shared a cell with three drug traffickers awaiting trial on Federal charges, watching every word in case he fatally let slip his former connection with the DEA.

As Special Agent Lesley Behrens explained when she called to see him with her clipboard and a new form to fill out, he was there because the county jail and the cells in the Federal building were all full. With that, she produced three sticks of fake dynamite, wired to an old-fashioned alarm clock, which the agents had found under the seat of his Mazda van.

'Would you mind telling me what *this* is?' she asked.

Coleman laughed. 'That's my Beirut alarm clock,' he said. 'Scared the shit out of you, right?'

'Where did you get it?'

'A buddy of mine gave it to me in Lebanon.' His smile faded. 'It's a joke, okay? A practical joke?'

'You mean you brought it back on an airplane?'

'Oh, God,' he said.

That was Tuesday.

On Friday, they put him in leg-irons and handcuffs and delivered him back to the Federal courthouse for a bail hearing before Magistrate Steele, who had the pre-trial services officer's report in front of him. After conferring briefly with Boohaker, who had driven five-and-a-half hours from Birmingham to be present, Coleman went on the witness stand and testified that he had indeed worked for the Drug Enforcement Administration.

'And what did you do for them?' Boohaker asked.

'I was a contract consultant involved in narcotics intelligence gathering and analysis in the Middle East,' he replied.

The young Assistant US Attorney (AUSA) representing the government winced, and looked around at the FBI agents at the back of the courtroom.

'And what were you doing at the time of your arrest?' Boohaker went on.

'I was preparing to go back to the Middle East,' said Coleman.

'For the US government?'

He hesitated. If he couldn't *break* the rules, he felt entitled to bend them a little.

'I'm not at liberty to answer that,' he said.

When Boohaker had finished, the AUSA was plainly in a quandary, but he still opposed bail, on the grounds that Coleman, with his overseas experience and connections, was an obvious flight risk.

In reply, Boohaker argued that, besides being a citizen of repute with no criminal record, Coleman was a resident of Alabama, held an Alabama driver's licence, and that his family lived there. In those circumstances, and as the charge could be tried as readily in Alabama as in Illinois, Boohaker could see no reasonable grounds why his client should be sent back to Chicago or why bail should be refused.

Magistrate Steele could hardly disagree. But he set bail at $25,000, plus a $75,000 surety, and ordered that Coleman's passport be withheld.

It was a relief to get the leg-irons off – but a $100,000 bond for a passport violation? They were definitely out to get him. But *why*?

Mary-Claude and the children were waiting outside the court-house. Through Boohaker, Coleman had arranged for a Lebanese-American friend to collect his family from the beach-house and drive them to Mobile, where they stayed in a hotel the first night and then, when his bail hearing was postponed until Friday, at their friend's house for the second night.

The separation had been an ordeal for them both. Knowing how terrified Mary-Claude had been by his arrest – inevitably a prelude to something far worse in her own country – and how vulnerable she must have felt with three babies to look after, Coleman had worried so much about her that he had scarcely had time to consider his own position.

The same was true for Mary-Claude. After three days of sleepless anxiety about him, she had almost reconciled herself to the idea of never seeing him again – although she *had* remembered to bring along a change of clothes. Untangling themselves from each other, they went off to an oyster bar for his first decent meal since the previous Monday night.

He then tried his DIA contact number, and was not much surprised to get a disconnected signal. At heart, he had known all along that as soon as the agency found out what had happened – assuming it had not had a hand in setting him up in the first place – he would cease to exist as far as the DIA was concerned.

He had no hard feelings about that. It had been understood from the day he signed on that if he were ever discovered, or if his activities as a spy ever threatened to embarrass the DIA, then Arlington Hall would disown him. Those were standard conditions of employment for any intelligence agent anywhere. It was just hard to accept that the rules applied at home as well as overseas, and to deliberate sabotage by an agency of his own government.

Not sure what to do next, he drove the family up to Birmingham to stay with his mother. And in a final request for guidance, particularly as he still had the DIA's video camera and other equipment that he was supposed to have taken with him to Beirut, he encoded a written message to Control and sent it off to his DIA Post Office mail drop in Oxenhill, Maryland.

Two months later, a letter was delivered to his mother's house, postmarked San Antonio, Texas, 16 July, and franked United States Air Force, Official Business. The address was in his own handwriting. Written as the return address on the envelope of his original coded message to Control, it had been cut out and pasted on the envelope.

Inside was a slip of paper with two sets of handwritten numbers: 332-22476 and 121-31323. Nothing else. And nothing else was necessary. Decoded, the message read: DEA – Cairo.

Coleman's suspicions had been confirmed. On being seconded to the DEA in Cyprus, he had been told to give Micheal Hurley copies of his alternative identity papers, including a copy of his CIA/Thomas Leavy birth certificate. If the DIA message meant anything, it meant that the DEA had used those papers, without consultation or authorization, as a cover identity for one of its people in Egypt. If a passport had already been issued in the name of Thomas Leavy, then his own application for a passport in the same name, with the same particulars, would presumably have triggered an investigation leading to his arrest.

The only remaining question was whether this had been done deliberately or was just the consequence of another ill-considered act by Hurley's cowboy operation in Nicosia.

Not that it made much difference. Either way, he was on his own. And after two months of brooding about it, making due allowance for the paranoia inseparable from intelligence work, he seriously doubted if there was anything unplanned in what had happened. Every time he visited his new pre-trial services officer in Birmingham and saw the puzzlement in his face; every time Boohaker expressed astonishment at the bail conditions and the government's conduct of the case; every time he woke up at night with the sure conviction that Hurley had him in his sights, the more he raked back over the past for some inkling of why they were out to get him.

He had begun to understand what Kafka was all about.

Schooled from childhood in the exotic intrigues of Beirut, Mary-Claude knew already.

'We were so sure there was more trouble coming,' she recalls, 'that we took turns sleeping, me and him and my mother-in-law. When we went to the market, we were sure someone was following us. At night, one of us would keep watch for any cars going around the house. Something was going to happen – to hurt us, to take my husband away, to ruin our lives. Every night, we would not sleep until four or five in the morning, and smoke two or three packs of cigarettes.'

Rather than sit home, waiting for trouble to arrive, Coleman decided to meet it half way. He called his old friend in New York, Bernie Gavzer, formerly of NBC News and now a contributing editor of *Parade* magazine.

'Hey, Les? Howaya? Howya doin'? You're supposed to be in Beirut. Why aren't you in Beirut?'

'I got arrested, Bernie, that's why.'

'Yeah? Well, it's about time. What they get you for? White slaving?'

'No. The FBI busted me. For making a false statement on a passport application.'

There was a brief silence at the other end.

'No kidding,' said Gavzer. Coleman had never told him about his DIA connection but Gavzer was aware of his undercover work for the Drug Enforcement Administration. 'Anything I can do?'

'I don't know. Maybe. I need a lawyer.'

'Hell, that's easy. I know a shit-load of lawyers.'

'Yeah, but how about one with Washington connections? Plugged into the Pentagon, maybe? Because that's what I need. Somebody who can get an inside track on all this.'

'Okay. Sure. I'll ask around. See what I can do.'

What Gavzer did was to line up a call from Marshall Lee Miller, former counsel to the Defense Intelligence Agency, or so Miller told

Coleman during a high-powered telephone conversation in which he offered to get William Colby, former director of the CIA, to testify for him if necessary.

'Only it won't come to that,' he said. 'Don't worry about it. We'll get to the bottom of this and clear the whole thing up so we don't have to *go* to trial. So it never even sees the light of day.'

'Well, that'd be great. But how do you know you can do that?'

'Because I'm connected in the right places, Les – that's how I know. I got all kinds of contacts here. So just sit tight. I'll get back to you.'

Coleman had a good night's sleep for the first time in weeks. This was obviously the DIA's way of baling him out without having to show its hand. In the best Hollywood tradition, the US Cavalry had ridden to the rescue in the nick of time.

True to his word, Miller had William Colby talk to Coleman on the telephone to explain the strings he could pull. If it turned out that things had gone too far for them simply to wipe the slate clean, then they would have the case moved to Washington. 'They don't know how to deal with these things in Chicago,' he said.

Cheered by their confidence, Coleman decided to test his theory that it was Hurley and the DEA who had wrecked his career. He presented himself at the DEA's field office in Birmingham and asked to see the agent from whom he had picked up his airline tickets and expense money before flying out to Cyprus to join Hurley's operation two years earlier.

The agent recognized him at once and seemed astonished to hear what had happened.

'Oh, this is crazy,' he said. 'Somebody's fucked up as usual. I'll send a wire to Washington. Find out what the hell's going on.'

'Yeah, okay,' said Coleman. 'Only I think it's something to do with DEA Cyprus, and the guys out there probably don't even know what's happened – about the FBI and the passport charge and everything. So if you tell Mike Hurley about it, maybe he can help straighten this thing out.'

'Sure. I'll put it on the wire tonight. Just leave it with me, okay? I'll call you as soon as I hear something.'

What the agent heard in response to his telex surprised him rather more than it surprised Coleman.

'Hey, Les, I don't know what's going on here,' he said, when Coleman called next day. 'I got this message back that you're a real bad egg and we're not supposed to have anything to do with you.'

He laughed uncomfortably. 'I don't know what you did, Les, but they say to tell you, don't try to get the DEA involved in your case.'

'Listen, I'm trying to get the DEA *off* my case, all right? But thanks anyway.'

Now he knew who, if not why. And it was some comfort to know that Arlington Hall had played no part in setting him up. Except in the first shock of his arrest, he had never seriously believed that anyway. With the profound contempt of the military for a civilian agency, the DIA would never have connived with the DEA to destroy one of its own agents. This *had* to be a combined DEA/FBI set-up, based on the DEA's unauthorized use of his alternative identity papers.

But Coleman was still no closer to understanding why Hurley had chosen to move against him *now*, more than a year after the row between them. Marshall Lee Miller seemed unable to account for it either, although he continued to convey the impression that he knew more about the case than he cared to admit. Coleman was astounded, for instance, when the court in Chicago denied their motion for the case to be moved to Washington, but Miller, in spite of what he had said in the beginning, passed on the news as though he had known all along what the outcome would be.

The Colemans' cigarette consumption began to go up again. The same eerie feeling was coming back that they were caught in an unseen web, that their future was being decided *for* them, somewhere else, without their knowledge. Valiantly trying to retain some sense of control over his own life, Coleman started to call all his old friends in the media, particularly those with Washington connections, in the hope that he might just stumble on something that would help make sense of the nightmare, that would offer some clue as to what was happening, and why.

Among those he called was Charlie Thompson, a friend at CBS who put him on to Sheila Hershow of ABC's 'Prime Time'. Coleman already knew her as they had worked together on the 'Jack Anderson Show' in 1983.

In April 1989, Hershow had been chief investigator for the House of Representatives Sub-Committee on Government Activities and Transportation. Some two weeks before the sub-committee was due to start hearings into the Flight 103 disaster, Ms Hershow had been unceremoniously fired, it was said because of a personality conflict with sub-committee chairman Cardis Collins, but some believed because of her tenacity in pressing, not only Pan Am, but the Federal Aviation Administration (FAA) and the airport authorities at Frankfurt and Heathrow with awkward questions about security.

She refused to be drawn on the subject when Coleman spoke to her, but, more than a year later, she had certainly not lost her interest in the Lockerbie disaster. There was some connection she had not been able to track down, she said, between the bombing and the DEA in Cyprus.

'You were out there around that time, weren't you?' she asked. 'I remember Brian Ross, over at NBC, saying he met you in Nicosia.'

'Well, yes, that's right. They were doing a story on the Lebanese connection – about heroin from the Bekaa Valley, you know? And as I was out there doing some academic research on narcotics trafficking and Lebanese politics, we got together and compared a few notes. But that was a while before the bombing.'

'Uh-huh. He said you did some work for the DEA as well.'

'Well, yes,' he said cautiously. 'Intelligence analysis – that kind of thing. Desk work. Nothing operational.'

'No, but intelligence analysis – that must have given you a pretty good insight into what they were doing out there, right?'

'Well, yeah. Pretty good.' It went against the professional grain to admit even *that*, but he owed the DEA nothing. And besides, he was curious. 'It's a small office. I was in and out all the time. Not a lot went on there I didn't know about.'

'Okay,' she said. 'I'm going to send you a picture. And I want you to tell me if you know who it is. If you ever saw him before. Will you do that for me?'

'Sure. Why not? Is it somebody I knew out there?'

'I don't know. You tell me.'

The picture was faxed to him two days later. It was of a young man, an Arab, about 20 years old, and, after pencilling in a moustache, Coleman recognized him at once.

'That's Khalid Nazir Jafaar,' he told Hershow. 'Nice kid. We used to call him Nazzie.'

'Well, well,' she said. 'That's interesting. You mind telling me *how* you know him?'

'Nazzie was one of the boys, one of Hurley's people. The DEA had a front operation in Nicosia, down the street from the embassy. The Eurame Trading Company. That's where I worked. And that's where I met Nazzie. Saw him there several times.'

'Well, well,' she said again. There was a funny note in her voice. 'The Jafaars – they're into heroin, right?'

'Biggest in the Bekaa. Or they were until the Syrians moved in. The Jafaars were Lucky Luciano's heroin connection. They go back a long way in the dope business.'

'This kid, Nazzie – are you saying he *worked* for the DEA?'

'Oh, sure. And probably for the CIA as well. Seemed like the whole damn family were CIA assets.'

'But why? I mean, why would they want to work for the US government?'

'Why? Hell, the Jafaars'll work for anybody against the Syrians – they hate 'em so bad. They'd do *anything* to get Assad off their backs.'

'Okay. So what did *he* do?'

'Nazzie? Well, he was under age to be an informant, so he was probably on the DEA books as a subsource. I know for a fact he ran two or three controlled deliveries of heroin into Detroit.'

'You mean he was a DEA courier?'

'Among other things. But how come you're interested in Nazzie?'

'You don't know?'

'No, I kind of lost touch with those people when I got back here, you know how it is. I've no idea what he's doing now.'

'He's dead,' she said.

'Yeah? Oh. Well, I'm sorry to hear that. Like I say, he was a nice kid. But I'm not surprised. It's a tough business.'

'Yeah. He was on Flight 103 when it went down.'

Coleman chewed that over.

'No shit,' he said.

That probably explained everything.

And when she went on to say that at least two intelligence agents had also died with Nazzie Jafaar, having switched to Flight 103 through RA Travel Masters of Nicosia, the DEA's travel agents on Cyprus, he knew without a doubt that his life was in danger.

The octopus already had its coils around him.

—— IV ——

The first Lester Knox Coleman was a Navy man.

A native of Moffat, Texas, he had signed on in 1917 to escape his family's dirt-poor existence in the Texas dust bowl. Liking the look of it no better when he came back from the war, he re-enlisted in the peacetime Navy, and, in 1924, was assigned to the USS *Shenandoah*, the Daughter of the Stars, one of two Navy airships developed from the German Zeppelins that, for many, seemed to point the way to the future of aviation.

He was on board when, in 1925, the *Shenandoah* cast off from her mooring mast at Lakehurst Naval Air Station, New Jersey, and headed out on a barnstorming tour of the Midwest to drum up public support for the Navy's lighter-than-air programme. Two days later, a violent storm broke her back over the cornfields of Ohio, littering the ground with the bodies of her crew.

Lester Knox Coleman survived, as no one who knew him would have doubted.

Lester Knox Coleman Jr, an engineer by profession, was another survivor. The day after Pearl Harbor, he quit his job with the Gulf Power Company in Pensacola, Florida, and, like his father before him in 1917, signed up for the Navy. His infant son was 18 months old before he even laid eyes on him.

Lester Knox Coleman III was born in the USNAS/Navy Point Hospital on 25 September 1943, while the other two were overseas, fighting their country's war against the Japanese, one in South America, the other in the South Pacific.

Like them, he was brought up to believe in America, to honour its principles, to be suspicious of foreigners and to distrust politicians, who, as far as the Colemans were concerned, had about as much common sense as a bucket of warm spit. There was nothing in his small-town Southern background, his traditional American middle-class home or his average educational achievement to raise as much as an eyebrow among the team of military investigators who later vetted him back to his diapers to determine his suitability for secret government service with the Defense Intelligence Agency.

When Coleman was five, the Gulf Power Company transferred his father from Pensacola to Panama City, a two-hour ride down the Florida panhandle on Highway 98. And for the next eight years nothing much else happened as far as Coleman can remember, except for the stroke that disabled his grandfather. He dawdled through Cove Elementary and Jinks Junior High to Eighth grade, showing no great aptitude for academic study; failed Ninth grade when his father moved the family north to New Jersey for a year, and did hardly better in Tenth grade at Pensacola High when the Colemans returned to Florida.

Indeed, the high point in his education until then was the discovery of progressive jazz. Under the tutelage of his friend Connor Shaw, ace drummer of the Pensacola High 'Tiger' Band, he was introduced to the music of Charlie Parker, Oscar Peterson and Thelonius Monk, and to other, more tangible pleasures of the Beat Generation.

Older than Coleman, and with a driver's licence, Shaw would pick up his protégé in his '51 black Chevy coupe as soon as the Friday afternoon bell rang and together they would set off for a night out in the French Quarter of New Orleans, three hours away along the Gulf shore highway. Nearing sixteen, Coleman read Jack Kerouac's *On the Road*, and took to wearing a hip pair of shades with his dirty sweatshirts and sneakers.

Then, one day, everything changed. His father came home and said, in his usual, unadorned fashion, 'We're moving to Iran.'

'Yeah? What part of Florida is that in, Dad?'

'I-R-A-N.'

'You mean, Iran like in Persia? Shit!'

The pain of withdrawal from his local bohemia was soon offset by Coleman's growing excitement at the prospect of travelling to faraway, romantic places of the sort his father and grandfather had so often talked about. But, as it turned out, the family was bound for the oil company settlement of Golestan, a suburb of Ahwaz, about two hours overland by Land Rover from the city and oil terminal of Abadan. With its neat, yellow-brick homes set in plots of real grass, its own supermarket, school and country club, Golestan might as well have been in Arizona as in the ancient kingdom of Shah Mohammed Reza Pahlavi.

Continuing his teenage rebellion, Coleman decided to become an Arab.

He set himself to learn colloquial Arabic by hanging out with the company drivers and labourers who spent a good part of every work day sitting around charcoal stoves sipping glasses of hot tea through cubes of sugar. It was a conscious decision. Rather than learn Farsi, spoken only in Iran, he chose Arabic as it was the language of many nations, from the Shatt-al-Arab waterway clear across the northern reaches of Africa to the Atlantic Ocean.

As Coleman's proficiency improved, and the Arabs, treated like dogs by the Iranians, lost their suspicion of the 'young Satan', so they allowed him deeper into their society. His new friend Ahziz, who lived in Laskarabad, took him to visit his uncle's village to drink tea and eat sheep's eyes and rice with the old sheik as they lounged on Persian carpets and watched the belly dancers.

Coleman practised his Arabic around camp fires at Refresabad, in the wilderness near Isfahan, and while riding third-class trains to Antimeshk. He grew accustomed to eating by the light of burning donkey dung with people who lived in huts or tents and bathed and urinated in open jubs as they had for a thousand years.

To placate his family and their Iranian friends, Coleman also learned a little Farsi, but as he approached his eighteenth birthday, both he and his father were only too conscious that his school credits were barely worthy of a high-school junior. If he was ever to amount to anything more than an Arabic-speaking bum, he needed to catch up with his formal education.

In the autumn of 1961, he was sent home to boarding school in Orlando, Florida – and contrived to get himself expelled in three weeks. He then went to stay with his uncle in Birmingham, Alabama, while he attended Shades Valley High School.

'On Friday and Saturday nights,' Coleman remembers, 'my friend Walton Kimbrough and me went cruising in his '53 Mercury, parking at Pig Trail Inn, elbows out the window, listening to Dave Roddy on the radio, sipping cherry Cokes and eating Bar-B-Cues. We'd cruise up Red Mountain, beneath the bare bottom of Vulcan Statue, past WYDE radio and into five points south, giving the royal digit salute to every blue Ramsey High jacket we saw. Then shoot down main-drag 20th Street, all the way to 10th Avenue North, pull into Ed Salem's Drive Inn, elbows still out the window, watching lake-plugged hot-rods peel rubber, driven by boys from Ensley and Hueytown with names like Billy-Joe and Leroy and Bobby.'

It couldn't last. For one thing, he no longer had much in common with his contemporaries. When he told them he lived in Iran, they would mostly look him up and down, shake their heads, and with doubt shading through scorn to open hostility, ask him 'Where's that?' And when he told them where it was, they would shake their heads again and dismiss what he said as 'a sack of porkey-pine shit'. He had never noticed before how parochial and ignorant of the world American kids were.

'It struck me about this time,' Coleman says, 'that they seemed to lie more than kids from other places. They didn't do it with purposed deceit – it was just part of America's fast-hustle, three-card-monte morality. When a person tells the truth, other people, looking at themselves in the mirror and seeing a liar, assume that the truth-teller is a liar, too. You see America differently after you've been away for a while. All us expatriate kids had the same experience. When we got home and tried to communicate with our peers who had never left the United States, they'd look at us like we'd just landed from Mars.'

To the relief of his parents, and to re-establish his roots, Lester Knox Coleman III, with his friend Walton Kimbrough, applied for admittance to The Marion Military Institute (MMI), in Marion, Alabama. Founded in 1842, and alma mater to a distinguished roster of generals and heroes in every American war since then, the MMI was both a cradle and shrine to the United States Army, and a cadetship among the highest honours the military establishment could bestow on a young American of the right calibre.

Having somehow passed the written examination, Coleman reported for duty at the start of the winter term and managed to curb his rebellious streak sufficiently, not only to make his grades and the Dean's List, but to put up five stripes as a Sergeant First Class Platoon Sergeant in his senior year. Coleman Senior pretended to take this for granted when his son rejoined the family in Iran that summer, but, for the first time in his life, Coleman sensed his father was proud of him.

He also re-entered the Arab world as if coming home. By the time he graduated from MMI with the Class of '63, his father had moved on to a job in Libya with Esso. When Coleman arrived out there, the limitless horizons of the Sahara and the brutal austerity of life among the nomadic tribes of the desert caught his imagination so completely that it was 1966 before the claims of higher education in the United States again outweighed those of the liberal education he was acquiring in Arabic and Middle Eastern affairs. As his father pointed out with increasing acerbity, he had a living to earn, and – not counting a brief spell at the American University in Beirut – nothing worth a damn to interest a prospective employer.

An aimless year at Jacksonville State University, Alabama, failed to remedy the deficiency, but it did at least point the way. Through a friend, Jim Sands, he was introduced to the trials, tribulations and occasional rewards of scrub broadcasting.

A big, round, jolly fellow, Sands supported himself, more or less, by working at one of the scores of marginally profitable, day-time radio stations that had sprouted their directional antenna arrays all over the South. Under Sands's benevolent auspices, Coleman tried his hand as disc jockey-cum-announcer-cum-newsman and realized at once that he had found his vocation. Nothing would do now but a career in broadcast journalism. As foreign correspondent for CBS in the Middle East, maybe. Or even for NBC, at a pinch.

But he had to start somewhere. And as the FCC required each station to have a licensed engineer on duty at all times, and as you were obviously more employable if you were both announcer *and* engineer, he dropped out of Jacksonville and enrolled at Elkins Electronics Institute in New Orleans to study for the FCC exams, which he passed with flying colours in 1967.

It was the first flush of a passion for advanced electronics that, with his other qualifications, was later to prove of special interest to the United States government. At the time, however, it was of more interest to one-horse radio stations in Pasagoula, Mississippi, and Bay Minet, Alabama, where the transmitter sat in the middle of a cow pasture and Coleman had to dodge the resident bull to get to work every morning.

Stripped to his shorts in the heat and confined to a toolshed studio that turned blue with static electricity during a thunderstorm, he spun records, recorded supermarket commercials, and, for a change of pace, did occasional remote broadcasts from remote places like the local John Deere tractor outlet. A year of this brought him to the comparative luxury of a Country and Western 5000-watt station in downtown Mobile, but there his new career stalled.

For one thing, he could see that he needed better academic credentials if he was ever to get back to the Middle East as a network TV correspondent, and for another thing, his best friend, Jim Sands, was now also his brother-in-law.

Sands had invited him over to his mother-in-law's place one Sunday and introduced him to his wife's sister, Jocelyn. Hitting it off on sight,

Lester and Jocelyn were married soon after, but even in 1967, it was tough for a married couple to live on $90 a week. When their daughter Karen was born in February 1968, it proved impossible. The following September, Coleman left his job at 'Woonie Radio' and took his new family to Jacksonville, where he went back to university as a mature student of 25 and rewrote the definition of working one's way through college.

While coping with the not inconsiderable load of his degree course, Coleman held down jobs in a photo lab, on a radio show from 6 p.m. until midnight, six days a week, and as a paid football announcer on Saturdays. For *her* part, his wife worked as private secretary to the football coach, as well as looking after their infant daughter, and together the Colemans managed a 110-unit apartment complex which provided them with rent-free accommodation.

Thus stretched, they somehow survived the three years it took Coleman to equip himself for the big time with a bachelor's degree in political science and economics. But by then it was 1971, in the middle of a recession, and despite his now glittering qualifications, CBS wasn't interested. Nor was NBC or even ABC. After fruitlessly trawling the job market, Coleman took his wife and child back to Mobile and rejoined 'Woonie Radio' as News Director at $125 a week. It felt like he had put himself and his family through some pretty exhausting changes for an extra $35 a week.

Working out of a converted broom closet, his one-man news department was expected to write and deliver eight newscasts a day, although, as he recalls:

. . . the major activity at Woonie Radio was still station manager Rocky Reich's running poker game. It was too rich for *my* blood, but I did manage to pick up an extra twenty-five dollars a week producing the Dot Moore Radio Show. That meant I had to push a shopping cart carrying a heavy Ampex 601 tape recorder around Bellas Hess department store while Dot interviewed local shoppers. I'd then take the tape back to the studio, dub in the commercial breaks and add the music. But I couldn't see it as my life's work somehow.

Mobile was not exactly a hot news town anyway. My hourly five-minute newscasts were filled with the usual Fuz 'n Wuz from the police blotter, the Wuz being the corpses from shootings, house fires and traffic pile-ups. Once in a while a bit of political juice from City Hall would spice up my news day, usually about

Lambert 'Lamby Pie' Mims, Mobile's Bible-thumping Mayor, whose gospel of civic trust finally landed him in a Federal penitentiary. After five months in the 'Home of the Woonie Bird', I was open to the first reasonable offer.

It came from the Boy Scouts of America (BSA), which, as Coleman later discovered, served not only the nation's youth but also the military-industrial complex that had so exercised President Dwight D. Eisenhower in the 1950s.

Seated one day in his broom closet, writing copy and eating Krispy Kremes, Coleman took a call from Mark Clayton of the BSA National Public Relations Office. An Eagle Scout from Mobile had been selected to meet President Richard Nixon on the White House lawn, said Clayton. Was Woonie Radio interested in covering this event?

'Sure,' said Coleman. 'I'll take a tape feed of our Eagle Scout meeting the President of the United States. Great stuff. I'd like to ask him how it feels to get chosen out of four million Boy Scouts to shake his President by the hand. We'll do an interview, okay?'

Tongue intermittently in cheek, Coleman taped a few questions and answers and then, jokingly, asked Clayton if the Boy Scouts of America were looking for someone with a bit of broadcasting experience.

'Well,' said Clayton, surprised. 'Now that you mention it, yes. You mean you'd be interested in taking a job with us?'

Coleman looked around his broom closet newsroom, with its mops and pails and industrial-sized bottles of Mr Clean, and sighed for his lost illusions.

'Sounds like an exciting opportunity to me,' he said.

Brought over from Britain in 1910 by Chicago newspaper publisher William D. Boyce with the idea of building character in his street-corner newsboys, Scouting had grown by 1972 into a nationwide movement, chartered by Congress, with a full-time professional staff of 4000 directed from BSA headquarters in North Brunswick, New Jersey.

After a preliminary meeting with Clayton in Mobile, Coleman was flown in for two days of interviews and put up in the Scout guest-house, next door to a museum full of Norman Rockwell paintings, in the middle of a 30-acre game preserve criss-crossed with neatly tagged nature trails.

The job opening he had stumbled upon was in the public relations department, which already had a staff of 20 writers and photograph-ers – many of them former military public information officers – under the general direction of Ron Phillippo, a cigar-smoking outdoorsman in a three-piece suit, whose secretary, Marcia Schwartz, and right-hand man, Russ Bufkins, USN (retd) between them ran the place. Being all 'print people', with no practical experience of radio or television, they needed somebody who could get the Scout story 'on the air' for $12,000 a year.

Satisfied he was made of the right stuff, BSA offered Coleman the job, and in March 1972, a big cross-country moving van delivered the family's worldly goods to their new home in Heightstown, near Princeton, New Jersey, about 20 minutes by Toyota south of New Brunswick on Route 130. If not quite as he had imagined, Coleman had made the big time as the BSA's National Event Public Relations Executive.

A former Cub Scout with a school troop at eight, he soon discovered there was more to modern Scouting than rubbing damp sticks together in the wilderness. It was a franchise operation. With a network of regional offices, heavily staffed with former military personnel, to oversee 'the product', the BSA sold franchises to Local Councils in cities and towns across the nation. These councils, in turn, employed full-time professional staff to recruit volunteers and sponsors to run and finance Scout troops at neighbourhood levels.

In overall charge of the operation was a Chief Scout, a full-time salaried executive of BSA, Inc., and a volunteer counterpart with the title of National President. In 1972, they were, respectively, Alden Barber, a polished, smooth-talking businessman who could have stepped out of any corporate boardroom, and Robert W. Sarnoff, chief executive officer of the Radio Corporation of America.

Coleman's connection with the big time was through the National Public Relations Committee, a volunteer group he was encouraged to cultivate for help and support. One of its members was Walter Cronkite, of CBS News.

'Can you imagine?'

Twenty years on, Coleman still remembers the excitement of hopping on a train to New York, taking a cab uptown from Penn station to the corner of 57th Street and 10th Avenue and walking in to tell the guard he was there to see Walter Cronkite.

'And then actually getting in to see him. Escorted down one narrow hallway after another, past Xerox machines, past dark studios with the ghosts of John Cameron Swazy and Edward R. Murrow, then into the CBS newsroom, into Cronkite's glass fishbowl of an office, and there he is – thinner and younger-looking in person, wearing a khaki suit, loafers kicked off, feet on the desk, talking to me about the next Explorer Scout Olympics in Fort Collins, Colorado.'

Most of the national events Coleman worked on were organized by the BSA's Explorer Division, the then-new co-ed Scout 'product' for young people between fourteen and twenty, offering hands-on experience in the career fields that interested them.

It was the Explorer programme that finally married the Boy Scouts of America to the military-industrial complex. The military saw Scouting as a training ground for leaders who were also good team-players, disciplined, respectful of authority and imbued with ideals of service to God and country, while the business community saw it as a politically neutral means of indoctrinating youth in the principles of free enterprise capitalism and the American way.

Nobody had a bad word for Scouting. It was the perfect public relations vehicle for acquiring civic virtue on the cheap while continuing the ruthless pursuit of corporate self-interest in government and the market place. In government, all the way up to Federal level, sponsorship of Career-Interest Explorer Posts proved so popular among image-sensitive agencies such as the police that a special unit was set up at BSA headquarters to administer 'Law-Enforcement Exploring' and to work alongside existing departments responsible for Congressional Relations, Military Relations, Mormon Relations (the Boy Scouts of America is the official youth movement of the Mormon Church), Corporate Relations and so on.

As Coleman would discover at first hand, it was not so much that Scouting was *controlled* by the octopus as simply incapable of denying it a favour. When a two-star general in Washington called a retired colonel in North Brunswick to ask if the BSA could find a job for one of 'our people' from overseas, the only possible answer was, 'Yes, *sir!*'

In his two years at headquarters, Coleman came across several 'spooks' cooling off in executive niches of the Boy Scout Movement, and later became one himself. He also came to appreciate the mutual benefit of having a Boy Scout troop on every significant US military base around the world. It not only helped with the BSA's numbers game but served as a benevolent advertisement for the American way of life, as well as a convenient cloak for low-level intelligence gathering.

As with any franchise operation, growth was the bottom line. In

1972, the BSA's national advertising slogan claimed that 'Scouting today is a lot more than you think', but in fact it was a lot less. Under pressure from head office to meet ever higher 'sales' targets, Local Council staffs had begun to create imaginary Scout troops, in much the same way as Teamster union officials had once created 'paper' Locals, and to pad the rolls of existing troops with phantom members.

By 1974, the BSA had 6.5 million Scouts on its books, of which two million existed only in the minds of hard-pressed District Executives. It was too many. When somebody at last blew the whistle, not even the National Public Relations Office could explain away so great a discrepancy. The Scouting hierarchy collapsed from top to bottom, sending Chief Scout Alden Barber into the decent obscurity of Santa Barbara, California.

In 1972, however, still untarnished by scandal, the BSA plugged Coleman into the military-industrial complex through Tom Geohagen, Department of Public Affairs, US Steel, Washington, D.C. A short, white-haired man with big ears and a booming radio announcer's voice – he had worked for years at NBC News – Geohagen was chairman of a high-powered committee of media experts put together to publicize the National Explorer Presidents' Congress, an annual meeting in Washington of Explorer Post leaders from all over America. The event was Coleman's first assignment, and Geohagen liked his style. Appointing himself Coleman's mentor, he was soon urging him to 'use this Scout business' as a stepping stone to higher things, perhaps in government service, where he could make the most of his command of Arabic and his background in the Middle East.

Wherever we went in Washington, Tom introduced me to his contacts [Coleman recalls]. We would go for lunch down the street from his office to the Army-Navy Club, and he knew everybody. You'd get these grey men in grey suits, sitting around smoking cigars in red leather armchairs under portraits of Nimitz and Patton, and they'd all say hello and pass the time of day. One, I remember, was General Danny Graham, an old spook buddy of Tom's, who had been sent over from the Pentagon to clean house at the CIA.

'Now there's a guy you ought to talk to,' Tom said afterwards. 'You'll like him, and I know he'd be real interested in your background. Tell you what – why don't I set up a meeting?'

'No, Tom,' I said. 'Thanks all the same. I still want to see how far I can go with journalism.'

But Geohagen kept on trying, determined his protégé should make the most of himself. His next manoeuvre on Coleman's behalf was to secure a staff position for him with the US Olympic Team at the 20th Olympiad in Munich that September. This was exciting but also embarrassing, for Mark Clayton, who had got him his job in the first place, had to be bumped out of the slot to make way for him.

'It was Clayton's assignment, Tom, and he's my boss,' Coleman protested. Half-heartedly. 'And why me? I've only been here six months.'

'Well, let's just say you have special talents that your committee feels would be better suited to this assignment,' said Geohagen. 'Let's just say there are people who want to see how you make out, how you handle yourself under fire, so to speak. So let's show 'em, okay?'

Of *course* it was okay. It was *damned* okay. To be in Munich with the US team at the Olympic Games was about as far as you could get from a broom closet in Mobile.

Geohagen's wish to see how Coleman handled himself 'under fire' turned out to be curiously prophetic, for the 1972 Olympiad was to be remembered, not for Mark Spitz's seven gold medals or Cathy Rigby's bare-bottom picture in *Sports Illustrated*, but for the slaughter of Israeli athletes by hooded assassins from Black September.

It was Coleman's first direct experience of Arab terrorism. Although he saw no more of the siege and carnage than anyone else in the Olympic Village, he had earlier taken the fullest advantage of his staff pass to explore the compound and to fraternize with athletes and officials from other countries, particularly those from the Middle East for the chance it gave him to practise his Arabic.

Although there were armed guards everywhere, security was a joke. Photo-ID badges were rarely checked, and no attempt at all was made to confine badge-holders to the specific areas of the Village for which they had security clearance. In theory, only someone with a press pass could gain access to the Olympic Press Centre, for example, but Coleman came and went as he pleased, in and out three or four times a day, every day, without ever being challenged.

Before the attack, he enjoyed the same freedom of movement to meet and drink coffee with his new Arab friends in their Olympic quarters – and also with Andrei, one of the Soviet team's 'trainers', who spent a lot of time in their company, drinking beer and picking away at salt fish wrapped in brown paper. After the attack, Coleman saw no cause to wonder how Black September had managed to smuggle explosives and automatic weapons into the compound, but he wondered long and hard about Andrei, who had mysteriously disappeared when the terrorists struck, and about the not-so-mysterious defection of the Arab teams, who now melted away for fear of Israeli reprisals.

Like everyone else, Coleman watched the drama build up to its bloody dénouement on television, still misusing his pass to keep abreast of the latest developments via the Press Centre's battery of monitors.

Under the critical weight of world attention, Munich's beleaguered police chief, Manfred Schreiber, was now at pains to lock the barn door after the terrorist horse had bolted. His officers were ordered to question everybody they could trace who had set foot in the Arab camp in the course of the Games, including Lester Coleman, public relations assistant with the US Olympic Team, on loan from the Boy Scouts of America.

In what turned out to be a curious link with the future, Coleman struck up a friendship with Hartmut Mayer, a local police officer whom he would meet again 15 years later in Cyprus, when Mayer was resident agent on the island for the BKA, and like Coleman, concerned with a DEA operation where sloppy security opened the way to an even bloodier atrocity than at Munich – the destruction of Flight 103.

For Coleman, there would be other curious links, too, between Munich and Lockerbie. In 1987, after renewing his acquaintance with Mayer, he was to work on the same poorly managed DEA operation with a Lebanese-American named Ibrahim El-Jorr, a key informant who claimed to have been one of the US Army support group sent into Munich after Black September took over the village.

In the troubled aftermath of Lockerbie, Coleman would also meet up with Juval Aviv, a private investigator hired by Pan Am, who was said to have been a member of the Mossad hit team turned loose after the Munich massacre by Israel's Golda Meir to track down and kill every member of the Black September squad responsible.

But the strongest link for Coleman was the continuing fascination of the American intelligence community with Arab terrorism.

On his first day back in the office after flying home with the Olympic team, he was called down to Washington by his sponsor.

'There's some people would like to hear about your experiences,'

Geohagen said, on their way out to Georgetown to have lunch at the Sheraton Park Hotel. 'Some of Danny Graham's boys. I told 'em you wouldn't mind. You can probably give 'em some useful insights, just from being there in Munich.'

'Think so?' Coleman shrugged. 'I'll be glad to talk to them, Tom, but there were a lot of people a lot closer to what happened than *me*. Are you saying they didn't have any of their own people in the Village? They must have done. I heard the KGB was all over the place.'

'Well, I expect they did. But I guess they didn't have anybody out there who spoke Arabic. Or spent much time talking to the Arab teams.'

It was only when somebody stopped by their table in the Sheraton's bar to say they were expected upstairs after lunch that Coleman began to wonder how Geohagen knew how he had spent his off-duty time in Munich, and it rather took the edge off his appetite.

After the meal, they adjourned for coffee to a suite on the third floor, where Geohagen introduced him to three men, who identified themselves as Bob, Nat and Herb, and then excused himself, saying he would see Coleman back in his office after they had finished. Nervous at first, but soon relaxing in their warmth and friendliness, Coleman told them about Andrei and tentatively identified him from a grainy ten by eight print that Herb produced from a file folder on his lap.

'You know who he is?' asked Coleman eagerly. 'Is he KGB?'

'It's not important,' Bob said. 'We keep tabs on all kinds of people. Can you tell us what you talked about?'

'Oh, Olympic-type things. You know, how it's good for East and West to get together, for people to exchange ideas, one to one, leaving politics out of it for a change. That sort of stuff.'

'You didn't talk politics? Not at all?'

'Well, depends what you mean by politics. Not cold war politics anyway. He asked me a lot of questions about what was going on here. Said he couldn't understand how people could be out of work or homeless or without proper medical attention and still be loyal Americans. He seemed to know a lot about black militant groups. Our 'dissidents' is what he called them.'

'Uh-huh. And how do *you* feel about 'em?'

'Me?'

Coleman spent 15 minutes defending his own political views before Bob finally turned to the subject of the Arabs he had talked to in Munich. And the same thing happened. After covering the ground, the three seemed to be at least as interested in examining Coleman's views on the Arab-Israeli question as the views expressed by the people he had met.

'Did you form any opinion about where the terrorists were from?' asked Nat, pouring him another cup of coffee.

'Well, I only know what I heard and saw on television,' Coleman said. 'But one of them sounded Libyan to me.'

'Libyan? Black September is a Palestinian group.'

'Yeah, I know. But King Idris took in hundreds of refugees from Palestine in the Fifties – the guy could still have been a member of the PLO. Seemed to me I recognized the accent. I worked with two Palestinians in Libya when my father was out there.'

They appeared to know about that, too, and after a lengthy discussion of Middle East politics, went on to ask him about what he had told Hartmut Mayer, of the Munich police, and how he felt generally about the Germans, their security arrangements and their attitude towards the Israelis.

The questioning went on for more than two hours, and ended with another round of warm handshakes as they ushered him into a taxi for the ride back to Geohagen's office on K Street, North West.

'It had all been very friendly,' Coleman recalls, 'but I left feeling drained, as if I'd just sat through a really testing examination. But I also felt relieved from telling everything I knew to people I thought could do something about it, who could stop another Munich from happening. I guess I was still naive enough, going on twenty-nine to believe in the fatherly image of the American government, as somehow all-protecting, all-knowing, and capable of fixing anything.'

By the time Coleman reached K Street, Geohagen had already heard from the octopus.

'They were very impressed,' he said. 'You know, Les, you really ought to consider working for those guys. You could have a big future there.'

'Well, thanks, Tom,' said Coleman. 'I'm flattered by their interest and I'm glad if I've been of help. But, like I say, I really am hooked on broadcasting. I want to see how far I can go.'

'Yeah, well, I told them that. But if you ever change your mind, Danny Graham says you're to go see him about it. Any time.'

— V —

After his appearance with Tom Brokaw on NBC's 'Nightly News', Coleman went back to his cover job with the Boy Scouts of America, and in the following months the fate of Flight 103 slipped from his mind. Although he read about the case in the Chicago newspapers from time to time, he made no serious attempt to keep up with it, for he was still unaware of his connection with the disaster.

As is rarely true in murder inquiries, the identity of the killers, their motives, the method and approximate details of the weapon employed were known to agents of several governments from the start, but for various reasons, some political, some self-serving, this knowledge was not fully shared with the Dumfries and Galloway Constabulary. Even so, such intelligence information as *was* made available ensured that within 72 hours, the Scottish police officers investigating by far the biggest mass murder in British history knew more or less who had done it and roughly how. From the start, the entire thrust of their efforts was to *prove* what they knew.

But odd things were happening at Lockerbie. Although the collection of forensic evidence was of paramount importance, it was hampered for two days while CIA agents, some dressed in Pan Am overalls, combed the countryside for the luggage of the dead American intelligence agents and a suitcase full of heroin. After a 48-hour search, assisted by units of the British Army, whatever they had found was flown out by helicopter, and in due course, one suitcase, emptied of its contents, was returned so that it could be 'found' again officially.

It belonged to Major Charles 'Tiny' McKee, an agent of the US Defense Intelligence Agency. It was severely damaged, possibly by an explosive device of the type sometimes fitted in luggage used by intelligence agents to destroy the contents before they fall into the wrong hands. As the search continued, documents relating to the

American hostages held in Beirut were recovered, along with over $500,000 in cash and traveller's cheques.

When the CIA's presence was reported on Radio Forth by David Johnston, who later published *Lockerbie: The Real Story*, he was interviewed at length next day by police officers who finally threatened him with legal sanctions unless he identified his sources. This Johnston refused to do and, oddly, that was the end of the matter. No further action was taken, and he heard no more about it, perhaps because to have carried out the threat would have drawn more attention to his story than was actually shown at the time, in the chaotic aftermath of the disaster.

Odder still, and more serious, it was later reported that 59 bodies which had been found, tagged and certified dead by a police surgeon on 22 December, were left lying where they had fallen in open country around Lockerbie until 24 December, when they were retagged, removed and recertified dead. But by then, according to the police count, there were only 58 bodies. Somebody had either miscounted or one had gone missing. Also puzzling, the name-tag observed by a local farmer on a suitcase full of heroin before that, too, went missing did not correspond with any of the names on the passenger list.

Another witness involved in the search within hours of the crash has spoken of finding handguns on six of the bodies, presumably those of the agents on board. He also saw Americans throwing tarpaulins over bodies and suitcases so that they could examine them in private, and warning searchers to keep clear of certain sectors, his own team included.

With the Americans scrambling to cover their tracks, the Germans also made sure they were not left holding the bag. Although the BKA, like H.M. Customs and Excise, had collaborated fully with their American colleagues in supervising the leaky DEA/CIA pipeline through Frankfurt and London to the United States, a spokesman for the German Ministry of the Interior calmly stated on 29 December that there were no indications that the bomb had been put aboard Flight 103 in Frankfurt – a position the BKA would maintain for almost a year, until finally persuaded it would not be saddled with the blame.

No one in the Anglo-American camp was ready to buy that. On the same day, 29 December, Michael F. Jones, of Pan Am Corporate Security in London, received a telephone call from Phillip Connelly, assistant chief investigation officer for H.M. Customs and Excise, who wanted to know if Jones had 'considered a bag switch at Frankfurt due to the large amount of Turkish workers'.

Asked to expand on this, Connelly said that before the disaster he had attended a meeting in Frankfurt with the other agencies concerned to discuss deliveries of heroin through Frankfurt airport involving the substitution of bags by Turkish baggage-handlers.

The next day, spokesmen for the British and American authorities followed up this thought by briefing the press in exactly opposite terms to those employed by the German authorities. On 31 December, *The Times* reported that the team investigating the Lockerbie air disaster had told the Scottish police that the bomb had definitely been placed on board in Frankfurt.

'The hunt for those responsible,' the story went on, 'is now centred in the West German city, where a Palestinian terrorist cell is known to have been operating for more than 18 months . . . The Frankfurt terrorist cell is known to be part of Ahmed Jibril's hardline Popular Front for the Liberation of Palestine – General Command, and to have carried out two bombing attacks on US military trains.'

The *Times* report added that Scottish police officers had flown to Frankfurt on 30 December in the hope of interviewing Dalkamoni and Ghadanfar, the two PFLP–GC members still in custody after the BKA raids on 26 October. They had been caught in possession of an explosive device 'similar to the one being blamed for the Lockerbie disaster'.

In the United States, a spokesman for the FBI went further and named Khalid Nazir Jafaar, a 21-year-old Lebanese-American citizen, as the possibly unwitting accomplice of the PFLP–GC.

His father, Nadir Jafaar, who owned a garage and other business interests in Detroit, said that his son had been visiting his grandfather in the Bekaa Valley and was on his way home for Christmas after spending a few days with Lebanese friends in Frankfurt. He feared that the terrorists might have used his son as a dupe and planted a bomb in his luggage. In any case, he intended to sue Pan Am for $50 million.

Commenting on the possibility that Jafaar's friends in Frankfurt might have tampered with or switched one of his bags, Neil Gallagher, of the FBI's counter-terrorist section, said: 'This is the type of relationship we are analysing as we look at the passenger manifest.'

If Lester Coleman in Chicago had heard or read about the FBI's suspicions then, ten days after Flight 103 had gone down, before the investigators stopped contradicting one another, and before politics intruded to distort or suppress their findings, the course of events might have taken a different turn.

Had he known that Khalid Jafaar, a DEA courier, had been aboard, and put two and two together, the Defense Intelligence Agency might well have reactivated him to take a hand in the game, as it had in the past when the DIA found itself embarrassed by the activities of TV evangelist Pat Robertson and Lt-Colonel Oliver North. In that event, Coleman might have had a role in cleaning up after the DEA rather than, in the end, being compelled to act as a witness against it. Even so, ten days after the disaster, the essential questions about the fate of Flight 103 had been answered; what remained was the burden of proof and the issue of contributory negligence.

The search for forensic evidence had gone well. On Christmas Eve, a foot-long piece of aluminium luggage pallet, scorch-marked by the explosion, was recovered, showing clear traces of the chemical constituents of Semtex-H plastic explosive. Further tests at the Royal Armament Research and Development Establishment (RARDE) at Fort Halstead in Kent also established, from fragments of polystyrene and tiny pieces of circuit board trapped in the wreckage of the luggage container, that the explosive device had been housed in a black Toshiba radio-cassette recorder, a two-speaker version of the Toshiba Bombeat bomb found by the German BKA in Dalkamoni's car. Tests at RARDE on pieces of blast-damaged luggage also proved that the device had been packed in a copper-coloured Samsonite suitcase.

This was a remarkable piece of scientific detection, considering there were an estimated four million pieces of wreckage from Flight 103 strewn clear across the Scottish Lowlands into northern England, but it was virtually the end of that line of inquiry. Bits of the bomb, bits of the clothing that had been packed around it, and bits of the suitcase the bombers had used were the only hard evidence the searchers would ever find at the scene of the crime. And it would probably have been enough, other things being equal, but German suspicions that the Americans, aided by the British, were still trying to duck the responsibility for the DEA/CIA operation that had gone so terribly wrong, filtered down to the Scottish police at ground level as plain bloody-minded obstructionism.

On 28 March 1989, Detective Chief Superintendent John Orr took the Germans to task about it at a conference in the Lockerbie Incident Control Centre. The minutes of the meeting show that he reviewed the evidence pointing to Frankfurt as the airport where the bomb was placed aboard and went on to detail the 'evidential connections' between the disaster and the activities of the PFLP–GC in West Germany, demanding that the BKA release their full files on the October raids and arrests.

'There was, he suggested, a strong circumstantial link, and it was essential to find out all possible information. He stressed that he was not saying conclusively that these people did commit murder, but there is strong circumstantial evidence.'

Orr also reported progress in matching passengers with their baggage. 'However, if a "rogue" suitcase had been introduced into the system, and if the suitcase containing the bomb did not belong to a passenger, then further close examination of baggage-handlers and others would be carried out.'

Circumstantial or not, the evidence against Dalkamoni, Ghadanfar and other members of the PFLP–GC cell in Germany had been strong enough to lead Britain's transport minister, Paul Channon, to tell five prominent political journalists over lunch at the Garrick Club two weeks earlier that arrests were imminent. They were the result, he said, of 'the most brilliant piece of detective work in history'. As their conversation was off the record, the information was attributed in media reports next day to 'senior government sources' – and was immediately attacked as prejudicial by all concerned.

Lord Fraser of Carmyllie, who, as Lord Advocate of Scotland, was in charge of the investigation, observed in the House of Lords that it was not likely to be assisted by such 'wild, irresponsible speculation'.

More directly to the point, 'Getting the bastards that did this is more important than taking credit for finding out who they are,' said an anonymous American 'intelligence source' quoted in *The Sunday Times*. 'It wasn't the Brits that found that out anyway,' he added, hinting at the inter-agency tensions that had bedevilled the inquiry from the start.

It was left to Pierre Salinger, chief foreign correspondent for the American ABC Network, to identify Channon as the background briefer. Trapped by then in a web of denials, the transport minister resigned shortly afterwards, but not, as it turned out, solely on account of his lunchtime indiscretions. He was probably also a casualty of an 'understanding' reached around this time between Prime Minister Margaret Thatcher and President George Bush, although both subsequently denied any such agreement.

According to Jack Anderson and Dale Van Atta in the *Washington Post*, 11 January 1990, the two leaders decided on the telephone in mid-March, 1989, to soft-pedal the Lockerbie investigation for several reasons.

One was so as not to prejudice negotiations aimed at securing the release of Western hostages in Beirut by arousing further animosity among the Syrian-backed or Iranian-sponsored terrorist groups who were holding them captive.

Another was that the shifting sands of Middle East politics now required the West to find some counterbalance in the region to the monster it had created in Saddam Hussein of Iraq – and the best available candidate for the job was Hussein's sworn enemy, President Hafez Assad of Syria.

While it was unfortunate that Assad permitted Ahmed Jibril's PFLP–GC to operate openly from Damascus and although it was clear that he controlled events in eastern Lebanon, where the hostages were held, in the joint State Department/Foreign Office view, the West now had little choice but to treat Syria as an object for diplomacy rather than of police work.

A third reason, no doubt, for not pressing the inquiry too rigorously was to shield Anglo-American intelligence operations in the Middle East from further embarrassment. The Scottish police were getting uncomfortably close to uncovering evidence of the DEA/CIA pipeline and the 'controlled' deliveries of Syrian heroin to Detroit – Monzer al-Kassar's price for using his influence with the Syrian leadership to help with the hostage problem.

Around the time of the Bush–Thatcher telephone call, Pan Am's investigators picked up the trail of the Lockerbie heroin and followed it to Cyprus. On making inquiries of the DEA in Nicosia, they were bluntly warned off on grounds of national security, a cry heard with increasing frequency as the airline tried to prepare its defence against the liability suits.

Sheila Hershow's interest in the same drugs lead may also have played a part in her unpublicized suspension a week later from the job of chief investigator to the House of Representatives Sub-Committee on Government Activities and Transportation. Two weeks after that, on 6 April 1989, she was fired for being 'uncontrollable' and 'dangerous'.

Further indications that the politicians had taken over were provided later in the year by Cecil Parkinson, Channon's successor as transport minister. In September, in response to misgivings expressed by the families of the Flight 103 victims about the apparent lack of progress in the investigation, he promised to arrange for an independent judicial inquiry at which sensitive intelligence information could be taken *in camera*, provided no word of his promise leaked out to the news media. Three months later, the minister (now Lord Parkinson) was obliged to tell them that he had been unable to convince his colleagues that such an inquiry was necessary and that the government had decided against it.

As the magazine *Private Eye* observed:

If, after a major tragedy, a secretary of state recommends a judicial inquiry into something which is his departmental responsibility, he is almost certain to get it. The exception would be if the colleague who resisted it was the prime minister.

But why would she block an inquiry? The only possible answer is that she was advised against it by MI5. Can it be that senior officers there, like their counterparts in the US and West Germany, are anxious to draw a veil over the Lockerbie incident? None of them wants anyone to know how a bomb, of a type which the security services already knew about, came to be placed in a suitcase which, if the current theory is to be believed, travelled from Malta to Frankfurt, where it changed planes, and then from Frankfurt to Heathrow, *where it changed planes again*, without being identified.

It was a fair point. Added to the Thatcher–Bush accord on a low-key pursuit of the bombers and the consequent need for all the agencies concerned to meet on common ground, it serves to explain why the Lockerbie investigation stalled in mid-1989 and never really got going again, leaving John Orr and the Scottish police to spin their wheels in frustration. After the Thatcher–Bush accord, the emphasis of government policy changed, none too subtly, from catching the bombers, whose identities and whereabouts were known, to pinning the blame for the bombing entirely on Pan Am and the undeniable inadequacy of its security arrangements at Frankfurt.

In this, the US government had powerful allies, commanding everybody's sympathy. Relatives of the victims of Flight 103 had legitimate claims for compensation against Pan Am and its insurers, but under the Warsaw Convention of 1929, the airline's liability was limited to a maximum of $75,000 for each passenger *unless* the claimants could prove wilful misconduct on the part of the airline.

The enthusiasm with which American law firms undertook to represent the families on a contingency basis in order to prove just that, coupled with the unstinting help they received from the US government in support of their claims, ensured that, from then on, Pan Am would be pilloried at the bar of public opinion to a degree just short of what might have been expected if it had wilfully blown up its own aircraft.

Any attempt on the part of the airline, its lawyers and insurers to shift any part of the blame back to where they thought it belonged, on the government agencies whose operational deficiencies had let the terrorists through, was promptly denounced in the news media as a sleazy attempt to duck responsibility for the disaster and thereby to avoid having to foot the bill for the generous financial settlements to which the grieving families were clearly entitled. (Pan Am later offered $100,000 in compensation to each of the families but this was rejected.)

Surprisingly, perhaps, the most temperate comment came from Bert Ammerman, president of American Victims of Flight 103, representing many of the families claiming compensation. 'If what Pan Am is saying cannot be substantiated, then Pan Am is through,' he said. 'But if what Pan Am is saying *is* true, then we have the most major scandal in the history of government in the twentieth century.'

He was right on both counts.

What Pan Am was saying was that, good, bad or indifferent (and they were certainly bad), its security arrangements at Frankfurt were probably irrelevant. Intelligence information strongly suggested that the bomb suitcase had been put on the conveyor *after* the baggage for Flight 103 had been cleared through the airline's security checks.

Within days of the disaster, lawyers acting for the families were seeking to get around the Warsaw Convention's $75,000 limit by alleging that Pan Am had wilfully disregarded prior warnings of a terrorist attack. (To hedge their bets, they also served notice that they would file claims against the US government as well for failing to pass on the warnings.)

On 2 November, the FAA alerted the airlines with a warning, similar to one already issued by the Germans, about the Toshiba radio-cassette bomb found in Dalkamoni's car. On 17 November, this was followed up with another bulletin describing the bomb in detail and urging all airlines to be extra vigilant. The British

Department of Transport underlined this with a warning of its own on 22 November and had a further detailed description of the bomb in preparation when it was overtaken by events.

On 5 December the American Embassy in Helsinki received an anonymous call about a plot to blow up a Pan Am aircraft flying from Frankfurt to the United States 'within the next two weeks'. On 7 December, the FAA advised all US air carriers of the threat, and the State Department circulated an unclassified warning to all its embassies.

This was taken particularly seriously in Moscow, where the entire American community was advised of the threat. Like the earlier alerts, the Helsinki warning was still in force when Flight 103 took off from Frankfurt on 21 December, and although it was later dismissed as a coincidental hoax, this was no consolation to the families of those who, unaware of the State Department's warning to its staff, had bought standby tickets for seats on Flight 103 vacated by American diplomats.

With the US, British and German governments prepared to stand pat on what they *had* done to alert everybody (except the travelling public) to the danger, attention then shifted from the weaker ground of Pan Am's wilful disregard of these warnings to the more promising ground of its wilful failure to observe the FAA's baggage-security requirements.

The first suggestion that the airline might be vulnerable to this line of attack had appeared in the *New York Post* only two days after the disaster. A report from Tel Aviv declared that an Israeli security firm had told Pan Am two years earlier that its security arrangements in Frankfurt and London were 'dangerously lax'.

This story was quickly followed by reports that baggage recovered from the wreckage could not be matched with any of the passengers aboard Flight 103. According to the *Sunday Telegraph*, 'The implications of this are causing investigators grave concern because police believe that matching luggage to victims is an essential first step towards tracing the bombers.'

It was Pan Am's concern over problems of baggage security that had led the airline in 1986 to commission a survey of its procedures from KPI Inc., the New York arm of an Israeli firm of consultants headed by Yossi Langotsky and Isaac Yeffet, former chief of security for El Al. Their 200-page confidential report was scathing. As copies began to turn up in newspaper offices around the world, lawyers for the families seized on it avidly.

'Pan Am is highly vulnerable to most forms of terrorist attack. The fact that no major disaster has occurred to date [1986] is merely providential,' was one of the more damaging conclusions.

Another was that Pan Am's security was in the hands of 'an organizational set-up which suffers from a lack of authority, and an alarmingly low level of training and instruction'.

And again: 'The striking discordance between the actual security level and the security as advertised by the corporation may sooner or later become a cause of harmful publicity. In the event of casualties or damage resulting from terrorist action, the question of fraudulent advertisement would assume even greater significance.'

And worst of all: 'There are no adequate safeguards under the presently operating security system that would prevent a passenger from boarding a plane with explosives on his person or in his baggage, whether or not he is aware of the fact.'

No matter how Pan Am protested after the report became public that changes had been made which 'satisfied both the security needs of Pan Am *and* the Federal Aviation Administration'; no matter that the co-author of the KPI Report, Isaac Yeffet, said after the Lockerbie disaster that Pan Am had been unlucky, in the sense that its security was neither better nor worse than that of other airlines – Pan Am appeared now to stand before the world virtually self-condemned of wilful misconduct.

Certainly, any deliberate evasion of security regulations exposing passengers to unnecessary risk would have merited that charge. And certainly, there were security lapses by Pan Am at Frankfurt on 21 December 1988 that were probably unpardonable after the airline had been warned of the dangers of terrorist attack. Nevertheless, Pan Am's procedures were essentially the same as those followed by every other airline (but one) at every other airport in the world.

As the DEA, the BKA, H.M. Customs and Excise and any international drug trafficker like Monzer al-Kassar will acknowledge, if it is possible for suitcases to be lost or stolen in transit, it must also be possible for suitcases to be switched or *added* in transit. With the security systems operated by every airline in the world (but one), there is no finally effective way of preventing corrupt airport workers from putting an unchecked bag in with legitimate luggage for a flight to America or of preventing corrupt airport workers in the US from intercepting that bag on arrival – and a bag smuggled aboard in this manner could as easily contain explosives as a shipment of heroin.

The only way to exclude, with reasonable certainty, the possibility of a bomb being placed on a passenger flight is to have the aircraft guarded around the clock, to hand-search everything that goes aboard, accompanied or not, and then to keep everything and everybody under continuous observation until the aircraft doors are closed for departure – and even then, the risk of human error or corruption would remain.

Among airlines, only El Al does that, and because of the time it takes to hand-search every piece of baggage, passengers are required to check in at least three hours before departure.

If all airlines were obliged to do the same, airport terminals around the world would come to a standstill. At Frankfurt alone, about 60,000 pieces of luggage are fed through the airport's baggage-handling system every day. If they all had to be hand-searched, existing flight schedules would have to be abandoned, and international air traffic on its present scale would soon become impossible – a level of disruption that terrorists would no doubt be delighted to achieve without risk or effort on their part.

Today, the danger of terrorist attack, like the danger of design faults, equipment failure, pilot error, traffic congestion, bad weather, metal fatigue, bird-ingestion and all the other acts of God and man against which it is impossible to legislate, is a risk every passenger takes in using so convenient, and so vulnerable, a service as air travel – which is not to suggest that governments and airlines are under anything but the most solemn obligation to minimize those risks in every possible way.

In the case of Pan Am Flight 103, both government and carrier failed in their duty, but in the 'national interest' and for reasons of 'national security', the airline was left to carry the full burden of blame.

At the very least, this was a gross dereliction of responsibility. The destruction of Flight 103 was not simply an attack on a commercial airliner but a deliberate act of war against the United States, whose government was, and is, accountable for the safety of its citizens at home and abroad.

To expect an unsubsidized commercial airline to assume a government's role in defending its citizens against state-sponsored terrorism, as well as the more specific function of airport security in a host country, is unreasonable. The airline's duty is to provide a third line of defence against the known danger, and, however defective this may have been in Pan Am's case, it can hardly be blamed for defects in the first and second lines of defence. For the US and German governments to disown any responsibility for letting the terrorists through, and then to blame everything on Pan Am after their own agents had connived at bypassing an already inadequate third line of defence was unconscionable.

But once the findings of the KPI Report became known, anything Pan Am chose to say or do was dismissed as a cheap attempt to pass the buck. All that the lawyers for the victims' families needed to do in order to get around the provisions of the Warsaw Convention was to show that Pan Am had been warned of the risk of terrorist attack and had not done enough about it. Now, with every reason to suppose they could make the charge stick, a legal action 'proving' wilful misconduct on the part of the airline would also have the effect of absolving all three governments of *their* misconduct.

By the end of 1989, with the investigation effectively stalled for political reasons, with public opinion conditioned to accept that the mass murder of 270 airline passengers was Pan Am's fault, and with the BKA at last prepared to acquiesce in a joint cover story, the American, German and British co-sponsors of the 'controlled delivery' run from Lebanon to the United States could relax a little.

No one was likely to talk. Everyone connected with the operation had some degree of culpability or negligence to conceal, and no one could be required to testify while they remained in government service. As they approached the first anniversary of the disaster, the only really worrying loose end was Lester Coleman, the one man outside the loop who knew about the heroin pipeline at first hand, who had fallen out with the DEA on Cyprus, who was no friend to the CIA, and who had just been reactivated by the Defense Intelligence Agency for Operation Shakespeare.

Could he be trusted to keep his mouth shut?

He had chosen to involve himself with the Lockerbie disaster by appearing on network television to answer questions about it. And barely three months later, Pan Am's lawyers and investigators had arrived on Cyprus asking about a dope pipeline to the United States.

A coincidence? Or had Coleman gone off the reservation?

With the 'national interest' at stake, who could afford to take chances? It was a job for the octopus.

— VI —

Coleman's first assignment for the United States government was in 1982, when the CIA sent him to the Bahamas to interfere in the islands' elections.

By then, his love affair with broadcast journalism had reached the point of separation and divorce, but not without some purple patches along the way. Among the most memorable was his final year with the Boy Scouts of America, before he left it for the first time in 1974. Though increasingly disturbed by its paramilitary functions, he had no reservations about accompanying Norman Rockwell, Mr America himself, on tour from sea to shining sea with his Boy Scout paintings, featuring Mom, Dad, apple pie and Old Glory.

Coleman's job was to act as a buffer between the grand old illustrator and his adoring female public and to arrange radio/TV coverage for the explosion of patriotic sentiment touched off by this travelling exhibition of *Boy's Life* magazine covers in cities across the nation. But he was still on the wrong side of the fence, and, as Walter Cronkite kept saying, 'If you want to be a network correspondent, you've got to get some experience first at a local TV station, pay your dues and move on up the ladder. You just can't start off at the top in New York.'

Taking the advice to heart, Coleman replied to all the likely want ads in *Broadcasting* magazine, tapped all the friends he had made in the media, and bombarded the industry with copies of his resumé, finally reaping the reward for perseverance with the offer of a job as late night news anchor back home in Birmingham, Alabama, with WAPI-TV.

He lasted six months. It was not that he objected to being a one-man show, writing, editing and delivering the news, sport and weather; it was just that he grew tired of being stopped on the street and criticized for the necktie he had worn the night before.

In radio, you didn't even have to *wear* a necktie. At the invitation of WSGN programme director Jan Jeffries, he moved on to become news director of Alabama's top radio station, with studios in the penthouse of the City Federal Savings & Loan Building, 'The Big Six-Ten', where he lasted three years.

There I was, free to cover stories I felt would have an impact [he says]. And a lot of them came through Aaron Kohn, director of the New Orleans Metropolitan Crime Commission, who really got my juices going as an investigative reporter. Following through on leads I got from him, we aired reports linking the state attorney-general to New Orleans crime figures, and ran a whole series of in-depth probes into corruption and serious social issues. There were some unserious ones, too – like the piece we ran on the wire-tap that Cornelia Wallace put on Governor George Wallace's bedroom phone. After I aired the story, he exiled her to Elba, Alabama, and called me up to say I was a nitwit shit, no bigger than a pinhead.

Others held a higher opinion. Coleman was making a name for himself in investigative journalism. During his tenure, the station won the International Edward R. Murrow Award from the Radio Television News Directors Association; the National Sigma Delta Chi Award for Public Service, and the National Headliner Award. But they earned him no laurels from management, despite Jeffries's enthusiasm. WSGN was one of six stations owned by Southern Broadcasting, a deeply conservative company that seemed sometimes to regard the weather forecast as a threat to the status quo. An invitation to join the Special Investigations Unit of WBZ-TV, Boston, in December 1978, probably arrived in the nick of time.

The move from 65th-market radio to 4th-market television was not only a significant leap upwards in his career but Coleman had been head-hunted on the strength of his growing national reputation to do what he liked to do most: non-deadline exposés of graft and corruption. He rented an expensive apartment in Concord, Massachusetts, just down the road from Walden Pond, and moved a somewhat reluctant Jocelyn up from Alabama with their two children – Karen, now ten, and Guy, aged three.

But there are exposés and exposés. WBZ-TV was part of the Westinghouse Broadcasting Network, and run with the same corporate zeal as Westinghouse displayed, wearing its defence contractor hat, in charging the Pentagon $9096 for Allen wrenches that cost 12 cents each in Handy Dan's. Coleman embarked on a six-month investigation of design faults and cost overruns in the supply of Boston's new mass-transit trolley cars by Boeing Vertol, a defence contractor, like Westinghouse, and better known as builders of military helicopters.

Coleman recalls:

Any city that agreed to buy Boeing's product got an automatic grant from Nixon's Urban Mass Transit Administration. Didn't matter that the trolleys didn't work. Didn't matter they were dangerous, that their plane plastic interiors gave off toxic smoke if they caught fire – any city that bought them still got its grant. So after digging around for six months, we went on air with a 35-minute report, lead story on the six o'clock 'Eyewitness News', exposing the whole thing. Big sensation. Media spin-off all around the country. The city of Boston sued Boeing and the federal government, and Westinghouse folded its Special Investigations Unit. I'd breached the Eleventh Commandment. Thou shalt not expose defence contractors.

Coleman won a New England Emmy for the programme, but it was time to move on – to Washington now for a stripped-to-the-bone security vetting before joining the White House press corps as correspondent for the RKO Radio Network. On the face of it, Coleman was now within reach of everything he had ever dreamed of in broadcast journalism, but in fact running around after Jimmy Carter for two years turned out to be the most boring episode of his professional career.

Reporters assigned to cover the President are not reporters at all [he insists]. They're hand-out takers – told what to report, how to report it and when to report it. Break the rules and goodbye press pass. There's no room for enterprise at all. The whole White House press operation is geared to feeding the television networks, making sure that the evening newscasts have the proper 'spin'. The rest – and there were 150 of us when I was there – were more or less along for the ride.

Never mind what the Constitution says, the role of the American media is to inform the electorate of what the Administration wants it to hear in the way the White House wants it done. The press office manages the media the way you manage a spaniel, by leaking tid-bits to TV correspondents as a reward for stories that flatter the President and punishing them for stories that make the President look bad by shutting them out of the house. You get some rebels but they don't last. They *can't*, if they're shut out of background briefings. So most of the White House press corps just scamper around like puppies in pin-stripe suits, caught up in the ego trip of trotting along at the heels of the leader of the free world. Ask any honest reporter who's covered that beat – it's a gruelling, back-breaking bore.

The nomadic life of a newsman had already cost Coleman his marriage. Jocelyn was tired of packing and unpacking and starting again somewhere else every two years. She wanted to settle down and raise her family, and he could not fault her for that.

'They say there are three things you can't keep if you want the job of White House correspondent – and I *wanted* it: plants, pets and wives. Everybody I knew there was divorced. But it went deeper than that. Jocelyn and I had married too young and we'd grown apart, that was the truth of it. We woke up one morning and found we weren't the people we had been before. We both tried to keep things going, but it didn't work out. And that was mostly *my* fault. I still have deep scars and regrets about the way I conducted myself. It was the worst time of my life.'

Resigning after the 1980 election, Coleman went off to Connecticut to win another New England Emmy with WFSB-TV, Hartford, and to write a book about the Mafia.

The Ethel Donaghue case made him an instant celebrity. Coleman's story of how a crooked probate judge had conspired with corporation counsel to bilk an old lady of $83 million by having her declared incompetent plucked at Connecticut's heartstrings, bringing him not only an Emmy but more criticism of his taste in neckties at supermarket check-outs and the friendship of FBI Agent Danny Mahan.

'Boy, have I got a subject for you,' Mahan said, when Coleman told him one night in their favourite bar that he wanted to write a book.

The subject's name was Richie Pedemonti, who had spent the last three of his 20 years in organized crime as an FBI informant. Refusing to go into the Federal witness protection programme after his cover was blown, Richie had fallen on hard times, made all the harder when his wife divorced him, unable to face life without a pink Cadillac and regular trips to Las Vegas. Although the FBI agents he had worked with had done their best to get him on his feet again, they were running out of ideas when Mahan took Pedemonti to meet Coleman at the Arch Street Tavern, behind the Bureau's Hartford office.

Fascinated by Richie's inside view of the mob scene, Coleman rented a small studio on Asylum Street and set to work on *Squeal*, a book anatomizing the mob's business interests in New England – his collaborator, as often as not, sleeping on the studio floor. Even with a grant from the Fund for Investigative Reporting in Washington to match a small advance from the publishers, Spoonwood Press, their standard of living was austere, and Coleman was obliged to do some additional, part-time reporting for WCVB-TV, Boston in order to keep the project afloat.

When his WFSB-TV source of income ran dry at the end of 1981 – Coleman had gone after a businessman implicated in a Federal housing scam, not knowing that he was the station manager's neighbour – the collaboration seemed headed for the rocks, but then the CIA came to the rescue. In mid-December, Richie was summoned to a meeting on Long Island to discuss the Pizza Connection case, and, as he was unwilling to go alone, Coleman agreed to tag along.

Two weeks later, Coleman took a call at his studio from a government agent who declined to identify himself but proposed a chat and a drink at the airport Ramada Inn. Coleman recognized him at once by the drip-dry suit, white shirt and wing-tip shoes.

'Understand you guys could use a little cash,' the agent said affably, after they had settled in a quiet corner of the bar.

'Yeah, well, without it, I'd say posterity is going to be deprived of a literary masterpiece. What do I have to do?'

'How about a few days in the Bahamas?'

Coleman put down his drink. 'You're going to pay me to go down to the Bahamas? In January? Who do I have to kill?'

The agent chuckled politely. 'Guy we know down there just lost his wife from cancer. Nice lady. Name of Rose. Helped us for years. She was a real *asset* – you know what I mean?'

'Okay.' That was when Coleman realized he was talking to the CIA. 'Sure. I know what you mean.'

'Fine. Well, she left a ton of papers and documents we need. And some people we know think you might be just the guy to help us out.'

'Yeah? How?'

'Soon as her husband gets the stuff together, we'd like for you to stop by their place and bring it out for us, that's all.'

'Well, I think I can handle that,' said Coleman cautiously. It seemed like a complicated way of dealing with a simple problem but he was broke and tired and not disposed to quarrel with the idea of a few days in the sun at the government's expense. 'Do I take Richie with me?'

'Hell, no. Not on your life. He's not to know anything about this.'

Rose's husband, now widower, turned out to be an American expatriate of about 30 years' standing, with business interests in the islands and a lovely old house across the street from the governor's mansion in Nassau. When Coleman stopped by, expecting to pick up a huge box of documents, he was handed a couple of rolls of film.

'Is that it?'

'That's it,' he said. 'That's what you came for. Have a nice trip.'

After ten days in Nassau, Coleman felt guilty about accepting the paper bag that the CIA agent offered him in exchange for the film when he arrived back in Hartford – until he looked inside.

'What the hell's this?'

'That's two thousand dollars,' the agent said. 'In Italian lira.'

'What am I supposed to do with Italian lira?'

'You're supposed to take a run over to JFK and change 'em into dollars.'

'Oh. Okay. Tell me, you know a guy named Danny Graham? *General* Danny Graham?'

'Yeah,' the agent said cheerfully. 'I heard of General Graham.'

A few days later, he called to fix another date at the Ramada Inn.

'How'd you like to go down to Nassau again?' he said. 'There's something else we'd sure like you to do for us down there, if you got the time. And I guess you could still use the money.'

'That's a pretty good guess,' agreed Coleman, who somehow had to tide himself over for another month or two until he could finish the book. 'What do you want me to bring back this time? Robert Vesco's head?'

'Ha ha,' said the agent. 'No, this time, you'll take some stuff down for us. Including your typewriter. You can stay in the cottage behind Rose's house and work there.'

'Sounds good to me.' He was still broke, and more tired than ever. 'What is it – this stuff you want me to take?'

The agent smiled benevolently. 'You got a public relations background, right? Used to work for the Boy Scouts, I hear.'

'That's right. That was before I got to be a legitimate journalist.'

'Well, you're not a journalist *now*, are you?' He seemed worried suddenly. 'I mean, you're writing a book, but that's not the same, is it?'

'No, I guess not.' Coleman was unaware at the time that the American intelligence community was under orders *not* to use the media as a cover for its agents. 'It's kind of a longer range project.'

'Well, that's good. Because here's a situation where we think you can really help us, with your media experience. And I think you'll enjoy it.'

As he certainly enjoyed the Bahamas, and as his first mission had been harmless enough, Coleman agreed to go without even asking what was expected of him. The widower would fill him in when he got there, the agent said.

'And we're going to give you some alternative identification to use instead of your passport,' he added. 'You'll be in and out a couple of times, so we'll get you a birth certificate in another name. That's all you need for the Bahamas – a birth certificate. So I want you to fill out one of these applications.'

He produced forms from three different states, and after some discussion they settled on one for Connecticut, as Coleman was more familiar with that state than with the other two.

'Should I use my own date of birth?' he asked.

'No, better not. This has got to be a whole new identity.'

'Well, I'm not too good with dates. If I can't remember my own birthday, that could be embarrassing.'

'Well, put down July the Fourth,' said the agent. 'You're not going to forget that one.'

He went away with the completed application form and came back in a couple of hours with a Connecticut birth certificate in the name of Thomas Leavy, born on the Fourth of July, 1948.

A few days later, Coleman set off on his first covert operation for the octopus, which was to discipline the prime minister and government of the Bahamas and remind them of their dependence on America's good will.

Lyndon O. Pindling had been framed in Washington's sights since offering sanctuary to the runaway financier Robert Vesco, and even before that had incurred American displeasure by consorting brazenly with money launderers and senior members of the Colombian cocaine cartels.

As the widower explained to Coleman on arrival, the CIA would feed them information on these associations and it was their job to use the dirt where it would do the most damage. He would see that it reached the ears of Pindling's political opponents, and in particular the Free National Movement, which could be counted on to make hay with it during the election campaign. Coleman's role was to use his public relations experience to get the maximum possible mileage from it in the Bahamian and mainland media.

Not having bargained on helping to run a dirty tricks campaign in somebody else's elections, and in any case feeling he had been suckered into it, Coleman hesitated for a day or two before finally persuading himself that Pindling was a rotten egg anyway and deserved all he had coming. Though scarcely aware of it at the time, he had crossed the line. It was easier, after Thomas Leavy's mission to Nassau, to accept that in the real world it was sometimes necessary to do good by stealth, and that it was all right for the United States to interfere in the domestic affairs of other countries because everybody knew it was constitutionally committed to the greater good of the greatest number.

Upon his return to Hartford, Coleman changed another bagful of Italian lira at JFK airport, finished *Squeal*, and in 1983, after the book appeared in the stores, took a job as field producer with 'The Jack Anderson Show'.

As a legitimate journalist again, this put him out of reach of his new friends at the CIA, who were now calling periodically to see if he was ready to change his mind and work for the Company full-time. And there were moments when he wavered. The trivialization of broadcast news by the networks had made him uneasy about the future; the world was too complicated to deal with in picture opportunities and soundbites. Reporting in depth was what he wanted to do, and what he felt he was good at. The rest was just showbiz. Already he was looking back on his time at WBZ-TV, Boston, as the good old days.

For a while, 'The Jack Anderson Show' gave him the scope he needed. Indeed, one story he worked on, in which he managed to get cameras inside a camp run by the Ku Klux Klan for training kids to be Klansmen, came close to his ideal of what investigative journalism was all about, but a few months later the show folded, yet another casualty in the trend towards news as entertainment. Faced with a choice between unemployment, WMAR-TV – a Baltimore station owned by the same company – and the CIA, Coleman chose Baltimore.

It was a mistake. Determined not to repeat its experience with 'The Jack Anderson Show', management had made up its collective mind to spare viewers the agony of thought by censoring any provocative, or even serious, material from local newscasts. The station wanted a 90-second exposé every night, and Coleman was free to do anything he liked in that spot, provided it had to do with sex, drugs or rock 'n' roll.

With a family to support (he and Jocelyn were separated but not yet divorced), Coleman tried his best and even met management half-way with an off-beat story about a local attorney, James B. McCloskey, who ran a quickie divorce business from his home at 301 Timonium Road, Timonium, Maryland.

Working with a partner, Fernando Cornielle, in Santo Domingo, McCloskey claimed he could get a divorce for anybody, even for those who didn't want to tell their spouses. It was not necessary to leave the country, and no court appearances were required. All petitioners had to do was sign a few papers, pay McCloskey his fee and bingo! Within a week, the decree would arrive by airmail, and, under the laws of the Dominican Republic, they were free to do it again.

His own best advertisement for the service, McCloskey had been married five times and would probably have gone on but for the fact that he was well past sixty and his last wife, an Internal Revenue Service (IRS) agent, was busting his ass through the courts. Tough, gruff, feisty and profane, he was almost the last person anyone would have suspected of being a spy-catcher, recruiting officer and consultant to the US Defense Intelligence Agency. Coleman certainly didn't when he aired his story about McCloskey's mail-order divorces or for some time after they became friends. None of it showed behind McCloskey's amiable façade, and even if it had, Coleman, like most other Americans to this day, had never even heard of the DIA.

Often at a loose end at weekends, he took to stopping by McCloskey's place on Saturdays to pick him up for lunch at a local Mexican café. Over tacos and Dos Equis, Coleman would complain about the assholes who ran WMAR, McCloskey would listen sympathetically, although convinced Coleman was wasting his time anyway 'with all this bullshit news business', and divert him with stories about his ancestors.

One of these Coleman wrote up for the *Baltimore* magazine.

According to McCloskey, his forebears had once owned the Liberty Bell in Philadelphia's Independence Hall and he was planning to sue the city to get his bell back. Before long, he had taken Coleman under his wing in much the same way as Tom Geohagen had appointed himself the younger man's mentor in the Boy Scouts.

'If you ever wanna do something meaningful with your life,' he said one day, after Coleman confided that his running battle with WMAR's management was likely to get him fired, 'all I gotta do is pick up that phone. I know a lotta people in D.C. who'd snap you up in a minute.'

'Like who?'

'Never mind. When you're ready to give up this bullshit, just say the word.'

A week later, Coleman was declared surplus to WMAR's requirements, but he was still not ready to say the word. For one thing, to have abandoned journalism at that point would have left him feeling defenceless against the CIA, which for months had been pressing him to the point of harassment. He had even complained about it to Laurie Bernard, a TV producer in Washington whom he was dating at the time.

It was getting close to blackmail. 'Well, now, you know, you worked for us a couple of times, and you're a journalist and all – I mean, how's that going to look if it gets out?' was the usual line. 'The media's not going to like that. On the other hand, you could have a secure future with us, with a pension at the end of it. And that's something you ought to consider very seriously. People in TV news don't get pensions. They get fired.'

In his late thirties, with a broken marriage and his career fizzling out, Coleman felt trapped in the wreckage. After several days of putting resumés together in McCloskey's office, of calling around the industry on McCloskey's telephone, and badgering his agent, David Crane, in San Francisco, for a network news opening overseas where he could do some serious work, Coleman touched bottom one night in a waterfront bar and showed up next morning at McCloskey's place ready to throw in his hand.

Among his telephone messages was one from Crane, who had got him a freelance assignment with Cable News Network (CNN) in New York.

For six weeks, Coleman worked out of the new CNN bureau across from Penn station, running around town with a camera crew doing one or two pieces a day, covering the UN and interviewing notables, from Mayor Ed Koch to visiting Israeli Premier Shimon Peres – and then lightning struck. Crane called to say that CBS had seen his work for CNN and had asked for a tape and his resumé. Its foreign desk was thinking of adding another producer.

'This is *it*,' Coleman told McCloskey, exultant.

It wasn't.

He was kept dangling for several months while CBS News reorganized itself around Dan Rather and News Vice President Howard Stringer. Then at last, on 19 August 1984, Don DeCesare, the assistant foreign editor, called to ask Coleman if he was free to go to Saudi Arabia as an assistant producer with senior correspondent Tom Fenton to cover the Hadj, Islam's annual pilgrimage to Mecca. The contract would run for six weeks, and he would work on the story with Rome Bureau Chief Peter Schweitzer out of the Jeddah Hyatt hotel.

'Take it,' said David Crane. 'They want to see what you can do.'

Coleman needed little urging, although he already knew that one of the things he would have to do was to keep the Jewish chief of the Rome Bureau well away from Saudi officialdom. Then, as now, the country was a tightly run police state, a true kingdom, where the house of Saud literally owned the country and its citizens, and where arbitrary arrest was an automatic response to breaches of political or religious protocol.

They gave me a CBS News ID [Coleman remembers] and the next evening I took an Air France flight to Paris, connecting four hours later with a flight to Jeddah. After nearly twenty years away from the Middle East, it felt like I was coming home at last. Then culture shock. On clearing customs and immigration, I stepped out of the terminal into the glaring heat to grab a cab, and there, strung over the four-lane highway, was a banner in Arabic which said, 'Please refrain from auto-racing'. Kids in Porsche 911s and Mercedes 350SLs, rich and bored, amused themselves by weaving in and out of the traffic at 100 miles an hour plus.

Otherwise, it could just as easily have been Tucson, Arizona. Riding over to the Hyatt, and talking to the driver to free off my rusty Arabic, we passed big American-style shopping malls, Kentucky Fried Chicken restaurants – even Taco Bell joints. The women, especially the young girls, were the only visible difference. With nothing to do but shop, they were in and out of the stores, cloaked from head to toe, soda straws sticking out from their veils as they sucked on their Slurpies, giggling, gossiping, buying designer jeans and Walkman stereos. I mean, what have we *done* to those people?

Schweitzer was not particularly pleased to see him and let it be known up front that *he* was running the show. Although he had declared himself 'an agnostic' to the Saudi authorities, his evident unfamiliarity with the Arab world made Coleman even more nervous for he had realized within hours of his arrival that all foreigners were under close surveillance. With Islamic fervour at its height, he knew there would be hell to pay for the whole crew – jail or worse – if the Saudis were given even the slightest room to suppose that Schweitzer was an Israeli spy.

The security police were everywhere [says Coleman]. All interviews and shoots had to be cleared in advance – there was no going out on our own, shooting pictures in the streets. Anybody caught doing that was put on the next plane out and had his cameras and gear confiscated.

My job was to go around to the Ministry of Communications every day with a box of tapes, sit down for hours on end and negotiate each shot. Every foot of video we wanted to up-link by satellite had to be previewed by Saudi censors. If they didn't like a shot of a Hadji shaving or pilgrims passing out in the heat, out it had to go. Anything sensitive, anything I knew we couldn't get by, we had to smuggle out in video-tape machines, hoping Customs wouldn't look inside.

Due in large measure to his knowledge of Arab ways, the assignment passed off without incident and Coleman returned to New York confident that he had shown CBS what he could do and that a full-time contract offer would now be forthcoming. But, if anything, morale on West 57th Street was lower than when he had left. Don't hold your breath, was the best Don DeCesare could offer. 'Who knows?' he said. 'I may be selling aluminum siding in Bridgeport myself next month.'

Coleman went down to Baltimore to see McCloskey.

'Okay,' he said. 'Who are these people you're always talking about?'

Ironically, he heard some weeks later that he was under consideration for a producer's slot with the CBS correspondent in Amman, but by then Coleman had been visited by two young men wearing double-knit sports jackets and highly polished black shoes who asked a thousand questions and took notes and had him fill in the permission forms they produced from their identical grey briefcases so that the US Army could proceed with a full security vetting.

At thirty-nine, he had finally committed himself to joining the octopus as a secret agent of the armed forces of the United States – and taken the first step on the road to exile.

— VII —

When President George Bush and Prime Minister Margaret Thatcher agreed on the telephone in March 1989, to keep the Flight 103 investigation within politically acceptable limits, the octopus was presented with a tricky problem of news management.

As the only official source of information about the disaster, as well as the only official source of information about government business in general, the American and British bureaucracies could count on the polite attention of every mainstream journalist, but the story had run for months and it was hardly possible to retract the tips, leaks, official statements and background briefings already given.

The consensus was that the Syrian-backed PFLP–GC had committed the atrocity for the Iranians; that the Libyans had probably had a hand in it by supplying the bomb components; that the individuals responsible had been identified, and that warrants could be expected at any time.

Undoing these now inconvenient views and expectations was not going to be easy, even without the continued meddling of congressional committees, boards of inquiry, lawyers for both sides in the compensation dispute and police officers still treating the case as a murder investigation. There was also the problem of what to do with the Germans, because there was no way of putting a suitable gloss on events without them.

At their baldest, the new policy requirements were that Syria and, to a lesser extent, Iran should be eased out of the picture, leaving Libya solely to blame, but without seeming to deny or tamper with evidence already made public and without appearing to allow expediency a higher priority than the ruthless pursuit of justice.

Given the usually uncritical reception of 'official news' by the media, and the patriotic reluctance of most people to believe the worst of their own governments, this should have been possible, but the solution to the problem rested in the hands of those who had created it in the first place, and in the end the task was to prove beyond them.

The first requirement was to get the Germans to cooperate, and the only way to do that was to show that the bomb had gone aboard Flight 103 in Frankfurt due to circumstances beyond their control.

After Detective Chief Superintendent John Orr had taken them to task in March 1989, for dragging their feet, the BKA in April sent him the files on the PFLP–GC cell they had broken up some eight weeks before the disaster – and by any reading, the circumstantial evidence against Dalkamoni, Ghadanfar and Khreesat was strong, not to say overwhelming. Although the first two remained in custody, charged with bombing American military trains in Germany, Khreesat and the other PFLP–GC suspects rounded up in the raids had, unaccountably, been released – a decision which, on the face of it, might well have cost 270 lives.

A possible solution was to show that the bronze Samsonite suitcase containing the bomb had been fed into the system at some other airport, and that it was therefore a failure on Pan Am's part which had allowed it to go aboard Flight 103 in Frankfurt without an accompanying passenger. If this could be 'proved', then the German authorities would be no more to blame than the British at Heathrow, who had also allowed the bag to be transferred from one aircraft to another for the trans-Atlantic leg of the flight.

To make this version of events plausible, a few awkward facts had first to be smoothed over. There could be no suggestion, for instance, that Frankfurt was the European hub of a 'controlled delivery' pipeline for drugs in transit from the Middle East. There could be no suggestion that 'clean' suitcases, properly checked through, were routinely switched in the baggage-handling area with 'dirty' suitcases containing heroin en route to the United States. There could be no reports of 'suspicious activity' in the baggage-handling area before Flight 103 left Frankfurt on 21 December. Nor could there be any videotapes available from the security cameras in the baggage-handling area.

A good deal of embarrassing speculation had already been made public. On 30 July 1989, for instance, the *Observer*, in London, had published an 'exclusive' under the headline: 'Lockerbie: Turks "planted bomb."'

Reviewing the results of a 'three-month inquiry' into the disaster, the report said the paper had obtained specific information from a range of Middle East sources who have told us that Turkish nationals were brought into the plot to bomb the Pan Am Boeing 747 at the end of September last year ... Contact is said to have been made, on the instructions of a German-based Iranian diplomat, by a member of the PFLP–GC ...

According to our sources, five Turks were entrusted with the task of planting the bomb on the Pan Am plane ... One has been described as a 'young Turkish engineer' and it is this man who is said to have physically planted a suitcase containing the bomb inside a cargo container on the London-bound Boeing 727 ...

German officials who questioned airport workers after the bombing have refused either to support or dismiss this account. American intelligence agencies want to reexamine and trace all likely suspects, but they appear to have received little co-operation from the Germans. The 'engineer' allegedly left Germany for Beirut via Cyprus shortly after the bombing.

What was needed to divert attention away from Frankfurt into politically safer channels was some 'new' evidence, preferably linked to the hard forensic evidence that had already been established and which, by association, would lend credibility to it. And as the police officers engaged in the field investigation could not be counted upon to cooperate in a political fix, that evidence had to be 'found' in a plausible way, even at the cost of further inter-agency bickering.

On 17 August 1989, eight months after the disaster, Chief Detective Superintendent John Orr received from the BKA what was said to be a computer print-out of the baggage-loading list for Pan Am Flight 103A from Frankfurt to London on the afternoon of 21 December 1988. Attached to this were two internal reports, dated 2 February 1989, describing the inquiries that BKA officers had made about the baggage-handling system at the airport. Also provided were two worksheets, one typewritten, the other handwritten, that were said to have been prepared on 21 December by airport workers at key points on the conveyor-belt network.

In the margin of the computer print-out, a pencilled cross drew particular attention to bag number B8849 – that is the 8849th bag to be logged into the computerized system at Terminal B that day. By reference to the worksheets, B8849 could be shown to have arrived in Frankfurt by a scheduled Air Malta flight from Luqa airport and to have been 'interlined' through to Flight 103. But neither the Air Malta nor the Pan Am passenger lists showed anybody who had booked a through flight from Luqa to New York that day. In other words, bag B8849 had arrived from Malta unaccompanied but tagged for New York and had been loaded aboard Flight 103 without being matched with a passenger. And as the job of matching bags with passengers is the responsibility of the airline, not of the airport authorities or of the host government, Pan Am had plainly been guilty of lax security amounting to 'wilful misconduct'.

This tied in nicely with the forensic evidence, which had already shown that the bomb had been hidden in a Samsonite suitcase filled with an assortment of clothing made in Malta, including a baby's blue romper suit.

Less than three months after the disaster, in March 1989, two Scottish police officers had flown out to the island to interview the manufacturer of the romper suit but had drawn blank. At least 500 of them had been sold to babywear outlets all over Europe. To trace the purchaser of the suit that had been all but destroyed in the explosion was clearly impossible. Now, with the baggage records pointing to a suitcase originating in Malta, the field of search was dramatically narrowed.

Two weeks after the BKA released the Frankfurt baggage print-out, two of Detective Chief Superintendent John Orr's men returned to Malta and, with the help of the manufacturers, traced the clothing to a shop in Sliema.

As 'luck' would have it, the proprietors not only remembered selling the exact items which the forensic team had shown were used as packing around the bomb but remembered the date on which they had sold them, 23 November 1988, a month before the bombing; remembered the purchaser – a Libyan, they thought – and, ten months after the event, remembered what he looked like clearly enough to brief an FBI video-fit artist to produce an acceptable likeness to Abu Talb of the PFLP–GC, who was known to have visited Malta not long before the bombing.

Leaving the shopkeepers guarded around the clock by security men, the police officers returned home with their questions answered so neatly that in other circumstances they might have been forgiven for suspecting the witnesses had been coached.

Never mind that Air Malta, the Maltese police and the Maltese government categorically denied that any baggage, unaccompanied or otherwise, had been put aboard Air Malta Flight KM180 to connect with Pan Am 103 in Frankfurt on 21 December 1988, and never mind that the airline's record-keeping showed this to be so – as David Leppard of *The Sunday Times* pointed out later, if the fatal bag 'had been smuggled on to the flight unaccompanied, it must have bypassed Luqa's baggage control system. No one could blame the airline company for the criminal activities of a terrorist gang.'

He was not prepared to exercise the same understanding for Pan Am in Frankfurt, however. 'Under international airline rules, bags unaccompanied by passengers should never be allowed on to aircraft,' he wrote (erroneously) in *The Sunday Times* of 29 October 1989. 'The new evidence casts serious doubt on the theory that the bomb was placed on board in Frankfurt and carried by an unwitting passenger who died in the crash.'

Leppard did not address the possibility that the bomb might have 'bypassed' Pan Am's baggage-control system at Frankfurt in the same way as he suggested it might have bypassed Air Malta's at Luqa; nor did the *Independent*, in London, two days later.

'Police investigating the Lockerbie bombing,' the paper reported, 'have confirmed they are investigating whether the bomb was first placed aboard an airliner in Malta, and then transferred to the Pan Am flight even though it had no accompanying passenger.' The story went on to quote a spokesman for the BKA as saying 'there are clues that a suitcase from Malta may have played a part. There are also clues that someone from Libya – or at least, someone with a Libyan accent – may have bought the items.'

John Orr declined to comment.

With this sensational breakthrough in the case, everybody but Pan Am and its insurers were off the hook. If the world could be persuaded to buy this scenario, then the responsibility would be shifted from the Iranians and Syrians to the Libyans, to the obvious benefit of Western foreign policy, not least in its attempts to secure the release of Western hostages in the Middle East; the security and police forces of the United States, Germany and the United Kingdom would be seen to be blameless, and the families of the victims would have a clear shot at a clear target in seeking proper compensation for their loss.

But there were problems.

The weight of circumstantial evidence against the PFLP–GC unit in Germany was still impressive and not to be wished away. If the bomb had been built there by Marwan Khreesat and hidden in the copper-coloured Samsonite suitcase that he had brought with him from Damascus, how did it get into the hands of the Libyans in Malta?

And why? It was winter time, when flight delays and missed connections were commonplace. Was it likely that any well-organized, well-funded, seriously determined terrorist group, capable of building a sophisticated explosive device to blow up an American aircraft over the Atlantic, would choose to put it aboard the target flight by sending it, unaccompanied, in a suitcase that had first to be smuggled on to an Air Malta flight (which might have been delayed or diverted) to Frankfurt (where it might have been mislaid or misrouted), in the hope that Pan Am would fail to search it or match it with a passenger and forward it, unaccompanied, on a feeder flight (which might also have been delayed or diverted) to Heathrow (where again it might have been misplaced or misdirected), still in the hope that no one would notice or examine the suitcase before it was finally loaded aboard the third, and target, aircraft for the New York leg of the flight?

As this is still the official view, such a plan must surely represent the most conspicuous victory of optimism over elementary common sense in the annals of terrorism. On the face of it, the PFLP–GC would have been better advised to post their bomb to the United States as a registered air parcel.

More particularly, there were problems with the computer records and worksheets from Frankfurt. For one thing, they did not tally with Pan Am's own baggage records, which although questionable as to their accuracy, were at least compiled in good faith. To this day no one knows exactly how many pieces of luggage there were aboard the doomed flight or consequently whether they have all been recovered or accounted for. Nobody even knows exactly how many suitcases were in the luggage pallet that contained the one with the bomb – it was 45 or 46 – or how many of these were brought in by the feeder flight from Frankfurt. (The number was also thought to include not one but *four* unaccompanied bags.)

The BKA estimate that 'about' 135 bags were sent through to the baggage room below the departure gate of Flight 103A, some belonging to the 79 passengers whose journey ended in London and the rest to the 49 who were going on to New York. There were no records of luggage sent directly to the departure gate, nor of interline luggage taken directly from one aircraft to another, nor of bags belonging to first-class passengers.

Of the 49 passengers bound for New York and beyond, 28 began their journey in Frankfurt, and 21 transferred from other connecting flights. As with the other interline passengers who joined the flight in London, their luggage was X-rayed before it went aboard but no attempt was made to match baggage with passengers, even though it had already been established that the Semtex explosive in the PFLP-GC Toshiba radio bombs was virtually undetectable by X-ray examination alone. (Later on, it would emerge that the X-ray machine operator had been instructed to pull out any bag that appeared to contain a radio. According to his testimony, he X-rayed 13 bags but none contained anything resembling a Toshiba radio.)

Of the 135 bags mentioned by the BKA, 111 had been logged on the Frankfurt computer and about 24 taken directly to the aircraft from three other connecting Pan Am flights. The list compiled by Pan Am at its check-in desks, however, showed not 111 but 117 items of luggage, and the discrepancy has not been convincingly cleared up to this day.

Although the 'discovery' of an unaccompanied bag from Malta was seized upon as a breakthrough in the investigation, there were in fact 13 items of unaccompanied luggage on the flight. According to the minutes of the fourth international conference of police agencies called on 14 September 1989, to consider the new Libyan link with the bombing, this cast 'doubt on the total reliability of hand-written entries of the baggage handlers on the computer print-out,' which had indicated only one such item. Details of the Malta connections were discussed, 'and it was explained that the bomb need not have been brought on in Malta, but must at least have come from Frankfurt'.

Well, *they* said it. Given that the flight wreckage was picked over initially by the CIA, that the total number of bags loaded aboard is not known, that the remains of others may yet be found in the wilder reaches of the Kielder Forest and the Scottish border country, and that there is still no reliable manifest for Flight 103 listing all the passengers by name with their seat numbers and baggage – given all this uncertainty, to suggest that the theory of a suicide bomber or of an unwitting 'mule' had been eliminated or that the baggage could not have been tampered with at Frankfurt or Heathrow or that the investigation had accounted for every piece of luggage on board and, except for the bag from Malta, matched every piece to a passenger is, to say the least, unpersuasive.

Indeed, the claims are almost as unconvincing as the provenance of the crucial computer listing itself.

If the new Malta/Libyan theory was to replace the established Iran/PFLP–GC scenario, it was necessary, first of all, to believe that no one thought to ask for the baggage-loading lists for Flight

103A as soon as terrorist action was suspected – which was almost at once.

It was necessary to believe that no one in any of the British, German and American police, intelligence and accident inquiry agencies who had a hand in investigating the disaster, or anyone who was in any way involved with airport management or security at Frankfurt or London, thought to secure the baggage lists as the one indispensable tool that would be needed to unravel the mystery of how the bomb got aboard.

It was necessary to believe that the only person who considered the lists to be at all important was a lowly computer operator at Frankfurt airport.

The *Observer*'s chief reporter, John Merritt, described how this came about in a story published almost two years after the disaster. He wrote, on 17 November 1991:

A major breakthrough in the hunt for the Lockerbie bombers came to light only because of the quick thinking of a conscientious computer operator at Frankfurt airport.

The vital computer evidence, proving conclusively that the bag from Malta, identified as Item B8849, was on board as the airliner was blasted apart on the last stage of its journey from Heathrow to New York would have been lost forever if the woman operator had not kept her own record.

Acting on her own initiative, the woman, an employee of the Frankfurt Airport Company, who for legal reasons cannot be named, was working at the computer system known as KIK on the day of the disaster. She knew records relating to baggage loaded on to flights were kept in the system for only a limited time [eight days] before being wiped. So when she returned to work the next day she made her own print-out of the information and placed it in her locker before going on holiday.

On her return, weeks later, she was surprised to learn that no one had shown any interest in the computer records. She passed the print-out to her baggage section leader who gave it to investigators from the West German Bundeskriminalamt. But it was not until mid-August, eight months after the bombing, that the German authorities turned over this information to Scottish police in charge of the investigation.

The woman employee's role became known only last week when lawyers for families of the American victims took evidence from her in Germany. She had kept her own copy of the print-out and still had it in her locker.

The *Observer*'s readiness to print this story contrasted sharply with its scepticism when Pan Am subpoenaed the CIA and five other US government agencies in the US District Court for 'all documents concerning warnings, tips, alerts and other communications as to plans by any person to place a bomb, make an assault or commit another form of terrorist attack at Frankfurt airport during November or December 1988'.

The request seemed reasonable enough, given that the airline and its insurers were facing damage lawsuits totalling some $7 billion, and possibly as much again in punitive damages, but it was instantly dismissed as a fishing expedition when it became known, five weeks after the subpoenas were served, that Pan Am was seeking through the courts to compel the US government to produce the documents necessary for its defence.

This step had been prompted by the now notorious Interfor Report commissioned by the airline from Juval Aviv, whose inquiries into the disaster had produced intelligence information that was sometimes more reliable than the conclusions he drew from it. When copies of the report were leaked to the press and to Congressman James Traficant, a member of the House Aviation Committee who was then seeking re-election, its findings captured media attention across the world.

'Pan Am Seeks to Prove US Was Warned of Lockerbie Attack' – the *Independent*, London.
   'Syrian Arms Dealer Linked to Pan Am Lockerbie Disaster' – the *Daily Telegraph*, London.
   'Lockerbie: How the Bomb Slipped Through' – *Daily Mail*, London.
   'CIA Drugs-for-Hostages Deal Allowed Bomb on Pan Am Jet' – *The Times*, London.
   'CIA Accused of Link to Drug Runner in Lockerbie Attack' – the *Guardian*, London.

In vain, Pan Am protested that it was embarrassed by the leak of its confidential report (which was certainly doing the airline's position no good at all) and, in vain, did its spokesman insist that: 'We are not supporting the findings, neither are we suggesting that they are nonsense. What we are trying to do is establish what is fact and what is fiction. That is why we asked for the subpoenas.'

No sooner had the furore died down than the *Observer* weighed in on 26 November with the results of a 'Special Investigation':

'Pan Am Lockerbie Report a Sham'
'How Lockerbie Bomb Story was Planted'.

In marked contrast to the sympathetic hearing the paper was later to give the story of how the computer baggage-list came to light in Frankfurt, its reporting team fastened on the Interfor Report and its author like piranha fish.

An investigator's report which claims that the CIA allowed terrorists to place the bomb on board Pan Am Flight 103 is today exposed as a sham, following an investigation by the *Observer* [it announced]. Pan Am's insurers commissioned the report from an Israeli intelligence expert based in New York. As a result of his findings, the airline issued subpoenas demanding information from the CIA and five other US intelligence agencies . . . As the agencies will strenuously contest any attempt to force information from them, Pan Am will be able to argue it was prevented from presenting a complete case.

And why not? Why would the agencies 'strenuously' contest the subpoenas if their hands were clean and they could prove the airline was wrong?

Described as 'incredible', 'unbelievable' and 'bizarre', the Interfor Report was summarized in the context of interviews with Juval Aviv – 'a chubby Donald Pleasance, wearing a grey suit and a Gucci watch' – and Congressman Traficant – a 'former sheriff, who was once accused by Federal tax inspectors of accepting $108,000 in bribes from organized crime figures.'

When the *Observer* team met with Aviv, 'he failed to provide any evidence to substantiate a single claim in his report.' And when Traficant was told that there were 'serious doubts about the report', he suggested the *Observer* might be working for the CIA. When pressed, Mr Traficant said: '"You've come here a day late, a dime short and you're a piece of shit." The *Observer* made its excuses and left.'

In the *Observer*'s summary, the Interfor Report claimed

. . . that an autonomous CIA unit based in Frankfurt, West Germany, struck a deal with a Syrian drugs dealer with terrorist connections [Monzer al-Kassar]. He was supposedly allowed to smuggle heroin into the United States in return for helping to negotiate the release of American hostages in Beirut. Knowing of his 'protected' route, the bombers used his network to place the device on board the plane. It also alleges that warnings that Flight 103 was the target of a terrorist attack were suppressed because they would have exposed the 'drugs-for-hostages' deal . . .

On first reading, the report is a detailed and strictly factual account of a complex plot to strike back at the US for the downing of an Iranian airliner over the Gulf in July 1988. Many of its facts are true, but they have no link with Lockerbie. Other details do not stand up to close examination. The report is riddled with errors.

The *Observer* team then itemized the errors they had found and the details which did not stand up to close examination.

1. The report claimed that al-Kassar had rented a car in Paris and driven to Frankfurt with components of the bomb. On examining the records of the rental firm for the day in question, 'No car hired on that date clocked up sufficient mileage to have made the trip.'

2. The report claimed that 'Corea' was the code name for the drugs-for-hostages deal. 'But Corea actually refers to communications between members of Trevi, the group of European intelligence, customs and police forces set up to monitor "terrorism, revolution and violence".'

3. The report claimed that documents proving Pan Am's case were held in the safe of Kurt Rebmann, 'a West German equivalent of an assistant attorney general, based in Berlin'. This was denied by Mr Rebmann, 'who is, in fact, a Federal prosecutor based in Karlsruhe'.

And that was it, apart from other unspecified 'facts' that appeared 'to have been cobbled together from newspaper cuttings, many of which have turned out to be wrong'. On the strength of these revelations, which seem little enough to warrant such a conclusion, the Interfor Report was never again to be referred to in the public prints, either in Britain or the United States, without being described as 'discredited' or 'a sham'.

Aviv may have failed to provide the *Observer* with any additional evidence to support his findings, but equally the *Observer* failed to provide any solid evidence to refute them, despite the obvious pains it had taken. It was also a little ungrateful of the paper to attack him so vigorously, for in his preamble to the report, Aviv had spoken of crossing the trail of several other private investigations into the Flight 103 disaster, notably those of the *Observer* and *The Sunday Times* – but 'only the *Observer*', he wrote, 'seems to continue trying to identify how the act was done and by whom.'

The Sunday Times was less dismissive of Aviv's work, although its reporter, David Leppard, agreed that 'the report at first appears so fantastic as to be ridiculous. Almost all the agencies involved have denied it. The CIA called it "nonsense"; one intelligence source said it was "fantasy". But the report, however bizarre, does contain remarkable detail, including names, dates, times of meetings, telephone and bank account numbers.'

The Interfor Report was commissioned by James M. Shaughnessy, of the New York law firm, Windels, Marx, Davies & Ives, who was acting for Pan Am as lead counsel in its defence of the liability suit. The report was an internal document, summarizing mostly unverifiable intelligence data collected in the field, designed to open up lines of inquiry that might lead to the discovery of evidence admissible in court, which the report self-evidently was not. Aviv began work in the spring of 1989 and when his findings were submitted to Shaughnessy on 15 September they provided the basis for the subpoenas served shortly afterwards on the CIA, the DEA and other government agencies.

The leakage of the report to Congressman Traficant and the press some six weeks later was a severe setback for Pan Am's legal team – indeed, the embarrassment it caused was so acute that conspiracy buffs might well have suspected the US Justice Department itself of leaking the report. A US magistrate thought otherwise, however. Amid a blizzard of media speculation, an evidentiary hearing was ordered, at which John Merritt of the *Observer* was questioned, and, after hearing the testimony, the magistrate concluded that Aviv's denial of having leaked the report was 'not credible'.

After defining its terms of reference – which had nothing to do with exculpating Pan Am, as was widely suggested even by those who had read them, but was 'to determine the facts and then to identify the sources, nature, extent, form and quality of available evidence' – the report reviewed the results of the official investigation to date and the theories then current as to who was responsible. Then followed a review and assessment of the anonymous intelligence sources who had contributed to Aviv's findings, rated on a scale of reliability from 'good' to 'excellent'. In some cases, their anonymity was barely skin-deep. 'Source 5', for example, rated 'excellent', was described as 'an experienced director of airport security for the most security-conscious airline'.

Next came a 'Background History' to the disaster, starting two years beforehand, in which the politics and principal players were put in context. Libya's leader, Colonel Muammar Gaddafi, 'a major funder of terrorism', was said to have demanded better coordination among terrorist groups, and better 'deniability' for himself, with the result that the Abu Nidal group took over drugs and arms smuggling while Ahmed Jibril's PFLP–GC, backed by Syrian intelligence as its 'front team', concentrated on arms and terrorism.

Nidal's partner was Monzer al-Kassar, a Syrian arms and drugs smuggler, married to Raghda Dubah, sister of Ali Issa Dubah, then chief of Syrian intelligence, and a close associate of Rifat Assad, Syrian overlord of the Lebanese heroin industry and brother of Syria's President Hafez Assad. Al-Kassar's mistresses in Paris included Raja al-Assad, Rifat Assad's daughter, and a former Miss Lebanon who had previously been married to two prominent terrorists – most recently to a friend of Nidal's, Abu Abbas, who had planned the *Achille Lauro* hijacking.

Al-Kassar had many passports and identities, which Aviv listed in his report by serial number and date and place of issue, and operated through cover companies and offices, also listed by address and phone numbers, in Tripoli, Warsaw and Berlin. One of the principal drugs/arms smuggling routes ran through Frankfurt, with Pan Am being the favoured carrier. Tipped about what was going on, 'reportedly by a jealous Jibril', the BKA, in cooperation with the CIA and the DEA, began to monitor the operation and infiltrated 'at least two agents as well as informers, one of whom was Marwan Khreesat', the PFLP–GC's ace bomb-builder.

Aviv's Interfor Report went on:

The Pan Am Frankfurt smuggling operation worked as follows: an accomplice boarded flights with checked luggage containing innocent items. An accomplice Turkish baggage handler for Pan Am was tipped to identify the suitcase, then switched it with an identical piece holding contraband which he had brought into the airport or otherwise received there from another accomplice. The passenger accomplice then picked up the baggage on arrival. It is not known how this method passed through arrival customs, where such existed, but this route and method worked steadily and smoothly for a long time . . .

Khalid Jafaar was a regular 'passenger' accomplice for the drug route.

The BKA/DEA/CIA surveillance continued to monitor the route without interfering with it, according to the report, and by visibly increasing the police presence in other locations, the team sought to focus drug smuggling through Pan Am's baggage area at Frankfurt. The reason for this was mainly convenience, as it was already under close watch by the CIA because of cargo shipments via Pan Am to and from the Eastern bloc through Frankfurt, Berlin and Moscow.

In Aviv's opinion, the CIA team concerned with this operation was not closely supervised. 'It appears that it eventually operated to some, or a large, extent as an internal covert operation without consistent oversight, à la Oliver North . . . To distinguish what it knew as opposed to what CIA HQ definitely knew, we refer to that unit as CIA-1.'

In March 1988, the report went on, the CIA team was advised by the BKA of a secret meeting in Vienna between delegations from France and Iran that led to the delivery of weapons to Iran in exchange for the release of French hostages held in Lebanon. Having identified Monzer al-Kassar as a key player in the deal, BKA/CIA-1 approached him to see if he could also help arrange the release of American hostages in return for their protection of his drug routes.

According to Aviv, al-Kassar not only agreed to this but helped the CIA 'in sending weapons ostensibly to Iran . . . supposedly to further the US hostage release', and also used his arms routes to supply weapons to the Contras in Nicaragua, sometimes financing the shipments out of his drug profits. For these and other services, he was designated a CIA 'capability', which meant that he and his business activities were then virtually immune from interference.

'It is believed that US Customs at JFK were ordered by CIA to allow certain baggage to pass uninspected due to national security interests. Thus the drug-smuggling operation was now secure.'

That was in the summer of 1988, at about the same time as a special team of counter-terrorist agents led by Matthew Kevin Gannon, the CIA's deputy station chief in Beirut, and Major Charles Dennis McKee, of the Defense Intelligence Agency, left for Beirut 'to reconnoitre and prepare for a possible hostage rescue'.

Against this background, Aviv now set out the sequence of

events leading up to the bombing of Flight 103 as described by his sources.

On 13 December 1988, Jibril met with Khalid Jafaar and a Libyan bomb-maker known as 'the Professor' in Bonn – 'sources speculate that Jafaar was offered money to make a private drug run to raise money "for the cause".' The 'passenger accomplice' was now lined up. But the BKA's raids on the PFLP–GC cell in late October had made it necessary for another bomb to be brought in, and Aviv asserts that al-Kassar took care of this personally.

'His brother Ghassan's wife, Nabile Wehbe, travelling on a South Yemen diplomatic passport, flew from Damascus to Sofia on 13 November 1988, picked up the bomb components from [Ali] Racep and then flew to Paris. Al-Kassar picked up the bomb from her, and on 25 November 1988, rented a car from Chafic Rent-a-Car, 46 Rue Pierre Charron in Paris and drove to Frankfurt (carrying other contraband as well). He had previously been arrested twice by West German border guards but each time was suddenly released after a telephone call was made. Sources speculate that he apparently felt secure because he had "protection".' (The *Observer*, which later discovered that Chafic had no record of any such rental transaction, also managed to reached al-Kassar by telephone in Syria. Not unnaturally, he insisted he had been somewhere else at the time.)

Aviv's report went on to list the warnings that began to come in from the beginning of December 1988.

The first, from a Mossad agent about three weeks before the disaster, was to the effect that a major terrorist attack was planned at Frankfurt airport against an American-flag carrier. This warning was passed to CIA HQ and BKA HQ. The local CIA team is said to have suggested that the BKA visibly secure all the American carriers except Pan Am so that the threat, if it was genuine, would be focussed on an airline and airport area already under close surveillance.

The second warning, on or just before 18 December, came from associates of Nidal and al-Kassar, who wanted to save their protected drug route without seeming to lack zeal in the cause of militant Islam.

Having 'figured out the most likely flights for Jibril's bomb . . . they tipped BKA that a bomb would be placed on this regular Pan Am Frankfurt–London–New York flight in the next three days. They figured that BKA would increase visible security, thus dissuading Jibril in case that was in fact his target. So, two to three days before the disaster, and unwittingly, these terrorists tipped off the authorities to what proved to be the very act.'

The third warning, a follow-up of the second, was issued by CIA HQ, 'which sent warnings to various embassies, etc., but not apparently to Pan Am. CIA-1 thought that BKA surveillance would pick up the action and that BKA would stop the act in case the tip was correct.'

Meanwhile, al-Kassar had learned that the Gannon–McKee official hostage team in Beirut had found out about his relationship with the CIA unit in Germany and his protected drugs/arms smuggling route through Frankfurt. According to Aviv, the official team had advised CIA HQ of what was going on and when no action was taken to put a stop to it, Gannon and McKee decided to return home, outraged that their lives and rescue mission should have been put at risk by CIA-1's deal with al-Kassar.

'Al-Kassar contacted his CIA-1 handlers sometime in the third week of December,' the Interfor Report went on, 'communicated the latest news and travel information and asked for help. There were numerous communications between CIA-1 and its Control [in Washington].'

The fourth warning came two or three days before the disaster. A BKA undercover agent reported a plan to bomb a Pan Am flight 'in the next few days' and the tip was passed on to the local CIA team. Though anxious not 'to blow its surveillance operation and undercover penetration or to risk the al-Kassar hostage release operation', the warning was passed on and the State Department advised its embassies. As a result, BKA security was tightened even further around all the American carriers operating out of Frankfurt except Pan Am. Observing this, Jibril scratched American Airlines as his preferred target and finally selected Pan Am.

'We do not know exactly when this decision was made,' wrote Aviv, 'but the dates point to two or three days before the flight ... Jibril, through an intermediary, activated the Jafaar/Turkish baggage-handler connection via Pan Am. For the Turk and Jafaar, this was another normal drug run. Jafaar does not profile as a suicidal martyr type.'

The fifth warning, from an undercover Mossad agent 24 hours before take-off, was of a plan to put a bomb aboard Pan Am Flight 103 on 21 December. BKA passed this to CIA-1 who reported it to Control.

'The bomb was ready,' Aviv's report went on. 'Within 24-48 hours before the flight, a black Mercedes had parked in the airport lot and the Turkish baggage-handler picked up a suitcase from that auto and took it into the airport and placed it in the employee locker area. This was his usual practice with drugs.'

The sixth warning came from a BKA surveillance agent watching the Pan Am baggage loading about an hour before take-off on 21 December. According to Aviv's sources, he noticed that

... the 'drug' suitcase substituted was different in make, shape, material and color from that used for all previous drug shipments. This one was a brown Samsonite case. He, like the other BKA agents on the scene, had been extra alert due to all the bomb tips ... He phoned in a report as to what he had seen, saying something was very wrong.

BKA passed that information to CIA-1. It reported to its Control. Control replied: 'Don't worry about it. Don't stop it. Let it go.'

CIA-1 issued no instructions to BKA.

BKA did nothing.

The BKA was then covertly videotaping that area on that day. A videotape was made. It shows the perpetrator in the act. It was held by BKA. A copy was made and given to CIA-1. The BKA tape has been 'lost'. However, the copy exists at CIA-1 Control in the US.

Jafaar boarded the flight after checking one piece of luggage. The suitcase first emerged from hiding and was placed on the luggage cart in substitution for Jafaar's only after all the checked suitcases had already passed through security. The suitcase was so switched by the Turkish Pan Am baggage loader ...

The special, designated communications codename which BKA/CIA-1 had set up for their operations as described above is known at CIA HQ as 'COREA'. All communications concerning the surveillance operation and as described above as between or among BKA/CIA-1 and CIA-1 Control were made via COREA. Thus all documents concerning all communications described above ought to be marked at the top COREA.

This completes the recitation of intelligence as to the act.

After listing other possibly useful details, such as the banks and account numbers used by al-Kassar, President Hafez Assad, Abu Abbas and Ali Issa Dubah to deposit their drug revenues in Spain, Switzerland, Austria, Beirut and Damascus, the Interfor Report declared

. . . it is our firm conclusion and opinion that our sources are correct as to why, how, where, when, by whom and what act was committed, and who had what prior warnings and when and what they did about it . . .

From the perspective of intelligence analysis, our findings are conclusive. From the perspective of journalists, it is publishable speculation. From the perspective of trial lawyers, it probably remains inadmissible speculation or hearsay. Fortunately, the intelligence provides leads to admissible evidence. The videotape is the gem. But all the evidence is guarded by formidable constraints. Only carefully planned and tenaciously and narrowly pursued efforts will make acquisition possible.

The remaining six pages of the report consisted of Interfor's practical recommendations as to how Shaughnessy should proceed in seeking to obtain that evidence, including the issue of discovery subpoenas.

In the light of affidavits sworn to later by Lester Coleman and many other witnesses and investigators, the Interfor Report – a confidential document never intended for public consumption – can be challenged more for errors of interpretation than errors of fact (although there were probably more of the latter than the *Observer* was able to find).

Lester Coleman believes that, by grouping the CIA agents in Germany together under the designation of CIA-1, Aviv endowed them with a collective, conspiratorial purpose which almost certainly did not exist, and that he entirely omitted the contribution to the Flight 103 disaster of the US Drug Enforcement Administration and its country office in Cyprus.

With the sinister expansion of 'narco-terrorism' everywhere in the world during the 1970s and 1980s, the work of the two agencies overseas had become ever more closely entwined, with the CIA emerging as the senior partner in view of its superior resources, its loftier purpose and its greater freedom of covert action. As often as not, the requirements of narcotics law enforcement were subordinate to those of foreign policy and national security, as defined in Washington but reinterpreted by the octopus in the light of changing local circumstances.

In Coleman's view, the Lockerbie disaster was not the consequence of a malign conspiracy by a rogue CIA team in Germany – as many assumed Aviv was saying from a careless reading of the Interfor

Report – but the result of misguided decisions and misplaced confidence in their own abilities on the part of a loose alliance of US government agents in the field, often working with different agendas and priorities, and always without adequate supervision, on an ad hoc, day-to-day basis.

It was only *after* the event, in his opinion, that Washington engaged in a deliberate conspiracy, and that was to avoid the potentially disastrous political fall-out from Lockerbie by covering up the incompetence, complacency and bravado that had let the terrorists through.

Aviv was also perhaps confused by his sources' reference to COREA, a matter the *Observer* seized upon in its attack on the Interfor Report. COREA may well have referred to communications within the Trevi group, as the paper suggested, but as Coleman pointed out later, it could also have been a mishearing of *khouriah*, a Lebanese slang word for 'shit', which is, in turn, the international slang word for heroin.

With the media only too happy to savage Aviv's report as a device to allow Pan Am to escape its obligations, the government was under no necessity to descend into the arena and battle it out line by line.

'Garbage,' said the CIA.

'Rubbish,' said British intelligence.

'We never received any credible threat against Flight 103 on 21 December or any other date,' said the State Department, diplomatically hedging its bets with the weasel word 'credible'.

With the report made public, Juval Aviv's usefulness to Pan Am as an investigator was virtually at an end, a consequence he might have foreseen if he had, indeed, leaked it to the press. In an attempt to flesh out its findings with hard evidence, he met Shaughnessy with a polygrapher, James Keefe, in Frankfurt in January 1990, and interviewed the three Pan Am baggage-handlers who, on 21 December 1988, were thought to have been in a position to put the suitcase bomb aboard Flight 103.

They were Kilin Caslan Tuzcu, a German national of Turkish origin, who had been in charge of incoming baggage; Roland O'Neill, a German who had taken his American wife's maiden name, and was load master for the flight, and Gregory Grissom. All three voluntarily submitted to polygraph examinations.

Tuzcu was tested three times, O'Neill and Grissom twice. On reporting the results to the Scottish police, Shaughnessy was asked to sign a statement about the tests in the presence of an FBI agent, and readily agreed. The only visible result, however, was that, upon his return to the United States, James Keefe, the polygrapher, was served with a subpoena at Kennedy airport to appear before a Federal grand jury in Washington.

When he did so, he testified that Tuzcu 'was not truthful when he said he did not switch the suitcases'. And in Keefe's opinion, 'Roland O'Neill wasn't truthful when he stated he did not see the suitcase being switched, and when he stated that he did not know what was in the switched suitcase.' He thought the Grissom results were inconclusive.

A second polygrapher brought in by Shaughnessy to review Keefe's findings agreed with his interpretation of Tuzcu's and Grissom's tests but found those on O'Neill inconclusive. (Grissom was later eliminated from Pan Am's inquiries when it was shown he had been out on the tarmac at the time.)

The interest displayed by the FBI in the *fact* of Pan Am's polygraph tests rather than in the results was not shared by the British authorities, however. Convinced that the Scottish police would wish to interview Tuzcu and O'Neill on the strength of this lead, the airline found a pretext to send them to London so that they could be questioned and, if necessary, detained, but nobody seemed in the least bit interested. After hanging around all day, they returned to Frankfurt that night. (Intelligence sources suggested later that O'Neill was an undercover BKA agent, which, if true, might account for the lack of British and American interest. Otherwise, it must be assumed that the British investigators were as committed as the Americans to the politically more convenient theory that the bomb had arrived unaccompanied from Malta.)

Predictably, the results of the polygraph tests were leaked to the press, and just as predictably, on 28 January, the *Observer* heaped scorn on the airline's initiative: 'Both the timing of the pair's interrogation [by polygraph] and the circumstances surrounding it have refuelled suspicions about Pan Am methods in defending the lawsuit brought by relatives of the 270 people who died when Flight 103 was blown up over Lockerbie.'

Unable to resist having another tilt at the Interfor Report, which 'was exposed as a sham by the *Observer* two months ago', the paper went on to say that the report 'weaves a fantastical tale around the assertion that the CIA, operating a drugs-for-hostages deal through Frankfurt airport, allowed the bomb to proceed, thus overriding or corrupting the airline's own security controls'.

Whether that was a fair statement of Juval Aviv's position or not – he still believes that Tuzcu and O'Neill are prime suspects in the mass murder – it was certainly typical of the prevailing view that Pan Am was indulging in spy-fiction fantasy to pervert the course of justice.

But in the scale of probabilities, was it any more likely that the management and staff of a major international airline, its insurance underwriters and the best legal brains that money could buy would seek to evade the legitimate claims of the victims' families and counter the determination of three governments to pin all the blame on Pan Am *by inventing a fairy tale*?

Is it any more fantastic than Aviv's report to think that they would hire, not just Aviv, but a small army of investigators to run around the world looking for some shred of happenstance to clothe that invention?

Or that they would persevere with it for years in the face of almost universal condemnation and ridicule and at a cost of millions of dollars in the hope that one day they would find someone like Lester Coleman, who might transmute some of that fantasy into fact?

— VIII —

The octopus had had him in its sights for so long that the security vetting should have been a formality, but a month went by without a word. And that was the first thing Coleman learned about the Defense Intelligence Agency: it never knowingly took chances. It would sooner not employ him than take an unnecessary risk, said McCloskey. He had known them junk a whole operation that had taken hundreds of people months to put together just because there was an outside chance that if anything went wrong the DIA might break cover.

McCloskey was unperturbed by the delay. This wasn't the CIA, he said. The CIA was a showboat civilian agency. These were the professionals, the military, the combined intelligence arms of the United States Army, the United States Navy and the United States Air Force. Together, they formed the largest and most discreet intelligence agency in the world; 57,000 people operating out of Arlington Hall, Virginia, and Bolling Airforce Base, Washington, D.C., on a budget five times bigger than the CIA's. No restrictions, no oversight – and nobody even heard of it. Why? Because it didn't make mistakes. And because the director reported to the joint chiefs of staff, who didn't tell anybody anything they didn't have to know. And that included the Secretary of Defense.

But wasn't that dangerous? asked Coleman. To have a covert agency that big and powerful, and not directly accountable to *anyone*? Not even to the President of the United States? Their commander in chief?

The White House leaked like a colander, McCloskey said. It was full of politicians, and politicians came and went. Same thing with Congress. The military had never trusted politicians. It didn't trust *civilians*. Period. The military was America's backbone, its power and its honour. It didn't take sides. It didn't have to make promises it couldn't keep or gamble with the national interest to get elected.

You could count on the military to see things straight, to see things through and to do things right. The DIA was only dangerous to the nation's enemies.

But where did the CIA fit in? And the National Security Agency? Didn't the DIA have to share these responsibilities?

The National Security Agency took care of the electronic and satellite stuff, McCloskey replied. And all that was filtered through the DIA before it went to Langley. The NSA did an important, technical job. As for the CIA, its main use as far as the military was concerned was as cover, as a front operation. While Congress, the media and the whole world watched the CIA, America's real spy shop could get on with its work the way it was supposed to – in secret. Everybody knew about the CIA. It was good for a scandal a year at least because it leaked from top to bottom. It was a public agency, pinned down by White House directives and Congressional committees. Its director was a public figure. Everybody knew about William Colby, Richard Helms, George Bush, William Casey, William Webster, Robert Gates – but who even knew the *name* of the DIA director?

'Not me,' said Coleman.

'Damn right,' said McCloskey. 'Not that I guess you'll ever get to meet him anyhow. Or even see the inside of Arlington Hall, come to that. The only DIA personnel you're ever likely to meet will be your handler and maybe a couple of agents you'll work with.' (And he was right. It was only after the DIA froze him out that Coleman finally learned that the name of his boss, the agency's director of operations, was Lt General James Kappler.)

A week before Thanksgiving 1984, a call came in on McCloskey's private line instructing Coleman to drive out to Washington's Dulles International airport and stand beside a potted palm near the United Airlines ticket counter, where he would be contacted at 11.15 a.m. precisely.

Coleman thought it was McCloskey playing a joke. He started to ask if he should wear a red carnation in his buttonhole or a false nose or something but the caller hung up.

At 11.15 a.m. precisely, he took up position by the potted palm and waited to see if he could spot his contact before his contact spotted him. It was a tie. He advanced to meet the first young man he saw with a grey briefcase, they shook hands cordially, and descended by escalator to street level, where his escort hailed a cab.

On arriving at the airport Ramada Inn, they took the lift to the fifth floor, walked back down the stairs to the third floor and along the hall to a room towards the end. After knocking on the door, his escort unlocked it himself and ushered Coleman inside.

Sitting by the window [he remembers], was a thin fellow in his shirt-sleeves, about my age, a bit taller than me, same colour hair as mine, a beard, too, who gets up and introduces himself.

'Hey, buddy,' he says. 'How are you? Glad you could make it. My name's Bill Donleavy.'

Before I could say anything he flips on the room TV, I guess to mask our conversation, and again I have to smile because this is straight out of John Le Carré. Anyway, Donleavy is to be my Control, my principal contact with the DIA for the next five years.

A quiet, careful, calculating man, Donleavy would quickly earn Coleman's trust and respect, in large measure because Coleman never caught him out in a lie but also because he always felt that Donleavy really cared, that he was genuinely concerned about Coleman's personal safety and the welfare of his family. But it was soon clear also that while Donleavy had to know everything about him, he was to know next to nothing about Donleavy.

Over the five years of their association, Donleavy revealed very little about himself, other than that he had served in Vietnam with the Special Operations Group, Military Assistance Command, and had worked in intelligence for most of his military career. Nor did he ever reveal very much about the agency that employed them both, other than that the range of its interests was wide enough to merit ex-CIA Director Richard Helms's rueful description of the DIA as 'the 900-pound intelligence gorilla'.

That was one of the ground rules Donleavy discussed at their first meeting. Everything would proceed on a strictly need-to-know basis. Coleman would have no contact with the DIA other than through him or those he would introduce from time to time. He would not meet or be aware of the identity of other agents unless they worked together, and possibly not even then. He could tell no one of his affiliation under any circumstances, not even the closest members of his family. If he were ever compromised or if it was ever suggested that he worked for military intelligence, the DIA would disown him; it would categorically deny that he had ever worked for the agency or had ever had any dealings with it in any capacity whatsoever.

In return, the DIA would pay him $5000 a month, plus expenses (but in a way that could not be traced back to the agency); it would put him to work on matters of national importance (for which he would never receive any public recognition); it would train him in the most advanced security and intelligence techniques, and go to almost any lengths to keep him out of harm's way because the DIA was only as good as its agents and none of them were ever considered expendable. If Coleman was ready to accept the offer on those terms, all he had to do was sign an undertaking, binding for life, that he would never disclose the nature of his employment or assignments to anyone at any time and the agency would be happy to welcome him aboard.

As McCloskey had told him most of this already, Coleman signed.

'Okay, so what now?' he asked. 'Where am I going?'

Donleavy smiled. 'Later,' he said. 'When you get back from Europe.'

'Europe? Where in Europe?'

'Spain. For your training.'

'When?'

'First of the year. But there are things to do yet.'

They included a polygraph examination by an operator from Fort McClellen, Alabama – six hours wired to the box in a hot, stuffy hotel room, while he answered the same sets of questions over and over again, with the sweat pouring off him.

Then another session at a different hotel with Donleavy, who told him he was now officially assigned to the Department of Defense Human Resource Intelligence (HUMINT) Program of the Armed Forces of the United States. His unit was MC/10, whose activities, he later learned, were part of Trine, a compartmented, special-access programme requiring clearance beyond Top Secret. MC/10 reported to the Special Technical Operations Center (STOC), The Pentagon. His code name was Benjamin B. He would use that to sign all receipts and agency documents from then on in.

'What about Thomas Leavy?' Coleman asked. 'I've still got that birth certificate. The one the CIA gave me to use in the Bahamas.'

Donleavy shrugged. 'Let me have it,' he said. 'It may come in useful some day. Who knows? I'll give it back to you later.'

Coleman was also given a contact number to call, but only in an emergency (703–455 8339), and a mail-drop address (PO Box 706, Oxenhill, Maryland 20745).

'Otherwise, don't call us, we'll call you,' Donleavy said. 'And if I can't get to you myself, if I have to send somebody, he'll say, "Hullo, I'm a friend of Bill Donleavy's." And you'll say, "I don't know any Bill Donleavy." Then he'll say, "His friends know him as Kevin." After that, you can talk. But if you've got any doubts, any question in your mind at all, just act like the name means nothing and pass it off. Never take a risk you don't have to. Not ever.'

Coleman practised this procedure several times before Christmas when meeting experts from Intelligence and Security Command (INSCOM) attached to Army Intelligence Center and School (JITC), Fort Huachuca, Arizona. They took him through such things as JUG (Intelligence User's Guide), MEBE (Middle East Basic Intelligence Encyclopedia), ACOUSTINT (Acoustical Intelligence), OPSEC (Operations Security), CIPINT (Encrypted Intelligence Communications) and HITS (Human Intelligence Tasking System).

He was also told to look out for a help-wanted ad in *Broadcasting* magazine placed by the Christian Broadcasting Network, a private venture owned and operated by Pat Robertson, the popular TV evangelist and moral conscience of the far right. CBN would be looking to hire a Middle East correspondent and when the ad appeared, Coleman should apply for the job.

'You're going to get born again,' said Donleavy. 'Kind of a nice touch that, seeing you're just starting out with us.' He seemed quite proud of it. 'When they get your resumé, a guy with a British accent will give you a call and invite you down to Virginia Beach. Do like he says, and he'll help you see the light.'

The call came just before Christmas. Right after the holidays, Coleman flew down to be interviewed at CBN's Virginia Beach headquarters, a sprawling, neo-Colonial, campus-like complex with broadcasting facilities to rival anything he had seen in the major networks. The guy with the British accent, besides working for MI6 under the code name of Romeo, was at the time general manager of CBN's Middle East Television (MET) based in Jerusalem, and had flown over to hire a correspondent for its bureau in Beirut.

'It's all set,' Romeo said, as they strolled in the grounds. 'All you've got to do is play the role. And not just with the Robertsons – with everybody you meet down here. These are pray-TV people, every last one of 'em – and they're all paranoid, so watch your step. They all think they've been called by Jesus to work for Pat Robertson.'

'Including you?'

'Doesn't it show? You'll find 'em friendly enough on the surface but don't let that fool you. They're fanatics, and very suspicious of strangers. They're going to work you over pretty thoroughly to make sure you're not the devil in disguise, so let's show 'em a little evangelical fervour, shall we?'

Romeo was not exaggerating. Coleman was asked to supply the names and addresses of past and current friends, a floor plan of his house, the names of his spouse, children and close family members, his medical records, dental charts and a typical daily schedule of family activities.

He then sat for a round of personality profile tests and apparently showed the requisite degree of apostolic zeal for, at the end of this two-day inquisition, a benevolent Romeo introduced him to Pat Robertson's son Tim and the three of them went off to meet the great man himself at a local restaurant, where they prayed over the salad bar.

During lunch, the Robertsons explained that MET operated from studios in Jerusalem, with a transmitter in Marjayoon in Israeli-occupied South Lebanon, an office in Nicosia, Cyprus, and a news bureau in the Christian enclave in Beirut, to which Coleman would be assigned. The station aired Christian and family programmes to the mostly Arab populations of Lebanon, Syria and Jordan, thereby enraging Islamic fundamentalists to such an extent that they had several times bombed the transmitter even though it was located in the Israeli security zone.

'It was a funny coalition,' Coleman found. 'You had right-wing Christian Americans, the Israelis, and right-wing Christian Lebanese fascists, funded, trained and uniformed by the Israeli Army, all working together and in bed with outfits like CBN.'

Over dessert, Pat Robertson explained at some length that his interest in the region stemmed from his belief that the Second Coming of Jesus Christ was imminent in the Holy Land, and he intended to cover it *live*.

As far as Coleman could make out, MET seemed to be a *pirate* station, operating, in violation of international law and numerous treaties, without a licence from any government. There was no advertising, and the programme material, other than the Robertsons' religious and family output, consisted of wrestling on Saturday nights, NFL football and endless reruns of American soaps and situation comedies. As far as its audience was aware, the whole operation was funded entirely by the American faithful (of whom the most generous, as Coleman discovered later, was faithful Bill Casey, director of the CIA, and his friends at the Jewish Defense League).

Coleman's job was to file stories from MET's Lebanon bureau, not just for the pirate station, but for a new national network news programme the Robertsons were planning to set up in the United States.

They always had some major project going [he remembers]. Pat would say he had been talking to Jesus, and Jesus had told him He wanted him to do this or do that, so CBN would then go out and hire the people they needed. These people would quit their jobs and sell their houses and move to Virginia Beach, where they'd buy new homes and settle down happily and go to work for Pat because Jesus had called them. He'd pay everybody lots of money and they'd all live very comfortably. Until one day he'd walk into the office and say, 'I just talked to Jesus. He doesn't want me to do this anymore. You're all fired.'

The Robertsons' mission in the Middle East was still clear and urgent, however, when they talked to Coleman over lunch.

'How soon can you join us?' Tim Robertson asked. 'We really need to get you out there, to get you started on God's work as soon as we can.'

'Praise the Lord,' said Coleman. 'I need thirty days to prepare myself.'

Donleavy had already told him to set January aside for his crash course in DIA HUMINT operations. CIA agents graduate in classes of 40 from spy school at Camp Perry, Virginia, not far from Williamsburg. As a DIA HUMINT agent, Coleman was trained alone, one on one, having little contact with anybody but his instructors and no contact at all with anyone outside his chain of command.

On 15 January 1985, he flew out to Malaga and made his way to Torremolinos, where he was picked up by an American contact, a friend of Bill Donleavy's, better known as Kevin, who drove like a madman down the winding coastal highway to Estepona, deposited him on the doorstep of a small hillside cottage overlooking the sea, and drove away immediately with a cheerful wave. With a rueful nod, Coleman went inside and slept the sleep of the jet-lagged.

The following morning, at 8 a.m., he dragged himself out of bed and went downstairs to see who was hammering so vigorously at the door.

'Sorry to disturb you,' said another obvious Englishman, looking him up and down with professional detachment. This one had steel-grey, Fuller's brush hair, a bulging briefcase and a generally more purposeful air than Romeo. 'I'm a friend of Bill Donleavy's.'

Donleavy had already explained that the DIA enjoyed a special relationship with MI6, sharing the view that secrets were meant to be kept, not turned into headlines in the morning papers. The British had never quite grasped the logic of Congressional oversight of the CIA. The notion of their own intelligence chiefs being questioned at televised hearings before a Parliamentary committee was so comically at variance with British ideas of a secret service that they had turned gratefully to the DIA as a discreet, professional alternative to Bill Casey and his Langley cowboys, whom they distrusted almost as much as the Pentagon did.

But there were limits.

'I wish your people could have waited another fortnight,' grumbled Coleman's visitor. 'The border reopens next month, and I can drive here in under an hour from Gib. As it is, I had to fly from Gib to Tangier, and from Tangier to Malaga and drive over from there. And a bloody bore it was, too, I don't mind telling you.'

'Sorry,' said Coleman humbly. 'How about another cup of coffee?'

The man from MI6 had come the long way around in order to brief him on the finer points of the political situation in the Middle East, a British sphere of interest since the late 19th century. When they got down to considering which neighbourhoods in Beirut were controlled by which of the warring Christian and Muslim factions, his visitor raked through his tattered briefcase and tossed a bundle of Bartholomew's folding maps on to the kitchen table.

'There you are,' he said. 'Compliments of HM government. Available at all good stationers. Easy to read and a bloody sight more accurate than the rubbish you'll get from the CIA.'

It was a useful lesson. If he was ever stopped and searched, no one would think twice about finding a Bartholomew's street plan in his pocket. But a map of Beirut by a military cartographer?

The lesson was underlined by a succession of visitors to the cottage over the next two weeks, most of them from Wiesbaden and Lisbon. As a correspondent for the CBN, Coleman was not about to engage in hand-to-hand combat with enemy agents or in high-speed car chases with armed Muslim militiamen, but for his own protection he was issued by one of his instructors with a small, five-shot, stainless steel, single-action, North American Arms .22 Magnum revolver, courtesy of 7th Brigade, Special Forces Detachment, from Bad Tolz, near Munich.

He was supposed to carry it in a canvas holster worn under the zip fly of his trousers, but Coleman never could get used to the idea of walking around with its barrel pointed at his private parts. On the rare occasions he went out with it, he wore the holster on his ankle instead.

In the event of an attempted kidnap or close combat he was supposed to aim at the eye or behind the ear of his assailant, but, having some notion of the hitting power of its Magnum round, rather doubted if he could do it. Although brought up with firearms, he had never really liked them, and managed to lose this one before he left for Beirut.

The main thrust of his training was in cryptography and communications. Although his assignment would entail the dispatch of lengthy reports to Control almost daily, the use of secret short-wave transmitters or fancy electronic gadgetry was ruled out. Unless the means of transmission were as secure as the codes he used, his cover would be constantly at risk, along with the integrity of his reports. If his true role as an American agent were ever suspected, not only would his life be in danger, but – even more serious from the DIA's point of view – he might also be used by the opposition as a channel for disinformation.

The same considerations also ruled out the use of the American Embassy's secure communications system from Beirut. Donleavy had already made it clear that Coleman was to keep well away from the embassy and its staff after he arrived in Lebanon as they were under continuous surveillance by Arab and Israeli intelligence agents. Anything but the most casual and routine contact with US government officials in the field was, therefore, to be avoided, and under no circumstances was he to reveal his true affiliations to any of them, up to and including the ambassador.

Being entirely on his own, therefore, and unable to use any method of communication with Control that might draw attention to himself, Coleman needed a simple yet virtually unbustable code system that would enable him to send untraceable despatches to Washington every day via the ordinary international telecommunications networks without alerting anybody listening in to the traffic and without having to use any item of equipment more incriminating than a Bartholomew's street map.

For an FCC licensed broadcast engineer working with the DIA's cryptographers, the solution was child's play. Between them they devised a simple grid code based on random number access via a telephone touch-tone keypad, the variable alpha-numeric sequence being determined for each transmission by the day of the month and the month of the year. All he needed was a Radio Shack pocket calculator with a touch-tone number pad, of the sort that any businessman might carry in his briefcase, and a two-speed microcassette recorder of the type that any self-respecting media correspondent would carry in his pocket.

After encoding his message, Coleman had simply to record the touch-tone bleeps, using slow speed, then direct dial Donleavy's answering machine in Maryland from a public telephone, place the recorder over the mouthpiece, play the tones on high speed as soon as the answering machine beeped, hang up and erase the tape. In this way he could transmit a lengthy, secure message in 30 seconds or less – far too short a time for anyone to trace a call even if they had been waiting for it. (Later on, they supplemented this system with a software program in Coleman's laptop computer that randomly scrambled his plain language reports as they were sent via a modem direct to his contact number in Washington.)

But first he had to have something to communicate, and so was taught about 'dead drops' for the exchange of messages. A basic means of communication among members of the DIA cell in Beirut, these offered the advantage that the people using them did not have to meet, and messages could be left there at any convenient time. Popular locations included an international telephone booth in the central telephone exchange, where messages could be taped under the shelf, and the soap and detergent section of a supermarket in Jounieh. This became one of Coleman's main pick-up points for material coming from West Beirut, and was the unromantic setting for his first meeting with Mary-Claude, who worked there for a time.

He also learned about 'live drops', receiving or passing information face to face, and the 'brush pass' – by far the riskiest means of exchange.

Then there was 'environmental situation awareness' – or how to work covertly in a hostile environment. The key to this was an intimate knowledge of the terrain, with carefully selected drops, meeting and contact areas, and prearranged escape routes and safe houses, taking into account the opposition's strong points and weak points.

An intimate knowledge of the enemy was also crucial, for to

overestimate him could be as dangerous as to underestimate him. This in turn meant understanding local culture and history and how differences in thought and outlook had to be taken into account in running an operation – a factor nowhere more important than in the Middle East.

Still using off-the-shelf technology, he was taught how to photograph documents with an ordinary 35 mm. camera in available light. He was also shown the basic spy tricks of how to pass a message in a paperback book by pinpricking letters or words, the holes being visible only when the pages were held up to the light. (A variant of this was the overlay message, where the holes were pricked through a sheet of paper that the message receiver would then lay over the appropriate pages of his own copy of the book.)

A more sophisticated method was to use the book as a one-time code pad, reducing a letter or word to a number sequence by listing page number, line number and the letter or word number on that line. He liked this system, for he could keep up with the paperback bestseller list at the same time. He also enjoyed typing invisible messages on the back of innocuous letters by means of his IBM typewriter's lift-off correction tape.

The remainder of Coleman's crash induction course was taken up with briefing sessions on Operation Steeplechase, the mission for which he had been so hastily prepared.

The DIA had been monitoring activities at the Virginia Beach headquarters of the Christian Broadcasting Network which suggested that Pat Robertson's organization was heavily engaged in raising money and providing support for the Nicaraguan Contras through Major-General John K. Singlaub, president of the Taiwan-directed World Anti-Communist League, and Lt-Colonel Oliver North, with the covert assistance of DCI William Casey and the CIA. James Whelen, a close friend of Casey's, had been installed at CBN to tap its database for fund-raising, and it was a measure of the importance attached to Robertson's contribution that, in 1985, the Contras named a brigade in his honour.

Coleman's job in Beirut was to track the Middle Eastern ramifications of the conspiracy, working through a network of informants who reported to Tony Werner Asmar, the DIA agent in place. A Lebanese of German extraction, Asmar owned AMA Industries, SAL. – a hospital supply business which gave him access to every part of the country and every section of Beirut, regardless of which faction, Christian or Muslim, controlled it.

Until Coleman arrived, on 25 February 1985, the main duties of the Asmar cell had been to monitor the Muslim radical groups supported by Iran and Syria, to report on the movements of their leaders – in particular, those of Sheik Mohammed Hussein Fadellah – and to keep track of the Western hostages then being taken in Beirut. After Coleman's arrival as Asmar's Control and his communications link with DIA headquarters, this work continued but with the added responsibility of trailing Oliver North and his boss Robert McFarlane, President Reagan's National Security Advisor, as and when the Iran-Contra conspiracy brought them to the region to buy illegal arms.

Coleman was also required to provide intelligence support for 7th Brigade Special Forces detachments in Lebanon, working through DOCKLAMP (Defense Attaché System), American Embassy, Beirut. These Green Beret units were there ostensibly as advisers to the Lebanese Army but actually as a commando team to free the American hostages if the political situation in Lebanon ever changed sufficiently to warrant the use of force.

As CBN's Beirut correspondent, Coleman was well placed to observe and report on all these activities. Robertson's Middle East Television had close ties with Lebanon's right-wing Christian groups, which were largely funded by drugs trafficking, and in particular with the Christian Lebanese Forces, a militia largely funded by Israel.

CBN's 'office manager' in Beirut, Gushan Hashim, and his 'assistant', Antoine, had both been recruited from the Christian Lebanese Forces, and, as Coleman observed when he took over, the bureau was better equipped with arms than with cameras. He also quickly discovered that the main function of CBN's telex links was to enable Antoine to contact 'Odette' in Tel Aviv via Zurich on behalf of the Mossad, ingeniously rendering his Arabic into its phonetic English equivalents in order to use the English-language keyboard.

DIA's concern about the Iran-Contra conspirators was focussed in particular on Oliver North's Georgia 'mafia', whose representative, Michael Franks, also known as Michael Schafer, arrived in Beirut soon after Coleman. Described as a 'TV cameraman', Franks stepped off the boat from Cyprus wearing full army battle fatigues with a mercenary patch on his black military baseball cap.

He had been sent out by Overseas Press Services Inc. (OPS), a television consultancy company run by W. Dennis Suit, formerly a CIA operative in Central America. An associate of Oliver North, General Singlaub, Contra leaders Adolfo and Mario Calero, and

William Casey, Suit specialized in organizing field trips for journalists to US-supported military and paramilitary operations around the world, notably in Afghanistan, Angola, Central America and the Middle East.

As consultants to Pat Robertson's television operations, OPS clearly felt that Franks's inability to distinguish one end of a camera from another was offset by the expertise he had acquired in counter-terrorist techniques at SIONICS, a mysteriously funded training school near Atlanta run by another North associate, retired Lt General Mitchell Werbell III.

It was all the same to Coleman. The Beirut bureau never filed a story in all the months he was there, and Franks was never around long enough to prove an embarrassment. Socially, they got on well enough, to the point where Franks felt free to talk openly about OPS and the Contras. His boss, W. Dennis Suit, while under cover for the CIA in Nicaragua as an ABC-TV cameraman, had apparently been caught handing out bugged Zippo lighters to the Sandinistas and ABC had fired him. When not regaling Coleman with gossip of this sort, Franks spent most of his time fighting along the so-called 'Green Line' with the Christian militias.

For his part, Coleman had his hands full coping with the flood of intelligence data from Tony Asmar, who quickly became a close friend. The Asmar cell was efficiently run, thoroughly professional and highly productive. Besides a network of informants inside every political and religious faction, the armed militias and the Lebanese Army, he also ran a string of Filipino domestic workers recruited from American Baptist missions in Manila. To have a Filipino housekeeper was a mark of prestige among Lebanon's leading political, military and business families, and as she invariably attracted the intimate attention of the head of the family, her reports, often of pillow talk, were invaluable.

When I first got to Beirut, Tony stationed one of them with me for a while [Coleman recalls]. Mainly for my protection. Before I even opened a suitcase, a package arrived at the chalet with a .380 calibre Beretta and another .22 Magnum pistol inside – to add to the folding umbrella with the stiletto in the handle. I kept the Beretta in the bedroom and sometimes wore the twenty-two in an ankle holster, but Kathy was much better at that sort of stuff than I could ever hope to be.

She was a deadly little thing. Good with knives, guns or bare hands. Black belt karate. Close armed combat expert – kill you in a minute. And yet the sweetest little thing you ever saw. I could step out of the shower in the morning and my slippers would be waiting at the bathroom door. She was always very attentive, and kept everything clean and spotless.

Mary-Claude soon put a stop to that.

As there was no way of avoiding face-to-face contact once in a while, Coleman and Asmar had decided that to fraternize openly as friends would probably attract less attention than if they were observed meeting in secret. At the first opportunity, therefore, Asmar invited Coleman to join him and his fiancée Giselle for Sunday dinner with Giselle's family. And to provide possible observers with a plausible reason for subsequent visits, Giselle made sure her sister Mary-Claude was there to make up a foursome who might also meet elsewhere on other occasions.

Virtually on sight, the two put flesh and blood on the stratagem by falling in love.

Neither could quite believe it. On the surface, Coleman, going on forty-two, divorced, a disillusioned, cynical and worldly American, a secret agent sailing under false colours, had nothing whatever in common with a petite, vivacious, voluptuously attractive, 22-year-old girl, strictly brought up by a typically close and protective Lebanese Catholic family in the claustrophobic confines of East Beirut during a civil war. His first reaction was to lie about his age. He told her he was thirty-seven.

But that was the least of their problems. He told Mary-Claude everything else about himself, except that he was an American spy, and left it to her to decide how much she would tell her family, who strongly disapproved of divorce, were concerned about the age difference between them, even though he had pruned it, and were naturally suspicious of his intentions. Even so, they were determined to marry from the start, and as quickly as possible as far as Coleman was concerned, for he had no way of knowing how long his assignment to Beirut would last.

The family's reaction was reserved, polite and curious [he remembers], but Mary-Claude was always headstrong and usually got her way, no matter what her father said. As I spent more time with them and they saw it was a serious matter – I told her father I respected the traditions of his society and

I think that went in my favour – so they came to accept me.

Even so, it was a style of courtship entirely alien to me. Though Christian and emancipated compared with the rest of the Arab world, the family was very strict by American standards. Mary-Claude and I were not allowed to meet without a chaperone – one of her brothers or sisters always had to be there. Once or twice we met surreptitiously for lunch and went for a walk afterwards but that was the only time we were ever alone. Out of respect for her father, we complied with his wishes in order to show the seriousness of what we felt for each other. Once he was convinced of that, we had a traditional Lebanese engagement party, at which I gave her the traditional set of gold jewellery and stuff, and that made us official.

Mary-Claude was unhappy with the idea of keeping anything from her family, but knew that Coleman's divorce would be one problem too many for her father to handle. Asked, years later, what she had thought on meeting Coleman for the first time, she replied, 'I thought he was an old fart,' and they both laughed uproariously.

'He lied to me about his age. He was a foreigner – with a previous marriage. There were many problems. But I always did like older men. I wanted a peaceful life with a wonderful husband who took care of me. I enjoy being spoiled. I like the attention. And I got it. I lived through hell.'

They both laughed again, but ruefully this time.

The DIA was delighted with the idea of having a married agent. Donleavy wanted to know all about Mary-Claude so that he could run a security check, but as her sister Giselle was already unknowingly in the loop, the vetting was a mere formality.

'Go ahead,' he said. 'Congratulations. That's great cover. With family there, you can go in and out of Beirut whenever you like and nobody's going to think anything about it.'

By then the question of cover was important. Although hired to do news stories for CBN, Coleman was using the camera equipment mainly to shoot background footage for intelligence reports and to keep up appearances. Even if he *had* filmed a story, he had no way of getting the tape to the studios in Jerusalem except via Cyprus. A running joke among correspondents in Beirut was, Middle East Television: Yesterday's News Tomorrow.

Until Operation Steeplechase got under way in April, the work

Coleman was paid by CBN to do consisted mainly of training the Christian militia to run a TV station, called LBC, for the Christian enclave. This operation was backed by the Israelis, who were trying to set up a microwave link to feed video from Jerusalem to its agents inside Lebanon. But he was kept busy enough handling the huge volume of data from Asmar's cell, and servicing the drop for what was officially described as an in-country mobile training team (MTT) from 7th Brigade, Germany.

The drop was at Juicy-Burger, a hamburger stand run by an American couple known as Bonnie and Clyde at Dora, on the road between Jounieh and East Beirut.

These Green Beret guys were supposedly advisers to the Lebanese Army [said Coleman], but they were really there to handle the wet jobs. If the politics had ever been right, they might have been used to rescue the hostages but the situation was always too sensitive, too precarious to risk using force. So they were simply there in case they were needed. They took care of loose ends. If there was anything for them, I'd take it over to Juicy-Burger and Sergeant-Major Duke, from 7th Brigade, would stop by for a hamburger and pick it up.

I remember one time I took in some special bullets that somebody needed. Six rounds in a coffee-can full of coffee with lead foil to beat the X-rays. Mercury-loaded or something, about .380 size shells hollowed out, with a wax tip. Couldn't help wondering what they were used for. But I'm happy I wasn't there when they were.

He was certainly there when the starting gate went up for Operation Steeplechase. On 22 April 1985, Coleman and office manager, Gushan Hashim, flew to Cannes to join Tim Robertson at a meeting in a private apartment with Pierre Dhyer, of the Christian Lebanese Forces militia; Mario Calero, representing the Contras, and a British agent from MI6 working undercover with the DIA.

The purpose of the meeting was to discuss a consignment of arms confiscated by the Israelis from the PLO and turned over to the pro-Israeli faction of the Lebanese Forces. The idea was to buy them secretly for the Contras and send them out to Honduras disguised as relief supplies on a ship chartered by CBN, but the problem was that the Hoobaka faction had declined a cash offer, preferring to exchange the weapons for an unspecified commodity to the value of $1.5 million, to be brokered by CIA asset Monzer al-Kassar.

After an animated discussion, Hoobaka's terms were accepted in principle and the meeting adjourned, the CBN contingent to advise Oliver North with a view to setting the wheels in motion, and Coleman to advise DIA with a view to applying the brakes. Control responded by calling him to Frankfurt. On the strength of his report, the DIA had decided to scrap the whole vehicle.

'This CBN thing is getting to be a real pain in the ass,' Donleavy said.

He paused to light another in his endless chain of Merit cigarettes, brushing the stub ash off what could have been the same pair of double-knit trousers he had worn at their first meeting.

'So is Ollie North and that whole damn bunch of kooks and weirdoes. We got this lightbird colonel running around loose, telling two and three-star generals what to do, and they're getting pissed off about it. So don't be surprised if we pull his plug. Starting with this cockeyed deal with the Hoobaka bunch. We want you to close 'em out, old buddy. Nothing sudden, nothing dramatic – we don't want to make waves. Just let it die from natural causes, okay? Let 'em get on with it, but from now on, things should start to go wrong.'

Early in June, al-Kassar flew out to Bogotá, Colombia, on a Brazilian passport, No. CB5941792, in the name of Muce Sagy, one of several aliases. By prior arrangement, $1.5 million had been transferred from Oliver North's secret Contra fund at the Bank of Credit and Commerce International (BCCI) in Panama to al-Kassar's own BCCI account in Lima, Peru, which he held under the name of Pierre Abu Nader. From there, the money was credited to a BCCI account managed for one of the Colombian cocaine cartels by Frank Gerardo, a DEA informant, for the purchase of several hundred kilos of cocabase.

As Pierre Abu Nader, al-Kassar then returned to Europe on his Peruvian passport and subsequently reported on the success of his mission to North, who was then in Cyprus, staying in the ambassador's private apartment at the US Embassy in Nicosia. Coleman observed him there on 15 June.

Two months later, on 17 August, the shipment of cocabase arrived from Colombia aboard an East German freighter that put in to Tarbarja, Lebanon, an illegal narcotics port operated by the Hoobaka faction. The load was then taken by road to Zakorta, just east of Tripoli, processed into high-grade cocaine in the Hoobakas' own laboratories and passed through to its agents in Sofia, Bulgaria, en route to Monzer al-Kassar's distribution hub in Warsaw for bartering in the Eastern bloc.

On 23 August, Coleman reported to Control that the arms were to be loaded within ten days on the same freighter, which was now waiting to sail for Porto Lampura, Honduras, under the banner of the CBN's Central American relief programme, Operation Blessing.

The rest was up to Donleavy and the DIA, for by that time Coleman had so demoralized CBN headquarters with telex messages about Gushan Hashim and his colleagues stealing the store in Beirut that he knew it would take only one more serious shock, like preventing the arms from leaving Tarbarja, to bring the whole enterprise down. In accordance with instructions, he had ensured that the Lebanese would take the débâcle philosophically, for they already had their cocabase and so would lose nothing by it, and that the Contra supporters would have to attribute the loss of the arms shipment, and of North's $1.5 million, to an act of God.

Meanwhile, Coleman had a pressing problem of his own. From the moment Donleavy gave North, Casey and CBN the thumbs down, Coleman had known that the days of his Beirut assignment were numbered. And now that he had found Mary-Claude, there was no way he was going to leave her in a war zone, not knowing when or if he could get back to her. The shelling had been bad that summer, and she had already had one narrow escape.

Coleman had been running around the city one day with Michael Franks when the bombardment became so heavy that he decided he should move the family down to the comparative safety of his beach chalet, which was sheltered to some extent from incoming fire by a number of tall apartment buildings. As the shells rained in from the Druze artillery, he drove through the winding streets of the quarter and found Mary-Claude hiding with her sisters in a neighbour's basement. Fifteen minutes after they left, the house took a direct hit and was virtually demolished.

But even the random brutality of the shelling provided the DIA with an opportunity for the kind of black humour enjoyed by the octopus. Coleman had been surprised to learn that Nabi Berri, boss of the Amal militia, held a resident alien's Green Card issued by the US immigration authorities and owned five garages in the Detroit area.

'And yet here he was, in the middle of kidnapping US citizens and up to his neck in the TWA 747 hijack and all that stuff. Berri really pissed us off. The problem was, what could we do to screw him without getting the US involved in the civil war?

'Well, what we did was leak the trajectory coordinates of every house on Berri's street except his to militia factions Amal happened to be fighting at the time, including Hezbollah. And sure enough, every damn house in the neighbourhood was hit *except his*. You can imagine what the neighbours thought. They went ape-shit. After that, nobody was going to mow *his* yard.'

The in-coming bombardment was less amusing, however, when Coleman himself seemed to be the target.

Mary-Claude was determined to have a proper wedding in a proper wedding dress at Christ the King, a beautiful, cathedral-sized church overlooking the sea. Equally determined to bring the marriage forward before his mine exploded under CBN, Coleman found himself faced with the usual string of time-consuming formalities, and prevailed upon her father Philippe to accompany him up to the monastery overlooking the city to seek a special dispensation from the bishop.

No sooner had they set out than shells started falling along the road, the barrage accompanying them half-way up the mountain. Taking their survival as a favourable omen, Coleman managed to convince the church hierarchy of his good intentions and they set off again down the mountain with the necessary dispensation, only to pick up the barrage where it had left off. Muttering prayers forgotten since childhood, he drove down the winding mountain road with Philippe, the shells still falling around them, and presented Mary-Claude with the necessary papers like a knight errant back from the Crusades with a trophy for his lady.

And only just in time. As Coleman had anticipated, CBN was finally panicked into acting on the reports he had been sending over about the reckless indiscretions of Hashim and his cronies in the Lebanese Forces. Fearing a major political scandal, the Robertsons ordered Coleman to close down the Beirut bureau at once and evacuate its equipment to Cyprus, abandoning the cache of arms on Tarbarja beach.

The shelling was then at its height, which at least spared him the complications of having to contend face to face with Hashim, who was hiding in his basement. But it did rather spoil the bride's toilette and the wedding party. Mary-Claude's hairdresser failed to get through, and except for Tony Asmar, only the immediate family were in the church when the bride and groom arrived in

Range Rovers manned by Lebanese Forces militiamen armed with Kalashnikov rifles. The best man, hurriedly pressed into service at the last minute, was Michael Franks, alias Schafer, the OPS mercenary.

The Colemans' wedding night was spent in the chalet, with Tony Asmar's men tramping in and out delivering videotape machines, cameras and other equipment from the CBN office. At 5 a.m., trucks arrived to take all the boxes to the Jounieh docks, where they were loaded on the ferry to Larnaca, and as the sun came up, the happy couple watched the coast of Lebanon fade behind them in the morning haze. For Mary-Claude, it was the first time she had set foot outside Beirut's Christian enclave.

Following Donleavy's instructions, Coleman reported on arrival in Cyprus to Colonel John Sasser, the Department of Defense attaché at the American Embassy in Nicosia. He was also debriefed by Micheal T. Hurley, the Drug Enforcement Administration attaché, though without revealing his connection with the DIA. As far as Hurley knew, Coleman was an employee of CBN's who had been evacuated from Lebanon after the closure of its Beirut bureau.

At Donleavy's suggestion, Coleman then took Mary-Claude to Corfu for a two-week honeymoon before they went home to the United States to begin their married life in an apartment not far from James McCloskey's house in Timonium, Maryland.

Everything had gone according to plan. Fearful that his political ambitions, including a presidential candidacy, would be wrecked if CBN's connection with bartering drugs for guns on behalf of the Contras ever came to light, Pat Robertson lined up Gushan Hashim to take the rap, severed his connections with Colonel North, General Singlaub and their associates, and fired every non-believer who knew anything about it, including Coleman – cushioning the blow with a $6000 severance check.

'Keep it,' said Donleavy. 'You did a great job, buddy. I want you to know that some very high-level people over here have asked me to thank you for a job well done. We rate the mission a major success. So take a couple of months off. Show Mary-Claude a good time. We're going to need you out there again after Christmas.'

—— IX ——

Stalled by the higher priorities of Anglo-American diplomacy, the deliberate withholding of information by British and American intelligence agencies, and the seeming intransigence of the German BKA, the police investigation into the bombing of Flight 103 again ground to a halt in December 1989. In a newspaper interview marking the first anniversary of the Lockerbie disaster, the Lord Advocate of Scotland, Lord Fraser, conceded that 'we have not yet reached the stage where proceedings are imminently in prospect'. In other words, 'We know who did it but can't prove it in court.'

Touched by the general mood of frustration, he added that he had even thought of abandoning the hunt 'because we don't want to kid people that there is an active investigation if really policemen are just shuffling files around'. As a sop to 'serious public concern', he announced that a Fatal Accident Inquiry – the Scottish equivalent of a coroner's inquest – would be convened in the new year.

'Lord Fraser was initially opposed to such an inquiry,' wrote the *Sunday Correspondent* on 17 December, 'and his change of mind is indicative not only of intense pressure from victims' relatives but is also an admission that the inquiry, which has so far cost £7.75m, has reached a dead end. There is still no positive evidence to link the suspects firmly to the crime, although Lord Fraser did say in his interview that the investigation was in "a very active phase".'

George Esson, Chief Constable of Dumfries and Galloway, agreed. 'We are cautiously optimistic, based on the amount of evidence and information that we've already got, of identifying the culprits. Intelligence is one thing, but turning intelligence into hard evidence is quite another issue . . . The gathering of the forensic evidence has been done, much of the analysis of that evidence has now been done. The obvious lines of inquiry are not exactly running out, but there's a limit to the time that can take and we are reaching that stage. You eventually exhaust the leads you have.'

Esson's caution and forbearance were remarkable, given that the investigation had become a political football. In the year since the disaster, his officers, led by Detective Chief Superintendent John Orr, had collected 12,402 names in the police computer at the Lockerbie Incident Centre, made 350 visits to 13 countries and launched inquiries in 39 others. (About the only people they had *not* talked to – and never did – were Juval Aviv and Lester Coleman.)

Otherwise, they had taken over 14,000 statements, logged about 16,000 items of personal property belonging to the victims, and taken some 35,000 photographs – and the only solid lead they had left was a link between the bombing and four Palestinians who had just been convicted of terrorist crimes in Sweden.

One of them, Mahmoud Said al-Moghrabi, had confessed to the charges against him and, in so doing, had connected two of the others, Marten Imandi and Abu Talb, with the PFLP–GC cell in West Germany. Just before the BKA raids, Imandi's car, with Swedish licence plates, had been observed parked outside the bombers' apartment in Neuss, and in October 1988, Talb had visited Malta, bringing back samples of clothing that he told Moghrabi he intended to import from the island for Sweden's rag trade.

When the Swedish police raided Talb's apartment in May 1989, they found a calendar with a pencil ring around the fatal date, 21 December 1988, and when they returned later with the Scottish police on a second raid, they found some 200 pieces of clothing manufactured in Malta.

Reporting these developments in *The Sunday Times*, David Leppard, the most assiduous of the newsmen still working on the Lockerbie story, wrote:

Talb flew out of Malta on November 26 last year – only three days after a man walked into a boutique in the tourist resort of Sliema and bought clothes which were later wrapped around the Pan Am suitcase bomb ... He also visited a flat in Frankfurt, West Germany, where the bomb was almost certainly built.

Talb is a member of the Popular Front for the Liberation of Palestine–General Command (PFLP–GC), the group Western intelligence believes was paid millions of dollars by the Iranians to carry out the Lockerbie bombing.

By now, Leppard was also convinced that the bomb had been put aboard Flight 103 in an unaccompanied suitcase sent via Air Malta to Frankfurt, an 'exclusive' printed two weeks earlier (after the extraordinary resurrection of the airport's computerized baggage lists), but the *Observer* was not so sure. 'The Maltese connection is the strongest lead so far in the search for the bombers,' the paper conceded, 'although there is nothing to support newspaper reports that the bomb itself originated on the island.'

It fell to David Leppard to close out the media's coverage of the disaster for 1989. On 17 December, under the headline 'Police close in on Lockerbie killers', he wrote:

Police now have the necessary evidence to charge suspects with the murder of 270 Lockerbie air disaster victims. After a series of exclusive disclosures over the past seven weeks, *The Sunday Times* understands that officers heading the investigation – despite a cautious attitude in public – have told their counterparts abroad that under Scottish law 'charges are now possible against certain persons . . .'

The revelation . . . was made at a secret summit in Meckenheim, West Germany, of the heads of security services involved in the inquiry from Britain, West Germany, America, Sweden and Malta.

A week later, on Christmas Eve 1989, he added: 'Police hunting the bombers of the Pan Am jet which blew up over Lockerbie last year have uncovered important new forensic evidence linking a group of suspected Palestinian terrorists in West Germany to the bombing.

'Ministry of Defence scientists now believe a white plastic residue recovered from the crash site is the same material as that in alarm clocks bought by the group at a shop in Neuss, near Düsseldorf, two months before the bombing.' Scottish detectives, Leppard went on, 'believe the white residue provides "a hard link" between the bombs found at Neuss and Frankfurt and the Lockerbie bomb'.

A year later, the same forensic evidence and a hitherto discounted CIA report of a secret meeting in Tripoli in 1988 would serve to pin the blame exclusively on the Libyans, as was then required by changes in Middle East policy, but on the first anniversary of the disaster, there was no reason to doubt the sincerity of the Lord Advocate when he insisted that 'Our commitment and determination to bring the evil perpetrators of this mass murder to justice continues undiminished.'

The same commitment had been expressed a few months earlier by President George Bush in setting up his Commission on Aviation Security and Terrorism, with instructions to report by 15 May 1990. This, too, was in response to public pressure for results in the Flight 103 investigation, and, like the promised Fatal Accident Inquiry in Scotland, was offered reluctantly, lest its findings should conflict with the politically acceptable solution required by London and Washington.

In Britain, the government managed to put off the Scottish hearings until October 1990, and even then, no evidence was to be offered that might prejudice possible extradition hearings, which covered pretty nearly everything. In Washington, where the appearance of openness in government is more highly prized, the necessary political constraints on the president's Commission were built in with the choice of its members. With Ann McLaughlin, Reagan's former secretary of labor, in the chair, it included four career politicians, among them a former secretary to the Navy, and a retired Air Force general.

Though empowered to call witnesses and to subpoena records, the Commission dutifully concentrated, not on the criminal investigation, but on Pan Am's security lapses in Frankfurt and London and on the shortcomings of the Federal Aviation Administration. Even so, some revealing snippets emerged from the hearings. The panel learned, for example, from Raymond Smith, then deputy chief of the US mission to the Soviet Union, that 80 per cent of the reservations made by Moscow embassy staff on Pan Am flights during the 1988 Christmas holidays were cancelled after the so-called Helsinki warning early in December.

'It named a carrier,' said Smith. 'It named a route. And it covered a time period when many Americans in Moscow would be going home for Christmas. Here, it seems to me, we have a moral obligation to let people know.'

On his responsibility, the warning was drawn to the attention, not only of diplomats, but of the entire American colony in Moscow. As Andrew Stephen wrote in the *Observer*, 'These revelations have helped to explain the mystery of why there were so many empty seats on Pan Am Flight 103 from Heathrow to New York on 21 December 1988.'

Also significant were reports of a clash between testimony given under oath by Thomas Plaskett, Pan Am's chairman, and Raymond Salazar, security chief of the FAA. Some months before the disaster, the airline had decided to allow unaccompanied baggage aboard its international flights with an X-ray check instead of the physical search seemingly required under the rules. Plaskett testified that the FAA had agreed to this at a meeting with Pan Am's security chiefs, but Salazar denied that any such exemption had been given, dismissing Plaskett's testimony as 'not credible'.

Credible or not, when the FAA fined Pan Am $630,000 for violations of its rules in Frankfurt and London during a five-week period beginning on 21 December 1988, it did *not* cite the airline for failing to search unaccompanied baggage or for failing to reconcile interline baggage with interline passengers.

Stung by Salazar's denial, Pan Am promptly accused the FAA of engaging in a cover-up.

That was in April. On 16 May 1990 – two weeks after Lester Coleman's arrest on a trumped-up charge – the report of President Bush's commission was duly published, and duly spared Washington and London any further embarrassment in their diplomatic courtship of Syria. Stopping just short of pronouncing Pan Am guilty, the Commission found that the airline's security lapses, coupled with the FAA's failure to enforce its own regulations, were probably to blame for the disaster.

'The destruction of Flight 103 may well have been preventable,' its report concluded. 'Stricter baggage reconciliation procedures could have stopped any unaccompanied checked bags from boarding the flight [sic] at Frankfurt . . .' On the other hand, the commission could not 'say with certainty that more rigid application of any particular procedure actually would have stopped the sabotage'.

Its caution was justified, although clearly there had been plenty of room for improvement.

Until interline passengers checked in at Frankfurt [the report observed] Pan Am had no record of them, or their baggage, in its computer. Nevertheless, Pan Am personnel made no attempt to reconcile the number of interline bags being loaded into any plane with the number of bags checked by interline passengers who actually boarded the plane. Bags with distinctive interline tags were simply X-rayed on the baggage loading ramp, taken directly to the aircaft and loaded.

Pan Am employees did not determine whether any given interline bag loaded on to Flight 103 was accompanied by the passenger who presumably had checked it onto an earlier flight into Frankfurt or for that matter, whether that bag had ever been accompanied by any passenger.

In his book, *On the Trail of Terror*, published in 1991, David Leppard described that statement as 'a searing indictment' of the incompetence of Pan Am's security staff at Frankfurt in letting the bomb through, but the Commission itself was less damning. An FAA inspector checking on the airline's security arrangements in October 1988, had written in his report that 'the system, trying adequately to control approximately 4500 passengers and 28 flights per day, is being held together only by a very labour-intensive operation and the tenuous threads of luck'. Nevertheless, 'It appears the minimum (FAA) requirements can and are being met.'

Six months after the disaster, as the commission noted, FAA inspectors were generally less accommodating. In June 1989, one reported that while the security systems of four other US carriers at Frankfurt were 'good', Pan Am's was 'totally unsatisfactory' – so much so that 'all passengers flying out of Frankfurt on Pan Am are at great risk'.

This change of attitude by a Federal government agency before and after the disaster may or may not have been influenced by a change in the Federal government's political requirements before and after the disaster, but there were other inconsistencies also in the commission's report.

The bombing had occurred against a background of warnings that trouble was brewing in the European terrorist community and 'nine security bulletins that could have been relevant to the tragedy were issued between 1 June 1988 and 21 December 1988'. Elsewhere, however, the commission insisted that no warnings specific to Flight 103 and no information bearing on the security of civil aviation in general had been received by US intelligence agencies from any source around that time.

The report also solemnly recorded the CIA's assurances that its agents had not gone to Lockerbie after the disaster, but stopped short of denying that at least two of them had been among the victims.

After reviewing the findings of its nine-month inquiry, the commission made over 60 recommendations for improving airline security in general, for revising the Warsaw Convention and overhauling the machinery of inter-agency cooperation. Most of these were sensible but some were mere sabre-rattling.

'National will and the moral courage to exercise it are the ultimate means for defeating terrorism,' the report declared. It urged 'a more vigorous US policy that not only pursues and punishes terrorists but also makes state sponsors of terrorism pay a price for their actions ... These more vigorous policies should include planning and training for pre-emptive or retaliatory military strikes against known terrorist enclaves in nations that harbour them. Where such direct strikes are inappropriate, the commission recommends a lesser option, including covert operations to prevent, disrupt or respond to terrorist acts.

'Rhetoric is no substitute for strong, effective action,' it added, with a certain poignancy, for rhetoric was all the president's Commission had to offer in the changing circumstances of the Bush administration's Middle East policy. In deference to the government's requirements, there was no mention in its report of Syria or Iran or even Libya, or of any terrorist group known to be backed by any one of them. Nor was there any mention of drugs or drugs smuggling from Lebanon through Frankfurt to New York, Detroit and beyond. This was still the one component of the Lockerbie affair that had not been publicly addressed by the authorities but which, nevertheless, refused to go away.

After the flurry of excitement aroused by the discovery of a Swedish connection, the investigation had again stalled. Marten Imandi and Abu Talb, both sentenced to life imprisonment for terrorist activities in Scandinavia, steadfastly declined to assist the Scottish police in their inquiries, and although the circumstantial evidence against them remained strong, the lead petered out in yet another dead end.

Worse still, in June, the Swedish government moved to deport to Syria ten Palestinians it had picked up on suspicion of involvement with terrorism, including two who had been identified as associates of Dalkamoni and Khreesat. According to the BKA, these two had arrived in Germany from Syria and stayed at the PFLP–GC apartment in Neuss until a few days before it was raided in October 1988. Getting out just in time, Imandi had smuggled them into Sweden by car, where they had gone to ground near Uppsala. As one of the two had since been identified as a former Syrian intelligence officer, the Scottish police were naturally keen to interview them in the hope of establishing further connections between the bombers and PFLP–GC headquarters in Damascus.

Reporting this development in the *Observer*, on 17 June 1990, John Merritt wrote that

> . . . anger at their imminent deportation will be increased by the revelation that their links with the West German terrorist cell found in possession of Lockerbie-type bombs, and their whereabouts, have been known to Western intelligence services for 18 months.
>
> Sources close to the Swedish investigation said intelligence agents were tipped off about the men's movements since leaving Syria and the way in which they were smuggled into Sweden a few weeks before the Lockerbie bombing. And they cannot explain why they have been arrested only now – just to be sent back to Syria . . .
>
> Swedish investigators are also convinced that there is intelligence information on 'several other suspects' with material important to the Lockerbie investigation currently living in Sweden. But there is 'a reluctance' on the part of intelligence sources to reveal details to the police inquiry.

Answering, in effect, the question of why the two were being sent back to safety in Syria to join Khreesat and the other West German cell members, and why Western intelligence sources were reluctant to cooperate with the police, Merritt concluded his report by observing that 'with the British government entering fresh negotiations with Syria, and Damascus signalling its interest in sending an ambassador to Washington, Swedish investigators were last week asking how much other information is being kept from the police inquiry for political reasons'.

The Scottish police had been asking the same question from day one of the investigation.

Two weeks after his Swedish report, Merritt drove yet another nail into the coffin prepared for Pan Am. On 1 July 1990, he wrote:

> Fresh evidence from the investigation into the Lockerbie bombing indicates that the suitcase containing the bomb was allowed on the doomed Pan Am flight because of a failure to match baggage to passengers.
>
> Within the last week, detectives have established that only one item of luggage, pieced together from the wreckage after

one-and-a-half years of painstaking forensic work, cannot now be positively linked with a passenger from Flight 103. That item is the Samsonite suitcase which held the bomb.

The clear implication . . . is that the beleaguered US airline broke American aviation security law . . . Written procedures under the Federal Aviation Act expressly prohibited the US carrier from transporting any baggage not matched with a passenger who boarded the flight.

This was not the first time the media had made that mistake – the requirement at the time was that unaccompanied baggage should be searched before going aboard – but, as Merritt accurately surmised, 'This development will greatly strengthen the case for families of the dead who are suing Pan Am.'

The following month, Saddam Hussein of Iraq occupied the neighbouring sheikdom of Kuwait, Syria declared itself on the side of the allied forces committed to rolling back the invasion, and from that moment on, nothing more was heard from official sources on either side of the Atlantic about Syrian complicity in the Flight 103 bombing.

'The Syrians took a bum rap on this,' declared President Bush, pointing the Anglo-American finger at Libya, which was now to be solely to blame for taking advantage of Pan Am's 'wilful misconduct' at Frankfurt airport.

Everything seemed safely wrapped up, except for the almost universal scepticism which greeted the news that the Libyans were the culprits and the still persistent rumours of drug smuggling via Pan Am flights from Frankfurt.

With half-buried Syrian tanks guarding the poppy fields of the Bekaa Valley; with the Syrian President's brother, Rifat Assad, controlling the production and export of Lebanese heroin to the United States; with the Syrian arms and drugs dealer, Monzer al-Kassar, identified as Assad's marketing manager, and with al-Kassar inextricably linked with Ahmed Jibril's PFLP–GC and other Syrian and Iranian-backed terrorist groups, any serious suggestion that drug smuggling through Cyprus and Frankfurt to the United States had been in progress during December 1988, could only re-implicate Syria and thereby undo all the good work of disinformation and obfuscation carried out by the octopus.

In the national interest, anybody promoting any such idea had to be severely discouraged.

On 25 September 1990, Marshall Lee Miller introduced his client, Lester Coleman, to Pan Am's attorneys in Washington, and dropped out of sight.

Coleman neither saw nor heard from him again.

— X —

Having successfully worked himself out of the job of CBN's Beirut correspondent, Coleman went back to the Middle East in December 1985, as Condor Television Ltd, a one-man production company with an 'office' in the Kastantiana hotel, Larnaca, Cyprus.

Set up by his guru, James McCloskey, as an offshore Gibraltar corporation, with bank accounts (Nos. 00569798 and 02843900) at the First American Bank of Maryland (a BCCI subsidiary), Condor was to be Coleman's front for resuming control of Tony Asmar's network of agents in Lebanon.

As before, his duties were to direct and evaluate the flow of intelligence data, channel it back to the DIA in Washington, and act as paymaster for what was now by far the most valuable Western intelligence asset in the Middle East. To avoid any possibility of its being compromised by payments traceable to the DIA, Coleman used Visa traveller's cheques drawn on BCCI, Luxembourg. These were delivered to him by DHL, the international courier company, in shipments containing ten packets of ten unsigned $100 cheques. Every month, Asmar's secretary would take the Sunboat from Jounieh to Larnaca to collect the payroll from Coleman for distribution within the network, each cell member then signing his cheques and counter-signing them on presentation to a Lebanese bank for payment.

No sooner had he set up these new procedures than Coleman was summoned to the American Embassy in Nicosia by the Department of Defense attaché, Col. John Sasser, to whom he had reported on leaving Beirut as a CBN 'refugee' a few months earlier. Although Donleavy had told him to stay clear of American officials overseas in case they were under surveillance by foreign intelligence agencies, Coleman assumed that Sasser had cleared the meeting with Control and drove up from Larnaca to keep the appointment, expecting to be briefed on some unexpected emergency. Instead, Sasser showed him a home videotape of a Hezbollah demonstration in Beirut and asked if he could identify anybody.

Annoyed that his cover might have been jeopardized for such a trivial reason, Coleman left Sasser's office with the intention of coding an immediate complaint to Donleavy – only to run into Micheal T. Hurley on the stairway. This was even more embarrassing, for Donleavy's strictures about keeping away from the embassy had focussed particularly on the risks of associating with the Drug Enforcement Administration's 'cowboys', the DIA's contempt for the CIA under William Casey being exceeded only by its detestation of the DEA.

Greeting Coleman like an old friend, although they had met only once before, Hurley said Sasser had told him about Condor Television and its plans for covering events in Lebanon, and how about joining him for lunch? As much to find out how much Sasser *had* told him as to learn what Hurley was up to, Coleman agreed, and over a sandwich from the embassy canteen in Hurley's basement office, discovered that the DEA attaché was trying to put together a videotape documenting narcotics production in the Bekaa Valley.

'Think you can help us out with that?' Hurley asked. 'You got anybody over there can shoot some pictures for us?'

'Well, I don't know,' said Coleman cautiously. 'We're just setting up here – we don't have much equipment or anything yet. Why don't I get back to you when I have this thing up and running?'

When he reported this encounter to Control, Donleavy hit the roof and summoned him to Frankfurt.

They had met there before for face-to-face debriefings during Operation Steeplechase, and the routine was always the same. Coleman would check into the Sheraton airport hotel and call a contact number, identifying himself as Benjamin B, and almost immediately, Donleavy would call back.

'Howya doin', buddy?' (He always called Coleman 'buddy'.) 'Have a good trip? Here's what I want you to do. In exactly thirty-five minutes, I want you to leave and go to the airport terminal. Take the escalator down to the lower level. Get on the train and get off at the third [or fourth or fifth] stop. Cross over and go back two [or three or four] stops. Get off, cross over again and come on in to the Meinhof. Get off, go through the gate, and I'll meet you, okay?'

'Okay?' Coleman shakes his head at the memory of it.

Like hell I was okay. Two stops, did he say? Is this the right train?
I could have wound up in Wiesbaden for all I knew. But I'd get
off at the Meinhof, looking straight ahead and keep on walking
and I'd feel this presence move up beside me. In a trenchcoat.
'Hey, buddy,' he'd say, and get real animated. 'How's everything?
How's Mary-Claude?' And there we were, two friends coming off
the train together.

After leaving the station, we'd just walk around for ten or
fifteen minutes, doubling back on our tracks, heading in through
the lobby of a big hotel and straight out again through the rear
entrance, until finally we'd come to some itty-bitty hotel in a back
street with a desk in the hallway, and we'd do the elevator routine.
Up to the fifth floor, then walk down to the third, where he'd taken
a couple of rooms. It was always the same with him. I used to call
it the spook walk.

And once we got there, the routine was always the same. We'd
have a drink. He'd chain-smoke a couple of Merits while we
chatted about what had happened since our last meeting and
then he'd hand me over to the guy in the room next door for
a routine polygraph. Happened every three or four months. 'See
you later,' he'd say, and often it was five or six hours later. There
would be the guy with the black box in a suitcase and the chair
facing the wall that I would sit in while he sat in a chair behind
me. He'd fit the electrodes to my fingers, a band around my chest
and a blood-pressure gauge to my left arm and then we'd go at
it, heat full up, windows closed, sweating like pigs because that
was supposed to make the polygraph more accurate.

Same questions over and over again. A lot of them related to
the data I'd been passing but also he'd want to know who I'd
been talking to. Had I been in contact with officials of other
governments? Any close contacts with foreign nationals? If so,
when, how and why? The whole thing was designed to smoke
out double agents, to make sure you hadn't gone over and
started to work for the other side. I didn't mind. Seemed like
a sensible precaution to me. After that, I'd take a shower, we'd
have a meal sent up, get a good night's sleep and start fresh in
the morning.

Donleavy had thought seriously about the chance encounter with
Hurley, and, on balance, had decided that they might turn it to
account, although . . .

He was mad at Sasser for calling me in [Coleman remembers]. 'In future, if he wants to know anything,' Donleavy said, 'he can go through channels.' And as it looked like Sasser had told Hurley something about me, Control passed the word that I had handled some contract work for the Defense Department in the past, just minor stuff, but that it was all finished now.

'So if Hurley asks you again if you can do something for him,' he said, 'tell him, okay. Otherwise he's going to get suspicious. But you don't tell him Condor is a DIA operation or let him think you're with DIA HUMINT. And under no circumstances do you tell him about any assets we have in place in Lebanon. If he wants to know who your contacts are over there, make 'em up.'

'Fine,' I said. 'And I'm going to have to make up the cameras and equipment, too, because we don't have any.'

'That's all right, buddy,' he said. 'Just string him along until we get things squared away. There could be a positive spin to it because now you can keep an eye on Hurley for us. We've been picking up some bad vibes on that guy. But watch yourself. That whole bunch is into cowboys and Indians. Just don't get too close.'

Returning to Cyprus on 16 February, Coleman engineered another meeting with Hurley and told him Condor would be glad to do what it could to help.

'Hey, that's great,' Hurley said. 'We heard some good things about you – and you'll find we pay better than the military. We got all kinds of people shooting stuff for us out there. Mostly media people, so you probably know 'em already. One way or another, we get to see most of their stuff before it gets Stateside. So pass the word to your guys. Tell 'em we'll buy anything they can get on narcotics. People. Places. Labs. Illegal ports. We want the whole picture. And here's a few bucks to grease a few palms.'

Signed up as a 'contract consultant', Coleman was paid $4000 in the next two months for supplying Hurley with absolutely nothing. His 'guys' in Lebanon, the Asmar network, were not to be risked on routine intelligence for the DEA, and Coleman had no other contacts there that he cared to expose to the Syrian-backed heroin cartel in the Bekaa Valley.

Donleavy was right [Coleman says]. They were cowboys. Rock 'n' roll cowboys, with beards, long hair, leather boots and jeans –

the embassy people couldn't stand them. Not their sort of bridge partners at all. And to see 'em hanging out upstairs with the spooks in their tennis shorts – God, what a picture. America in action overseas.

But Hurley was no fool. At first sight, he was the kind of big, bull-headed Irish-American you'd expect to see in a blue uniform directing traffic, but he had Cyprus pretty much in his pocket and was planning to retire there after he'd put in his twenty years. He was shrewd, in a self-serving way, and friendly enough. But if anybody crossed him, or if he thought the embassy establishment was trying to put him down, he'd stand on his desk and raise hell.

He was always screaming about how they dumped on him. How he had the worst office space in the building, and the worst housing of all the embassy staff. When Hurley got off on one of his tirades, Dany Habib, his number two, would stand in the doorway and roll his eyes, and Connie, his secretary, a typical career civil service type, would cluck around like a mother hen. 'Now, Mike, don't *do* that. Get off the desk. You just cool down now, you hear me?'

But nobody could tell Hurley what to do. Not Connie, not me and certainly not anybody in Washington. They were all assholes at DEA headquarters, according to Hurley. They'd never understood him or what he was trying to do, he once told me. That was in the beginning, during our honeymoon period. But after two months and $4000 and still nothing to show for it, he was getting a little hacked off at Condor Television.

Control came to the rescue. On 4 April 1986, Coleman was summoned to Frankfurt for another 'spook walk' and polygraph.

'How long since you were in Libya?' Donleavy asked, once the formalities were over.

Coleman shook his head. 'You probably know better than me,' he said. 'Not for years. Not since the late sixties.'

'Well . . . Hasn't changed much. Think you can find your way around Tripoli?'

'I guess so. I still know some people there anyway. Why? What's going on?'

Donleavy seemed not to hear. 'Do you have a way to get in?' he asked. 'Or do we need to set something up? There isn't much time.'

'Well, I wouldn't want to use Condor. I mean, I still don't have any cameras or gear, do I?' It was getting to be a sore point. 'How about as a newsman? I can probably get freelance credentials. There's a couple of radio people I can call.'

'Okay. Sounds good. But get right on it, buddy. Because when I say go, I want you *gone*.'

He closed his briefcase. The meeting was over.

Coleman laughed. 'You mean, I'm not supposed to know *why* I'm going?'

Donleavy sat down again and lit another Merit. He had the air of a man about to break a rule of a lifetime.

'You're going in there to observe the effect of Operation El Dorado Canyon,' he said.

Coleman waited, but that was all. 'Okay. So what the hell's El Dorado Canyon?'

'We're going to give Gaddafi a slap,' said Donleavy. 'Maybe take him out.'

'No shit.' Coleman whistled. 'What's he done now?'

Control shrugged. 'They reckon the disco bombing was enough.'

'In West Berlin? The Libyans didn't do that.'

'I know,' said Donleavy.

Coleman flew back to Cyprus on 6 April to rejoin Mary-Claude in Larnaca. She was particularly glad to see him as she had just been told she was pregnant.

The next day, finding it difficult to concentrate on anything as mundane as a punitive airstrike against Gaddafi, he called Evelyn Starnes, managing editor of Mutual Radio, in Arlington, Virginia. Ms Starnes, who had once worked for him in the news department of WSGN Radio in Birmingham, Alabama, agreed at once that he should cover pending events in Libya for Mutual Radio and promised to get the necessary credentials to him within 48 hours. He then called his father, now living in retirement at Lake Martin, and got the name of a former Libyan engineering colleague, whom Coleman immediately telexed, saying he was coming out for a visit.

Control said all that was just fine, and to stand by for instructions.

On 16 April, Coleman met Donleavy in Zurich for a last-minute briefing. His mission was now critically important, he was told, because the CIA had pulled its operatives out of Tripoli in advance of the attack. Never mind that they might have tipped off Gaddafi by doing so, there was nobody now left on the ground to report back directly to the United States government on the effects of the bombing. It was all up to Coleman.

Well, thanks, he said. Libya was a big country. Expect him back in six months.

He could have three days, Donleavy said. They were not so much interested in damage assessment. They could do that by satellite. What the bird *couldn't* do was measure the impact of the raid on Libyan morale. How would the population react? Would its response be positive or negative? If Gaddafi survived, would it weaken or strengthen his position as leader? Would the bombing succeed as a deterrent, discouraging popular support for terrorism, or would it provoke a desire for revenge? Coleman's job was to get out on the streets and talk to people, to come back with a feel for what the bombing had achieved.

Donleavy posed these questions as if, like Coleman, he knew what the answers were already.

In the wake of the F-111s that had flown out from their British bases to bomb targets in Tripoli and Benghazi, Mutual Radio's correspondent arrived on the scene on 17 April with a *laissez passer* from the Libyan Consulate in Zurich. He had no difficulty getting in. Mourning the death of his adopted daughter in the raid, Gaddafi was inviting the world to come and see what the Americans had done to him.

After dutifully inspecting the destruction at the El Azziziya barracks, where the Libyan leader lived, at the port of Sidi Balal and at Tripoli airport, as well as the damage done to the French Embassy and to civilian homes adjoining the target areas, Coleman left the media pack clamouring for phone lines at the El Khebir hotel or doing 'stand-ups' on the roof and went off on his own. (To avoid getting bogged down with routine reporting at the expense of his DIA mission, he had telexed Ms Starnes from Zurich to say he had been denied entry, a diplomatic untruth that still gives him a twinge when he thinks of it.)

Luckily, his father's former colleague at Esso Libya invited Coleman to stay with him, for there had seemed a pretty obvious danger in starting a cold canvas of opinion so soon after the raid. Feeling was running high in the city against the American 'butchers'. Whatever internal dissent there might have been had clearly been silenced by a unifying sense of outrage over the city's 37 dead. Coupled with a wave of popular sympathy for Gaddafi as a bereaved father, resentment at what was seen as Washington's bully-boy tactics appeared to have rallied the Libyans behind him with a solidarity he had rarely enjoyed before.

Networking out through the families and friends of Libyans he knew, talking to people in their homes, in coffee shops, in the markets and on the streets, Coleman met no one prepared to acknowledge even the smallest justification for the American action. From all that he heard, it was clear that Gaddafi's position had been secured for him in a way that his palace guard and secret police could never have managed on their own. Any question of a coup or a move towards popular democracy had been snuffed out.

With his knowledge of Arab ways, Coleman was not surprised. What *did* surprise him a little, and which argued a political maturity that even sensitive Western observers were sometimes inclined to overlook, was that, in three days of systematic canvassing of Libyan opinion, he encountered little or no personal hostility. The anger and resentment expressed at every level, from street vendor to middle-class intellectual, was almost entirely directed at Washington, not at him as an individual American. It was almost as if they considered him to be as much a victim of *his* government as they were of theirs, as if *he* could no more be held responsible for Reagan's actions than they could for Gaddafi's.

He told all this to Donleavy on his return to Zurich on 19 April. They talked for hours, and as he piled on the detail in his report, so Donleavy became ever more thoughtful and preoccupied.

'Okay, buddy,' he said eventually. 'Send Hurley a postcard. Tell him you're not coming back.'

'Say again?'

'Deactivate yourself. I need you back home for a spell.'

'Okay. But why don't I tell him myself? I can call from Larnaca.'

'No, no. I want you to head right on out of here to D.C. We got a lot of debriefing to do.'

'Now, wait a minute, Bill,' Coleman protested. 'What about Mary-Claude? I can't just leave her behind. She's pregnant.'

'Sure.' Donleavy nodded. 'So give her a break. This way, she can take her time packing your stuff and follow on when she's good and ready.' He checked his watch. 'Call her. You got an hour. If you get your ass in gear, you can make it out of here tonight.'

'Hold on, Bill. What about Tony Asmar? I can't just leave *him* high and dry either. We got a shit-load of stuff coming through about the hostages.'

'I know, buddy, but this is more important. Call Mary-Claude and write Hurley goodbye. You'll find your ticket downstairs by the time you check out.'

Coleman sighed.

'Come to think of it,' said Donleavy, 'maybe it's not too smart to get a US entry stamp in your passport right after this. You better fly back via Canada and go in on your Leavy ID.'

Donleavy tried to make up for it later by arranging a champagne thank-you weekend for the Colemans at the DIA's expense in an exclusive little Georgetown hotel, but by then they were almost too tired to enjoy it. Mary-Claude's pregnancy had been troublesome from the start, even without the stress of a month's separation and having to cope by herself with the move back from Cyprus, and Coleman was exhausted from a gruelling month of detailed debriefings by a stream of DIA officers and analysts at an assortment of Ramada Inns in the Baltimore/Washington area.

He was also for the first time vaguely troubled about the DIA's priorities in the Middle East, particularly with respect to the Western hostages in Beirut. As far as Donleavy and his masters were concerned, clearly nothing was more important than preserving the integrity of Tony Asmar's network of agents in Lebanon. They were Washington's eyes and ears.

We could have gotten the hostages out any damn time we wanted to [Coleman insists], but nobody was willing to rock the boat with a rescue operation. We knew where they were. We knew who their guards were. We knew what they had for lunch. We knew when and where they were going to be moved before their guards did. But the DIA wouldn't risk any action based on information that might have been traced back to one of Asmar's people. If we'd blown the network because of the hostages we would have left ourselves blind in the middle of a minefield. So there had to be another way. And it was in trying for another way that the CIA let in people like Monzer al-Kassar and, without meaning to, set up the whole Lockerbie scenario.

One of the factors that led me to sign up with the DIA was the idea that I might be able to do something for my friend Jerry Levin, who had been taken hostage in Beirut by Hezbollah, but as it happened he was released before I got out there. He and I had met in Birmingham, Alabama, while he was news director of WBRC-TV and I was news director of WSGN radio. When he landed the job of Beirut bureau chief for Cable News Network,

I remember I said to a colleague that if Jerry was ever taken hostage, his kidnappers would probably wind up paying CNN to take him back – and I was only half wrong. He had a wicked tongue when roused and could talk a blue streak. The story going around at the time was that he had ticked off the Lebanese bureau staff to the point where they sold him to Hezbollah for a bit of peace and quiet!

Officially, he was supposed to have escaped by sliding down bedsheets from an upper window, but the truth is that CNN's vice president, Ed Turner – no relation to *Ted* Turner – had to pay a hefty ransom for him. The deal was set up by Ghazi Kenaan, Syria's head of security in Beirut, who naturally took his cut off the top.

Another wave of kidnappings began soon after I got out there in 1985. Terry Anderson was taken, then Brian Keenan and John McCarthy in April 1986, followed by Terry Waite in January 1987.

Waite was a special case, of course. It's no secret now that he hooked up with Oliver North and Bill Casey of the CIA in an effort to trace the hostages – all of them unaware that the DIA, through Tony Asmar's network, already knew where they were. North wanted to have Waite wired to keep track of his movements electronically, but Waite, very sensibly, refused. So naturally they went ahead and did it anyway, without Waite's knowledge. Before he left Larnaca airport on a US Navy helicopter for the hop over to the American Embassy in East Beirut, his briefcase was rigged with a microchip Gigaherz transmitter no bigger than a butter biscuit.

That was stupid, and typical of North's cowboy mentality. As soon as Waite vanished, the trail went cold, because the first thing his kidnappers did was separate him from his briefcase.

It took Tony Asmar a month to find out where he was. Islamic Jihad had stashed Waite in the basement car park of a four-storey building in Baalbeck, in the Bekaa Valley. After that, they moved him to a building near Rue Michelle Boutros, and later on to the cellars of two different hospitals in West Beirut, both of them supplied by Tony's company, AMA Industries.

These hospitals were funded by Iran to treat battle casualties – Hezbollah, Amal militiamen and Syrian troops, depending on who happened to be fighting whom at the time – and they were ideal places for holding hostages. Not only Waite, but Anderson, McCarthy, Keenan, Mann and most of the others were also hidden there at various times, housed underground on two soundproofed levels. There were reliable supplies of electrical power, food and water, and if anybody got ill, help was available just upstairs.

The hostages were also pretty well protected from the fighting in the city. After all, who was going to bomb or attack a hospital? And when it came to moving them around, who was going to take any notice of vehicles coming and going from a hospital? The set-up was perfect.

It was even good enough to ease the conscience of the people on *our* side who decided to leave them where they were. If the hostages were reasonably safe and reasonably well cared for, why jeopardize our policy and priorities in the Middle East by trying to rescue them by force? An armed raid on a hospital was bound to cause an international outcry, particularly if we came out empty-handed.

Even so, Waite had everybody worried. I remember one time I reported that he had developed a cough and back came a directive that we should try to make an audio recording of it. Can't imagine why. Maybe somebody in the Pentagon figured they could find out how ill he was just by listening to it. Another time they asked if the hospital had taken delivery of a large bed. The Lebanese being quite short and Waite being quite tall, I guess they thought that this would show if Islamic Jihad was treating him right.

With his respiratory problem, he was lucky they didn't move him much. As I recall, they took him out in a refrigerator once, but the usual method with the hostages was to wrap them in blankets or carpet, strapped up with grey plumber's tape, cover them in sheets, then wheel them out in the middle of the night and stuff them in a van or the boot of a car for the journey. Before, during and after each move, the signals would really fly between us and Washington. We had to keep tabs on Waite at all times.

Not so with John McCarthy. The Brits' attitude was, well, he was a journalist. He had been warned the night before not to attempt to go to the airport but had done so anyway. The impression we got was that they thought it was pretty much his own fault. Like Anderson, Keenan and the others, he was a low priority. If it hadn't been for Jill Morrell and the people at WTN, London would have left him to rot.

All the noise being made about the hostages at that time was just political rhetoric. Nobody could move in those Beirut sectors without the consent of the Syrian occupying forces. If the Syrians had not permitted Hezbollah to have a presence in the southern suburbs of Beirut, there would have been no Iranian presence there. When the Syrians said, 'We don't know where the hostages are but we'll be glad to help locate them,' all they had to do was pick up the phone. Never mind what the US government says or what the public thinks – that's how it worked. The hostages could not have been held for ten minutes without Syrian permission.

General Ghazi Kenaan, commander of Syrian military intelligence in Lebanon, was on top of every move the whole time. How do I know that? Because we had somebody living in his house. Because he was screwing one of Tony Asmar's Filipino operatives.

The truth is the hostages were cynically exploited by both sides for political and tactical purposes. Okay, so we couldn't afford to compromise the Asmar network with a rescue operation, but there was another reason, too, why we had to leave them where they were. We needed to keep Hafez Assad, the Syrian president, in place. He's probably the most astute politician in the Middle East, and we knew we could do business with him.

If we'd upset his applecart in busting out the hostages, then the radical fundamentalists might easily have taken over in Syria and given us a much worse problem. So, well before the Gulf War, when he turned out to be a useful counterpoise to Saddam Hussein, Assad was serving our purpose by keeping Ayatollah Khomeini quiet. Much easier for us to deal with a conniving, self-serving bastard like Assad than try to cope with a religious fanatic. Those were the priorities. The hostages had to stay where they were, and we had to play the game. But I can't say I enjoyed it.

After their weekend in Georgetown, the Colemans moved in to his family's lakeside cottage at Lake Martin, near Auburn, Alabama, to await his next assignment. Donleavy kept in touch by telephone, sometimes talking to Coleman's father by mistake as they both sounded very much alike.

'My Dad would say to Donleavy, "I think you want to talk to the other Les." Then he would hold the phone out to me and say, loud enough for Donleavy to hear, "Hey, it's the spook."'

Although the DIA clearly had plans for him, it was evidently in no hurry to send him back to the Middle East. That summer, Donleavy arranged for Coleman to enrol for graduate study, with a teaching assistantship, at Auburn University, one of the many land-grant universities involved in secret government research. No one at the university was to know of his DIA connection, and to avoid any written record that might compromise his cover, Donleavy arranged for him to be paid during this period with American Express money orders drawn at 7-11 stores around Falls Church, Virginia.

On 31 August 1986, just three weeks before the Fall Term was due to begin, Donleavy called from Washington and told him he had to make an urgent trip to Lebanon.

'No way,' said Coleman. 'Mary-Claude is due in four weeks. I can't take her with me and I can't leave her here, so forget about it, Bill. I'm just not available until the baby's born.'

'I know how you feel, buddy. And I wouldn't ask you if we didn't have a real serious problem here. If there was anybody else we could send, I *would*, you know that. But it'll only take a couple of days.'

'Bill – '

'Listen, I don't want to talk about it on the phone. Come on up here, and we'll work something out.'

On 3 September they met for dinner at the Day's Inn on Jeff Davis Highway in Crystal City, Virginia.

'Sorry to do this to you, buddy,' Donleavy said. 'But we got a national emergency on our hands with your name on it.'

'Bill, I'd like to help you out but – '

'Well, we just don't have a lot of choice here. You'll be back in a week, I guarantee you. And Mary-Claude'll be just fine. Maybe you can get somebody to move in with her for a couple of days. Family, maybe.'

'Now wait a minute, Bill – '

'We got you on a flight out of Dulles via Heathrow the day after tomorrow. That'll get you back here by the fourteenth.'

'That's not a week. That's ten days.'

'At the latest. Cut a few corners, and you can maybe pick up a day or two along the way.'

'Well, that depends on what you want me to do, doesn't it?'

Donleavy chuckled. 'You're going to like this one. But eat your steak. I'll tell you about it in the morning.'

This was the military. Orders were orders. Coleman ate his steak.

Next morning, Donleavy came up to his room to lay out the assignment.

'Two things,' he said. 'First, you're going to get the video equipment you want for Condor and take it out there. Tony Asmar's lined

— 133 —

up a couple of people in Beirut to shoot some pictures for us near the airport. When they're through doing that, bring the equipment out again and come on home with the videotape.'

'Okay. Good.' Coleman looked at him curiously. A national emergency? 'So where is it? This equipment.'

'Here's what you do.' Donleavy opened his briefcase and placed an envelope on the bed. 'There's twenty-two hundred dollars. That'll buy you a Sony video system from Errol's Video Supply Store in Falls Church. Take a cab, have it wait for you, and you'll be back here in an hour.'

Coleman shook his head. But for his trust in Donleavy, he would have dropped out at this point, military or no military.

'You said *two* things. What's the other?'

'I'll tell you when you get back.'

An hour later, Coleman returned to the hotel with the Sony system from Errol's. He produced the receipt, Donleavy carefully itemized the equipment on a small yellow legal pad and Coleman signed for it with his code name, Benjamin B.

'Okay,' said Donleavy, putting the pad away in his briefcase. 'You're all set. Now here's the national emergency.'

He produced a Mattel Speak 'n' Spell toy computer, and Coleman sat down slowly.

'What the fuck is this? Some kind of joke?'

'No joke, buddy.' Donleavy was deadly serious. 'I want you to take this out to Tony Asmar.'

'Come on, Bill. Are you kidding me? I'm risking my marriage for *this*?'

'Remember a year ago?' Donleavy said. 'When you pulled the plug on CBN and the Contra deal? Well, this is it. The bottom line. This is where you get to wrap the whole thing up.'

'With *that*?'

'Yep.' He patted the toy. 'You got a little something extra in there.'

'Great.' Coleman weighed it in his hand suspiciously. 'It's not going to blow up on me, is it?'

'Nothing like that. We put in an extra chip, that's all. When you sit down with Tony, punch in your code word, he'll punch in his, and you'll retrieve the data we loaded in. He'll know what to do with it.'

'Oh, God. Suppose I forget the code word. You know what I'm like with those things.'

'You won't forget this one. You're from the South. What's the Southern slang word for peanut?'

'You mean, goober?'

Donleavy beamed.

Next day, Coleman flew to Heathrow with the camera equipment and the Mattel Speak 'n' Spell, arriving on the morning of 6 September. From there, he took a direct flight to Larnaca, Cyprus, and after four hours' sleep, caught the midnight ferry to Jounieh. Asmar's fiancée, Giselle, Mary-Claude's sister, met him off the boat, and as it was now Sunday, they joined the family for lunch at their house in Sarba.

On Monday, 8 September, Coleman got to work with Asmar in his office at Karintina. After testing the video equipment, they sent Asmar's volunteer cameramen off to start shooting the locations Control had specified in the western sectors of Beirut, places where, Coleman assumed, the hostages were being held. They then put the Speak 'n' Spell on Asmar's desk, set it up in accordance with the maker's instructions, and punched in their code words.

Out poured a detailed account of visits made by Robert McFarlane and Lt-Col. Oliver North to Iran, travelling on Irish passports, to organize the sale of TOW missiles and launchers to the Iranian government in exchange for the release of American hostages; details of money transfers and bank accounts, with dates and places – most of it based on incidents and conversations that could only have been known to the Iranian or American negotiators.

'My God,' said Coleman. He had known North was seriously out of favour at the Pentagon, but here was another glimpse into the pit. 'What are you supposed to do with this stuff?'

Asmar looked at him soberly, and Coleman did not press the point.

He left Beirut with the camera equipment and videotapes on 11 September, arriving back in Cyprus on the 12th. Next day, he flew to Heathrow, and after an overnight stop in London, travelled on to Montreal, and from there, as Thomas Leavy, to Baltimore-Washington International airport, where he checked in, as instructed, at the Ramada Inn. Donleavy, accompanied this time by another agent, arrived there early next morning, the 15th, for a full day's debriefing, and that night Coleman headed south for Alabama to rejoin Mary-Claude at the Lake Martin cottage.

On the 23rd, he began his postgraduate studies as a teaching assistant at Auburn University, and on 2 October, also on schedule, Mary-Claude presented him with a daughter, Sarah.

Meanwhile, one of Asmar's operatives had delivered the Speak 'n' Spell material to a relative who worked for *Al Shiraa*, Beirut's pro-Syrian Arabic-language news magazine. When the story ran on 3 November, it was picked up at once by the Western media, touching off an international scandal of such embarrassing proportions that President Reagan was forced to act. On 25 November 1986, he fired North, accepted the resignation of Rear-Admiral John Poindexter, McFarlane's successor as National Security Adviser, and spent the rest of his administration trying to dodge the political fallout from Irangate.

'Most people assumed it was the Iranians who blew the whistle on North, McFarlane and Poindexter,' Coleman says. 'Some even said it was the Russians who leaked the story after the failure of the Reykjavik summit. But it wasn't. It was the Pentagon. It was the DIA. It was me, with my little Speak 'n' Spell.'

— XI —

Pan Am was getting a bad press – rightly so for its slovenly security at Frankfurt, but wrongly so for its attempts to establish the truth of how the bomb got aboard. While the general presumption was that its negligence had let the terrorists through, the intelligence indications were that its security arrangements – good, bad or indifferent – had been bypassed.

In its sympathy for the families of the victims, the public was inclined to forget that any passenger aircraft with the Stars and Stripes on its tail would have served as a target as well as another. To that extent, Pan Am, its insurance underwriters and the 16 members of the Pan Am crew were also victims of an act of war against the United States.

It would therefore have followed civilized custom if the government of the United States had sought both to relieve the burden of the disaster on all those affected by it and to pursue and punish those responsible. But for reasons of its own, Washington in the end did neither. It sought, first, to exonerate itself from any general or particular blame for the tragedy and, second, to temper the pursuit of justice, for victims and murderers alike, with considerations of political expediency.

This failure to respond appropriately not only called the government's good faith into question, opening the way to all kinds of lurid speculation about its actions and motives, but further victimized Pan Am. No matter what the deficiencies were in its security arrangements at Frankfurt, the airline and its insurers were at least entitled to prepare their best defence against a charge of wilful misconduct. But with all the relevant documents and witnesses controlled by a government determined to evade any suggestion of responsibility for what had happened, no adequate defence was possible. Pan Am was delivered to the courts hamstrung, bankrupt and ripe for dispatch as a scapegoat.

When James M. Shaughnessy came to the case, ten days after the disaster, certain agents of the government already knew how and where the bomb had been placed on Flight 103. But it was soon evident that the government was not about to share any of its information or, indeed, to cooperate with Pan Am in any meaningful way. From day one, at a political level, the purpose of the investigation was, not to uncover the facts, but to 'prove' that Pan Am was to blame for letting the terrorists through.

Left with no choice but to accept the responsibility or to pursue its own independent inquiries, the airline instructed Windels, Marx, Davies & Ives to prepare its defence and to investigate the suggestions of government complicity that were already coming to light. If Washington was determined to show that Pan Am's deficiencies were solely to blame for the bombing, Pan Am's *only* defence was to show that Washington was at least equally at fault.

The telephone call on 29 December 1988, between Michael F. Jones, of Pan Am Corporate Security in London, and Phillip Connelly, assistant chief investigation officer of H.M. Customs and Excise, was the first substantial lead that Shaughnessy had to work with. With the methodical professionalism of a former detective sergeant with 20 years' experience in London's Metropolitan Police, Jones had made a full note of a conversation in which Connelly asked, 'Have you considered a bag switch at Frankfurt?'

A subsequent call, also noted down in detail at the time, established that before the disaster Connelly had attended a meeting in Frankfurt between various agencies monitoring a drug-trafficking operation through the airport which involved the switching of baggage. Follow-up inquiries leading to Cyprus ran into a dead end, however, when DEA Nicosia refused to discuss the matter on grounds of national security. (Two years later, Connelly would dispute Jones's recollection of these conversations, but by then the octopus had more or less got its act together. In the immediate aftermath of the tragedy, there was no reason why Connelly should not have been helpful or why Jones should have falsified an entry in his notebook.)

In April 1989, Shaughnessy learned from a colleague that Juval Aviv, an Israeli-American investigator with a reputation for getting results, had told him that some of his contacts in the intelligence community had important information about the crash of Flight 103. After nine prominent law firms had each recommended Aviv highly, Shaughnessy hired him and his company, Interfor, Inc. to develop those leads, and Aviv took off for Europe. Although some of his referees had said he was 'extremely zealous' and needed to be kept within specific guidelines, at the time, that had struck Shaughnessy as a commendation rather than a reservation.

Two months later, Aviv submitted his now notorious report.

Not surprisingly, Shaughnessy found it 'extremely disturbing, because it suggested serious wrong-doing by the government and suggested that Pan Am employees placed the bomb on Flight 103'. Whereas the pending liability suit against the airline depended on the theory that the bomb had penetrated Pan Am's security, the Aviv report indicated that it had *circumvented* Pan Am's security. As this conclusion was supported to some extent by the earlier Jones-Connelly conversations and other intelligence data, Shaugnessy and his colleagues now felt obliged to put Aviv's findings to the test.

'In order to properly defend our clients,' Shaughnessy explained later, 'we decided that we should serve subpoenas on a number of Federal agencies in an effort to determine whether the government had any documentation which would either confirm or dispute what Mr Aviv had reported.'

Because of its sensitive nature, access to the report was confined to the attorneys working on the case. At Pan Am, only the chairman and chief executive officer, Thomas G. Plaskett; the senior vice president, legal, John Lindsey, and Gregory W. Buhler, deputy general counsel, were allowed to read it, and only they were advised of Shaughnessy's decision to subpoena government records. (On first hearing of Aviv's findings, Plaskett reportedly exclaimed: 'You mean to tell me the CIA has been using Pan Am planes to run drugs? I thought I was running an airline.')

Significantly, Plaskett later told Shaughnessy 'that he had person-ally informed Secretary of State James Baker and Director of Central Intelligence William Webster of the contents of Mr Aviv's report and of our intention to serve subpoenas on a number of Federal agencies'.

Whether or not this advance notice had any bearing on the government's response, when the subpoenas were served on 29 September, the FBI, the DEA, the State Department, the National Security Agency, the CIA and the National Security Council each made it clear that they had no intention of complying with them.

And whether or not this advance notice had any bearing on the leak of Aviv's confidential report to Congressman James Traficant and the media in November, the subsequent publication of its findings around the world undermined the credibility of Shaughnessy's attempt to test the report's conclusions to the point where no one seemed inclined to take it seriously.

Angry at being put at such a disadvantage, Shaughnessy twice confronted Aviv about the leak, and twice Aviv denied having had anything to do it.

In November, the government moved to quash Pan Am's subpoenas before Chief Judge Thomas C. Platt in United States District Court, Eastern District of New York. Two conferences were held in an attempt to resolve the dispute, with the court attempting to determine what privileges, if any, the government was claiming.

Based on papers submitted for review *in camera*, Judge Platt felt the government might have a valid claim that the subpoenaed documents were protected from discovery by the state secrets privilege, but counsel for the government seemed unwilling to accept the suggestion. Indeed, the government showed so little cause for its refusal to provide discovery that the court felt it might have to stay the civil litigation against Pan Am until the conclusion of the criminal investigation. Chief Judge Platt then directed the government to search for documents bearing on how and where the bomb was placed on Flight 103 and on warnings received by the government before the night of the disaster.

Instead of complying with this order, the government 'distilled the specific accusations' it had identified in Aviv's report and instructed each of the Federal agencies to respond to that 'distillation' with declarations that there was nothing to support it. As this severely restricted the scope of what the agencies had been directed to search for, Shaughnessy felt confirmed in his suspicions that the government had something to hide and sought to obtain depositions from the officials who had signed the declarations. At a further conference, however, on 5 April 1990, the court ruled against him because the original subpoenas, and the government's motion to quash, were still outstanding.

With both sides now hopelessly deadlocked, the court convened another conference on 27 July. After advising counsel for the government that Washington could not keep on withholding relevant evidence, Chief Judge Platt ordered the government to produce all documents relating to how and where the bomb was placed on Flight 103 for inspection *in camera* by 1 October 1990.

Convinced that he was getting somewhere at last in his search for admissible evidence, Shaughnessy now turned to several other lines of inquiry. After the strange indifference of the police investigators to the results of the polygraph examinations of Tuzcu and O'Neill in Frankfurt, and the even stranger attempt by the FBI to intimidate the ex-Army polygraph expert who had carried them out, Juval Aviv had played no further part in the preparation of Pan Am's defence. Already something of an embarrassment after the publicity surrounding the leak of his report, he became something of a liability when the results of the polygraph tests also leaked out to the press. Confronted yet again by Shaughnessy, Aviv yet again denied any hand in the disclosure and on 31 May 1990, resigned as Pan Am's investigator, mainly because Shaughnessy refused to take his advice.

'Here I am, leading the charge up the hill,' he was reported as saying, 'and I look back, and where are my troops? They are hiding behind bushes, waiting to see how Juval makes out.'

After the leak of the Interfor Report, counsel for the victims' families attempted to take a deposition from Aviv but Shaughnessy moved to quash the subpoena on the grounds that Aviv's work was protected from discovery by the so-called attorney work-product doctrine. In reply, the plaintiffs argued that either Pan Am or Aviv had waived that protection by knowingly leaking the report to the media, and Chief Judge Platt referred the issue to Magistrate Judge Allyne Ross for a ruling.

After hearing several witnesses, including Aviv and the *Observer*'s reporter John Merritt, who had interviewed him in November 1989, Magistrate Judge Ross found that Aviv had divulged at least part of his report to Merritt and had thereby waived work-product protection. In her written opinion, dated 27 July 1990, Ross described Aviv's testimony as 'not credible', which most of the media took to mean that his leaked report was 'not credible'. In fact, she was referring only to his denials of having leaked the report. At no time had she addressed herself to the credibility or otherwise of anything *in* the report. (Curiously, although Magistrate Judge Ross ruled that plaintiffs *did* have the right to take a deposition from Aviv, their counsel never attempted to do so. The widespread belief that Ross had declared the Interfor Report 'not credible' was, perhaps, of greater value to their case than anything Aviv might have sworn to.)

But even before Aviv dropped out of the picture, Shaughnessy had substantially broadened the scope of his inquiries.

'As might be expected in an investigation involving international terrorism, the murder of 270 innocent people and a possible government cover-up,' he told the court, 'most of the individuals we contacted or who contacted us, demanded complete anonymity. For me to reveal the identities of those individuals would not only be a breach of confidence and trust in me but, in some cases, might jeopardize the careers of those involved or even jeopardize their safety.'

Though he offered to identify his sources to Chief Judge Platt *in camera*, Shaughnessy was only too well aware that the certainty he felt about Flight 103 had yet to be converted into a certainty he could prove in court. A former DIA agent, for instance, had confirmed the involvement of the US intelligence community in narcotics trafficking, but not for attribution. Similarly, a former CIA agent had given him a detailed, off-the-record account of the agency's involvement with arms and narcotics trafficking in the Middle East.

More dramatically, in the spring of 1990, a senior DEA intelligence analyst confirmed that most of what Aviv had said in his report about narcotics trafficking through Frankfurt airport was true.

At about the same time, Shaughnessy also commissioned a former German intelligence agent to carry out an investigation for him in Europe. When his report was submitted, it dwelt at length on the key figure of Monzer al-Kassar and his involvement with Palestinian terrorist groups, supporting Aviv's assertion of al-Kassar's connection with the bombing of Flight 103. Of even greater interest was the flat statement that the BKA, working with German intelligence, had established that the bomb had been carried to Frankfurt from Damascus via Cyprus.

Four other sources provided documents and information, mainly about warnings received before the bombing. One also supplied a report entitled 'Pan Am Flight 103', prepared in January 1989 by the intelligence unit of the Lebanese Forces, which had to do mainly with the substance of intercepted telephone calls to and from the Iranian Embassy in Beirut.

On page 10, the report stated: 'Two days after the downing of Pan Am 103, the Iranian embassy in Beirut receives a phone call from the Interior Ministry in Teheran, intercepted, during which the ambassador is told to hand over to the PFLP–GC the remaining funds, size and scope not specified, and is being congratulated for the "successful operation".'

All four informants confirmed that the United States had the Iranian Embassy in Beirut under electronic surveillance prior to the disaster. They also confirmed that an American named David Lovejoy had made a series of calls to Hussein Niknam, the Iranian chargé d'affaires, about a team of American agents, led by Charles Dennis McKee and Matthew Kevin Gannon, who had arrived in Beirut on a mission concerned with the hostages.

Lovejoy's last recorded call was on 20 December 1988, when he advised Niknam that the agents had changed their travel plans and would catch Pan Am Flight 103 from London next day, 21 December. Niknam at once put in a call to the Interior Ministry in Teheran and was monitored passing on Lovejoy's information.

One of Shaughnessy's sources, with close links to Israeli intelligence, actually claimed to have heard the tapes of these telephone intercepts, and another, well-connected with the US intelligence community, confirmed not only that the Iranian Embassy's calls had been monitored at that time but also the substance of the Lovejoy–Niknam conversations.

Other documents to which Shaughnessy was given access included a series of DIA Defense Intelligence Terrorism Summaries (DITSUMs) issued in the second half of 1988 warning against renewed threats of attack on US interests, particularly as a consequence of the shooting down of the Iranian Airbus in July. On 1 December, just three weeks before the disaster, a DIA DITSUM stated that 'reports of surveillance, targeting and planning of actions against US persons and facilities are continuous'.

All four sources also independently confirmed that on 9 December 1988, Israeli Defence Forces had captured documents in a raid on a PFLP–GC base near Damour, Lebanon, which disclosed plans to bomb a Pan Am flight out of Frankfurt by the end of that month. One of the four said that Flight 103 was specifically mentioned, and all agreed that the Israelis had immediately warned the governments of the United States and West Germany.

The consensus was overwhelming, but Shaughnessy could call none of his informants to the witness stand, even if they had been willing to testify, because almost everything they had told him – no matter how detailed and how well corroborated by information from other independent sources – would have been ruled out as inadmissible hearsay.

Although there was little room to doubt that the government of the United States, with the assistance of the British and German governments, was engaged in the biggest cover-up of modern times, there was no possible way Shaughnessy could prove it to a judge and jury unless the US government opened its files – and thereby virtually incriminated itself.

Everything seemed to hinge, therefore, on Chief Judge Platt's decision to order the government to produce all documents relating to the bombing of Flight 103 by 1 October 1990, for his review *in camera*. But in December, Shaughnessy was astonished to learn that the subpoenas he had served on seven Federal agencies (the DIA had been added to the others in March 1990) had been quashed without further hearing of argument.

The circumstances were odd, to say the least. The court's order, signed 12 December 1990, showed that, after the 27 July conference, the government had approached Chief Judge Platt privately to suggest that, rather than produce the documents he had specified, its agents should simply brief the court on certain matters connected with the bombing.

Without advising Shaughnessy of this proposal, much less inviting his opinion of it, the court had agreed to the government's suggestion and, as Shaughnessy put it later, 'was briefed on undisclosed matters on unspecified dates by unidentified agents of the government . . . I still do not know [September 1992] who briefed this court, when the briefings took place or what was told to this court during those briefings.'

All he knew was that 'in the end, this court quashed the subpoenas based upon *ex parte in camera* briefings given to it by the government'.

Chief Judge Platt had already shown signs of distress over the government's intransigence. A year earlier, when the discovery dispute was at its height, he had been asked to comment on the documents he had seen so far.

I am troubled about certain parts [he had said], and I don't think anything can be – there could be a redaction, but I think what was left after the redaction would be virtually useless. And I don't know quite what to do because I think some of the material may be significant. Some of the material I haven't seen, of course, because the government hasn't even shown me all of the material. They have just given me the reasons why, which, as I see it, I am not at liberty to reveal at this stage.

But depending on what is behind that material, those reasons, if you will, there may be – *it might change this case completely* [author's italics]. There is a possibility. I don't say that it's a reality. There is a possibility, depending on what hypothesis you assume and I have no way of knowing which hypothesis is correct . . .

A year later, he resolved his uncertainty in favour of Washington. But Shaughnessy had lost a battle, not the war. As any claim under the Federal Tort Claims Act had to be filed within two years – in other words, by 21 December 1990 – he obtained leave from the court to commence a third-party action against the United States government. The thrust of this was that if the passenger liability suits went against Pan Am, the airline would seek to recover the cost of the compensation awards from the government on the grounds that the Flight 103 disaster had been due to the misconduct of government agencies.

The complaint, filed on 19 December, stated that the government had had a duty to inform Pan Am of information in its possession that a terrorist organization was planning to place a bomb on a Pan Am flight from either Frankfurt or London, specifically on Flight 103 on 21 December 1988, and had 'negligently failed to inform Pan Am'.

Secondly, the complaint charged that the government had been 'negligent in supervising and controlling an operation utilizing criminals, terrorists and terrorist sympathizers at various locations, including Frankfurt Rhein-Main airport, which circumvented all baggage security controls and which was utilized by a terrorist organization to place the bomb on Flight 103'.

Support for this theory, of an unexpected kind, had been provided a few weeks earlier by network television.

On 30 October, NBC News reported: 'Officials of the Drug Enforcement Administration told NBC News today they are conducting an inquiry of a top secret undercover heroin operation in the Middle East to find out whether the operation was used as cover by the terrorists who blew up Pan Am 103 almost two years ago.'

The report went on to say that

NBC News has learned that Pan Am flights from Frankfurt, including 103, had been used a number of times by the DEA as part of its undercover operation to fly informants and suitcases of heroin into Detroit as part of a sting operation to catch dealers in Detroit.

The undercover operation, code-named Operation Courier, was set up three years ago by the DEA in Cyprus to infiltrate Lebanese heroin groups in the Middle East and their connections in Detroit. According to law-enforcement and intelligence sources, the Pan Am baggage area in Frankfurt was a key to the operation. Informants would put suitcases on the Pan Am flights, apparently without the usual security checks, according to one airline source, through an arrangement between the DEA and German authorities.

Law-enforcement officials say the fear now is that the terrorists that blew up Pan Am 103 somehow learned about what the DEA was doing, infiltrated the undercover operation and substituted the bomb for the heroin in one of the DEA shipments.

The following evening, 31 October, Pierre Salinger of ABC News, weighed in with a story of his own:

In 1987, the US Drug Enforcement Administration set up a dummy company called Eurame here in Nicosia, on the Mediterranean island of Cyprus. According to law-enforcement sources, it was part of Operation Corea, an undercover operation designed to track the flow of heroin. The DEA recruited undercover couriers who would be monitored as they carried the drugs from Lebanon, through Cyprus and Europe and on to drug dealers in Detroit. ABC News has confirmed that one of those couriers was a young Lebanese-American named Khalid Jafaar.

He was one of those killed aboard Pan Am 103.

The report went on: 'Operation Corea worked like this. German police would be notified that an undercover courier was arriving at Frankfurt airport. German agents would escort his baggage through all security checks, and one of them would personally place the baggage on the plane.'

Before the broadcasts, both Brian Ross of NBC News and Pierre Salinger of ABC News had contacted Gregory W. Buhler, deputy general counsel of Pan Am, to inform him that they had obtained evidence from sources within the United States government that a DEA undercover operation was involved in the crash of Flight 103.

They also told him that they had talked to Lester Knox Coleman, a former agent of the Defense Intelligence Agency in the Middle East, seeking confirmation of certain details of the story before airing their reports – in Salinger's case, at a face-to-face meeting in London.

A couple of months earlier, Buhler had been introduced to Coleman by Marshall Lee Miller in Washington, and since then had been urging Shaughnessy to talk to Coleman because he had 'a great deal of interesting information concerning the crash of Flight 103'.

As they were both due in London in connection with the case, and as Coleman was also there seeing Salinger, Buhler suggested that it might be a good opportunity for the three of them to get together.

Shaughnessy agreed, and on 1 November 1990, met his first – and so far his only – independent witness for dinner at the Hyde Park hotel.

— XII —

'You know, buddy, you don't have to do this if you don't want to,' Donleavy said. 'Those guys are bad news. Anything goes wrong, they'll just leave you face down in the shit.'

'So what else is new?'

It was already too late. Mary-Claude was hopping with excitement at the idea of showing off their new daughter to her family.

'Hey!' Donleavy did his best to look hurt. 'We're the guys who *hate* to make mistakes, remember? The DEA, hell – it's just one *big* mistake. Which is why we want you out there. To keep an eye on 'em.'

'Sure.'

Heads we win, tails you lose. But there had been little doubt he would go from the moment Micheal Hurley had called during the Thanksgiving holiday to say he had at last been funded for a major operation in the Middle East and would Coleman be interested in going back to Cyprus as a DEA contractor?

Maybe, Coleman had replied cautiously, but it was not up to him. He had been involved in other things.

Hurley already knew that, but he was sure the logistics could be worked out if Coleman agreed.

So was Donleavy when Coleman told him about Hurley's call. The DEA had already expressed an interest in getting him back there, he said. If Coleman was willing, he was ready to second him to Hurley to protect the security of DIA's mission in the Middle East. While working on the DEA/CIA operation Hurley had mentioned, Coleman could keep tabs on DEA's Cyprus station and provide 'back channel' reports on what it was up to.

The Colemans were willing. During the first week of December 1986, Donleavy came down to the Windfrey hotel at River Chase,

Alabama, just south of Birmingham, for the first of several briefing sessions.

The DIA was worried about DEA personnel getting caught up in secret intelligence missions, he explained. None of them had been trained in covert operations other than when dealing with criminals. Its misgivings dated from the DEA's links with the CIA under the late DCI William Casey, whose Contra operations, as Coleman well knew, had been childish and reckless.

In contrast, the DIA's covert activities had never been compromised and it had never become embroiled in public controversy. In order to keep things that way, the agency was obliged to keep track of other US intelligence operations that might prove embarrassing and to head them off as necessary.

If Coleman accepted the assignment, under no circumstances would he permit anybody to have any direct contact with or knowledge of DIA operatives in the region or allow anyone to suspect that he was reporting 'back channel' to Donleavy in Washington.

'You'll also need a better cover story,' he added, 'if you're going to be seen around with Hurley and his crowd. So I want you to enrol for the winter term at Auburn for one course. Thesis Research. It's for your master's degree. And your thesis topic is "The Role of Illegal Narcotics Trafficking in the Lebanese Political Crisis".'

Coleman smiled.

Donleavy seemed pleased with it, too. 'Just tell your faculty adviser you got a research grant from the DEA, and you'll be spending the term at the American Embassy in Nicosia.'

And so it was.

In January, Donleavy called from Washington to say he had met with Hurley and his people to discuss Coleman's assignment to NARCOG Nicosia, and if he still wanted the job, he should collect the family's travel expenses and airline tickets from the DEA's Birmingham field office. In Cyprus, he would live in government housing, use a green staff pass to enter the embassy, and receive mail via FPO New York 09530, a federal postal address for US government employees overseas. Anything else he needed, he should work out for himself with Hurley.

'Okay,' said Coleman. 'How much does he have to know?'

'About you? No more than he knows already. Just your vital statistics and your alternative ID. In case they want to use you undercover.'

'The Thomas Leavy ID?'

'Right. He probably knows about it anyway. They're in pretty tight with Langley. But that's *it*. Not a word about me or the agency or anything you've done for us or why you're there or anything.'

'Fine,' said Coleman. 'And the back channel reports?'

'I'll come down and talk to you about that,' Donleavy said.

He arrived with a Radio Shack hand-held computer phone dialler and a two-speed microcassette recorder for Coleman to use with the code that had worked so successfully before, based on a standard telephone touch-tone pad.

On 21 February 1987, the Colemans were met off the plane at Larnaca airport by Special Agent Dany Habib, Hurley's number two at DEA Nicosia.

An Arabic-speaking Tunisian-American, Habib was the son of Phillip Habib, a former government agent who had played a big part in breaking up the French Connection in Marseilles during the 1960s. Shrewd, devious and Arab-looking, Dany Habib and Coleman took to each other on sight, despite their professional caution, sensing they could work together.

Hurley was waiting for them on the tarmac near the terminal in his big blue BMW 520i. When the Colemans' baggage arrived, without the formality of having to clear Customs, Coleman jokingly observed that the DEA attaché must have the island in his pocket, a suggestion that Hurley took quite seriously.

'You bet your sweet ass,' he said. 'I got customs and immigration working for me and the Cypriot National Police. Once you got that, you got the whole damn country by the balls.'

'So hearts and minds must surely follow,' said Coleman politely. Hurley did not improve on further acquaintance.

'You better believe it. Anybody gets out of line, we just run his ass clear off the island. So any problems, you come to me. I'm your sphincter muscle, okay? Everything passes through me. I'm your total interface with this operation.'

It was hard to tell if he meant this as a warning, a threat or an offer of assistance. Habib remained impassive, and Mary-Claude, with Sarah in her lap, looked out the window. She had long since realized her husband worked for the government, but he had never discussed it with her, much less told her he was a spy. The space between them was filling up with unasked and unanswered questions.

The Colemans were driven to Filanta Court, on Archbishop Makarios Avenue, and handed the keys of No. 62B, a large three-bedroomed apartment with a balcony overlooking the port of

Cub Scout Lester Knox Coleman III aged eight.

Boy Scout executive Lester Knox Coleman III in 1988 on the eve of Operation Shakespeare, his last mission as an agent of the United States' Defense Intelligence Agency.

beachfront villa in Beirut where Coleman lived in 1985 during his first DIA
ercover assignment. Posing as Middle East correspondent for the Christian
adcasting Network, he was on a mission to serve as linkman for the DIA's
anese spy network and to frustrate an Iran-Contra arms deal engineered by Oliver
rth.

e identity badge and pass issued to Coleman in 1987 when he taught a course in
lio and video surveillance at the National Intelligence Academy in Fort Lauderdale,
rida.

Coleman's DIA spy kit. Consisting of off-the-shelf commercial equipment that anyone might buy, it included the Sony video camera that was still signed out to him at the time of his arrest by the FBI in 1990 on a trumped-up passport charge.

vo of Coleman's DIA-issue tape recorders and 'bugs'. The Sony voice-activated
chine was used to record the conversation with DEA attaché Micheal Hurley seven
onths before Lockerbie in which Coleman warned him of the 'disaster waiting to
ppen'.

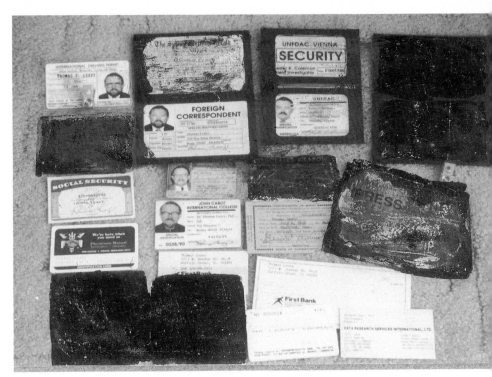

The identity papers seized by the FBI at the time of Coleman's arrest in May 1990. Most of them are in the name of Thomas Leavy, a cover identity originally provided by the CIA in 1982 and reinforced by the DIA in 1990 for Operation Shakespeare.

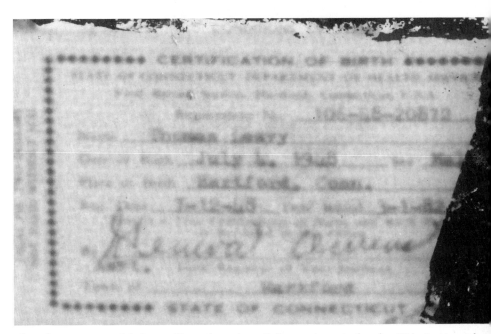

The Thomas Leavy birth certificate issued to Coleman in 1982 by the CIA. In 1990, he was charged with applying for a copy of a birth certificate in that name and using it to make a fraudulent passport application. The FBI has yet to explain why he would have needed another copy when he already had one.

are moment of relaxation for Lester and Mary-Claude Coleman in the
amo–Galaxen refugee camp after they sought political asylum in Sweden in 1991.

Front-page news, 19 October 1992. Eighteen months after the Colem arrival *iDAG*, Sweden's national afternoon newspaper, tells the stor the first American citize to seek asylum in that country since the Vietna war.

Larnaca from which everybody getting on or off the ferry from Lebanon could be observed through binoculars.

On the way in from the airport, Hurley had warned him that the back bedroom was full of electronic gear that nobody knew how to use. Coleman's first job for NARCOG would be to get it operational as a listening post to monitor Lebanese radio traffic and to keep track of shipping movements in and out of Lebanese ports. Among the equipment was a maritime receiver that automatically picked up ship transmissions while continuously scanning a preset frequency range and recorded everything on tape, including the position of each vessel.

'Taxi George' was waiting inside the apartment and 'Syrian George' arrived a few minutes later. While Mary-Claude saw to the baby and busied herself around the apartment, Habib made the introductions.

Syrian George would man the listening post every day, play back the tapes and provide translations as required. A former officer in the so-called Pink Panther Brigade under Rifat Assad, he held a master's degree from the University of Kiev and, as Coleman quickly discovered, worked harder than anybody because he was desperate to get to America and Hurley kept promising to get a visa for him if he made himself useful.

Taxi George, a likeable Iraqi Chaldean Christian who worked as an interrogator for the Cypriot National Police Narcotics Squad, was another key informant. Fluent in Arabic, Greek and English, he visited the US several times a year as a DEA courier, making controlled deliveries of Lebanese heroin to dealer networks in and around Detroit, but had proved even more useful to Hurley as a taxi driver.

Lebanese drug traffickers visiting the island to close a deal would check into a hotel like the Palm Beach or the Golden Bay on Dekalia Road, and, on going out to dinner, would find Taxi George at the kerb. With no reason to suppose he was anybody but a Greek-Cypriot, they would go on talking business in Arabic, and Taxi George would time their cab ride according to the intelligence value of their conversation.

Hurley had promised him a visa, too.

Then there was Ibrahim El-Jorr, who had an American passport already. An erratic Lebanese with a wife and family in Beirut and a Dutch mistress in Nicosia, he wore jeans and cowboy boots and drove around at high speed in a Chevy 4 × 4 with expired Texas licence plates. He claimed to have been at the Munich Olympics in 1972 while serving with the US Army, and seemed particularly proud of a photograph of himself in officer's uniform (without apparently realising that the insignia were incorrect).

El-Jorr was Hurley's principal link to a network of DEA informants/CIA 'assets' in Lebanon, many of them members of the warring clans of the pro-Syrian Kabbaras and the anti-Syrian Jafaars in the Bekaa Valley.

Two of them, Zouher Kabbara and his cousin Nadim Kabbara, had unfortunately been arrested in Rome about a month before Coleman arrived on Cyprus, but he did meet Sami Jafaar, a short, stocky, fast-talking Shiite drug runner with a hairy chest festooned with gold chains and medallions.

Technically, Sami was a confidential informant (CI) for Michael Pavlick, the DEA's country attaché in Paris, but he was to play a vital part in Operation Goldenrod, a project preoccupying the NARCOG task force in Nicosia when Coleman arrived there, and which was to touch off the chain reaction of events that exploded over Lockerbie 21 months later.

In January 1986, President Reagan had signed a secret directive – 'They can run, but they can't hide' – instructing the octopus to identify terrorists responsible for crimes against American citizens abroad and to bring them to justice in US courts. By October, when the administration's Operations Sub-Group on Terrorism met in the White House Situation Room, the target list had been whittled down to one, Fawaz Younis, whom the CIA described as 'a key player in the back-street world of terrorism . . . who reported directly to the leadership of the Shiite Amal militia'.

In fact, he was a Beirut used-car dealer who had once been a member of the Syrian-backed Amal militia headed by Nabi Berri, a Shiite Muslim cabinet minister in the Lebanese government (and a less well-known businessman in Detroit, Michigan).

Though not a high-level suspect, Younis *was* wanted in connection with the hijacking of a Jordanian airliner with three Americans aboard in 1985. He had also been identified as one of those who had guarded the hostages after the TWA 747 hijack in June of that year, which made him an accomplice in the murder of US Navy diver, Robert Stetham. More to the point, he was the only accessible target the CIA had been able to find, and the DEA had an informant – Sami Jafaar – who was both willing and able to nail him.

Sami's cousin and business associate, Jamal Hamadan, had known Younis for six years. They had once shared an apartment in Beirut, and when Hamadan later moved to Poland to run the Jafaars' heroin export business to the Eastern bloc through their offices in Warsaw, Younis had paid him an extended visit there. The Jafaars' main competitor in Eastern Europe was, as always, the Assad cartel, which worked out of a front company on Stawkis Street and another, ZIBADO, on Friedrichstrasse in East Berlin.

Sami Jafaar was confident he could persuade Hamadan to renew his friendship with Younis, and that, between them, they could cook up some pretext to lure Younis out of Lebanon into neutral territory for an FBI snatch. Hamadan became equally confident they could do so when the CIA offered them both 'asset' status, which meant virtual immunity from prosecution or the risk of ever having to surface in court and testify as witnesses.

The Hamadan clan, like the Jafaars, had been involved in a losing struggle against the Syrian cartel ever since Rifat Assad and Monzer al-Kassar had taken over the Bekaa Valley in 1975 with the help of the Syrian Army. One of the reasons why Sami and Jamal were so happy to cooperate with the Americans was that Younis belonged to the Syrian-backed Amal militia, which had burned Jafaar and Hamadan poppy fields and destroyed their processing labs, and here was a chance for revenge.

The fact that the DEA and the CIA were heavily involved with both camps would have meant nothing to Sami and Jamal. As far as they were concerned, and like most Arab players in the narcotics game, the DEA was welcome to play one side off against another, so long as *they* could watch safely from the sidelines. Business was business.

By the time Coleman picked up the threads of the plot in February 1987, there was still no clear plan of attack, although it was generally agreed among Hurley and his colleagues that luring Younis into a drug deal was probably the key, and that a lot of political hassle would be avoided if he could be taken, say, in international waters. Precisely how he was to be enticed aboard a suitable vessel remained in doubt, particularly as the DEA neither owned nor controlled a suitable vessel.

Finding one was Coleman's first assignment for Operation Goldenrod, in between setting up a NARCOG listening post in his back bedroom and instructing the Cypriot Police Force Narcotics Squad (CPFNS) in electronic surveillance. At CPFNS headquarters near the Nicosia Hilton, a cupboardful of expensive audio and video equipment paid for by the UN Fund for Drug Abuse Control was gathering dust and Hurley was anxious to get it out in the field, even though wiretaps were strictly illegal in Cyprus.

No, it was okay, he said. The government would turn a blind eye if the targets were foreign nationals, and particularly a despised Lebanese like Fawaz Younis.

In 1986, Coleman had struck up a friendship at the Larnaca marina with Fohad Beaini, a lively boat-builder better known around the docks as Abou Talar. A short, wiry Lebanese in his fifties, Talar lived aboard a partially finished 81-foot yacht, *King Edmondo*, with a tall, blonde Danish woman who towered over him and was known locally as 'Foofoo', as she was thought to be somewhat strange. He had pumped all his savings into building the boat, using bits and pieces scrounged from all over the Middle East, and was suspiciously eager to part with it. When Hurley approved of Coleman's find and hurriedly arranged for the CPFNS to buy *King Edmondo* for $80,000, Talar pocketed the money, kissed Foofoo goodbye and disappeared into Lebanon before anybody thought to take the boat out on trial.

Although the funds had come from Hurley's budget, the yacht was bought in the name of Andreous Kasikopu, a retired Cypriot marine police captain who looked remarkably like Claude Rains. This was in the interests of deniability. The DEA was free to use it for any covert operation it wished, but if anything went wrong, Hurley could always say, 'Oh, you mean that *Cypriot* boat.'

In fact, something went technically wrong almost at once. A week after taking delivery, Kasikopu telephoned the American Embassy to report that the transmissions of both engines had broken down, and although new, were beyond repair. When Coleman checked with the American manufacturers in Indiana, he discovered that they were really tank engines which Talar had somehow scrounged from the Israeli Army.

After spending more of the taxpayers' funds to make the *King Edmondo* seaworthy, and to rig her out with state-of-the-art marine communications equipment, Coleman handed the boat over in late March to Hurley, who renamed her *Skunk Kilo*. At about the same time, Jamal Hamadan put in the first of the 60 telephone calls he would make from Paris to Fawaz Younis in Beirut before the trap was sprung.

As the plan now called for Jafaar and Hamadan to meet Younis in

Cyprus before consummating their phony drug deal aboard *Skunk Kilo*, and as close electronic monitoring of their conversations would be essential to avoid last-minute surprises, Hurley was determined not to risk a breakdown in surveillance, after what had happened with the boat. Some sort of dress rehearsal was clearly required for the Cypriot police officers who were only just coming to grips with wiretap technology, and, right on cue, one of Hurley's informants passed the word that Abou Daod, a Lebanese drugs trafficker, was coming to Cyprus to set up a deal.

With CPFNS Inspector Penikos Hadjiloizu, Hurley rented several rooms in the Filanta hotel, across the street from Filanta Court and the NARCOG listening post in 62B. Under Coleman's direction, a carrier-current monitor, with microphones hidden in the sitting-room and bedroom table lamps, was installed in a first-floor suite facing the street. When the lamps were plugged in, the hotel's own electrical circuits carried the microphones' output to a receiver and voice-activated recorder in another room down the hall. As the telephone was also wired to interface with the bugs, any sound in the suite was thereby automatically recorded, the only human intervention required being a periodic change of tape.

All was in readiness when Abou Daod stepped off the Suny boat from Jounieh. Picked up by Taxi George, he was steered successfully to the Filanta hotel, where the receptionist duly assigned him to the 'hot' suite. And in the room down the hall, Sergeant Mikalis, the Cypriot police officer appointed by Inspector Hadjiloizu to sit on the wire and bring the recorded tapes across the road for translation, watched the reels begin to turn as Daod placed calls to his associates in Athens, Paris and Sofia.

A big, blustering, opinionated cop, full of self-importance, Mikalis soon grew bored with wiretap duty. After two days, in which it had become clear that Daod was organizing a drug shipment from Lebanon via Cyprus to Bulgaria, a well-worn route through the Eastern bloc into Western Europe, he decided to go home and sleep with his wife instead of staying on the job, as instructed, in case of overnight calls. At 11 p.m., he made sure there was still plenty of tape left on the machine and departed, returning at 8 a.m. the following morning to take it across the street to Syrian George.

After listening to it on his headphones for a few minutes, Syrian George stopped the tape, looked Mikalis up and down and turned to Coleman.

'Daod called Sofia at 3.03 a.m.,' he said, in Arabic. 'He told his contact he was on Olympic Airways' seven o'clock flight to Athens. You want to tell this dumb-fuck donkey son of a Shiite whore that Daod just left the country right under his nose?'

'What did he say?' asked Mikalis excitedly. 'Is there news?'

'Yeah,' said Coleman. 'He said to tell you that Mr Daod's plane is just landing in Athens.'

The sergeant looked baffled. 'What is this meaning?' As it began to sink in, his eyes opened wider. 'He's gone? He's left Cyprus?'

'Without even saying goodbye. You want me to tell Penikos or will you?'

'No, no, no,' Mikalis said wildly. 'Gimme the tape – I must investigate this. Gimme the tape.'

They had better luck with Fawaz Younis. By the time Jamal Hamadan, accompanied by Sami Jafaar, arrived in Cyprus to meet his old friend at the Filanta hotel, Sergeant Mikalis had been banished to police school in Germany, and his successors in the room down the hall from the 'hot' suite had been drilled by Coleman to within an inch of their lives. Every incriminating word that Younis uttered within range of the room bugs was meticulously recorded, transcribed and translated as evidence to be used against him in an American court.

Encouraged by Hamadan, Younis made much of the minor role Nabi Berri had assigned to him in the Air Jordanian incident and admitted he had helped guard the hostages after the TWA 747 hijack. He also allowed that the used-car business had failed to keep him in the style to which he had grown accustomed and rose to the prospect of a lucrative drug deal like a shark to a bucket of entrails.

To cement their renewed friendship, Hamadan then took Younis on a five-day spree through the bars and cabarets of Larnaca, topping off this dizzy round of DEA-financed hospitality by pressing $5000 into his hand as a parting gift – an act of impulsive generosity that sent Hurley thundering upstairs to confront his CIA colleagues.

'I'm not gonna get hung with this whole thing out of *my* budget,' Coleman heard him insist, as did half the staff of the embassy. 'I'm just along for the ride, that's all. This guy belongs to *you*.'

As Coleman subsequently reported to Control, this pretty well summed up the relationship between Hurley and the spooks in Nicosia. With the national and strategic interest of the United States as part of its more elevated terms of reference, the CIA would co-opt DEA informants at will or take over a DEA operation that suited its purpose or use the DEA as a cloak for its own interests or activities without much regard for the lesser claims of law enforcement. It was already clear to Coleman from his analysis of the drugs-related intelligence coming out of Lebanon that the traditional heroin route to the US via Cyprus, Frankfurt and London was used regularly by both agencies, that the traffic was not always in narcotics and that it moved both ways.

After visiting Hamadan twice more on Cyprus (to complete the softening up and the wiretap evidence), Younis was targeted for an FBI snatch on 13 September. A team from the Bureau's anti-terrorist squad flew out from Quantico, Virginia, a week beforehand to take charge of the arrangements and Hamadan placed his final call to Younis in Beirut, telling him to drop everything and come at once. He was to meet 'Joseph', a big-time drugs trafficker, aboard his yacht to conclude a deal that would solve all his problems for ever.

Younis arrived in Larnaca on the 10th and joined Hamadan in another two-day, nonstop pub crawl that turned the knife in Hurley's wound and brought them, on schedule, to the Sheraton resort hotel in Limassol on the night of the 12th. Next morning, decked out like a sacrificial goat in his gold chains and designer finery, Younis left the Sheraton marina by speedboat with Sami Jafaar and Hamadan to meet the octopus.

The logistics of his complicated destiny involved not only *Skunk Kilo*, anchored by its FBI crew in international waters, but the USS *Butte*, a Navy ammunitions ship that had been shadowing the yacht by radar, the aircraft carrier USS *Saratoga*, standing by with a Navy S-3 jet and an escort of two F-14 Phantoms to fly him to Andrews Air Force Base near Washington, D.C., two KC-10 tanker aircraft to refuel the S-3 on the way, and 15 carloads of FBI agents to meet him on arrival.

Blissfully unaware that the full panoply of America's military might was about to deliver him up to the majesty of American justice, President Reagan's token terrorist was welcomed aboard *Skunk Kilo* by an undercover FBI team that was so wrought up by the occasion that in placing Younis under arrest they managed to break both his wrists, though he offered no resistance or showed any enthusiasm for the 12-mile swim back to Limassol. After that, it took the agents four days to extract a confession from their prisoner on the USS *Butte* before turning him over to the US Navy for the 13 hour 10 minute flight to Washington, a new solo record for a carrier-based aircraft carrying a second-hand car dealer.

After the arrest, Hamadan and Sami Jafaar returned to Limassol in the launch and were driven to the American Embassy in Nicosia. Coleman recalls:

It was mid-afternoon when they arrived at the compound's rear gate. Cypriot security guards checked the BMW's undercarriage with a large mirror, lowered the iron teeth into the pavement and waved them through. An agent punched the buzzer next to the embassy's rear steel door. The men stepped inside, took the stairs to the right that led to the DEA office and rang the bell. Connie buzzed them in for a joyous greeting from Hurley, Colonel John Sasser, the Defense attaché, and one of Buck Revell's FBI team, but there wasn't much time for celebration because Hamadan was wanted elsewhere for debriefing.

Hurley handed him a Turkish passport with a West German visa and he was escorted over the green line into Turkish-occupied northern Cyprus. After spending the night at an embassy cottage in Kyrenia, he was put on a Turkish Air flight to Istanbul connecting with a Lufthansa flight to Frankfurt. He then spent three days at Fort King being questioned by people from the DIA, the FBI, the CIA and the DEA, and after that a bunch of US Marshals took him away into the Federal Witness Protection Program. And as far as I know, Hamadan has never been heard of again from that day to this.

As for Sami Jafaar, the feeling was that he had not been compromised, although, with hindsight, it seems possible that Syrian intelligence had noticed his involvement. At any rate, he and his clan went to the top of the class as far as the DEA and CIA were concerned.

Back home, the massed ranks of the Federal government's press officers had been deployed to exploit the triumph of Goldenrod and the supposed deterrent value of President Reagan's 'They-can-run-but-they-can't-hide' anti-terrorist programme. To make sure that none of the macho details went to waste, the full, inside story of Washington's awesome display of military prowess was entrusted to Steven Emerson of US News & World Report, who had shown in the past that he knew how to treat a government 'scoop' with respect, and who could be relied upon to resist the kind of sceptical impulse that sometimes afflicts reporters with a wider readership.

In the summer of 1987, while outwardly researching his master's thesis on Lebanese narcotics trafficking, Coleman met several newsmen of a less trusting nature, among them Brian Ross of NBC and his producer Ira Silverman. They already knew one another. Coleman had met Ross in 1981 while writing his book *Squeal*, in which he described how Las Vegas superstar Wayne Newton had sued Ross and Silverman over an NBC story connecting him with organized crime. The two had arrived in Cyprus, with the cooperation of the DEA, to prepare a documentary on 'The Lebanese Connection', and as Hurley did not want to be bothered, he deputed Coleman to look after them.

With his television news background and now intimate knowledge of Middle East drugs trafficking, Coleman helped Ross and Silverman prepare what was generally considered to be as balanced and authoritative a survey of narco-terrorism as the media had ever presented to the American public, a contribution which they both generously acknowledged on several occasions afterwards and which subsequently led to Coleman's appearance on NBC News after the Flight 103 disaster, although neither of them were aware then or before of his DIA/NARCOG affiliations.

For the most part, however, Coleman's experience with the media was disillusioning. While the intelligence community was specifically forbidden to compromise staff newsmen or to use media staff credentials as a cover for its agents, cutbacks and bureau closures had left most of the world's press, radio and television dependent on local freelance reporters and cameramen, to whom the restrictions did not apply.

Coleman himself had used freelance credentials supplied by Mutual Radio to get into Libya after Operation El Dorado Canyon a year earlier, and he would meet very few stringers during his various spells of duty in the Middle East who did *not* supplement their incomes from journalism by supplying material to government agencies like the DEA.

One morning, for instance, after monitoring radio traffic all night in the NARCOG listening post he had set up in his back bedroom, Coleman reluctantly opened his apartment door to a caller who introduced himself as David Mills, a British photographer for *Newsweek*.

It seemed they had a mutual acquaintance in 'freelance' W. Dennis Suit, president of Overseas Press Services, whom Coleman had met as a 'consultant' to Pat Robertson's Christian Broadcasting Network and with whom he had kept in touch, on DIA instructions, because of Suit's involvement with Oliver North's ragtag army of conmen, yahoos and armchair mercenaries from Georgia.

Mills had apparently met a very loquacious Dennis Suit in a bar in Tegucigalpa, Honduras, and listened to him brag about the worldwide connections he had made in the course of his career as a self-proclaimed CIA agent. On hearing that Mills was headed for the Middle East, Suit had suggested he should look Coleman up in Cyprus because he was doing some research there and had a lot of good contacts.

'Oh,' said Coleman wearily. 'That's great. How are you? Come in. Would you like a cup of coffee?'

Doing his best to stay awake, he chatted to Mills until satisfied that the other was convinced of his academic credentials and then, to get rid of him before Syrian George arrived to transcribe the night's tapes and give the game away, sent him over to see Hurley, who wanted to know if Mills, in the course of his travels in and out of Lebanon for *Newsweek*, would like to shoot a few pictures for the DEA.

Seeing no conflict of interest in this, or any serious ethical problem in working covertly for the DEA, Mills joined the rest of the press corps on Hurley's freelance payroll and subsequently turned in some useful photo coverage of illegal port facilities in Lebanon.

Although Coleman still had qualms about the misuse of media credentials, foreseeing a time when immigration officials around the world would automatically assume that any visiting journalist was a spy, it would have been hypocritical to complain. But he did protest vigorously to Hurley when he discovered that a full-time British staff cameraman for a major news service was also secretly shooting stuff for the DEA, using his employer's equipment.

'There's a directive about that,' he said. 'I don't want to get involved. If Washington finds out, there'll be hell to pay.'

'He's a foreign national,' said Hurley impatiently. 'Fuck it.'

In the end, Coleman had to let it pass, although he contrived not to pay for the footage, and duly noted the DEA's systematic corruption of the media in one of his back-channel reports to Donleavy. It hardly mattered anyway, for in addition to his bootleg coverage, Hurley was also helping himself to anything he wanted in the *legitimate* footage brought out of Lebanon by television news teams.

As Coleman says:

If CBS, NBC, ABC, the BBC – anybody – wanted to up-link video they'd shot in Beirut they could go either to Damascus or

Nicosia. That was the choice. And a lot of times, particularly after shooting in the east, they were cut off from getting to Damascus so they had to put their tapes on the boat to Larnaca and up-link it from Cyprus.

Well, Hurley had this arrangement with Customs . . . All those guys had DEA certificates of appreciation on their walls – he'd greased the skids all the way. Anybody came in with videotape, Customs would grab it and say, 'Well, we have to look at this before you take it in.' 'But this is urgent news material,' the guy would say. Tough shit. He'd have to wait two or three hours while Customs ran it across the road to me so I could make a quick video dub for Hurley or his spook friends before they returned the original and let the guy on through to Nicosia.

Same thing with MEMO, Middle East Media Operations, just down the street from the embassy in Nicosia. It worked like a news bureau. You could rent office space and video equipment there. You could file your stories from there. They had secretaries, drivers, people to answer your phone – it was a complete support operation on the ground, and most of the networks had a desk there. And everybody was working for Hurley, although most of them didn't know it. Anything going through MEMO ended up in the American Embassy. Assignment details. Progress reports. Private conversations. Notes. Videotape. Everything – right down to scrap paper from the waste baskets. He had the whole thing fixed.

But NARCOG was not the only group using Cyprus as a base for its intelligence operations. When Beirut, the capital of Middle Eastern intrigue, was turned into a battleground in 1975 by the Lebanese civil war, the entire international espionage community moved out lock, stock and barrel to Nicosia. It used to amuse Coleman to saunter through the Churchill hotel around midday.

'It was like something out of an old Peter Lorre, Sidney Greenstreet film,' he remembers. 'There were Libyans, Lebanese, PLO, KGB, Bulgarians, Romanians, British, Americans – you could go by there and watch all the spooks watching each other have lunch.'

It was not so amusing, however, to have them on his doorstep.

One morning, it became clear that NARCOG was not the only group using *Filanta Court* as a base for its intelligence operations. Coleman had gone up on the roof the previous evening for one of his periodic checks of the antennae he had rigged for the listening post. All seemed to be in order, but next morning, after having trouble with one of the receivers, he went up again to make sure he had not inadvertently disturbed anything.

To his astonishment, a 30-foot latticework tower, neatly secured with guy wires, had sprouted there overnight, topped by a two-stack array of five-element, horizontally aligned, directional antennae, one pointed towards Nicosia, the other towards the Lebanese coast.

Was it possible that Hurley had forgotten to tell him they were putting in some decent professional equipment at last?

No, it wasn't possible.

Hoping no one was watching, Coleman climbed the tower's inspection ladder to look at the frequency allocation on the antennae. He then climbed down again, and followed the coaxial cables across the roof to the point where they went over the rear wall of the building and in through one of the bedroom windows of the apartment next to his.

Returning thoughtfully to his own back bedroom, he tuned one of his receivers to the frequency he had read off the antenna and hooked it up to a tape machine. Then he telephoned the embassy.

'Well, who the fuck did that?' Hurley demanded, when Coleman explained what had happened.

'Hell, I don't know. I got the frequency, so I'll ask Syrian George to listen in. See what he comes up with. And maybe you can get Penikos to find out who's renting the apartment.'

'Better than that, I'll have him kick their ass off the island.'

'Well, why don't we see what's going on first?' Coleman suggested. 'Whoever they are, these guys know their stuff. Could be interesting.'

'Listen, you spotted *them*, maybe they spotted *you*. I don't want to take chances.'

'Don't worry about it.' Coleman was not used to such solicitude. 'Let's give it a few days. We'll be okay.'

'Hell, I'm not worried about that.' Hurley sounded astonished. 'I got a bunch of shitheads flying in from headquarters to take a look around. I told 'em about the listening post, so I don't want it compromised, okay?'

Over the next few days, Syrian George taped an assortment of Arab cab-drivers in Tel Aviv broadcasting on taxi frequencies with bits and pieces of low-level intelligence picked up from observations while driving around town and from eavesdropping on their fares' back-seat conversations. And twice a day, somebody would transmit a very brief, very high speed coded message from the apartment next door via the VHF array aimed at Nicosia.

Coleman recalls:

I took the tapes up to the embassy for analysis, and sure enough, it turned out that Yasser Arafat's PLO had installed a listening post right next to ours. They had these cab-drivers in Israel using taxi frequencies to pass on intelligence to Cyprus, and as it came in, so they'd pass it up the line to the PLO office in Nicosia.

Hurley went dip-shit crazy. He had his top brass coming in from Washington to look at the operation and the first thing they'd see at Filanta Court was this 30-foot PLO radio mast. So he pulled all his strings, and although it was politically very sensitive, he got the Cypriots to close the Palestinians down and kick them off the island.

Well, he needn't have bothered. His guys showed up from Washington and they didn't want to see shit. It was a junket. When they came to the apartment, Mary-Claude was cooking up a storm in the kitchen, Sarah was squalling in her crib in the front bedroom and in the back it was wall-to-wall Star Wars, with all the electronic gear we had in there. So they walk in, wearing their Izod shirts and white walking shorts with clean sneakers, just like it was Miami Beach, and it was, 'Howiya? Howya doin'? Hey, what's going on here?' and all that bullshit, but what they really wanted to know was, where's the nearest topless beach?

I thought they'd probably want to see the video I was splicing together from the footage we were getting on opium growing in the Bekaa Valley, but these were cops on a government-paid vacation. They could watch that kind of stuff any time, back home at headquarters. They were there to get laid, that's all. It's an awesome sight, the US government at work overseas.

The deputation from DEA headquarters had luckily chosen one of the cooler days of a very hot summer for their inspection visit. The NARCOG budget had apparently not stretched to air-conditioning, and there were times when life in Filanta Court was almost insupportable. At the height of the heatwave, with Hurley in Washington, Coleman finally had to notify the embassy that he was closing down the listening post and moving into the hotel across the street to save the equipment as well as the family from overheating.

But Donleavy, no less than Hurley, was anxious to get him back. From his response to the huge volume of encrypted data that Coleman was sending twice a week to his DIA number in Maryland, Donleavy was interested in his reports, not just for their own sake, but as a means of cross-checking the official inter-agency pooling of information by the DEA and CIA.

'Donleavy wanted to know everything. All he could get his hands on. Who the DEA were using and why. Names and descriptions of informants, their reasons for working with Hurley and the nature of their relationship. Details of DEA operations in Lebanon, cross-checked with whatever feedback I could get from my guys over there. Anything and everything to do with on-going cases. Control wanted a complete run-down, and knowing the way Hurley operated, I think the DIA probably had a better handle on it from my back-channel stuff than DEA headquarters did through its own official channels.'

Although the principal objective of NARCOG remained the same, to piece together a detailed picture of Lebanese narcotics trafficking and its role in politics and terrorism, the emphasis in the DEA's contribution began to change after Dany Habib was reassigned to San Francisco in May. His replacement as Hurley's number two was Special Agent Fred Ganem, a tall, polite, soft-spoken Lebanese-American who had spent the previous five years in Detroit, on the receiving end of the Middle East narcotics pipeline.

While Hurley remained preoccupied with inter-agency projects like Operation Goldenrod, Ganem soon made it clear to Coleman that he had little patience with Hurley's intelligence operations. Ganem saw his role in Nicosia as an extension of his role in Detroit. He was interested primarily in law-enforcement, in using the pipeline through Cyprus to identify and arrest distributors of Lebanese narcotics in the United States. He was therefore interested in stepping up controlled deliveries, and for that he needed intelligent, well-motivated CIs who could pose as suppliers. Like the Hamadans and Jafaars.

Masked by the explosion in cocaine abuse, and by Washington's simple-minded preoccupation with the Colombian drug cartels, heroin addiction in the US had risen steeply during the 1980s. Reflecting American demand, the acreage of the Bekaa Valley's opium poppy fields was doubling year by year. During the summer of 1987, Coleman helped identify 25 Lebanese laboratories with a combined annual output of six or seven metric tons of refined heroin, representing about half the country's gross national product.

Most of this was exported to the United States via the Cyprus-Frankfurt pipeline, nicknamed *khouriah* ('shit') by the couriers who used it, or via Turkey, the Balkans, central Europe and then on to New York and points west.

The profits were stupendous. Without needing to do more than put down sporadic resistance from the more independent clans, the 30,000 Syrian troops guarding the Bekaa for the heroin cartel were allowed to augment their pay by up to $1 billion a year in protection money. And this was chicken-feed next to the revenues earned by government-connected Syrians and Syrian-backed terrorist groups actually engaged in the traffic. Illegal narcotics contributed at least $5 billion a year to the Syrian economy, almost all of it in American dollars and other hard currencies. Without access to the American market for heroin and hashish, Syria and its Lebanese protectorate were as good as bankrupt.

But Washington's strategic interests in the Middle East ruled out the kind of interventionist policies pursued in Central and South America. With about 60 per cent of its energy requirements supplied by a region racked with religious, ethnic and political conflict, the United States was as helpless in the face of state-sponsored narcotics trafficking as it was in dealing with state-sponsored terrorism. While Syria made the appropriate public disclaimers, insisting it was serious about eradicating drugs and denying sanctuary to terrorists headquartered in the Bekaa Valley, Washington could take no independent action without risking the charge of meddling in Syria's internal affairs and thereby still further inflaming Arab sensitivities throughout the Middle East.

In any case, with Muslim extremists threatening to dominate the region, the Western world needed Syria either in *its* camp or at least on the sidelines.

After watching DEA Nicosia at work, Coleman readily understood why the DIA felt it necessary to monitor Hurley's activities. Anything directed at rolling up narcotics distribution networks in the United States was politically neutral and therefore acceptable. The recruitment of 'mules' and CIs and their employment in a stepped-up programme of controlled deliveries down the pipeline offered little risk of embarrassment, provided the 'stings' were well organized and proper security precautions were observed. But the conversion of DEA informants into CIA assets, and their use in operations directed against Syrian nationals or Syrian-backed groups on the supply side of the narcotics traffic, was altogether more sensitive, and it was this area that, under Donleavy's direction, became Coleman's special study in the late summer of 1987.

Monzer al-Kassar and Rifat Assad were two of the names that cropped up most frequently in the cascade of raw intelligence from informants and intercepts that he was analysing for NARCOG and back-channelling to Donleavy. On principle, Hurley refused to share information with the Germans and British, except when he needed their cooperation for controlled deliveries through Frankfurt and London, but, braving his disapproval, Coleman made a point of renewing his friendship with Hartmut Mayer, the German police officer whom he had met in Munich during the 1972 Olympics and who was now the BKA's liaison officer on Cyprus.

Although the contact was more social than professional, the two inevitably talked shop when they met, and as Coleman zeroed in on al-Kassar as possibly *the* key player in the Middle East's narco-terrorist game, he decided to visit Mayer in his office at the German Embassy one day to see if his friend could be persuaded to take a more generous view of international cooperation than Hurley's.

Mayer obligingly pulled al-Kassar's file and, among other bits of useful information, told Coleman about two more of the Syrian's aliases, including the numbers of the passports held in those names, and details of al-Kassar's recent journeys to and from South America. These were of particular interest because they confirmed suspicions that Syrian traffickers were developing close commercial ties with the Colombian cartels, trading heroin base for cocaine base and bartering either or both as required for arms supplies to terrorist and revolutionary groups around the world.

Operating from one of several palatial villas in Marbella, Spain, al-Kassar was publicly one of the DEA's most wanted fugitives and privately one of the CIA's most useful 'capabilities', having supplied hundreds of tons of US and Eastern bloc arms to Iran, as part of Oliver North's efforts to secure the release of American hostages, and to the Nicaraguan Contras as part of Oliver North's efforts to unseat the Sandinistas.

Though arrested in Denmark, Britain, France and Spain for narcotics and arms offences, al-Kassar had made himself too valuable an asset to European and American intelligence agencies for them to allow him to go to waste in prison, so that he went about his illegal business with a brazen assurance matched only among international criminals by his partner, Rifat Assad, younger brother of the Syrian president, who also owned a villa outside Marbella, and whose daughter, Raja, was al-Kassar's mistress.

After an unsuccessful attempt to depose his brother Hafez Assad from the presidency in 1984, Rifat had been banished to Paris, a punishment akin to being kicked out of purgatory and forced to live in paradise. Installed in a town house off the Rue St Honoré and accompanied everywhere in his armoured Mercedes by bodyguards armed with automatic weapons, he endeared himself to French society by throwing the kind of party that went out of style with Caligula while continuing to act as front man for the Syrian heroin cartel that underwrote his brother's fanatical Alawist regime in Damascus.

A volatile, erratic but undeniably charismatic figure, with a loyal following among the Syrian troops enriching themselves in the Bekaa Valley, among the Palestinian terrorists financed by Lebanese drug trafficking, and among Arabs living in Detroit and Los Angeles who distributed the product, Rifat Assad was also too valuable an asset to fear official displeasure from any quarter, Syrian, French *or* American.

Number three in Coleman's Syrian rogues' gallery was General Ali Issah Dubah, then chief of the Mogamarat, the Syrian secret service (and now President Assad's deputy chief of staff). One of Assad's closest confidantes (and Monzer al-Kassar's brother-in-law), Dubah was the cartel's principal enforcer, frequently co-opting Ahmed Jibril's PFLP–GC, the Abu Nidal faction and other Palestinian terrorist groups to do his dirty work as well as using them routinely as part-time agents in his 'legitimate' intelligence operations.

As the summer wore on and Dubah's name kept cropping up in raw intelligence data from DEA/NARCOG informants, Coleman eventually reported to Donleavy that, without ever leaving the country, the Syrian spymaster seemed to have his hand in the pockets of everybody engaged in the Bekaa's drug traffic, from Damascus to Dearborn.

General Ghazi Kenaan, head of Syrian military intelligence in Lebanon, and a subject of Coleman's close attention from the day he arrived in Beirut as a DIA agent, was the fourth key figure in the heroin cartel. With Monzer al-Kassar and Rifat Assad fronting for the group in Europe, it fell to Kenaan, as the man on the spot, to supervise the supply end of the business, to keep the Bekaa peaceful and productive, to suppress dissent, discourage private enterprise and mediate disputes. With 30,000 troops at his disposal, and everybody dependent on drug revenues, including the Palestinian terrorist groups based in the valley, Kenaan was the most powerful man in Lebanon.

Having learned from his first assignment that the general effectively controlled the hostage situation in Beirut, Coleman now came to realize that, in a broader frame but in the same sense, Kenaan also controlled the nature and scope of narco-terrorism itself – or, at any rate, could do so when it suited President Assad's purpose.

Next to Assad's Syria, Colonel Gaddafi's Libya had become little more than a refuge for Palestinian extremists, a useful quartermaster's supply depot for arms and explosives, and a convenient whipping boy for Western governments anxious to be seen taking a strong line on terrorism without risking their strategic interests in the Middle East.

It was also beginning to worry Coleman that while he and the whole NARCOG apparatus of government agents and informants were watching the Syrians, Syrian agents and probably many of the same informants were watching *them*. He had already advised Donleavy in his bi-weekly reports that Hurley's security arrangements were derisory, that all sorts of people with no clear allegiance were wandering in and out of NARCOG, ostensibly selling information but just as likely collecting it; that agents and bona fide informants were being put at risk because of this, and that future DEA or inter-agency operations might well be fatally compromised from the start.

But Hurley himself was apparently unmoved by any such fear. For one thing, he found it hard to accept that anyone who lacked the advantage of being American could pose much of a threat, and for another, he needed every scrap of material he could get from any quarter, even the newspapers, to sustain the nonstop barrage of reports he was firing into headquarters.

Coleman remembers:

We burned up the Xerox machine. 'Gimme paper,' he'd say. 'The more paper we send 'em, the more money we're gonna get next year – that's all those shitheads understand. So keep it coming, you hear? Never mind what you think about it, I want everything you can lay your hands on. Just make a copy and send it over.'

In the end, this passion of his for generating paper got to be so ridiculous that we had T-shirts made up, with the DEA logo and OPERATION MAKAKOPI in big letters across the chest.

Couldn't find a size large enough for Hurley so we got him a nightshirt instead. Everybody in the embassy thought it was funny as hell, but he was pissed with it. Came out of his office, waving it in the air. 'Got nothing better to do, goddammit?'

Flushed with the success of Operation Goldenrod, in late summer, Hurley and his CIA colleagues lent Sami Jafaar and other members of his clan to the DEA office in Bern, Switzerland, for Operation Polar Cap, aimed at closing down an arms/drugs-dealing business run by Arman Jirayer Haser, a CIA asset and long-time associate of the Syrian cartel, who had been making millions out of secret American arms shipments to Iraq. A Turkish national living in Monaco on a Canadian passport, Haser had somehow attracted the attention of the Monte Carlo police and the CIA was nervous that if the arms operation had been blown, he might expose the agency's role in it.

The DEA's quid pro quo was to be a huge money-laundering operation run, under Haser's direction, by the Magharian brothers, Berkev and Jean, in Switzerland for Monzer al-Kassar. Besides handling a substantial slice of Syria's drug revenues, Haser and the Magharians also laundered drug profits for the Colombian cocaine cartels through a number of Swiss banks controlled by Arab interests. If Haser could be brought down by the Swiss for money-laundering, so the theory went, then he would have no reason to dig the hole he was in any deeper by embarrassing the CIA with gratuitous revelations about the agency's arms deals with Saddam Hussein.

Beginning in September 1987, the CIA's Department of Justice Liaison Officer, Richard Owens, began feeding evidence against Haser and the Magharians to the DEA so that its country attaché in Bern, Gregory Passic, could pass it on to the Swiss authorities.

On 19 October, barely a month after the arrest of Fawaz Younis had made him a DEA star, Sami Jafaar was seen lunching in Marbella with Monzer al-Kassar and Stanley Lasser, a big-time money launderer with close ties to the Cali cocaine cartel in Colombia.

Jafaar was seeking a way in through al-Kassar to Haser and the Magharians, ostensibly to have them launder the clan's drug profits, and, through Lasser, to explore the unholy alliance that appeared to be in the works between the Syrian and Cali cartels whereby each would not only take the other's product but also share intelligence, smuggling routes and defensive tactics.

Jafaar scored with both barrels. With al-Kassar's blessing, he met the Magharians in Bern and Zurich to set up accounts for his family, each meeting taped and monitored by Coleman's assistant Syrian George, who had been flown in from Cyprus for this purpose. When the Swiss police agreed to tap Lasser's telephone in his Zurich apartment, Syrian George stayed on in Switzerland to sit on the wire while Sami Jafaar and other members of his clan kept watch to identify Lasser's Arab visitors.

On the strength of this, the Swiss issued arrest warrants for all the DEA/CIA targets, and before returning in triumph to Paris, Jafaar rounded off his winter's work by trapping Haser into a highly incriminating recorded conversation about heroin and morphine base shipments.

Over Christmas 1987, with his stock standing higher than ever, Sami introduced Michael Pavlick, the DEA country attaché in Paris, to his cousin, another eager and potentially valuable recruit to the anti-Syrian cause. He was Kalid Nazir Jafaar, still in his teens, and the favourite grandson of the clan's patriarch, Moostafa Jafaar.

Though living with his father in Dearborn, near Detroit, Kalid visited his mother and grandfather in the Bekaa Valley several times a year, a family duty providing him with perfect cover for the job of courier in the DEA's stepped-up programme of controlled heroin deliveries. Too young to be hired as a full-blown CI, he was signed up on the spot as a 'subsource', a convenient arrangement whereby he was paid by a DEA CI, rather than by the agency itself, so that, in the interests of 'deniability', his name did not have to appear on any official payroll records.

Congratulating themselves, and the Jafaars, on a six-month run of unparalleled success, DEA Nicosia greeted 1988 in a mood of cavalier optimism. With the NARCOG anatomy of the Syrian cartel now virtually complete, with a major Lebanese clan working for them and a better organized monitoring and intelligence network feeding them more reliable information, Hurley and his CIA colleagues prepared for the new growing season in the Bekaa with a sense of having seized the initiative at last.

There was just one problem they knew nothing about.

The Swiss money-laundering network run for Monzer al-Kassar by Arman Haser and the Magharian brothers was altogether too valuable an asset for the Syrians to have left unprotected. As Coleman had feared, while the DEA and the Swiss police had been watching and collecting evidence, KGB-trained agents of the Mogamarat, commanded by al-Kassar's brother-in-law, General Ali Dubah, had been watching *them*. Although the Magharians were arrested, al-Kassar and Haser had been under protective surveillance the whole time and were both spirited away before the trap closed.

The Syrians had also observed the Jafaars. The link between Sami Jafaar and the DEA, suspected by the Mogamarat at the time of the Fawaz Younis affair, had been confirmed – and the result, a year later, was catastrophic.

— XIII —

Suddenly Libya was solely to blame.

Along with other newspapers, the *New York Times* had signalled the change of tack a year earlier, on 10 October 1990, shortly before President George Bush met President Hafez Assad to discuss Syria's contribution to the multinational task force confronting Saddam Hussein in the Gulf.

New evidence, it reported, indicated that Libyan intelligence agents may have assembled and planted the bomb that destroyed Pan Am Flight 103.

The 'new evidence' had been previously described by the French news magazine *L'Express* on 28 September. A fragment of plastic circuit board found at Lockerbie was said to be identical with the circuit boards used in timing devices seized with a quantity of explosives from two Libyans at Dakar airport in February 1988. Further inquiries, by the CIA, had established that these digital electric timers were prototypes, unique to Meister et Bollier of Zurich, who had made 20 of them for a Libyan intelligence organization in 1985.

'State Department officials were unavailable for comment,' the *New York Times* reported, thereby hinting at the source of the leak, but if the story had been aired as a trial balloon, it failed to lift off.

The *Independent*, in London, obliged with another blast of hot air. On 14 December, a week before the second anniversary of the disaster, it ran a six-column headline: 'Jet Bomb May Have Been Gadaffi's Revenge.' Elsewhere in the paper, a seven-column headline, in even bigger type, stated, 'Libya Blamed for Lockerbie,' under the legend: 'Gulf crisis inhibits American action despite "conclusive proof" of bomb fragment's source.'

Under the first heading, the paper printed the text of a fax sent to Tripoli two months after the disaster by the head of the Libyan interests section at the Saudi Arabian Embassy in London claiming the bombing as a victory for Libya.

'The dispatch of the fax appears to have been disregarded at the time by the team of detectives investigating the bombing,' declared the *Independent*, concluding, unwarily, that 'after two years of pursuing members of Jebril's West German cell, and their associates across Europe, Scandinavia and the Mediterranean, it appears that these men were not responsible for planting the bomb.'

Further proof of Gaddafi's guilt, in the paper's view, was the mysterious Libyan who had bought the clothes wrapped around the bomb from a boutique in Malta less than a month before the tragedy. Quoting from the *L'Express* story, the *Independent* described him as 'an associate of one of two Libyan secret agents picked up in Senegal in February 1988, in possession of a trigger device identical to the one recovered from the Lockerbie wreckage'.

Under the *Independent*'s second major headline, this overstatement was partially corrected by reference to 'a detonator fragment' found at Lockerbie, but even so, this 'proof' that 'Libya was behind the bombing of Pan Am 103 over Lockerbie' was described as 'conclusive' by the 'high-level sources' who had inspired the story.

To avoid 'alienating the Arab members of the Gulf alliance,' the paper went on, 'no indictments have yet been issued against the prime suspects, *and the force of Scottish detectives in charge of the criminal investigation into the bombing has not formally been given the new evidence by other elements of the international inquiry team, which includes the FBI, CIA and German and British intelligence* [authors italics].' (The 'new evidence' was greeted with derision in some quarters when it became known that the *L'Express* story had originated over lunch with a senior official from the American Embassy in Paris. Suspicions of a CIA 'plant' deepened further when word leaked out that the matching of the Lockerbie circuit board fragment with the timers seized in Dakar was based on little more than a photographic comparison.)

A Libyan connection had, in any case, been assumed from the start, by Lester Coleman as well as most other experts aware of Libya's role as supplier of arms and explosives to terrorist factions around the world. In fact, the only genuinely new element in the Lockerbie investigation was Iraq's annexation of Kuwait on 2 August 1990, and the requirement this imposed upon the American intelligence community to put an acceptable face on

Washington's alliance with Syria and its desired *rapprochement* with Iran.

With those two off the target list, the only available scapegoat was Muammar Gaddafi, always seen as a likely accessory before, during and after the fact of the Flight 103 atrocity, but never – until December 1990 – seriously proposed as the prime mover. From then onwards, all the 'evidence' offered as 'proof' that Libya was responsible for the mass murder at Lockerbie would come, not from the Scottish police or forensic scientists, but from the FBI and the CIA – and they had to work hard.

Even after the *Independent's* uncritical puff for what it had learned from 'high-level sources', America's trial balloon was slow to take off. Two days later, Julie Flint in The *Observer*, shot it down.

'British and American experts believe that Libya's involvement in the Lockerbie disaster was only tangential,' she wrote. 'Despite last week's banner headlines claiming Libya "was to blame" for the bombing of Pan Am Flight 103 two years ago this week, it is still thought the outrage was almost certainly ordered from Iran and planned from Syria.'

Citing Paul Wilkinson, professor of international relations at St Andrew's University and head of the Research Foundation for the Study of Terrorism, as a leading proponent of this view, she reported that he had known about the timer match for almost a year. As for the fax claiming the bombing as a victory for Libya,

. . . Professor Wilkinson said it was not 'disregarded' – as the *Independent* claimed on Friday – but 'given a low rating because it was such a piece of opportunist propaganda'.

'There is something suspicious about wanting to shift the entire focus to Libya when we have so much circumstantial evidence for the involvement of Iran, Syria and the GC group, Ahmad Jibril's Damascus-based Popular Front for the Liberation of Palestine – General Command [he said].

'A lot of fine forensic work will not be revealed until charges are brought to court, but the investigators have a pretty good idea about the sources of the case. There is also a pretty conclusive picture that here was a group – the GC – intent on bombing an American airliner.

'The truth is probably that there was an unholy alliance,' says

Professor Wilkinson. 'Groups such as the GC have often been assisted by sympathetic groups, and it is not necessarily the case that the whole construction of the bomb was Libyan and that Libya was responsible for designing it.'

'Supporting this theory,' Julie Flint concluded, 'is the fact that the Libyans arrested at Dakar were not carrying a radio-cassette bomb, as the *Independent* claimed, but component parts – ten detonators, 21 pounds of Semtex and several packets of TNT. Intelligence sources also say the CIA has evidence that Jibril designed much of the Lockerbie bomb.'

If so, the CIA was not about to admit it. With its trial balloon grounded again, the next attempt to patch it up came from Vincent Cannistraro, who claimed to have been in charge of the CIA's contribution to the Flight 103 investigation until his retirement in September 1990.

Having refurbished two bits of year-old evidence to support the new Libyan thesis, he now weighed in with a two-year-old intelligence report about a meeting in Tripoli *before* the bombing – in mid-November 1988 – at which the Libyans were said to have taken over responsibility for the attack from the PFLP–GC after Jibril's West German cell was broken up.

According to Cannistraro, the report had been dismissed as unreliable at the time but now, in the light of the 'proven' Libyan connection, was the missing link that placed the blame squarely on Gaddafi.

He did not explain why the CIA had waited until December 1990, to draw this conclusion when the 'proof' had been available for at least a year, nor did he explain why no advance warning based on this report, reliable or not, had been passed down the line to those responsible for airline security. The so-called Helsinki warning, also dismissed as unreliable (and apparently for better reason), had at least saved the lives of those who would otherwise have occupied the vacant seats on Flight 103.

And possibly it was just a coincidence that Cannistraro's revelations, fully in keeping with the CIA's tradition of conducting America's secret business in public, were made at about the same time that his former colleagues in the Drug Enforcement Administration set out to discredit Lester Coleman as an obstacle to general acceptance of the Libyan/Air Malta explanation of the Lockerbie disaster.

On 21 December 1990, Steven Emerson appeared on Cable News

Network and in a broadcast received in 151 countries described Coleman as a disgruntled former DEA informant responsible for recent allegations in the media that the DEA was somehow involved in the bombing of Flight 103.

And possibly it was also significant that after the Royal Armament Research and Development Establishment (RARDE) forensic team had identified the tiny fragment of micro-circuitry as part of the bomb's triggering mechanism, it was not the Scottish police who discovered the source of the murder weapon but the CIA's intelligence analysts. It was Cannistraro and his colleagues who pointed them towards Dakar and the timers seized from two Libyan intelligence agents.

It was Cannistraro and his colleagues who also identified the mysterious Libyan who bought the clothes in Malta to wrap around the bomb, based on a photofit picture produced by the FBI from the shopkeeper's phenomenally detailed description of his customer ten months after he saw him for the first and only time.

It was Cannistraro and his colleagues who also identified this man as an accomplice of the two Libyans arrested at Dakar (and subsequently released) who took over from Ahmed Jibril after he asked for Gaddafi's help.

And it was Cannistraro's CIA colleagues who, with the FBI, eventually identified two other Libyans who were later indicted for the bombing by an American grand jury.

But that was a year later. In December 1990, nobody was much impressed by America's trial balloon for there were serious problems of credibility with the Libyan theory.

All the forensic evidence showed in support of the theory was that the timer used in the Lockerbie bomb appeared to be identical with a batch sold to the Libyans three years before the bombing, and that the clothing wrapped around the bomb came from Malta, which had close links with Libya.

Forensic science had no answer to the question of what happened to the timer *after* it was supplied to the Libyans by the Swiss, any more than it could say with certainty what happened to the Semtex plastic explosive after that was supplied to the Libyans by the Czechs. Both could have passed through any number of hands before being finally installed in the Toshiba radio-cassette player used to house the Lockerbie bomb.

The same was true of the clothing around the bomb and the Samsonite suitcase that contained the device.

Given Libya's established role as quartermaster to the world's terrorists, the forensic evidence alone could – and *did* – point as readily to the PFLP–GC as to the Libyans themselves. It identified the components of the bomb – not who made it or how it was put aboard Flight 103.

As accessories, the Libyans who supplied those components were as guilty as hell, as guilty morally and legally as anyone directly involved in commissioning or committing mass murder. But there was nothing in the available forensic evidence to prove that Libya was the sole author of the atrocity or even among the prime movers.

Beyond that, the official Libyan theory rested mainly on the proposition that the suitcase containing the bomb had been sent unaccompanied on an Air Malta flight to Frankfurt, where, undetected by Pan Am's inadequate security arrangements, it was loaded on to a feeder flight to London and then transferred to a third aircraft for the New York leg of the journey.

Apart from the inherent improbability that trained intelligence agents would simply add an armed suitcase bomb tagged for New York–JFK to a pile of international luggage waiting to be loaded in Luqa and then trust to luck that, unescorted, the bomb would get through the baggage-handling and security arrangements of two other major airports and be loaded aboard the target aircraft before the timer triggered an explosion, there remained the problem with the provenance and reliability of the Frankfurt baggage-list that was said to have identified the suitcase in the first place.

Apart from the inherent improbability that the Lockerbie investigators never thought to ask for it, that it was left to a clerk to print out a copy on her own initiative before the computer wiped the record, only to return weeks later from holiday to find that still no one had asked for it, and that the BKA, after being given the list, sat on it for months before passing it along to the Scottish police, there remained the problem of the FBI teletype which left open the possibility that no such bag from Malta was ever loaded on Flight 103.

According to this five-page document, sent from the US Embassy in Bonn to the FBI director on 23 October 1989, 'From the information available from the Frankfurt airport records, there is no concrete indication that any piece of baggage was unloaded from Air Malta 180, sent through the luggage routing system at Frankfurt airport and then loaded on board Pan Am 103.'

The baggage computer entry 'does not indicate the origin of the bag which was sent for loading on board Pan Am 103. Nor does it indicate that the bag was actually loaded on Pan Am 103. It indicates only that a bag of unknown origin was sent from Coding Station 206 at 1:07 p.m. to a position from which it was supposed to be loaded on Pan Am 103.'

The handwritten record kept at Coding Station 206 was no more explicit. According to the teletype, 'the handwritten duty sheet indicates only that the luggage was unloaded from Air Malta 180. There is no indication how much baggage was unloaded or where the luggage was sent.' On the agent's reading of the evidence, 'there remains the possibility that no luggage was transferred from Air Malta 180 to Pan Am 103 and *that a piece of luggage was simply introduced at Coding Station 206* [author's italics].'

The teletype also disclosed that, on a guided tour of the baggage area in September 1989, Detective Inspector Watson McAteer and FBI Special Agent Lawrence G. Whitaker had actually seen this happen. They had 'observed an individual approach Coding Station 206 with a single piece of luggage, place the luggage in a luggage container, encode a destination into the computer and leave without making any notation on a duty sheet'. From this they concluded that a rogue suitcase could have been 'sent to Pan Am 103 either before or after the unloading of Air Malta 180'.

Although one government-inspired commentator tried later to dismiss the FBI teletype as 'an early memo . . . that sketched one possible scenario, as of October 1989', and which subsequent events had rendered 'irrelevant' and 'pointless', it was less easy to reject the categorical denials by Air Malta, the airport staff at Luqa, the Maltese police and the Maltese government that any unaccompanied bag had been sent to Frankfurt on 21 December 1988, or, indeed, that *any* Maltese connection with the Lockerbie bombing had been established at all, other than that the clothing in the suitcase bomb had apparently originated on the island.

There was a question also about the device itself. In the official view, the use of the Swiss timer pointed clearly to Libya, not only because it had been supplied to its security agency in the first place, but because the PFLP–GC favoured a barometric-pressure triggering system for its Toshiba bombs.

Thomas Hayes, however, the forensic expert responsible for identifying the tiny piece of Swiss circuit board, was not prepared to commit himself on this point. In his book, *On the Trail of Terror*, David Leppard wrote later that, privately, Hayes believed the Lockerbie bomb had been a dual device, triggered by a barometric switch and then running on a timer, but that not enough of it had been recovered to be sure.

The possibility that Khreesat or Abu Elias or some other PFLP–GC bombmaker had incorporated a Libyan timer as well as Libyan Semtex into the Lockerbie bomb remained open, therefore – with the balance of probability tilted towards Jibril's group rather than the Libyans in view of its previous use of Toshiba radios as bomb housings.

But by now, the whole Lockerbie investigation was dogged by a sense of futility felt nowhere more keenly than at the Scottish Fatal Accident Inquiry which, just before Christmas 1990, recessed for a month after hearing 150 witnesses in 46 days.

Ian Bell wrote in the *Observer*:

Before it adjourned, it heard former Pan Am employees accuse the airline of refusing to pay for adequate security measures. Disgraceful, if true; but almost irrelevant. Pan Am did not kill its own passengers. The inquiry is unlikely to tell us who did . . .

Only a handful of reporters now cover the inquiry, and their stories slip day by day down the news schedules, overtaken by fresh nightmares and by disasters which are simpler, easier to comprehend. The iron laws of the press have prevailed. Predictably, the international media circus, with its Olympian disdain for the parochial, has long since moved on.

The words and images of 1988 are stored in the cuttings libraries and video vaults, sinking into history. The big world of geopolitics, where the truth about Lockerbie probably lies, demands the presence of the troupe elsewhere. For all we know, the political masters of those who destroyed Flight 103 are now our allies in the Gulf crisis. For all we know, they may have been our allies two years ago . . . The only important fact to have emerged from the inquiry is that those who know the truth will never willingly give evidence . . .

As the months have passed, it has become clear that something like a campaign of disinformation has been waged, for reasons which can still only be guessed at. With only the single, terrible fact of 21 December known for certain, journalists have scavenged and speculated. Some have been used. Hence the sense of futility haunting the Lockerbie inquiry.

Nothing said there, one feels, will approach the truth about

Flight 103. The Scottish legal system, for all its solemnity, has neither the strength nor the resources to solve the puzzle.

Neither had the House Government Operations sub-committee in Washington which, a few days before Coleman was publicly denounced in a CNN broadcast, opened hearings into allegations that the DEA was involved in the fate of Flight 103.

On 18 December, Stephen H. Greene, assistant administrator of the operations division of the DEA, described at some length how a 'controlled delivery' worked and agreed that the DEA often used the technique. But he strenuously denied that anything of the sort had been going on anywhere in Europe around the time of the Lockerbie disaster.

Under pressure from Congress and the media, he said, the agency had reviewed its files and questioned its agents overseas to see if there was any basis in fact for the NBC and ABC newscasts and other media reports asserting that Khalid Nazir Jafaar had been involved in a DEA operation known as Corea or Courier.

The result, according to the DEA spokesman's sworn testimony, was a classified 350-page report, reviewed and confirmed by its sister agency, the FBI, showing that Jafaar had never been used as an informant or subsource and that no DEA agent or office had ever had any contact with him. Jafaar's two pieces of luggage had been identified by the Lockerbie investigators and neither showed any sign of explosives or drugs. Nor had there ever been a DEA operation or unit called Corea, or anything similar to that name. According to Greene, there had been three controlled deliveries through Frankfurt between 1983 and 1987, none involving Pan Am flights, and none after that.

This blanket denial might have been more persuasive if the report, or the files on which it was based, had been made available for inspection by some suitably qualified independent investigator, but the subcommittee fared no better in this respect than had counsel for Pan Am. Accused of hen-stealing, fox and vixen had once again insisted on going back to their lair alone to look for feathers.

If anything, suspicions of a cover-up were reinforced by the DEA's determination to act as counsel, judge and jury in its own cause, and nobody was much surprised when, three days before the deadline imposed by the Federal Tort Claims Act, Pan Am obtained leave from the United States District Court, Eastern Division of New York, to file a third-party liability claim against the US government in connection with the crash of Flight 103.

In an update of the story on the second anniversary of the disaster, *Barron's*, the American business magazine, quoted Vincent Cannistraro's dismissal of Juval Aviv's Interfor Report as 'absolute nonsense', and the more recent NBC and ABC newscasts that shared some of its conclusions as 'total rubbish and fabrication'.

Victor Marchetti, however, another CIA veteran, strongly disagreed. Formerly executive assistant to the deputy director under Richard Helms, Marchetti told *Barron's* he had always thought that 'the essence of the Interfor report was true . . . I'm not concerned about a detail here or there that may be wrong'. With Iraq's invasion of Kuwait and the enlistment of Syria in the alliance opposing Saddam Hussein, 'the cover-up is now more true than ever. Which is why the lid is really on.'

A Middle Eastern intelligence analyst, who asked for his name to be withheld as he was employed by another agency, was even more emphatic.

'Juval Aviv is a very astute investigator who has come up with some very plausible explanations,' he said. 'I could find nothing that I knew to be untrue. And I found many details that I knew to be true. Do I think the CIA was involved? Of course they were involved. And they screwed up.'

Asked to comment on the *Independent*'s report that Libyan terrorists had put the bomb aboard Flight 103 by means of an unaccompanied bag sent from Malta, Aviv himself thought it was yet another attempt to distract attention from the truth.

> The timing of this story [he told *Barron's*], at the same time as the Lockerbie inquiry, on the eve of the second anniversary of the crash, just as the threat of a Pan Am lawsuit emerges, is not a coincidence. They had to try to take attention away from the accepted theory that Jibril and the Syrians were responsible. That theory was never disputed until three months ago.
>
> It does not make sense to send a bomb unattended from Malta through Frankfurt to London – two stops where it could be found [he went on]. This means they just sent it off, hoping it would pass all the checks and get on the right flight. How often does a bag get lost and fail to make a connecting flight? Professional terrorists don't take such chances. Also, according to the Libyan story in the *Independent*, the detonator was just a simple timer – not a

barometric pressure trigger. What would happen if there was a delay somewhere on that long trip from Malta through Frankfurt to London?

Preserving a balance throughout that had not been conspicuous in other media surveys of the Lockerbie investigation, *Barron's* concluded its article with a statement from Paul Hudson, a lawyer from Albany, New York, whose sixteen-year-old daughter had died in the crash. Without hard evidence, he remained sceptical of the Interfor Report's findings, but nevertheless called for a genuine public inquiry.

'We're counting on the Congress to shed more light on this,' he said. 'The subpoenas that would have shed light have been blocked. What we're looking for is a congressional review of the DEA and the FBI investigations, and then, if they decide there is any basis to the allegations, a special counsel. Right now, the House and Senate judiciary committees have jurisdiction over the FBI and the DEA. But the congressional intelligence committees are like a black box. Things go in without anything coming out. They never issue any reports. They never hold any open hearings. They don't seem to be a vehicle that's going to get the truth out. Whatever they do is totally within the intelligence cloak.'

No such hearings were held, of course – on either side of the Atlantic. Instead, Washington relied on the public's dwindling interest in the two-year-old disaster, the shortness of its memory, and what Ian Bell had described as 'the iron laws of the press' to blur the improbabilities that riddled the authorized version of events. Though it never really flew, the Libyan trial balloon had served its purpose. Eleven months later, the indictment of two Libyans for the mass murder of 270 people at Lockerbie struck most Americans as little more than a formality, giving practical effect to what they – and most of the media – already thought they knew.

It was now openly an all-American show, although Robert Mueller, assistant attorney-general, paid tribute to the Scottish police, who deserved, he said, 'the most unbelievable praise of any law-enforcement agency in the world'.

Believable or not, the praise was echoed by his boss, acting Attorney-General William Barr, who, coupling their work with that of his own investigators, congratulated the team on a 'brilliant and unrelenting operation'. Other American officials hailed the indictments as 'one of law enforcement's finest hours', but those who still cared were not convinced. Neither was Israel. Nor the PLO. Nor even Germany.

The official sequence of events, as set out in the American indictment, began with the sale of 20 custom-built Swiss electronic timers to the Libyan Ministry of Justice in 1985. In 1988, they were issued to Libyan intelligence agents abroad, many of them working under cover as employees of Libyan Arab Airlines (LAA), along with detonators and plastic explosives.

Lamen Khalifa Fhimah, one of the two men named in the indictment, was said to have stored the explosives at Malta's Luqa airport, where he was LAA station manager, and to have built the bomb with the second defendant, Abdel Basset Ali al-Megrahi, Libya's chief of airline security, hiding it in a Toshiba radio.

On 7 December 1988, al-Megrahi was alleged to have called at the Sliema boutique and bought the odd assortment of clothes that were used to wrap around the radio bomb. On 15 December, Fhimah made a note in his diary, reminding himself to take some Air Malta luggage tags from the airport. On 17 December, al-Megrahi flew to Tripoli for a meeting, followed by Fhimah next day, and both returned to Malta on 20 December with a suitcase for the bomb. On 21 December, the fatal day, they were said to have placed the suitcase with its Air Malta tags among the luggage being loaded on to international flights from Luqa airport.

Besides the Libyan connections established by the forensic evidence, the US Justice Department now had *two* witnesses.

The first was known to be Tony Gauci, son of the owner of Mary's House, the boutique in Sliema from which the clothing in the bomb suitcase had allegedly been purchased. Gauci had remembered the sale so vividly that, almost ten months later, he had given the Scottish police a probable date for it, 23 November 1988, and provided a FBI videofit artist with a detailed description of his customer – he believed, a Libyan.

According to reports in the media at that time, the resulting likeness was thought to be that of Abu Talb, a PFLP–GC terrorist who had visited Malta twice before the bombing and was subsequently arrested in Sweden while in possession of large quantities of clothing purchased in Malta.

In the indictment, however, the sale was said to have been made on 7 December 1988, and the purchaser was identified as Abdel Basset Ali al-Megrahi.

The government's surprise second witness was Abdu Maged

Jiacha, described as a Libyan intelligence officer who had worked undercover as assistant station manager for LAA at Luqa.

In the autumn of 1991, he had defected to the United States – 'for financial reasons' – and identified Fhimah and al-Megrahi as the bombers.

The investigators had also come into possession of what was said to be Fhimah's personal diary, improbable though it must have seemed to them that a trained intelligence agent would keep one or put anything in writing, let alone the incriminating English word 'taggs' (sic) in the middle of an entry in Arabic and then, according to media reports, leave the diary behind for the investigators to find. (Jiacha's 'financial reasons' were understood to be a reward of $4 million and resettlement in California under the Federal Witness Protection Program.)

The issue of warrants for Fhimah and al-Megrahi on 14 November 1991 was accompanied by a statement from President Bush's spokesman, Marlin Fitzwater, insisting that Iran and Syria were not involved. The Pan Am bombing, he said, was part of a consistent pattern of Libyan-sponsored terrorism that could no longer be ignored. President Bush was discussing a co-ordinated international response with other Western leaders and all options were open, including the forcible seizure of the two men from Libya.

Amplifying this statement, Washington officials claimed that Libya had tried in various ways to implicate Syria and Iran – by using a Toshiba radio-cassette recorder, for instance – but there was no evidence of their involvement. Everything, including intelligence data, pointed to a solely Libyan operation in retaliation for President Reagan's bombing of Tripoli in 1986.

'The Syrians took a bum rap on this,' President Bush famously declared.

Any suggestion that such a conclusion might have been politically directed was simultaneously rejected on both sides of the Atlantic. Lord Fraser of Carmyllie, Scotland's Lord Advocate, said he would have resigned if exposed to political pressure, and Assistant Attorney-General Bob Mueller insisted that no one had even *tried* to influence the investigation.

The sceptics were not convinced.

'Does George Bush take us for fools?' asked Bonnie O'Connor, of Long Island, New York, when a *Newsday* reporter invited her opinion. Her brother had died in the wreck of Flight 103.

Dr James Swire, who had lost a daughter at Lockerbie and was the leading spokesman for the British families, told *The Times* that he still believed the atrocity had been carried out by the PFLP–GC, acting as mercenaries for the Iranians, although he was anxious to see the two Libyans brought to trial by any means short of force. He thought Jibril had probably used them to confuse the chase.

Professor Paul Wilkinson agreed. 'There are no grounds for assuming that Libya was the only country involved,' he said, suggesting again that there had been 'an unholy alliance' between Iran, Syria and Libya.

The Israelis concurred. 'The revelation that Libya was involved does not necessarily mean that previous allegations against Syria and Iran are false,' said Anat Kurz, of the Jaffee Centre for Strategic Studies in Tel Aviv. 'It may be all three countries worked together.'

Yossi Olmert, head of the Israeli government press office, thought so, too. 'We are not surprised by the findings,' he said. 'It is what we call sub-contracting.'

Volker Rath, the German public prosecutor, tactfully said nothing at the time but later announced that Germany was suspending proceedings against the two Libyans for lack of evidence.

With the exception of a few journalists perhaps over-committed to the official Anglo-American view after following it so assiduously for three years, the press, too, was mostly unenthusiastic.

'The arrest warrants are unlikely to quell speculation that more than one country was involved,' wrote Alan Philps, diplomatic correspondent of the *Daily Telegraph*. Citing an additional reason for the change of tack, he went on to suggest that 'laying the blame at the door of Libya will lift a burden from the shoulders of diplomats working to reconvene the Middle East peace conference and to release the last remaining British hostage in Lebanon, Mr Terry Waite.

'Had either Syria or the Palestinians been shown to be involved,' he said, 'it would have added a complication to the peace conference, perhaps provoking an Israeli walk-out.'

The magazine *Private Eye* was more scathing, having already denounced the Thatcher and Bush governments for agreeing 'that they will not pursue any further the terrorists who bombed the plane over Lockerbie since they are known to be close to the Syrian government' (28 September 1991).

A week after the indictments were published, its 'Lockerbie Special Report' noted that

... in recent weeks, Bush and Major have been under some pressure from the families of people who died at Lockerbie. One US group of families recently visited Britain and started to agitate for action. The statement about the two Libyans was the two governments' answer. The wretched Lord Fraser, the Lord Advocate of Scotland, was ordered to read out 'results' of his police inquiry which were completely different from those already read out to newspapers all over the world ...

In the House of Commons, Douglas Hurd went out of his way to exculpate the 'other governments' (Syria and Iran) which his colleague Paul Channon had denounced in March 1989.

(Sceptical from the start of official announcements about the disaster, *Private Eye* added this footnote to a later story [8 May 1992] about the suitcase of drugs found among the wreckage at Lockerbie: 'PS: Lord Fraser of Carmyllie has been promoted in John Major's new administration to be minister of state at the Scottish office.')

More temperately, Adrian Hamilton in the *Observer* reminded his readers 'that the US charges of Libyan complicity in the Rome bar bombing of 1986 – used as a pretext for the US raid on Tripoli – proved groundless. It was Lebanese terrorists, probably at the behest of Syria, who planted the device which killed an American serviceman ... The assault on Libya is all too conveniently timed to let Iran and Syria off the hook and speed the release of hostages.'

A.M. Rosenthal, in the *New York Times*, felt that too many people had taken part in the investigation for the truth to remain hidden for ever. 'Among those I have talked to over the past years,' he said, 'I have found none who believed that Libya alone paid for, planned and carried out the crime – exactly none.'

Pierre Salinger of ABC News seemed equally unconvinced that it was Libya's sole responsibility after he went to Tripoli in December 1991 to interview the two accused and to discuss their indictment with Colonel Gaddafi. Though he had his doubts about al-Megrahi – his 'answers to questions were not always convincing' – he found Fhimah 'a simple man, and it was hard to believe that he had been involved in a terrorist case. Both Mr Megrahi and Mr Fhima told me they would be happy to meet Scottish or American investigators and talk to them about the case.'

Their willingness to do so was confirmed by Libya's foreign minister, Ibrahim Bechari, who said that Western investigators were welcome in Libya and that the Libyan judge looking into the allegations, Ahmed al-Zawi, would like to have more US or Scottish evidence in the case so that he could conduct a solid interrogation of the two men.

Gaddafi himself, when questioned by Salinger, said: 'I am angry about the accusations against Libya, but I am satisfied that things are moving according to law. I am satisfied there is a legal way to deal with this.'

Donald Trelford, editor of the *Observer*, was told much the same thing by Gaddafi in a further interview a month or so later.

'He challenged the US and Britain to produce evidence against the Libyans,' Trelford wrote. '"The truth is, they don't have it," he added. Libya has arrested the two men named by the Scottish Lord Advocate last November . . . and begun a judicial investigation of its own. Gadaffi invited British and US lawyers to attend the inquiry and interrogate the accused, and welcomed representatives of victims' families.'

Even the Palestine Liberation Organisation (PLO), though working to a different agenda from that of other critics of the official line, felt that the Libyan contribution to the Lockerbie disaster had been of a low-level technical nature.

In an 80-page report leaked to the press on both sides of the Atlantic, the PLO described a number of meetings between Ali Akbar Mohtashemi, the Iranian minister of the interior, Ahmed Jibril of the PFLP–GC and other officials in the late summer of 1988 to plan a revenge attack on an American airliner. According to the PLO's sources, the Toshiba radio-cassette bomb used to destroy Flight 103 had been built by Khaisar Haddad, also known as Abu Elias, a blond, blue-eyed Lebanese Christian member of the PFLP–GC, who passed the completed device on to an Iranian contact in Beirut.

This suggestion fitted neatly with the BKA's identification of Abu Elias as an associate of Hafez Dalkamoni, head of the PFLP–GC's West Germany cell until the arrests of October 1988, and with the Lockerbie investigators' belief that Abu Elias took charge of the attack after that.

Whatever its motives in preparing the report, no one could seriously challenge the quality of the PLO's sources in the Palestinian community. Even for those most deeply committed to the official view, these revelations could only reopen the vexed question of why the Scottish police and the FBI had changed their minds so comprehensively after claiming for at least 18 months that the bombing had been carried out by Ahmed Jibril's PFLP–GC at the instigation of Iran and Syria.

There were other questions, too.

If Libya was solely responsible for the bombing of Flight 103, why did the US government resolutely refuse on grounds of national security to open the relevant files for judicial or congressional examination, if necessary *in camera*, in order to dispose of alternative theories, rumours and speculation about the real cause of the Lockerbie tragedy?

If Libya was solely responsible, why had the government lied to Congress and the media about the activities of the Drug Enforcement Administration in Cyprus?

If Libya was solely responsible, why had the US government gone to such lengths to silence one of its own intelligence agents on the subject of the DEA's operations in Cyprus, and when that failed, to discredit what he had to say?

If the government's hands were clean, why did it insist on hiding them behind its back?

— XIV —

At the end of August 1987, the Colemans returned home from Cyprus.

Mary-Claude was sad to leave because, after spending much of the summer visiting her family with Sarah, she was not looking forward to an indefinite stay in Alabama, where she knew hardly anyone and where, after Beirut and Larnaca, the sheer difference in the scale of everything made her feel uneasy and exposed. But as a dutiful wife, she managed to put a good face on it, particularly after her husband promised they would return again in the spring. And that was settled. Coleman had agreed to Hurley's request that he renew his DEA consultancy contract for the 1988 opium-growing season, and had cleared this with the DIA.

Donleavy was highly complimentary about Coleman's work that summer. The back-channel reports on DEA operations that he had transmitted twice a week from his arrival in Cyprus were on file in a classified computer data bank, codenamed EMERALD, at Bolling Airforce Base, near Washington, and the first order of business upon his return was a systematic debriefing at a hotel near Fort Meade to fill in the gaps. Knowing Hurley, Coleman was pretty sure that the DIA now had a better grasp of what was going on at DEA Nicosia than the DEA itself.

Concerned above all else with preserving the integrity of the Asmar cell in Beirut, Donleavy cross-questioned him closely about the calibre and affiliations of the DEA's network of Lebanese CIs, and in particular, about El-Jorr, the Kabbaras and Jafaars. Now that Coleman had been seen working with DEA agents in Cyprus, there was a clear risk that he might also have been identified by one of their Beirut informants as a friend of Tony Asmar's. In which case, if the informant happened to be working both sides of the fence, the connection might prove embarrassing for Asmar. Or worse.

As Coleman had been at pains to point this out before taking on the DEA assignment, he could hardly disagree, but the risk had seemed acceptable at the time and he had taken particular care to underline his academic credentials whenever he met Hurley's people. And there seemed little doubt that the results *had* justified the risk. The Kabbara case in Italy, for one, had proved of particular interest to the DIA, for it showed that DEA Nicosia, in conjunction with the CIA, was in the habit of operating outside its law-enforcement brief.

Zouher Kabbara and his cousin Nadim Kabbara had been arrested at Rome airport with half a kilo of heroin about a month before Coleman arrived on Cyprus. After hearing the evidence, the Tribunale Penale di Roma found that they had obtained the drugs from Hurley for the purpose of entrapping Italian nationals, among them Mario Cetera, the husband of Joan Schumacher, American heiress to the Prentice Hall publishing fortune.

Cetera was subsequently cleared (only to die later in mysterious circumstances) but the real worry, for the DIA, was that the Italian court also found that the drug trafficking had been merely a cover, to justify payments to the Kabbaras as DEA informants. Their real function, it went on, was to assist the CIA in selling military equipment to Iraq through their Rome company, Kabbara International Export (KINEX).

KINEX quoted several telephone numbers on its letterhead, one of which (80 49 88) was assigned to the American Embassy in Rome, which paid the bills for it. A link was also established with APEXCO, a DEA front company in Larnaca, when Zouher Kabbara told the court that he could contact Hurley there as necessary by telex.

Donleavy was equally intrigued by the DEA's relationship with the Jafaars, bitter enemies of the pro-Syrian Kabbaras, but like them, hiding their CIA status behind their cover as DEA informants. He took Coleman several times through Sami Jafaar's part in the Fawaz Younis affair and the circumstances of Jafaar's subsequent posting to Switzerland for Operation Polar Cap, which was just getting under way as the debriefing took place. As with the Kabbaras in Rome, Jafaar's involvement in Polar Cap for the DEA masked a deeper CIA interest in hiding its role as an arms supplier to Iraq.

The DIA was also anxious to get its hands on Syrian George, who had gone to Switzerland with Polar Cap to sit on the wiretaps. As a Russian-trained former officer in the Syrian Army, he had seemed to Donleavy a potentially useful source of background military and political intelligence from the moment Coleman first reported in about him.

'But he belongs to Hurley,' Coleman said. 'You could ask him, but he'll turn you down.'

'You mean, he won't talk to us?'

'No, I mean Hurley won't hand him over. He's too useful.'

'Then how are we going to get hold of him?'

'Well, that's no problem – if you're not worried about upsetting Hurley.'

Donleavy was so obviously *un*worried about upsetting Hurley that Coleman laughed.

'Fine,' he said. 'Hurley's always stringing him along, saying he'll get him a green card. If you give George a visa, he's yours. And once he's gone, what can Hurley do about it?'

'Okay.' Donleavy looked at him thoughtfully. 'Then we'll give him a visa.'

'*We?*'

'Well, you've got to do something this winter. And if you're going back to Cyprus next spring, you'll need a new cover.' He found the paper he was looking for in his briefcase. 'How does Director of the Office of Visiting International Scholars, University of Alabama, Birmingham, grab you?'

'Birmingham? My Mom'll like it.'

'Well, there you go. It's a good slot. Means you'll work with all kinds of academics from overseas – scientists, graduate scholars, professors. And who knows what you'll pick up? Maybe you can find a few sources for us. You know, people we can persuade to keep in touch after they go home? And maybe keep us posted with scientific and industrial data? Stuff like that?'

Coleman nodded ruefully, and Donleavy smiled.

'Anyway,' he said, 'as director, you got the power to authorize J-1 visiting scholar visas – it goes with the job. So you'll give Syrian George one of those when you get back.'

'My pleasure. Can't wait to see Hurley's face.'

'Okay. But first you're in for a couple of months in Florida. There's something you can do for us down there.'

'You know,' said Coleman, 'working for you guys is a real strain.'

He found himself on loan to the faculty of the National Intelligence Academy (NIA) in Fort Lauderdale as director of Video Operations. The NIA was housed on the premises of Technos International, a manufacturer of electronic surveillance equipment sold only to US government agencies and countries with special export clearances.

After setting up NARCOG's listening post in Larnaca, training the Cypriot police to use their UN-funded radio equipment, fitting out police boats and *King Edmondo* with satellite tracking gear and installing short-wave transmitters in Beirut and Larnaca for DEA intelligence traffic, Coleman had acquired something of a reputation in the area of advanced electronics. At the NIA until just before Christmas, he worked with Martin McDermott, on loan from the Irish police in Dublin, instructing mixed classes of US Army personnel, Federal agents and state law-enforcement officers in the latest audio and video surveillance techniques.

In setting up his assignment at the University of Alabama, Donleavy had assumed that Coleman would return to Cyprus with Mary-Claude and Sarah in February 1988, but analysing the personal histories of foreign scholars produced such interesting results that the DIA several times postponed his departure. Coleman had no objection. He felt it necessary in any case to establish himself on campus before leaving for Cyprus, in order to avoid arousing suspicion among his university colleagues, and to connect with the Fulbright Commission, which administered its scholarship programme through offices in American embassies overseas.

To further strengthen his cover, he also became a member of the National Association of Foreign Student Advisors, and attended its conference in Washington, taking advantage of the opportunity to confer with Donleavy and DIA agent Neal Miller, who later took over as Control for Operation Shakespeare. It was only when Hurley called Coleman direct at the end of March 1988, telling him to get his ass over there in a week or he would find somebody else, that Donleavy agreed to release him.

There was too much going on at DEA Nicosia for Control to risk losing the back-channel reports the DIA needed to maintain its overview of American operations in the Middle East. Nor could it afford indefinitely to be without a direct, local link with Asmar's network, which was still using the agency's video equipment to keep track of the hostages in Beirut as well as monitoring the activities of DEA/CIA operatives.

Exactly one week later, on 5 April 1988, the Colemans arrived back in Nicosia, moving into an apartment just vacated by Ibrahim El-Jorr, the Lebanese-American DEA informant whom Coleman had met briefly the previous year and who was now to be his co-worker in Operation Dome, reassessing the Lebanese narcotics trade at the start of a new opium-growing season.

The scene of operations had also changed. Instead of working from home or at the DEA office, Coleman was given a desk at the Eurame Trading Company Ltd., a DEA/CIA 'front' newly set up by the Cypriot Police Narcotics Squad in a luxury three-bedroomed penthouse apartment down the street from the US Embassy. It gave him the creeps from the start.

Intended as a place where DEA and CIA agents could meet unobserved with informants and clients, as a message drop for CIA arms dealers supplying Iraq and the Afghan rebels, as a waiting room for DEA CIs and couriers from Lebanon, and as a transit point, not just for heroin, but for cash, documents and bootleg computer software moving to and fro along the Beirut–Nicosia–US pipeline, Eurame, as run by El-Jorr, was more like a low-life social club than a secret intelligence centre.

Coleman recalls:

Officially, my job was to work with El-Jorr on raw intelligence data supplied by DEA sources in Lebanon. I had to evaluate this stuff and sit on his case because he was always behind with everything. People would come over and be debriefed in the office. Then we'd draft reports, prepare maps, collect photographs, collate lists of growers and traffickers, plot their relationships, determine which illegal ports they were using and who they were paying off, make eight copies of everything and finally send it up the street to the embassy.

We were monitoring everybody, from the opium farmer in the Bekaa to the end-customer in Detroit or Los Angeles. The DEA's on-going, controlled deliveries were going right past the end of my desk. 'Who *are* these people, Ibrahim?' I'd ask him when the couriers came in, because I wanted him to introduce me. 'Mules,' he'd say. 'Carrying *khouriah.*'

As a place to observe what the DEA was up to in Nicosia, Coleman found the Eurame Trading Company ideal, but from his very first day on the job, he had an uncomfortable feeling that the same might be true for the opposition. Security was non-existent. All sorts of people, Cypriot and Lebanese, wandered in and out all the time, sometimes escorted, sometimes not, and although El-Jorr seemed to know most of them, there were clearly some who had simply been told to drop in and introduce themselves.

When Coleman took this up with Hurley, he brushed it aside.

'Listen, if I could trust Ibrahim to handle this alone, you wouldn't be here,' he said flatly. 'He's a flake. But he knows all kinds of people over there and he's getting me what I need. So don't worry about it. It's your job to evaluate the stuff and keep him on the ball. If he gives you any problems, lemme know and I'll kick his ass.'

'It's not Ibrahim I'm worried about, Mike. I'm talking about security. You're getting all kinds of people in there, including some he doesn't even know. And that's bad. So what I think we ought to do is –'

'Yeah, yeah. I'll take care of it. You just concentrate on getting those reports out. I want you to milk that sonuvabitch.'

There was little Coleman could do in the circumstances except fill out an IAP-66 authorization form for Syrian George and take him over to the embassy for a J-1 visa to admit him to the United States for a course of study at UAB.

The expression on Hurley's face when George told him the news was reward enough in itself, but there was an altogether different reaction from the DIA when Coleman reported in about El-Jorr and his key role as the DEA CI fronting for Eurame.

You could feel the pillars shake at the Pentagon [he recalls]. I got back a two-word coded message. 'Watch him.' So I did. I arranged for Tony Asmar to send over Walid, one of our best Muslim assets, to track him day and night. And sure enough, he watched Ibrahim visit the Lebanese Embassy several times a week, and he photographed Ibrahim's Dutch girlfriend meeting with a member of the PLO delegation in a side street near the Churchill hotel. Turned out later she was a Mossad agent, but even so . . . What the hell was going on?

As Hurley obviously knew nothing about it, it began to look as if Ibrahim was working both sides of the street. When I reported this to Control, Donleavy told me to warn Hurley, who told me to mind my own business. I guess he was still mad at me about Syrian George. Anyway, when I saw he wasn't going to do anything about it, I figured it was up to me to make friends with Ibrahim and find out what he was doing.

The number of DEA-controlled deliveries of heroin down the

pipeline to the United States had increased noticeably during the winter as a result of Fred Ganem's special knowledge of the Lebanese communities in Detroit, Houston and Los Angeles. Members of the Jafaar clan and other DEA couriers would arrive at Larnaca with suitcases full of high-grade heroin, white and crystal, and be met off the boat from the Christian-controlled port of Jounieh by officers of the Cypriot Police Narcotics Squad, who then drove them up to the Eurame office in Nicosia.

Greeted there by El-Jorr, they would gossip over coffee until summoned to the embassy to receive their instructions from Hurley. After that, the Cypriot police would take them out to the airport and put them on flights to Frankfurt, where the bag-switch routine used by 'legitimate' smugglers was employed to bypass the airport's security arrangements and load the 'dirty' suitcases on to trans-Atlantic flights.

On arrival in New York, Detroit, or points west, the DEA 'mules' would be met by DEA agents in the baggage claim area and escorted through Customs, the loads being kept under continuous surveillance until deals were struck and the heroin changed hands.

Hoping to enlist Coleman as an ally in his grievances against Hurley, which were many and various, El-Jorr lost no time in describing his own experiences during the Christmas holidays in a 'sting' operation against drug dealers in Southern California. Posing as a Lebanese cocaine buyer, he had flown to Los Angeles with a suitcase full of counterfeit US currency provided by DEA Nicosia and checked into a room booked for him by the DEA at the Sheraton Universal hotel.

Ten days later, when the agents moved in to round up their targets, El-Jorr checked out and returned to Cyprus, charging the hotel bill to his American Express card as instructed. But when he presented the bill to Hurley for reimbursement, Hurley refused to pay, insisting the DEA field office in Los Angeles should pick up the tab. And when El-Jorr sent the bill to them, they, too, refused to pay, claiming that most of the charges on it were unauthorized. Meanwhile, tired of waiting for its money, American Express cancelled his card.

It was a serious blow. El-Jorr felt the loss as keenly as he would have mourned his cowboy boots or his 4 × 4 Chevy with the Texas plates – the card was a basic prop of his all-American image. When Coleman tried to console him, suggesting that the DEA had a reputation for screwing its informants, he was immediately overwhelmed with supporting case histories. Sometimes informants and subsources in Lebanon had to go for weeks without pay because of budget cuts and red tape, El-Jorr complained, citing names, chapter and verse. Then, when word got out that Hurley again had a drawerful of money to pay for information, everybody in Beirut would try to get in on the act, making things up if they had to. And who got squeezed? El-Jorr, of course. And all the people who worked for him.

Coleman naturally lent a commiserative ear, and was soon able to provide Donleavy with a complete run-down on the DEA's network of informants in Beirut and the Bekaa Valley. Warmed by Coleman's sympathy, El-Jorr made a point of introducing him to all the CIs and 'mules' who arrived at Eurame on their way back and forth along the pipeline, including him in the conversation as they brewed up endless cups of Lebanese coffee.

Among the informants he met in this way was a Lebanese Army officer known as 'The Captain', with close connections to the Jafaar clan. Sami Jafaar's nephew, Khalid Nazir Jafaar, was a subsource of his, and one of whom El-Jorr seemed particularly proud as he was the favourite grandson of the drug clan's patriarch, Moostafa Jafaar.

A strongly built, blue-eyed young man who had chosen to live with his father in Detroit rather than stay with his mother and grandfather in the Bekaa, Khalid Nazir was a regular commuter between Beirut and Detroit. In the two months Coleman spent at Eurame, he met him there three times, including one occasion when 'Nazzie' volunteered the information that he was on his way to Houston with a load.

When not debriefing El-Jorr's subsources and evaluating intelligence data to meet Hurley's insatiable appetite for maps and quadruplicate reports, Coleman kept track of the other uses to which the pipeline was put. He had first reported to Donleavy on the use of counterfeit money for DEA stings during the 1987 season, after Dany Habib had produced a sample from his desk drawer, but it was soon clear from what he observed at Eurame that this, too, had become standard operating procedure in his absence.

Working with the Secret Service station at the American Embassy in Athens, DEA Nicosia now regularly employed huge sums of counterfeit US currency to make drug buys in Europe, the US and Mexico. When Coleman looked into this, DIA assets in Lebanon reported that much of it was being printed there, with large numbers of genuine $1 bills being bleached to provide the right paper for phony $100 bills. Fakes of even better quality, however, were coming out of Iran, where forgers had the advantage of using presses sold originally to Shah Reza Pahlevi's government by the US Mint.

Most of the counterfeit currency used by the DEA was supplied by Monzer al-Kassar, who received no separate payment for this service as it was covered by his regular CIA stipend deposited to his credit at the Katherein Bank, Vienna (A/c No. 50307495) and at the Swiss Bank Corporation in Geneva (A/c No. 510230C-86). From Hurley's point of view, this was a vast improvement on the bureaucratic mumbo-jumbo required to obtain cash for flash rolls and drug buys from DEA headquarters. After a successful sting, like El-Jorr's in Los Angeles, the DEA agents would turn the counterfeit currency over to the Secret Service and both could claim credit for the seizure.

Thinking back, Coleman often wonders how many of Hurley's confidential informants in Lebanon were, in fact, paid with funny money.

The business of Eurame was not just drugs and cash, however.

During the previous summer, Coleman had acted as technical adviser to the Cypriot Police Force Narcotics Squad (CPFNS) and helped train its officers in the use of communications, surveillance and other electronic gear paid for by the United Nations Fund for Drug Abuse Control (UNFDAC). On returning to Cyprus that spring, he found that the march of technology had continued in his absence and that all the CPFNS field offices had been hooked into a central computerized database installed by Link Systems, Ltd, a US government 'cut-out' company set up to carry out the contract for UNFDAC.

At CPFNS headquarters, he saw several of the officers he had worked with unpacking software from boxes marked PROMIS Ltd, Toronto, Canada. Sensing another Hurley enterprise that would interest Donleavy, Coleman poked around discreetly and discovered that Eurame had supplied, or was in process of supplying, copies of this software to other national police and military forces in the region, including those of Egypt, Syria, Pakistan, Turkey, Kuwait, Israel, Jordan, Iran and Iraq.

Puzzled as to why the DEA and CIA would choose to do this through a front operation in Nicosia rather than through official channels, Coleman duly reported all this activity to Control, but the response was so muted he could only conclude that the DIA knew about it already.

(Much later, he discovered that PROMIS had been developed

for the US Department of Justice by Inslaw, Inc. of Washington, D.C., as an information system for law-enforcement agencies and government prosecutors with heavy workloads to keep track of their cases. The systems sold through Eurame, however, were bootleg copies, made without the knowledge of Inslaw, to which a 'backdoor' software routine had been added. No matter how securely the front door might be barred with entry codes and passwords, American operators, holding the key to the secret back door, could break into the PROMIS systems operated by Cyprus, Egypt, Syria, Pakistan, Turkey, Kuwait, Israel, Jordan, Iran and Iraq whenever they wished, access the data stored there and get out again without arousing the slightest suspicion that the security of those systems had been breached – an incalculable advantage, not only in collecting and verifying intelligence data from those countries, but also in assessing the actual, as opposed to the professed, level of cooperation extended by their governments.)

Coleman had already transmitted to Control his first HOTSIT (hot situation report) to the effect that NARCOG and the Eurame operation, like everything else connected with DEA Nicosia, was coming unravelled. With Hurley's indifference to security, Coleman felt personally at risk.

> It was open house [he recalls]. From first thing in the morning until we closed at night, there were people drifting in and out all the time.
>
> We'd get Cypriot narcotics cops stopping by for a free cup of coffee or to make a call to their relatives in England on Uncle Sam's nickel. We'd get the day's batch of informants from Lebanon, picked up in Larnaca off the morning ferry. We'd get all kinds of weird people.
>
> From Asmar's reports, I knew that some of them were into arms trafficking as well as dope and that meant they had to have close ties with Syrian-supported terrorist groups like the PFLP–GC.
>
> It was crazy. With El-Jorr coming off the wall from working both sides of the street, it was only a matter of time before the whole operation came unglued. And I didn't want to be around when that happened. In the Middle East, you can get yourself killed that way. So what did Control advise? 'Communicate your concern to NARCOG Director Hurley.'

Coleman had already done that, but he tried again. At the embassy one day, he was talking to Fred Ganem when they were interrupted by a sudden commotion in the outer office. Moments later, an irate, gesticulating El-Jorr was ushered through to Hurley's inner sanctum by the long-suffering Connie, who pushed him in, closed the door and leaned against it, pretending to mop her brow.

Almost at once, the decibel level inside soared from an angry mumble to a full-blown shouting match.

'I can't do this any more,' yelled El-Jorr. 'I can't. What you're asking is impossible.'

'Listen,' Hurley roared. 'You will do what I TELL you to do, WHEN I tell you to do it. I don't want to hear anymore of your SHIT, Ibrahim.'

'But no one will WORK for you anymore. What's the matter with you, Mike? Don't you understand what I'm saying? They're all fed up with this shit. You want us to work like dogs . . . You want us to risk our lives, our families . . . There's no money. You don't pay. How am I to pay my people?'

'That's YOUR problem,' bellowed Hurley. 'You get money. How do I know what you do with it?'

They went on in this vein for several minutes while Ganem, occasionally shaking his head in disgust, tried to continue his conversation with Coleman. Then El-Jorr wrenched open the door and, ignoring everybody, left as abruptly as he had arrived, muttering to himself.

Hurley followed him out, and caught sight of Coleman in Ganem's office.

'You hear that?' he said gloomily. 'Either he's on something or Ibrahim's blown his stack. You better watch that guy pretty close.'

Coleman nodded. Even as they spoke, Walid was probably following El-Jorr back to Eurame. 'I told you you had a problem there, Mike,' he said. 'Now you better do something about it, and fast. That place is wide open.'

Hurley bristled, but let it pass. 'Has he taken anything out of there?' he demanded. 'Any files?'

'How the hell should I know?' Coleman said. 'He's the one with the office key.'

'Well, I want you and Fred to go around to his house right now and bring back whatever he's got over there. Tell him we're putting all the files in one place, or some such shit. Tell him anything you like, but make sure the apartment's clean.'

'Okay. But you better watch him, Mike. Several people have told me he's been seen at the Lebanese Embassy.'

'Yeah?' Hurley looked at Coleman doubtfully. 'What do you think he's doing over there?'

'Hell, I don't know, Mike. Why don't you ask him?'

'And why don't *you* stick to what I pay you for?' he retorted irritably, heading back to his office. 'What are you – some kind of wise-ass?'

Hurley had not forgiven him for the loss of Syrian George, and he was still under heavy pressure from Washington to show results, but in general Coleman made sure they got along for the sake of his back-channel reports to MC/10 Control. At a time when DEA Nicosia was so frenetically overextended in so many sensitive areas, he needed to stay close to Hurley, and the key to that was to make himself useful.

For that reason, he volunteered to look after Ron Martz, of the *Atlanta Journal-Constitution*, and his 'primary assistant', Lloyd Burchette, when they arrived in Nicosia at the invitation of the DEA to work on a series of reports about international drug trafficking. Coleman knew them already – they had been to see him at the University of Alabama while planning the trip – and so it was natural enough that he should now take on the chore of shepherding them around the island during their stay.

The DIA was also interested in their visit.

In October 1987, at the agency's request, Coleman had looked up his best man, Michael Franks, a.k.a. Schafer, who by then was back in the United States and running a military supply business called Minihawks in the Atlanta area. Soon after his call, they met for a meal at Shoney's Big Boy restaurant where Franks/Schafer introduced him to Burchette, who was then working from home as a one-man security service, and to Jack Terrell, a former operative of Oliver North's in Central America. Affectionately known in the group as 'Colonel Flako', Terrell had acquired his military training by reading army field manuals while imprisoned in Alabama State Penitentrary. All three, it turned out, were close friends of Ron Martz, and it was as a result of this meeting that Martz and Burchette visited Coleman at UAB to solicit his help with their Cyprus trip.

The DIA's interest in them sprang from their association with a Chinese arms dealer named David King, also known as David Loo Choy, who represented the People's Republic of China and had played a part in the North network's illegal supply of arms to the Nicaraguan Contras in association with Monzer al-Kassar.

Though Coleman found out nothing more about him from Franks/Schafer and his friends, he would remember his conversations with them later when, after the Lockerbie disaster, it emerged that US intelligence agencies had intercepted a series of telephone calls to the Iranian Embassy in Beirut from an arms dealer and presumed double agent by the name of David Lovejoy (Loo Choy?) advising the chargé d'affaires of the movements of the American intelligence team who died on Flight 103. (He would also discover later that an alias for David Lovejoy was Michael Franks!)

Even after the scene with El-Jorr, Hurley did nothing to tighten up on security for the NARCOG operation. Indeed, the last straw as far as Coleman was concerned was when Hurley took a group of his Lebanese CIs, whose identities he needed to protect at all costs, to lunch down the street at a café full of officials from the Bulgarian Embassy.

Coleman had had enough. On the morning of 18 May 1988, he hooked up his tape recorder to the telephone at Eurame and called Hurley at the embassy.

'Hello, Mike?'

'Yeah.'

'The situation here is getting out of hand.'

'What do you mean?'

'Well, we've got people coming in and out of here like a train station. Pinko's people bringing in all sorts – I don't know who they are. Lebanese I know are close to the bad guys. Lebanese with names we have in the files, you know what I mean? We had an agreement. It really worries me that we are being exposed like this.'

As always, criticism made Hurley irritable. 'Let me worry about that,' he said. 'You just help Ibrahim get those reports out. I'll deal with the Cypriots. Who's over there now?'

'Just me and Ibrahim. Bitching and complaining as usual. Says he can't do this any more. Wants to quit. He's driving me nuts. Goddamn it, Mike, this isn't why I came back here.'

'You'll just have to do the best you can,' said Hurley.

'And what about protecting security? Me? Mary-Claude is in Lebanon.'

'That's *your* problem. I told you to come alone.'

'Wait a minute.' Coleman was taken aback. 'That was never our deal. We don't even have housing – remember our agreement?'

'That was last year. You know things have changed. Budgets . . .'

'Nice of you to tell me after I get back, after I haul myself over here,' he said angrily. 'Your promises, phone calls to me at the university . . . "Come on back," you said. So I took leave. Now this is a mess. Do you know who these Lebanese are up here?'

'Look, Coleman,' Hurley shouted. 'Don't fuck around with me. Just get those reports finished. Stay on Ibrahim's ass.' He breathed out heavily, and they were both silent for a moment. Then he said, almost apologetically: 'Keep an eye on him. Is he taking anything out of there?'

'How the hell should *I* know? He *could* be. I told you he's making regular visits to the Lebanese Embassy.'

'Yeah, we know about that.'

'Doesn't that *bother* you?' asked Coleman, walking around the desk to see if El-Jorr was eavesdropping, but he was still busy at the computer terminal in the next room. 'Who *is* this guy, Mike? Phony pictures in a US Army uniform. Running around in a Chevy Bronco with Texas licence plates – everyone has to know he's working for you. And that means they know I am, too. That was not our deal, Mike.'

'I'll worry about Ibrahim,' he said. 'Just process the paper.'

'No, I don't like it. This is not what I bargained for. We're going home. I don't need this.' Coleman felt he was working himself up quite convincingly. 'Strange Lebanese walking through here. Crazy Ibrahim bouncing off the walls, appearing at the Lebanese Embassy, and you apparently don't give a damn. This operation is coming apart. The whole fucking island must know about Eurame. I feel exposed, and all you can say is, don't worry about it? Remember the PLO operation that suddenly appeared next door in Larnaca? Who found that? *I* did. Don't you give a shit about security?'

'This is a *law-enforcement* operation,' said Hurley, and Coleman was so astonished he took a moment to reply.

'Do you think people with several tons of TNT know the difference? Or care? Fuck it, Mike. I'm out of here.'

He looked up to see El-Jorr standing in the doorway, looking at the wire that connected the receiver to the tape recorder on his desk.

'Don't fuck with me, Coleman,' Hurley roared, finally losing all patience. 'You'll never work for the government again. The Cypriots are already on my ass about you.'

'About what?'

'You ran off last summer and didn't pay the bill at Filanta.'

'That was *your* bill, goddamn it. I got clearance from Fred to move. The apartment was sweltering. We never got the a/c you promised. All the gear was overheating. My family was suffering from the heat –'

'You forgot the rule, Coleman,' Hurley interrupted. 'Fred doesn't approve budgets. *I* do.'

'You were in the States,' he yelled, genuinely angry now. 'What were we supposed to do? Sit in that hot apartment? Lose the gear? Shut down completely until you got back from leave? That's a lot of crap, Mike. Look, I'm not one of your Lebanese or Cypriots or Iraqi CIs. You requested my services, remember? And I was told, if I didn't like it, I could pull out any time. You talk to whoever you went to to get me involved in this candy-assed operation. Tell 'em – or *I'll* tell 'em when I get back to the States – I'm pulling.

'This is a disaster waiting to happen,' he added, in a prophecy that would come back to haunt him. 'Even your own people think this is bullshit.'

'Don't fuck with me, Coleman.'

There was another brief silence. 'I'm not fucking with you, Mike,' he said tiredly. 'I'm just leaving.'

'Lemme speak to Ibrahim,' said Hurley.

Disconnecting the wire, Coleman pocketed the recorder, handed the receiver to El-Jorr and walked out of the room.

A few minutes later, El-Jorr brought him a cup of coffee. 'You really pissed him off,' he said. 'You can't *do* that. He'll ruin you.'

'What did he say?'

'He wanted to know if you taped the call.'

'So what did you tell him?'

'I said I didn't know.'

Coleman threw the last of his personal things into his briefcase. 'Tell him the truth,' he said.

He encoded a message to Control saying he had decided to abandon the DEA assignment and would await clearance for departure. He had no intention of leaving immediately. Mary-Claude was in Lebanon with Sarah having too good a time with her family for him to wish to cut it short. The DIA was in no hurry either. When Control acknowledged his message, he was told not to leave until he had retrieved the video equipment from Beirut.

But then, on 26 May, everything changed.

When he called Mary-Claude, he learned that Tony Asmar had been fatally injured in a bomb explosion at his office in Karantina.

Coleman's dismay was profound. The unremitting pressure of their role in the politics and violence of Lebanon's civil war had bonded them into a partnership that meant as much to him personally as professionally. For once in the treacherous business of intelligence gathering, the question of mutual trust had been answered on sight. From the start, they had worked together like brothers, with respect and affection, and Coleman's grief was in no way lightened by a suspicion that the killers might have fingered Asmar through him.

To this day, he blames the Drug Enforcement Administration for Asmar's death.

'I blame it on the fact that someone linked me with the US government,' he says. 'And they were able to do that because DEA Nicosia used the Eurame office as a waiting room for unscreened Lebanese coming in from Beirut. My exposure exposed Tony Asmar, and I believe that is why he was killed. I blame the DEA for that.'

The murder was also a heavy blow for American interests in the Middle East. Asmar's death virtually closed down MC/10's operations in Lebanon by breaking off contact with his agents in place. From then on, the US government was blind in its policy-making about the Beirut hostages, for example, because there were no longer any reliable day-to-day reports about their location and condition.

This may well have had a bearing on Washington's decision later in the year to send out the hostage intelligence team, headed by Major Charles McKee of the DIA, who died in the bombing of Flight 103. Indeed, the loss of the Asmar network's continuing surveillance of NARCOG's operations in Lebanon may well have had a bearing on the bombing itself.

After my warnings and reports, and then Tony's murder, [says Coleman] I assumed that somebody would have the CIA on the carpet and close NARCOG down. After all, the US had just lost one of its most valuable assets in the Middle East. Never even crossed my mind that Hurley would carry on like nothing had happened – that he'd keep Eurame open and go on using the pipeline.

After NARCOG's security was blown, that was madness. But knowing the DEA, the attitude was probably that the fucking military was being fucking paranoid as usual and to hell with *them*. And I guess the DIA felt, well, go up in flames if you must but keep away from *us*. We're going to pull our agent and leave you to it. Because as far as I can see, that's all that happened. And then seven months later, everybody's in a jam because 270 innocent people died at Lockerbie – and I'm odd man out.

For three days, while Asmar lingered on in a Beirut hospital, Coleman stayed in the apartment and slept with a gun under his pillow. On 28 May, the DIA video gear arrived from Lebanon, and on the 29th, he flew home alone with it, having been assured that Mary-Claude and Sarah would be protected until such time as they could join him in the States with Mary-Claude's sister Giselle. If Coleman was next on the hit list, they would in any case be safer travelling on their own.

Debriefed in fine detail by Donleavy and DIA agent Neal Miller, largely to see what could be done to patch up a new link with the Asmar network, Coleman was told to keep the video gear pending a resolution of 'this goddamn DEA fuck-up' and to take charge of Syrian George, who, as it happened, had arrived two days earlier on his J-1 visa and was staying at the International House on the University of Alabama campus.

To avoid giving the impression that he had been suckered into coming by US military intelligence, and any reluctance he might feel in consequence to talk freely, Coleman was told to take George home to the family lake house near Auburn, Alabama, and to set him up for questioning by saying that the FBI routinely interviewed all students from the Middle East. Suspecting nothing, Syrian George responded happily to his debriefing by DIA officers posing as FBI agents, and was afterwards turned over to Special Agent Robert Sleigh, of the FBI's C3 counter-intelligence section in Birmingham.

And that was it. When Coleman drove to Atlanta airport on 13 June to meet Mary-Claude, Giselle and Sarah off the plane from Lebanon, he had a distinct suspicion that his usefulness as a DIA agent in the Middle East was at an end. And in September 1988, Donleavy seemed to confirm this by placing him on the 'inactive' list and arranging for him to rejoin the Boy Scouts of America as Director of Marketing and Public Relations for the Chicago Area Council.

By then, the DIA had satisfied itself that Asmar's murder was the work of drug-trafficking elements in the Lebanese Forces, the ultra right-wing Christian faction whose secret war council complex was barely half a block from Asmar's office in Karantina. The Eli Hoobaka group, involved in the 1985 North/Contra/CBN arms deal, were prime suspects, and the likeliest motive, as Coleman had suspected all along, was that a DEA informant in the Lebanese Forces had identified him at Eurame as a friend of Asmar's.

If that was the case, it seemed unlikely that he would ever be able to return safely to the Middle East, but three months later, the DIA showed it still had plans for him.

Appalled by the Flight 103 disaster, perhaps more than most as a result of his recent experiences, but still entirely unaware of any possible connection between his Cyprus assignment and the bombing, Coleman appeared with Tom Brokaw on NBC's 'Nightly News' without realizing that, inactive or not, he was still expected to clear such engagements first with the DIA.

Although he had made it a condition of his NBC appearance that his whereabouts not be disclosed, Neal Miller called next day to say that he had taken over as his handler and to reprimand him for doing the broadcast without permission. For security reasons, he insisted that Coleman change his telephone number and arrange for a new mailing address.

Astonished he had not heard from Donleavy himself about Miller taking over, Coleman sometimes wondered afterwards, in exile, if Donleavy had been a code name for Matthew Kevin Gannon, one of the intelligence agents who had died with Major Charles McKee on Flight 103.

It would have been like Donleavy to try to clear up the Asmar mess himself. And besides the coincidence of his getting a new handler, without explanation, right after the disaster, Coleman could not help remembering the schoolboy password routine he had been given on joining the DIA.

'I'm a friend of Bill Donleavy's . . .' his contacts were supposed to say. 'His friends call him Kevin . . .'

In the end, he decided that, too, was just a coincidence. Gannon's reported age was thirty-four. If he were Donleavy, he would have had to have been at least ten years older than that to have served in Vietnam.

At any rate, Coleman soon realized that Miller's fears for his safety were well-founded. Immediately after the NBC broadcast, his mother received a series of calls on her unlisted telephone number threatening his life and the safety of Mary-Claude's family in Beirut.

After she changed the number, Coleman himself began to get similar calls at the apartment he had taken for the family in Palatine, a commuter train ride from the Boy Scouts' office on

Lake Street, Chicago, although these, too, stopped after he took the DIA's advice and obtained an unlisted number. As his new Control explained, the faction of the Lebanese Forces involved in the aborted Contra arms-for-drugs deal in 1985 were known to have members who were DEA CIs, and they were probably tracking him through credit reports, listing his current address, employer and so forth, obtained through Bank Audi, a Beirut bank with a branch in New York.

With Mary-Claude pregnant again, that was worrying. It was one thing to suspect that he might be on a terrorist hit list, and quite another to realize that Asmar's killers knew where he was. The idea of being sent out again to the Middle East lost what little charm it had left.

Knowing what I do now [he says], I think the DIA was looking for a way to get me back to Beirut to salvage what it could from the Asmar wreck. But what I didn't know, and what Control probably didn't know either, was that by then the DEA, as well as the terrorists, was gunning for me.

You can see how it must have looked. I'd pulled out of NARCOG after a blazing row with Hurley. I'd turned up on NBC talking about Middle East narco-terrorism right after Flight 103 crashed. And now, in January and February 1989, Pan Am investigators start poking around in Frankfurt and Nicosia. I guess at that point DEA assumed I had jumped the reservation and was feeding information to Pan Am. But the fact is, at *that* point, I didn't even *know* I had any information to feed anybody. And even if I *had* known, as a DIA agent the only person I would have told was Control.

With a new mailing address and telephone number, the Colemans tried to get on with their lives. Mary-Claude still found it difficult to match the popular image of America with her experience of it. Living there undermined her self-confidence. The sheer scale of the country, its unpredictability, its generally unstructured attitude to life seemed to call everything she knew into question, turning her inward to the family for security and, for a social life, to other Lebanese who shared her sense of exile.

Being pregnant again helped in the first respect. When Coleman took her to the hospital for a routine scan, he said jocularly:

'What is it? Twins?'

'How did you know?' asked the obstetrician.

Breaking the three-generational run of Lester Knox Colemans, his sons, Joshua and Chad, were born on 16 September 1989, at about the same time as the DIA decided to dust him off for his next assignment.

Now experiencing at first hand with the Boy Scouts of America the role of 'spook-in-residence' that he had observed at a distance during his earlier incarnation as a BSA executive, Coleman was engaged mainly in recruiting local captains of industry as sponsors and committee chairmen. But whereas before he had seen Scouting as a gateway of opportunity to the big time, 20 years on, the movement seemed narrow and provincial somehow, more concerned with preserving an America that was fast slipping away, if it had ever truly existed, than with helping to shape the country's youth to face an uncertain future.

Distracted also by his own uncertain future, he began to spend less time on Lake Street and more on getting back into journalism. If the Lebanese Forces were seriously gunning for him, there was nowhere to hide in any case. And if he surfaced again in the public eye, maybe the DIA would lose interest and decide to retire him permanently. He started to write a regular column for a Chicago weekly newspaper, and embarked on a series of radio interviews, talking about Syria's occupation of Lebanon and its involvement in narco-terrorism.

'After years in investigative reporting, years of exposing deceit, and then, from 1984 to 1990, years of creating it, I was fried,' he remembers. 'All I wanted to do at that point was change direction. I wanted to put all that two-faced stuff behind us and settle down with Mary-Claude to live a half-way normal life. I let it be known I wasn't really interested in going out again, and hoped they'd get the message – that I was finished with it.'

But in New Orleans, he took part in a radio programme with Joe Boohaker, an attorney from Birmingham, Alabama, and the driving force behind the National Alliance of Lebanese Americans (NALA), a group determined to resist the drift of the Bush administration towards *rapprochement* with Syria.

Sharing Coleman's opinion of President Hafez Assad as the evil genius of state-sponsored terrorism, NALA had been formed to press for the withdrawal of Syrian and Israeli troops from Lebanon and for the restoration of democracy under the aegis of General Michel Aoun, who, in September 1988, had been appointed head of an interim military government in Beirut by outgoing President Amin Gemayel.

An austere Maronite Christian who commanded the loyalty of both Christian and Muslim brigades in the US-trained and equipped Lebanese Army, Aoun had many friends in the Pentagon but none in the State Department, which saw his ambition to let the Lebanese choose their own government without foreign interference as a threat to America's interests.

The fact that Aoun's position also commanded wide popular support among Lebanese otherwise determined to kill one another on sight merely reinforced his reputation in Washington as a troublemaker. And the Bush administration was confirmed in this judgment when, after it had refused to recognize his military government, Aoun turned to Iraq for help against the Syrians and the ultra-right Christian militias. As far as the State Department was concerned, Aoun was now clearly an obstacle to a satisfactory peace settlement in Lebanon – satisfactory, that is, to the United States, Israel and Syria.

Finding they had much in common, Coleman and Boohaker arranged to meet after the broadcast, and their subsequent friendship would doubtless have flourished anyway, even if the DIA had *not* pulled Coleman's string in the autumn of 1989 and instructed him to cultivate the connection.

The agency now wanted him back in Lebanon for two reasons. The first, and hardest to resist, was that Charles Frezeli, another MC/10 agent, had just been assassinated in Beirut, leaving three others cut off from contact who had to be brought out before they, too, were killed or induced to talk.

The second reason, strategically more important, was that the Pentagon wanted a closer look at what was going on between Aoun and Saddam Hussein. There were signs that Iraq was withdrawing the military support it had sent in to bolster the Lebanese Army against the Syrians, and the reasons for this could be established more discreetly in Beirut than in Baghdad.

In November 1989, Coleman reluctantly agreed to resign his commission with the Boy Scouts of America, giving as his reason that he was returning to journalism with a job in Germany. To flesh out the story, the DIA provided him with a German mailing address, Postfach 1151, Geilhausen 6460, from which all correspondence, including anything from the DIA, would be readdressed to Coleman's maildrop in Barrington, Illinois.

The next move, planned at a series of meetings with Control at the Washington Court hotel in Washington, D.C., was to use the Boohaker connection to worm his way into the heart of General Aoun's constituency in the United States as a stepping stone to the general himself.

Boohaker's NALA was one of several groups affiliated to the national Council of Lebanese-American Organizations (CLAO) headed by Joseph Esseff, of Los Angeles, California, whose wife Pat and brother, Monsignor John Esseff, ran the CLAO's associated relief operation, Mission to Lebanon. A Roman Catholic priest who had been in charge of the church's Beirut aid mission to orphans and refugees in the Middle East while Coleman was out there, Msgr Esseff had returned to the US to become director of the Pontifical Mission Aid Societies, responsible for Catholic aid and refugee work globally.

In January 1990, Boohaker introduced Coleman to the Esseffs in California, and at Joe Esseff's suggestion, Coleman took on the job of freelance public relations adviser and lobbyist for the CLAO. In this capacity, he attended meetings around the country to organize opposition to American attempts to remove Aoun from office in favour of a new Syrian-backed president, and later that month conferred in New York with Dr Muhamad Mugraby, Aoun's envoy to the United Nations, and the consul general for Lebanon, Victor Bitar.

Present at that meeting was Walid Maroni, officially an Iraqi member of the UN press corps, who told them that his government was prepared to support the CLAO financially as well as in other ways. Afterwards, Coleman urged his new colleagues to reject this poisoned chalice, but only the Esseffs heeded his advice. Unable to carry the rest of the council with him, Joe Esseff would later resign the chairmanship of the CLAO in disgust, but meanwhile, on 3 March, he took Coleman to Paris to introduce him to Aoun's senior advisers.

At 32 Rue St Honoré, they met with Raymond Eddi, a distinguished Lebanese parliamentarian in exile, and Marcel Boutros, Aoun's personal envoy, who invited Coleman to meet the general himself at the presidential palace in Baabda. When Coleman encoded a message to this effect to Control, he was instructed to conclude the arrangements at once, if possible before he left. He was then to return home at once via Montreal, using his Thomas Leavy identity on re-entering the United States so as to avoid any tell-tale entry stamp in his passport.

On 9 March, Coleman received a detailed encrypted message from Control setting up Operation Shakespeare, clearing his visit to Lebanon and instructing him to carry out the mission as Thomas Leavy, of Westinghouse Group W News.

The reason for this was that his real name was probably known to the Syrian forces controlling Beirut airport, and certainly to the pro-Syrian Christian Lebanese Forces under Shamir Geagea who controlled the port of Jounieh and had already threatened his life after the NBC broadcast.

Coleman was to proceed to Israel, cross into Lebanon, escorted by the Israeli-backed South Lebanese Army, and from there drive to Baabda under the protection of pro-Aoun elements in the Druze faction. Satisfied that these arrangements were as safe as any in the circumstances, Coleman decided to beef up his cover by inviting Peter Arnett, Cable News Network's correspondent in Jerusalem, to join him in interviewing the general – without, of course, revealing his identity as an intelligence agent or even suggesting that there might be a hidden motive for the visit.

On 16 March, Coleman was summoned to Washington for a final briefing and to complete his Thomas Leavy documentation. After an overnight stay at the Washington Court hotel (at the government rate as the reservation had been made by the Pentagon), he obtained a Washington driver's licence in the name of Leavy and was given a Social Security card (no. 326–84–2972) in the same name.

He remembers asking Control why he was not also given a Thomas Leavy passport, and being told that, as there was enough time for him to go through normal channels to get one, a legitimate passport was always a safer bet. Like the birth certificate, it would come in handy for future missions.

'If I survive *this* one,' he said, still uneasy about it, and Control had laughed dutifully.

Funds for Operation Shakespeare had been paid into Barclays Bank, Gibraltar, he said – Account No. 35078565 – and when the mission was over, the Colemans were to establish residence in Spain. The Koldon Moving and Storage Company should therefore ship their household and personal effects to Eglin Airforce Base in Florida, after which the Pentagon would take care of their delivery to a US base near Cadiz. As soon as the passport came through, Coleman should wait for the first convenient lull in the fighting in Beirut and then leave immediately. General Aoun was then engaged with the Syrians on the one hand and Shamir Geagea's Christian Lebanese Forces on the other.

On 26 March, back in Chicago, Coleman applied for a US passport in the name of Thomas J. Leavy, using the birth certificate given him by the CIA in 1982 and the documents issued in Washington. He then took the family south to Alabama for a short vacation before they all left the country. It had been agreed that Mary-Claude and the children would make their way independently to Spain, and wait for him to join them there.

On 12 April, Coleman went over to the courthouse in Jefferson County, Alabama, and for a $5 fee, legally changed his name to Thomas Leavy. He did this on the advice of his father, who shared his misgivings about travelling on a passport in that name. If anything happened to him during the mission, Coleman was worried there might be a problem in claiming on life insurance policies taken out in his real name. To make certain Mary-Claude and the children would have enough money to live on if any such problem arose, he took out some short-term life insurance in the name of Thomas Leavy.

But on 2 May, three armed FBI agents took Coleman into custody for 'wilfully and knowingly making a false statement in an application for a passport', and threw him into Mobile City Jail.

— XV —

Even after six months, it still felt like a mistake. At the back of his mind, he still half-expected Control to call one day and say the Justice Department had fouled up as usual but everything was all right now, that it was time to send him out again.

He didn't blame the DIA for what had happened, or for fading from sight when it did. Control had told him often enough that the agency would never surface in his defence if anything went wrong. If it acknowledged his existence, it would also have to acknowledge its *own* existence, thereby inviting precisely the attention it had to avoid. To do its job properly, the DIA needed to remain invisible.

Even so . . . Coleman knew the power it could exercise behind the scenes, and went on hoping through the summer of 1990 that Control would somehow find the right strings to pull. The appearance of Marshall Lee Miller to handle his defence against the passport violation charge had seemed more than just providential. By introducing him to Pan Am's lawyers before bowing out again, Miller had broken Coleman's alarming sense of isolation and put him in touch with at least a measure of the support he needed, support that the DIA itself was unable to give.

And he needed all the encouragement he could get, for the threats had started again. Between June and September, his mother, Margie Coleman, in Birmingham, Alabama, received about 20 calls on her unlisted phone from men threatening to kill her son, to kidnap his wife and children and to harm her for taking them in. An elderly lady in doubtful health, she was terrified, particularly when the calls continued after her unlisted number was changed. From what was said, and the callers' apparent familiarity with his work in Cyprus, Coleman had little doubt that they were confidential informants of the Drug Enforcement Administration.

On 12 June, this impression was reinforced by a call from the

Special Agent in Charge of the DEA's Birmingham field office, who strongly recommended that he plead guilty to the passport violation charge and at all costs 'don't get the DEA involved in your case'.

Angry now, Coleman travelled alone to Chicago on 21 June and, unrepresented, pleaded not guilty to the charge before Chief Judge James B. Moran after waiving a formal reading of the indictment.

> He asked me, 'Where's your attorney?' [Coleman recalls]. So I said, 'I don't have an attorney, your honour. I came here to plead not guilty. Don't need an attorney for that.' So the hearing was over in two minutes. I picked up my briefcase, started out the door and asked the FBI agent on the case to see me downstairs to a cab because I didn't feel very safe in Chicago. He wanted to know why, so I asked him how much he knew about me. 'Well, we know a lot,' he said. 'But there's a lot more we'd *like* to know.' 'Me, too,' I said. 'But I can't tell you anything. And I'm sorry about that because we could probably settle this thing in twenty minutes.'

His display of independence seemed to make matters worse. The telephone threats became more frequent; he and Mary-Claude were often followed when they went out, together or separately, and word began to filter back that FBI agents were questioning his friends, neighbours and former associates.

On the other hand, the government seemed in no particular hurry to press its charges against him. At a case status hearing on 17 August, the court appointed a public defender to represent him and then adjourned the proceedings until a further status hearing on 3 January 1991, at which time a trial date would be set. As Coleman discovered later, it was not uncommon for the Justice Department to leave a case dangling over the head of a former government employee whom it wished to intimidate.

What finally persuaded him that, without allies or resources, he would never escape its clutches was the government's refusal to produce any of the material he needed for his defence, even his DEA file. When his court-appointed attorney, Michael Deutsch, filed a discovery motion on 30 August for documents that might show Coleman had been acting under orders when he applied for the Thomas Leavy passport, the DEA, the DIA and the CIA all declined to comply on grounds of national security.

By now he was under no illusions about the reason for the

frame-up. Though nobody on the government side had shown his hand, it was hardly necessary. This was an obvious attempt to secure his silence in return for a plea-bargain and suspended sentence on the passport charge. If that failed, the next move would probably be to a Federal penitentiary where a fight in the yard or a sudden bout of pneumonia would secure his silence for good.

They could also get at him through his wife and children, as the threatening phone calls had made plain. Down to his last few hundred dollars, and with nothing but the good offices of a public defender standing between him and the octopus, it was time to evacuate the hostages. And to tell Pan Am what he knew.

Nobody else seemed to be interested. None of the agencies involved in the official investigation of the Flight 103 bombing, either British or American, had even attempted to question him about the activities he had observed on Cyprus, despite all the rumours of the DEA's involvement.

To save his neck and protect his family was perhaps not the noblest of motives for coming forward as a witness, but if the DEA had not sought to frame him under the misapprehension that he was feeding information to Pan Am and the media, and if the DIA had not lacked the will to protect him behind the scenes, the idea of coming forward would never have crossed his mind at all – indeed, he might never even have known that he had a contribution to make to the Lockerbie investigation.

As a secret agent of the Defense Intelligence Agency, his first, last and only duty would have been, as always, to the US government. But with his back to the wall, and with the octopus bent on destroying him through no fault of his own, his first, last and only duty was to his family. And yet he was still reluctant to make public his connection with the DIA.

By now he was convinced that it had merely acquiesced in the frame-up *after* his arrest. The likeliest explanation seemed to be that, in the autumn of 1986, Control had indicated to the DEA that Coleman had worked for the DIA in the past but, as he was no longer active, the agency had no objection to his taking up a consultant's job with Hurley on Cyprus.

As Coleman's real job was to file back-channel reports on the operations of DEA Nicosia, the DIA was hardly likely to have told Hurley that they were lending him a full-time agent. They never revealed the identity of their agents to anybody in any case.

As far as the DEA was concerned, therefore, Coleman had none of the status or protection of being a government agent; he was a civilian consultant on a short-term contract who, as instructed, and as a matter of courtesy, had provided the Cyprus country office with a copy of his alternative identity papers.

Without Coleman's knowledge, and without consulting the DIA (on this basis, they had no reason to do so), either Hurley or Dany Habib had subsequently used those papers – in particular, the copy they had taken of Coleman's Thomas Leavy birth certificate – to obtain a passport for one of their own people in Egypt, thus cocking the trigger for a possible violation alert when Coleman also applied for a passport in that name two years later.

No matter how paranoid he felt from time to time about the DIA, Coleman could not conceive that Control would have told him to get hold of a legitimate Thomas Leavy passport for Operation Shakespeare knowing in advance that it would blow the mission and lead to his arrest. He could only assume that, being unaware of his true status as a DIA agent, the DEA and its oversight agency, the FBI, had seen him as a soft target, and framed the passport violation charge as a means of silencing an awkward witness without realizing who he was or the damage they were doing.

He could even appreciate how tricky a situation this must have been for the DIA, although it did little to ease his sense of injury. The Pentagon would have been furious at losing an agent as well as a major mission, but there was little or nothing it could say or do to put things right without acknowledging that Coleman was an agent and thereby admitting that, for the better part of two years, the DIA had been spying, not on the country's official enemies, but on other agencies of the United States government.

On 11 September, Coleman petitioned the US District Court, Northern District of Illinois, Eastern Division, for a change in his bail conditions. To support himself and his family, now on the edge of penury, he urgently needed to resume his occupation as a freelance journalist specializing in Middle Eastern affairs, and for that, he had to be able to travel.

As the prosecution still seemed in no hurry to have a trial date set, Chief Judge Moran overruled the government's objections and ordered that Coleman's legal passport be returned, subject to his giving the prosecutor two weeks' notice of his intention to leave the country and to his reporting in to his pre-trial services officer every other week by telephone.

Two weeks later, Coleman arrived in Gibraltar to clear out the funds standing to his credit at Barclays Bank. He felt the government owed him that much at least – and as the DIA had not seen fit to close the account, perhaps Control thought so, too. At any rate, he now had a little breathing space. As the DEA was plainly out to get him, and had blocked all access to the files he needed to clear himself, the only avenue open to him was to work with Pan Am, in the common interest of getting at the truth, using his training and experience to piece together the best defence he could.

But at a distance, and with some of the pressure off, Coleman began to wonder how much difference it would make if he did. The charge was such an obvious frame-up that he had to ask himself if there had ever been any intention to try him on it.

The central problem for the government was the central element in its case – the Thomas Leavy birth certificate. If the DEA *had* used it to provide a cover identity for somebody in Egypt, it could hardly admit that in open court or explain how it had come by the certificate in the first place. And yet, without showing prior use, how could the prosecution explain why Coleman's application for a passport in that name had alerted the passport office to a possible violation?

Compounding the problem was the fact that, as far as Coleman knew, no such person as Thomas Leavy had ever existed. How, then, could the government explain why he came to be in possession of a genuine birth certificate for a non-existent person without embarrassing the CIA, which had given it to him in the first place? And if the government *had* provided it for his use, why was it now prosecuting him for using it?

With so many awkward questions hanging over the case, Coleman found it hard to imagine that the government would take it into court – and was not at all reassured by the thought. If the charge had been framed merely to intimidate, when it failed to do so, the octopus would presumably try something else. Perhaps something more drastic.

So far, Coleman's meetings with Pan Am's attorneys had been informal, and the information he provided fairly basic, but while poking about in Europe, he became aware that somebody else, either within the DEA or close to it, was also talking knowledgeably about a link between DEA Nicosia and the bombing of Flight 103.

Based on information from some source within the government, both ABC and NBC were researching stories on the DEA connection [Coleman remembers]. ABC tracked me down after seeing some of the papers in my case and wanted to know if I could confirm what they'd been told. Oddly enough, one of Pierre Salinger's researchers, Linda Mack, while trying to check me out, had talked to another of their staffers, David Mills – the former *Newsweek* photographer who'd looked me up on Cyprus in 1987 and sold some pictures to Hurley. Anyway, I met Salinger in London to go over the story with him and confirmed those parts of it I knew to be true. He was just checking his facts with me. He had the story already.

So did NBC. Again, I don't know where they got their information from but I confirmed that the DEA had been running controlled deliveries through Cyprus while I was there and that its operations had been wide open from a security point of view. Brian Ross wanted me to go on camera to say so, but I refused. I figured the last interview I'd given them, right after the bombing of Flight 103, had probably been the root cause of why my life had been turned inside out, and I wasn't looking for any *more* trouble.

Neither Salinger nor Ross knew of my role in Cyprus as a DIA agent, and I certainly didn't tell them. Nor did their broadcasts attribute any part of the story to me – there was no reason for them to do that because I'd told them nothing they didn't already know. But I should have guessed that Hurley and his crowd would again put two and two together and make 22. *Catch 22.*

After talking to the Pan Am legal team in London, I flew back to the States to be with my family, and a few weeks later, the DEA *did* do something more drastic. Apparently convinced that *I* was behind the ABC and NBC stories and the media follow-up around the world, they blew my cover in a television broadcast that also went out around the world. They set me up as a target. And my wife and babies, too.

On the second anniversary of the Lockerbie disaster, a few days after Pan Am obtained leave to file its third-party suit against the US government, Steven Emerson aired an 'exclusive' on Cable News Network about the wave of speculation linking the DEA with the bombing of Flight 103.

Favoured with the inside story of the Fawaz Younis kidnapping and other government 'exclusives', Emerson's special relationship with Federal law-enforcement agencies was again on display when he quoted unnamed Washington sources to the effect that allegations of DEA involvement in the Lockerbie disaster had been traced to one Lester Knox Coleman, a 'disgruntled former DEA confidential informant who was terminated'.

The terminology was interesting. 'Confidential informant', like 'cooperating individual', usually means that the snitch in question was, or is, engaged in drug trafficking and cooperating with the DEA in order to avoid imprisonment. Anything he has to say, therefore, even under oath, needs to be taken with a pinch of salt. The fact that Coleman was also said to have been 'terminated' further underlined the notion of his unreliability by suggesting that, even as a snitch, he was not to be believed.

More serious from the point of view of his personal safety, by blowing his cover and stressing that he no longer enjoyed the government's protection, the CNN broadcast, in effect, declared open season on Lester Coleman. It all but invited every cop-hating drug freak, every aggrieved drugs trafficker from the Bekaa Valley to Los Angeles, every ultra-right, gun-running, Contra-supporting machismo addict, and every thwarted narco-terrorist or Muslim extremist looking for a safe or cheap revenge to 'terminate' him also.

CNN also showed Coleman's picture.

From then on, any semblance of normal life became impossible. Without resources, unable to earn a living, at the mercy of at least two Federal agencies determined to silence him by one means or another, and now set up as a government-approved target for any stray kook or fanatic, Coleman had to find a more defensible position.

Emerson's story sent everybody into a tailspin [he says], including Mary-Claude's family in Lebanon. I never saw the broadcast, but it seemed to be a clear attempt to discredit me. There was even a suggestion that I was one of Juval Aviv's sources for the Interfor Report, although I had never met the man or even *seen* his report at that point.

The government's obvious intention was to identify me as the main source of all the criticism and speculation running counter to the official line on Flight 103 and then to destroy me. Or, if that failed, to destroy my credibility. So I said, Screw this – I'm getting us out of here. And judging by the calls we got after the programme, there wasn't much time.

The worst were those with Arab accents. 'Your son is dead.' 'We know where your children are.' 'If he ever comes to Lebanon, he's a dead man.' 'We're going to kill his wife's family.' 'We're going to take Sarah, grind her up and send her back as hamburger meat.' Stuff like that. And they weren't kidding. I know these people. They were working themselves up to do it. So I set up a little deception plan, charged my credit cards to the limit and smuggled Mary-Claude and the children out to Europe. I was pretty well broke by then, but thanks to the good offices of Msgr John Esseff, they were taken in by the Sisters of Charity, the Most Reverend Mother Teresa's order, who hid them out in a convent in Spain.

Now I had to do something about Mary-Claude's family, because after Emerson's broadcast, they started getting calls as well. And you don't fool with those because things are on a shorter fuse in Beirut. They didn't have any money either at this point, so to get them out, I had to slip back into the States without anybody knowing and sell off everything we owned – all the furniture and household stuff. Even so, it was only just enough. And there we were. Hiding out in Europe. Penniless, homeless and exhausted. But at least we were still alive.

Though still seriously at risk.

Careful to avoid being declared a fugitive, Coleman had kept up the fortnightly calls to his pre-trial services officer in Chicago, reporting truthfully but contriving to leave his precise whereabouts in doubt. A trial date had finally been set for 17 June 1991, but given the obvious flimsiness of the case, he was still concerned that somebody within the DEA might be tempted into direct action. Its army of lowlife informants was not short of potential assassins. And for all he knew, pro-Syrian elements, the Lebanese Forces and other narco-terrorist groups were also still looking to revenge themselves for the damage that he and the Asmar cell had done to their drugs, arms and hostage-taking operations in Beirut.

The Colemans needed sanctuary.

On 17 April 1991, he met Pan Am's legal team for five days in Brussels. Until his family was safe, he had declined to make any formal statement, but now he went with them to the American Embassy and swore out an affidavit about what he had seen as a DIA agent assigned to DEA NARCOG, Nicosia.

He also described a call he had made later to his friend Hartmut Mayer of the BKA asking him if he knew how the bomb had been put aboard Flight 103. As he was not involved in the investigation, Mayer had put him in touch with a colleague, Bert Pinsdorf, in Germany, who, in answer to the same question, said the 'BKA had serious concerns that the drug-sting operation originating in Cyprus had caused the bomb to be placed on the Pan Am plane.'

Using a new set of genuine Thomas Leavy documents based on his legal name change – the last thing he supposed the Federal authorities would be on the lookout for – Coleman then slipped back into the States, via Canada, for what he felt in his bones was probably the last time he would see his father and his country. After spending a few weeks there, he flew to Frankfurt on 29 May, where he rejoined Mary-Claude and the children, who had meanwhile been looked after by Mother Teresa's Sisters of Charity.

From Germany, they travelled by train to Sweden, where he applied for asylum, the first American citizen to do so since the Vietnam War.

— XVI —

The government's attempt to silence Coleman coincided with an attempt to intimidate Pan Am's counsel, by now almost the only serious challenger left to the official version of events before and after Lockerbie.

On 20 March 1991, three months after James Shaughnessy had filed suit against the US government, claiming it was culpable in the Flight 103 disaster, the Justice Department responded with a motion seeking either dismissal of the third-party action or summary judgment on the claim.

The sting was in an accompanying memorandum which recommended darkly that 'substantial' financial sanctions should be imposed on Shaughnessy and his law firm for daring to suggest the government was in any way at fault, and for what it alleged was a deliberate abuse of court procedures.

At this point, after successfully stone-walling all attempts to get at the evidence and saddling the airline's insurers with legal and investigation costs running into many millions of dollars, the government probably expected Pan Am to cut its losses: to abandon its own inquiries into the disaster and meet whatever level of compensation was awarded to the victims' families, rather than risk further millions of dollars in costs and sanctions, only to have to pay up in the end anyway.

And no doubt, if Pan Am, its underwriters and attorneys *had* mounted the third-party suit as a diversionary move, the calculation would have proved correct: for a commercial enterprise, however well funded, to have knowingly persevered with a lost cause against the Federal government, with its virtually limitless financial and legal resources, would have been, not just irrational, but in the insurance business, inconceivable. (It was even less likely in this case because, on 8 January 1991, Pan Am had finally crash-landed into bankruptcy.)

But the suit was neither a diversion *nor* a lost cause. It was based on the conviction that everybody but the guilty had something to gain from getting at the truth. On 22 April 1991, Shaughnessy went to the barricades with Lester Coleman's affidavit to oppose the government's motion.

The stakes were now very high. Shaughnessy had to satisfy the court that Pan Am's third-party suit had been filed, not just in good faith but on sufficient grounds to justify a reasonable expectation that the case could be won if the government were ordered to open its files.

He began his written argument by pointing out that 'the crash of Flight 103 was caused by a dastardly and cowardly criminal act of mass murder. That criminal act was not targeted at Pan Am, but at the United States.'

The reminder was necessary because, in that sense, Pan Am was also a victim of the attack and therefore entitled to whatever assistance the authorities could provide. As Shaughnessy observed, 'virtually all relevant discovery concerning prior threats to Pan Am Flight 103 and the methods by which the bomb was placed on that flight are in the exclusive custody of the government.' Besides controlling most of the witnesses, the government also held all the documents necessary to establish the facts, and 'for this reason alone', he argued, 'the government's motion should be denied until third-party plaintiffs obtain complete discovery.'

Shaughnessy's affidavit went on to review Pan Am's unavailing attempts to subpoena the records it needed, first, to prepare a defence against the negligence suits filed by the victims' families, and then to pursue its own claims against the government. Blocked for 18 months by the government's refusal to open its files and the court's refusal to compel discovery, Shaughnessy described how he had attempted to secure the documents by another route, by asking for them under the Freedom of Information Act.

In its reply, the National Security Agency had supplied copies of previous requests for the same documents, notably from Tom Foster of the *Syracuse Post Standard* and Emma Gilbey of the American Broadcasting Company, and copies of its response in each case. As these requests had employed virtually the same language as Shaughnessy had used in his original subpoenas, filed in September 1989, they added nothing to the pool, but the NSA's response to them was revealing.

In its reply to Foster and Gilbey, the agency stated that 'documents responsive to items 1, 3 and 4 of your request were located in our search for records.'

These items had to do, respectively, with prior warnings of terrorist attacks against American airliners at Frankfurt airport; with who put the bomb aboard the aircraft and how and when they did it, and with contraband shipments through Frankfurt airport, including Pan Am's baggage area.

Copies of the documents located by the NSA were not supplied, however, for reasons of 'statutory privilege' and 'state secrets'.

They were not supplied to Pan Am either, although included in the NSA's reponse to Shaughnessy's request was an internal NSA memorandum which read: 'These FOIA requests for documents related to the bombing of Pan Am Flight 103 include the specific items requested in the subpoena by Pan Am in connection with a civil suit against the airline by the families of victims of the bombing ... Documents related to items 1, 3 and 4 of the request were located.'

As Shaughnessy pointed out in his affidavit, this admission conflicted sharply with the government's denial that it had any knowledge or evidence of prior threats or warnings of terrorist attack.

'Once again,' he declared, 'one is led to the question: what is going on here? I respectfully submit that the answer lies in the documents – documents which the government has told this court do not exist but which the NSA, in response to the Foster and Gilbey FOIA requests, admitted *do* exist, and which the government has steadfastly refused to produce.'

The affidavit then addressed itself to the role of Juval Aviv, whose Interfor Report had inspired Pan Am's original subpoenas but who later proved an embarrassment when Magistrate Judge Allyne Ross found that his denial of having leaked its findings was 'not credible'.

'The principal result of the report,' complained Shaughnessy, 'has been that plaintiffs' counsel [acting for the families] and the government have consistently characterized everything that third-party plaintiffs have done since September 15, 1989 [the date of the original subpoenas] as being based on the "discredited" Aviv report. Indeed, the government has sought, both in open court and on this motion, to tar third-party plaintiffs with basing their third-party complaint exclusively on the Aviv report. However, Mr Aviv and his company resigned as investigators for me in June, 1990, and stopped doing any investigative work long before then.'

After touching on the Lockerbie investigators' curious lack of interest in the results of the polygraph examination of the three Pan Am baggage handlers in Frankfurt, the Shaughnessy affidavit turned next to a review of the information Pan Am had obtained from other sources in support of its claims.

The information third-party plaintiffs have been able to gather, despite the government's stone-walling [he wrote] 'indicates that the government knew of plans to bomb a Pan Am flight out of Frankfurt during December, 1988, and even may have known that Flight 103 was the target. In addition, the information indicates that the terrorists used a government undercover heroin operation to place the bomb on Flight 103 . . .

While general warnings of the risk of terrorist attacks on American targets in reprisal for the shootdown of the Iranian airliner were passed on to United States flag carriers by the FAA, the government was in possession of far more specific information than the FAA disclosed. In early December, 1988, the Israeli Defense Forces (the IDF) raided a base used by Palestinian terrorist forces in Lebanon and captured documents which disclosed plans to attack and bomb a Pan Am flight in December, 1988 . . . I have been told by four separate sources that this information was passed to the government.

His affidavit also cited the telephone intercepts of calls made by David Lovejoy to the Iranian Embassy in Beirut about the movements of the American agents who died in the crash as a further indication that the government knew from more than one source that Flight 103 would be the target of a terrorist attack 'yet failed to disclose this information to Pan Am'.

This brought him to Pan Am's claim for relief on the grounds that the government had also been negligent in supervising DEA's controlled deliveries of heroin through Frankfurt airport, an operation 'utilizing known criminals, terrorists and terrorist sympathizers'.

After the NBC and ABC broadcasts of 30 and 31 October 1990, Stephen H. Greene, the DEA's assistant administrator, operations division, had appeared before a congressional subcommittee to make a statement about the agency's activities in Cyprus. Having explained how controlled deliveries work, he stated, on oath, that the DEA had no ongoing operation in Europe 'during or immediately before December 1988' that 'even remotely resembled the one described in the media reports'.

Noting this denial, the Shaughnessy affidavit went on to list four cases involving Lebanese drug traffickers that the government had prosecuted in the Eastern District of Virginia *before* Greene's subcommittee appearance. In each case, the evidence had been obtained as a result of controlled deliveries 'using commercial airline facilities and connections in Frankfurt'. One of those convicted had been charged with running 'a heroin laboratory and trafficking operation in the Bekaa Valley' and 'had often shipped heroin to the United States using a shipping company in Cyprus'.

In all four cases, a key element in the prosecution had been a sworn affidavit by DEA Special Agent Hollis Williams, who described how checked baggage containing narcotics was shipped through Frankfurt airport en route from Lebanon to Detroit, where the defendants 'were major sources of supply for heroin'.

In short, Shaughnessy went on, the DEA admitted it had run controlled deliveries through Frankfurt *prior* to 21 December 1988, and had continued to do so during 1989, but supposedly not 'during or immediately before December 1988'.

'I respectfully submit,' he wrote, 'that the DEA's denial is incredulous [sic]. Moreover, I further respectfully submit that, based upon the other information contained below, it is simply false.'

The 'other information' included reports about the involvement of Turkish workers in placing the bomb aboard Flight 103, and the deposition of Michael F. Jones, of Pan Am Corporate Security in London, describing his conversation with Phillip Connelly, assistant chief investigation officer of H.M. Customs and Excise, eight days after the crash. (Pan Am had sought to obtain a deposition from Connelly himself but the British government had advised the court that, under UK law, government employees could not be compelled to testify. Later on, Connelly would dispute Jones's account of their conversation, but by then the Flight 103 investigation had become a political football.)

Shaughnessy's hammer in nailing the DEA's denial was the affidavit of Lester K. Coleman, sworn to on 17 April 1991. Here was direct, first-hand testimony about the DEA's activities in the Middle East that flatly contradicted the agency's public statements in almost every particular, and which drew attention to its glaring lapses in security while dealing with informants and others known to be associated with terrorist groups.

> I respectfully submit [concluded Shaughnessy] that the information disclosed above and in the accompanying Coleman affidavit amply demonstrates that third-party plaintiffs have a valid basis for each of their claims against the government. I also respectfully submit, that information demonstrates that the government has, at the very least, been less than candid . . . If the government wants this court, third-party plaintiffs and the public to believe that there is no basis for third-party plaintiffs' claims, then it should open itself up to complete and candid discovery.
>
> If the government has nothing to hide, then why is it hiding?
>
> I respectfully submit that, despite the various grounds asserted by the government thus far, the government is hiding because there was a foul-up within the government. The government knows that it, and only it, could have prevented the murder of 270 people, but it is politically impossible for the government ever to admit that fact or to produce evidence from which that fact could be proven or inferred.

Strong stuff. Which evoked a strong – and unexpected – response.

The Coleman affidavit, describing what he had seen and done while seconded to DEA Nicosia, was precisely what the government had feared and tried so ineptly to avoid. Having failed to silence him, it could now either acknowledge the truth or redouble its efforts to discredit him, a choice that detained the DEA as briefly as it did Coleman. Knowing the government's overwhelming priority would be to brand him a liar, he had not expected the DIA to be of much help.

'I thought there was no way in hell I would ever be able to verify the fact that I was a Defense Intelligence agent,' he recalls. 'Standard operating practice is complete disavowal – that had been made clear from the start. No record would be held of my name and affiliation with the agency. I was Benjamin B – and all the subpoenas in the world would find no trace of any Lester K. Coleman. I remember telling Shaughnessy I would never be able to prove I had worked for them, but then they did it *for* me.'

On 7 June 1991, in response to Shaughnessy's affidavit, the government produced two significant declarations attacking Coleman's testimony. The first was sworn to by Micheal Hurley, former DEA

TRAIL OF THE OCTOPUS

attaché to the American Embassy in Cyprus, and the other by Lieutenant-Colonel Terry E. Bathen, assistant general counsel to the Defense Intelligence Agency.

Predictably, in the light of the DEA-inspired broadcast on CNN, Hurley's declaration made as little as possible of Coleman's association with DEA Nicosia. The gist of it was that he had been taken on as a DEA 'cooperating individual' on 31 January 1986, after he claimed he could establish a network of subsources to collect data on opium production in Lebanon. According to Hurley, Coleman received the standard admonitions given to all DEA CIs and 'was further advised that he had no official status, implied or otherwise, as agent or employee of DEA'.

Between then and 9 April 1986, he was paid $4000 for information and expenses, after which Hurley received a postcard from Coleman in Switzerland, dated 19 April, which 'indicated that his DEA CI number was retired.' Nevertheless, he was not 'deactivated' until 1 November, when Hurley learned he had returned to the United States.

Though denying that the DEA asked the DIA for Coleman's help during the 1987 opium-growing season, Hurley admitted Coleman was 'reactivated' as a 'cooperating individual' on 20 February 1987, to carry on as before, providing strategic intelligence information and videotape coverage of Lebanese narcotics trafficking. From then until 11 August 1987, he was paid $53,070 for information and expenses, most of which 'was to be paid to Coleman's subsources for the information which they provided . . .'

According to Hurley, he made a final payment of $6900 to Coleman on that date in the presence of a 'cameraman/subsource' who was owed $5500 for his work. Instead of giving him cash, Coleman paid him by cheque. 'In my presence,' stated Hurley, 'Coleman told the cameraman/subsource that they would go to his bank upon returning to the United States later that month, where he could get the cheque cashed.'

But the following spring, the declaration went on, Hurley heard from the cameraman/subsource that the cheque had been returned for 'not sufficient funds'. He also 'received information that Coleman may have approached the *Soldier of Fortune* magazine, trying to sell information which he had specifically collected for DEA'.

Nevertheless, after Hurley 'received assurances from Coleman that he did not provide any DEA information to any person/group outside the DEA', he was reactivated for the new opium-growing season in February 1988, at which time he 'was representing himself as Director of International Studies at the University of Alabama . . . I directed Coleman to travel alone, without his wife and child, and to stay in a furnished apartment which had been specifically designated for Coleman's use.'

Later on, according to the declaration, Hurley discovered that Coleman had not only brought Mary-Claude and Sarah but had 'represented himself as a DEA/US Embassy employee in order to secure an outside apartment for himself and his family'. In the period from his arrival until 11 May, he was paid a further $4500 for information and expenses, but 'in May 1988, Coleman was deactivated as a cooperating individual by DEA for unsatisfactory behavior . . .

'The incidents which led to Coleman's deactivation included his illegal and less than forthright behavior with one of his camera-men/sub-sources, his outstanding arrest warrant that the Cyprus Police had issued for him and the articles that appeared in *Soldier of Fortune* magazine which contained information which Coleman had obtained for DEA.'

The arrest warrant 'stemmed from Coleman's failure to reimburse his landlord in Cyprus for the international telephone calls which he incurred while living in the apartment with his wife and child. The bills were for several thousand dollars.' As a result of these charges, he said, Coleman was declared an undesirable and banned from entry into Cyprus.

Turning then to the substance of Coleman's affidavit, Hurley declared, on oath, that

> . . . during the period of time that I was the DEA country attaché in Cyprus [1984 to 1990], the DEA Nicosia Country Office was not involved in any controlled deliveries of heroin either originating in or transiting Cyprus wherein Frankfurt was utilized as a European transit point for a controlled delivery to Detroit.
>
> I do not know nor am I familiar with the word or name 'Khorah' in connection with any activity undertaken by DEA during my tenure as DEA country attaché in Nicosia.
>
> Khaled Nazir Jafaar was never a DEA cooperating individual nor was he known to be a 'mule' (drug courier) for DEA. To my knowledge he was never a CI for any other agency during my tenure as DEA country attaché in Nicosia . . .

I hereby declare under penalty of perjury that the foregoing is true and correct.

Signed this 31st day of May, 1991, Micheal T. Hurley, Special Agent, Drug Enforcement Administration.

As Coleman explained to James Shaughnessy, after going over Hurley's declaration and correcting its deficiencies, this was no more than he had expected. The astonishing thing was that in the other declaration, by Colonel Terry Bathen, the DIA actually acknowledged that Coleman had been working for *them* – and at a time when Hurley had declared that Coleman was working for *him*.

I was very surprised they did that [Coleman says]. It was the first admission that the DIA had been running intelligence operations that monitored and duplicated CIA operations and that there was hostility and suspicion between them. In fact, by acknowledging *my* existence, I think the DIA acknowledged its *own* existence for the first time in public.

I also think it was a back-handed way of having a swat at the DEA for putting the skids under me with that phony passport rap. In making this disclosure, the DIA was sending them a message: 'Hey, one of our guys was watching what you did. We know what was really going on there, so watch your step.' The thing they were concerned about was the barter of drugs for arms. Narco-terrorism was a fact. The DEA and the CIA were involved in highly questionable relationships that could – and *did* – explode in their faces.'

Apart from the key admission that 'Mr Coleman was formerly associated with a Department of Defense intelligence activity', Colonel Bathen's declaration, like Hurley's, was concerned to minimize the nature and significance of that association. Appointed to the post of assistant general counsel long after the events in question, he numbered among his responsibilities 'the processing of litigation requests for classified national security information'.

'In response to the criminal and civil matters involving Mr Coleman,' he declared, 'I personally reviewed the automated and documentary files of the Defense Intelligence Agency ... My review of Department of Defense HUMINT records reveals that

... on or about October 25, 1985, Mr Coleman contacted Defense Intelligence Agency personnel by telephone and volunteered to provide information concerning the Middle East. Mr Coleman's offer to provide videotapes associated with his travels in that part of the world was favorably evaluated, and he became affiliated with a classified Department of Defense intelligence activity during December 1985.'

According to Colonel Bathen's review of the records, Coleman did not operate a network of intelligence agents, nor was he instructed to apply for a passport in the name of Thomas Leavy.

'Mr Coleman received limited monthly compensation for his activities from July 16, 1986, until November 1986,' Bathen went on, 'when he was placed in a dormant status pending resolution of various actions by him which were inconsistent with any continuation of his intelligence-related activities. While Mr Coleman's status was periodically reevaluated during 1987 and 1988, he performed no services for Department of Defense intelligence activities after 30 November 1986.'

This gobbledegook was followed by a denial that the DEA had ever asked the DIA for Coleman's help in the Middle East or that the DIA had ever directed him to break off his relationship with that agency. Colonel Bathen also denied that the DIA had reactivated Coleman in November 1989 or ordered him to proceed to the Middle East under the name of Thomas Leavy.

Content that the agency had acknowledged him, Coleman and Shaughnessy found the rest of the Bathen declaration more interesting for what it did *not* say. From the Hurley affidavit, the stamps in Coleman's passport and other documents and witnesses, it was clear that the operational arm of the DIA had not been entirely frank with its assistant general counsel.

I'm supposed to have contacted the DIA by telephone to volunteer my services? [Coleman scoffs]. Where did I get the number from? The Yellow Pages? And why drop eleven months from the record? So as not to hurt Pat Robertson's feelings? I was recruited in December 1984, not '85.

My passport shows I arrived in Lebanon in February 1985. I was under cover as an employee of the Christian Broadcasting Network. After that assignment, I came home in October '85 and met Control in McCloskey's home to set up Condor Television Ltd. And I'm not surprised the DIA described that as a classified intelligence activity because the agency had no Congressional authority at that time to set up front companies. What they did instead was use 'cut-outs' – companies set up by individual agents or third parties but funded and operated by the agency. The DIA was the acknowledged master of the cut-out and the CIA had copied them. It was a great way of getting out from under Congressional oversight, raising plausible deniability to the level of an art form.

But the interesting thing is that Bathen puts me with the DIA in December 1985 and Hurley says I went to work for the DEA in January '86. So according to their declarations, for four months, until I was pulled out to go to Libya in April, the government acknowledges I was working for both agencies at the same time – without Hurley knowing it, of course.

It's also interesting that DIA says I received limited monthly compensation from July until November 1986, while I was still on Hurley's books. In July, I was issued with a Sony camcorder. Bathen doesn't mention this but the DIA eventually admitted it to my attorney in Chicago. In September, I used the camcorder in Lebanon and brought it back to the States. On Control's instructions, I took it out again when I was assigned to DEA Cyprus in February '87 and left it behind with Tony Asmar's people in Beirut when I came home that August. The following spring, after Tony was killed, I retrieved it from Lebanon and returned with it.

So there I was, working with the DIA's equipment all through '87 and the early part of '88, and guess what? The camcorder was still signed out to me when I was arrested in May 1990. Now they say I performed no services for them after November 1986? I was debriefed by Donleavy on each of those operations – which I guess is what Bathen meant when he said I was 'periodically reevaluated' during '87 and '88. Plus there are all the back-channel reports I filed twice a week.

It's obvious to me that the office of general counsel, for its own protection, is out of the loop as far as classified HUMINT operations are concerned. Like he says, Bathen's declaration was based on information made available to him. But I'm still grateful the DIA owned up to the fact that I worked for them. They didn't have to do that. It's what's known in the trade as a 'limited hang-out' – admitting just enough of the truth to create an impression of candour without giving the game away.

Meanwhile, James Shaughnessy had been doing his best to get around the government's stonewall defence of its files by seeking Hague Convention letters of request to depose witnesses and suspects turned up by the Flight 103 investigation. In Frankfurt, on 6 May 1991, a series of written questions were put to PFLP–GC members Dalkamoni and Ghadanfar, who had been arrested in Germany in October 1988, and who were then on trial for a series of terrorist acts. Not unexpectedly, they refused to testify.

On 8 and 10 May, Shaughnessy attempted to depose Bert Pinsdorf and Hartmut Mayer of the BKA, with whom Coleman had discussed the Lockerbie disaster on the telephone. Under instructions from the German Ministry of the Interior, Pinsdorf refused to answer most of the questions put to him, while Mayer, who had originally referred Coleman to Pinsdorf, merely confirmed that he was the BKA's narcotics agent on Cyprus and that he knew Coleman had worked for the DEA there with Hurley and Ganem.

On 10 and 12 June, Shaughnessy went to Sweden to depose PFLP–GC members Abu Talb and Mahmoud Moghrabi, who were both serving prison terms for terrorist offences. They, too, declined to answer almost all the questions put to them.

Refusing to give up, Shaughnessy would later try, with no greater success, to depose Phillip Connelly of H.M. Customs and Excise; Dr Thomas Hayes, the scientist responsible for most of the hard forensic evidence in the Flight 103 investigation, and the two principals of the Swiss firm who made the timers sold to the Libyans, but meanwhile, on 7 June 1991, argument was heard in New York's Eastern District Court on the government's motion to dismiss Pan Am's third-party complaint.

After hearing both sides, Chief Judge Platt evidently shared Shaughnessy's view that the motion was premature for he declared that Pan Am was entitled to discovery from the government before the court ruled on the matter. Six weeks later, on 19 July, he went further and entered an order *requiring* the government to respond to Pan Am's subpoenas, for he had taken the point that, while the government continued to sit on all the evidence, Shaughnessy could neither proceed with his clients' claim nor prepare a proper defence to the civil suits.

For a while it looked as if the truth might finally come out, but by a series of manoeuvres the government now asserted the state secrets privilege. In Shaughnessy's absence – indeed, without his knowledge – government counsel made a selective showing of documents to the court *in camera*, and at a conference called on 20 September, Chief Judge Platt reversed himself. Without identifying the documents he had seen, he told Shaughnessy that the government had validly asserted the state secrets privilege, that there was nothing in the documents to support third-party claims, and that he was therefore denying Pan Am discovery.

Whereupon, Shaughnessy asked if this meant that the court was dismissing Pan Am's third-party claims, as he had made it clear that he could not proceed without discovery. To his surprise, Chief Judge Platt declared that, to the contrary, he was denying the government's motion to dismiss the suit, that the government would be kept in the litigation until the conclusion of the liability trial, and that he was putting the government under the continuing duty to produce any evidence it developed bearing on the third-party claim. When Shaughnessy asked for leave to appeal this decision to the Second Circuit, the request was denied.

That was on 20 September 1991. After that, he concentrated on preparing for the civil liability trial and, to all intents and purposes, the case against the government was abandoned. Nevertheless, the ground had to be cleared, for the court now set provisional trial dates in April 1992, for both the passenger liability suits *and* the third-party claims.

On 20 March, Shaughnessy again applied to the court for an order either granting discovery and severing the third-party suit for trial later or dismissing the suit altogether. There was no way, he said, that Pan Am, with or without discovery, could prove its claim with admissible evidence at a trial scheduled to start in one month. Opposing the motion, government counsel demanded for the second time that the court impose punitive sanctions on Shaughnessy and his law firm.

Chief Judge Platt again declined to do this, but on 16 April, denied Pan Am's motion in its entirety, neither granting discovery *nor* dismissing the suit. As this was clearly unacceptable to both sides, a further conference was called on 24 April, three days before the trial date set for both actions, at which the government once again asked for Pan Am's suit to be dismissed.

In reply, Shaughnessy once again reminded the court that the government had never answered the complaint, and that, as discovery had been denied, Pan Am's claims could not be proved by admissible evidence. With this, Chief Judge Platt finally dismissed the third-party action, but with the proviso that he would reinstate the suit if evidence was developed to support it.

And there matters rested until 27 April 1992, when the trial at last began of the Lockerbie families' liability suit against Pan Am – and when that week's edition of *Time* magazine promised its readers 'The Untold Story of Pan Am 103'.

The response to *Time*'s cover article, researched for five months by Roy Rowan, a veteran reporter and editor with 44 years' experience, ranged from the hysterical to the vindictive, with some of its more extravagant critics suggesting that Pan Am had somehow arranged for its publication on that date in order to influence the liability trial. Besides the timing of its appearance, Rowan's reliance on Juval Aviv and Lester Coleman as two of his sources was clearly the reason for all the excitement.

Lee Kreindler, lead counsel for the victims' families, immediately filed a motion for the discharge of the jury because of the unexpected publication of 'the most shocking and most prejudicial false information about the Lockerbie story'. This 'false information', he said, 'bears directly on the trial and it appears to have been given to *Time* by the defendants'. He asked for a judicial inquiry into the circumstances of its publication as, in his view, it was 'bound to poison the mind of every juror picked'.

Chief Judge Platt did not agree, and ordered the trial to proceed. He also banned all the attorneys in the case from speaking to the media, which had immediately pounced on the *Time* story and relayed its conclusions around the world.

In essence, Rowan's article had suggested that Flight 103 might have been targeted by Ahmed Jibril's PFLP–GC because of the American intelligence team on board, led by Major Charles Dennis McKee of the DIA. Still further undermining the official Libyan theory, Rowan also quoted at length from the FBI field report that cast doubt on the reliability of Frankfurt's baggage computer records, leaving open the possibility that a 'rogue' bag containing the bomb had been 'inserted in the baggage system'.

This rogue bag, he suggested, 'may have been placed on board the plane by Jibril's group with the help of Monzer al-Kassar, a Syrian drug dealer who was cooperating with the US's Drug Enforcement Administration in a drug sting operation. Al-Kassar thus may have been playing both sides of the fence.'

Much of the information about al-Kassar was provided by Juval Aviv, who still stood by his original assertion that a 'freewheeling

CIA unit codenamed COREA was instrumental in allowing the PFLP-GC to engineer the baggage-switch. But Rowan had also unearthed a fresh piece of verifiable evidence which supported the FBI field report and showed how a rogue bag *could* have been exchanged for an innocent one and loaded aboard Flight 103.

Two identical Samsonite suitcases full of Christmas presents were among 11 bags belonging to passengers on a delayed Berlin–Frankfurt feeder flight that were left behind when their owners caught an earlier connection to London. These unaccompanied bags were entered into Frankfurt airport's computer system and sent on via Flight 103. But only *one* suitcase of Christmas presents was recovered at Lockerbie. 'The other was mysteriously left behind in Frankfurt, and arrived safely in Seattle a day later.'

Further undermining the government's contention that the bomb was contained in an unaccompanied suitcase from Malta was Rowan's revelation that James Shaughnessy had taken depositions from 20 officials who had been on duty at Luqa airport on 21 December 1988, 'including the airport security commander, the bomb-disposal engineer who inspected all the baggage, the general manager of ground operations of Air Malta, the head loader of Flight 180 and the three check-in agents. Their records showed that no unaccompanied suitcases were put aboard the flight, and some of the staff Shaughnessy interviewed are prepared to testify under oath that there was no bag that day destined for Pan Am Flight 103.'

Rowan next turned to what he had learned from Lester Coleman while researching the article, most of it echoing what Coleman had set out in his affidavit, and then came back to Juval Aviv's theory that Major McKee's intelligence team, learning of al-Kassar's connection with the CIA COREA unit, had decided to fly back unannounced to Washington to expose the secret deal between them.

'Apparently the team's movements were being tracked by the Iranians,' he wrote, citing the David Lovejoy calls to the Iranian Embassy in Beirut. 'Lovejoy's last call came on 20 December, allegedly informing the Iranians that the team would be on Pan Am Flight 103 the following day.' The result, Rowan suggested, was that the terrorists set out to kill them because of their planned hostage-rescue mission, although, he added, 'the FBI says it investigated the theory that McKee's team was targeted, and found no evidence to support it.'

Coleman does not believe it either, nor does he believe there was any freewheeling CIA unit codenamed COREA. From his personal observations, he believes that local CIA agents, working with local DEA agents, kept the *khouriah* pipeline open long after its security had been breached, and that the terrorists, who had been tracking the Jafaars, took advantage of one controlled delivery too many to switch a suitcase containing heroin for another containing a bomb. The deaths of five American intelligence agents, in Coleman's opinion, was an unexpected bonus.

But a contribution from another of Rowan's sources struck an eerie chord in his memory. The *Time* article described how Richard Gazarik, a reporter for the *Tribune-Review*, of Greensburg, Pennsylvania, had found in the lining of Major McKee's wallet, after it was returned to his mother, what Gazarik had assumed were the codenames of McKee's intelligence team: Chuck Capone (presumably McKee himself), Nelson, Dillinger, Bonnie (although there was no woman in the group) and Clyde.

During his first DIA assignment in Beirut, Coleman had serviced a dead drop for the Green Berets at Juicy-Burger, a hamburger stand in East Beirut. The owners were an American couple codenamed Bonnie and Clyde.

In London, the *Observer* greeted the *Time* cover story with barely concealed disgust. Two years earlier, its reporter John Merritt had interviewed Juval Aviv in New York and found him wanting, and *Time* had not mellowed his opinion.

'By *Time*'s own admission,' he wrote, 'the article makes much use of the Aviv information. But it is not just its timing that raises questions. It is clear that Mr Aviv's strange concoction remains the central plank of the insurers' defence. And therefore, as well as obscuring the issue of Pan Am's negligence with bizarre and unsubstantiated claims, it enables the defendants to claim an unfair hearing because the US government is "covering up" vital evidence.'

As Shaughnessy had been at pains to show that Aviv's connection with Pan Am had ended two years previously and that since then much other information had been assembled from many other sources, Merritt's strictures seemed unwarranted. Referring to the Interfor Report, he again insisted that 'both it and Mr Aviv were discredited by an *Observer* investigation more than two years ago. The *Observer* subsequently gave evidence on Mr Aviv in a New York hearing related to Lockerbie which led to him being "deemed not to be a credible witness".'

This could well serve as a textbook example of obfuscation.

The *Observer* investigation had identified some minor flaws in the peripheral detail of Aviv's report and, on the strength of this, had simply poured scorn on the rest.

The purpose of the New York hearing 'related to Lockerbie' had been to determine whether or not Aviv's Interfor Report could be treated as a privileged work document after its findings had been leaked to the press. Merritt gave evidence which showed that Aviv had leaked at least some of its findings to *him*, and it was Aviv's denial that he had done so which Magistrate Judge Ross deemed not to be credible. The substance of the Interfor Report was not discussed.

On the other side of the Atlantic, the *Washington Post* on 26 April 1992, carried a more measured, though still hostile, response to the *Time* article by David Leppard, of *The Sunday Times*. Though also committed to the official version of events, Leppard at least acknowledged that a few other people had contributed to Rowan's article besides Juval Aviv. Not that he set much store by what they had to say.

'The *Time* story, which laid out little new evidence, draws heavily on the case assembled by Pan Am's lawyers,' he wrote dismissively, before proceeding in his own article to draw heavily on the case prepared for the victims' families by 'veteran air-crash lawyer Lee Kreindler'.

'A review of the case files, evidence and other materials,' Leppard declared, 'shows that Kreindler's case is built on the premise that the bomb suitcase reached Frankfurt via Air Malta Flight 180 from the Mediterranean island and was transferred – unaccompanied by any passenger – to Pan Am 103 at Frankfurt. He will try to prove Pan Am committed the cardinal sin of airline security: allowing an unaccompanied, unaccounted-for bag into an airliner cargo hold. Kreindler's theory parallels the criminal conspiracy case assembled by the FBI and Scottish police . . .'

Leppard then turned to the alternative theory that the bomb bag had been switched for another in the airport's baggage-handling area and duly noted, without comment, the 'previously undisclosed FBI memo' which concluded, after a review of the airport's baggage-handling records, that 'the possibility' remained that *no* luggage had been transferred from Flight 180 to Flight 103.

This reminded him of the polygraph tests that two of Pan Am's Frankfurt baggage-handlers flunked when questioned about a possible suitcase switch. 'When the airline later flew the two men to London on a pretext,' he went on, 'British authorities refused to interrogate the pair. *Time*'s unstated implication: The British were cooperating with US intelligence to protect any covert links to the bomb plotters.'

Well? If *Time* had got it wrong, what did *Leppard* read into the British authorities' refusal? He did not say. Nor was he inclined to speculate about the conclusion drawn by the FBI memo which indicated a 'possibility' that the entire Libyan theory was wrong, if not a deliberate fabrication.

Demonstrating the 'unusual and controversial lengths' to which Pan Am's lawyers were prepared to go, he wrote, they had even tried through the London courts to 'force' him to divulge some of his own 'sources and materials'. As this was an attempt by Pan Am to clarify an opinion expressed to Leppard by Dr Thomas Hayes, the lead forensic scientist in the Flight 103 investigation, and already published in Leppard's book, it is not clear why he would have wished to withhold this source material in the first place. Nor did he explain why he thought it 'unusual and controversial' for Pan Am to want to know more about Dr Hayes's reported belief that the Lockerbie bomb was a dual device, incorporating both a barometric switch *and* a timer, when the Libyan/Air Malta theory rested in part on the bomb-maker's use of a Swiss timer alone.

As in any attempt to establish the truth, until the facts come out, who can say whose cause they will favour?

Certainly, Leppard appeared to favour the official line, for he went on to remind his *Washington Post* readers that a shopkeeper in Malta had identified one of the two Libyans indicted for the bombing as the purchaser of the clothing wrapped around the bomb (without mentioning that the shopkeeper had previously identified somebody else), and that a Libyan defector 'with detailed inside knowledge of the plot' was standing by to testify against his former colleagues (without referring to the reported $4 million reward for his testimony).

Leppard also subscribed to the government view that Juval Aviv was 'a primary source for Pan Am's lawyers'. While conceding that *Time* had not mentioned Khalid Nazir Jafaar in its article, he used Aviv's finding that Jafaar had been the unwitting instrument in getting the bomb aboard to link Aviv with Lester Coleman, whose affidavit supported that conclusion.

'Coleman in an interview told me he has no first-hand knowledge of the circumstances of Flight 103,' wrote Leppard. 'Moreover, if

Aviv's bag-switch thesis is true, one of Jafaar's checked-in bags would have been left behind at Frankfurt and therefore unaccounted for in the Lockerbie debris. But both of Jafaar's checked-in bags were recovered undamaged from the crash scene. Scottish investigators who interviewed Frankfurt airport staff found no one who could recall him with a bronze Samsonite suitcase.'

When Coleman spoke to Leppard on the telephone, he certainly agreed he had no first-hand knowledge of the circumstances of Flight 103 – he had been back in the United States for seven months when the attack occurred. But that was not *all* that he told him. He also said that he *did* have first-hand knowledge that Jafaar was a DEA courier making controlled deliveries of heroin to the United States in 1988 – which was, after all, the point of his affidavit.

As for Jafaar's baggage, his father was reported to have said that Khalid had travelled with two soft holdalls that he would normally have taken with him into the cabin – and Khalid's two soft holdalls were, as Leppard said, 'recovered undamaged from the crash scene'.

Given the inadequacy of Pan Am's baggage records – a central plank in the plaintiffs' liability suit – there is nothing to indicate that he did not *also* check in a Samsonite suitcase. And given that the terrorists did not expect him or the aircraft to survive the flight, there was no reason why they *should* have left a suitcase behind at Frankfurt. They would simply have added the bomb bag to the rest of the Flight 103 passenger luggage, relying on the explosion to destroy all the evidence, including any discrepancies in the loading list.

As the government's attorneys had insisted before Chief Judge Platt, just ten days before Leppard's article appeared: 'Pan Am's own records and procedures are in such disarray that the only thing they prove is that Pan Am had no idea what baggage was on the aircraft.'

Further evidence of this disarray, as Leppard noted, was the story *Time* had unearthed of the two unaccompanied suitcases full of Christmas presents that had been routed on from Frankfurt to the US via Flight 103. Unimpressed by the fact that one had unaccountably been left behind, he wrote: '*Time* offers no evidence of how a quick-moving bomb plot could have hinged on the chance availability of an appropriate bag for the necessary switch.'

This was either disingenuous or he had missed the point. *Time* had not suggested any such connection. Rowan's article was concerned only with showing that a rogue bag *could* have been 'inserted into the automated baggage-control system, as the secret FBI report indicates was possible'.

And not just 'possible'. The report described how, in September 1989, Detective Inspector Watson McAteer and Special Agent Lawrence G. Whitaker actually *witnessed* a baggage-handler bring in a piece of luggage, encode a destination for it into the computer, and toss it on to the 'secure' conveyor without making any notation on the worksheet.

The procedure for bag-switching was in place, and had been used many times by narcotics smugglers and DEA couriers. But in this instance, as the terrorists expected Flight 103 to crash into the Atlantic, there was no *reason* for them to substitute one suitcase for another, let alone to leave anything behind that might give the game away. The only requirement was to get the bomb bag aboard.

Leppard concluded his article for the *Washington Post* with a dutiful nod to the Libyan theory by suggesting that the bombing of Flight 103 could as readily have been a revenge attack for the American air raids on Tripoli 1986 as an Iranian-inspired revenge for the downing of its Airbus.

'The assertions supplied by Aviv and Coleman,' he wrote, 'require a different explanation, one which *Time* relates to its readers.'

This is not so. As Coleman had been at pains to point out in his telephone interview with Leppard, he had always believed that the attack on Flight 103 was inspired and financed by the Iranians, and carried out by Syrian-backed terrorists using bomb components in all probability supplied by the Libyans. He had never subscribed to the *Time*/Aviv theory that the flight was deliberately targeted by Monzer al-Kassar because an American intelligence team was aboard, although he has no doubt that al-Kassar's drug-smuggling arrangements at Frankfurt were employed to put the bomb in the cargo hold.

'There is not a scrap of evidence that Kassar was anywhere near Frankfurt at the time of the attack,' Leppard concluded, 'nor is there a witness who will say that he conspired in the bombing.' (That is certainly true. No professional criminal would risk being caught at the scene of a crime if his presence was not required, least of all a CIA asset. And the only possible witnesses against al-Kassar are either his co-conspirators or his CIA control, none of whom seem likely to come forward voluntarily.)

'No other witness can testify to the real motives behind the attack.' (That, too, is true – unless or until Ali Akbar Mohtashemi, Iran's former Minister of the Interior, or Ahmed Jibril, head of the PFLP-GC, decide to publish their memoirs.)

'Such are the Byzantine tales that await the jury in the case of Pan Am 103,' concluded Leppard, having himself contributed to some of them.

On the next day, 27 April 1992, jury selection began in the civil liability case before Chief Judge Thomas C. Platt, United States District Court, Eastern District of New York.

— XVII —

Lester Coleman's day in court had been scheduled for 17 June 1991, in Chicago, but having just found sanctuary for himself and his family in Sweden, he was not disposed to gamble with it.

Even if he *had* wished to run the risk of answering the government's trumped-up charge, he was neither fit enough nor solvent enough for any more travel. Acute lumbago, coupled with a kidney infection, had confined him to bed soon after his arrival, and he was down to less than $150. Except for their clothes, the family had nothing left to sell.

On 11 June, his Chicago public defender, Michael Deutsch, advised the court that Coleman was ill in Sweden, and Chief Judge James B. Moran rescheduled the trial for 22 July, ordering Coleman to produce proof of his illness and to appear at a pre-trial hearing set for 16 July.

It was impossible.

'We are disillusioned and exhausted, homeless and broke – and there seems to be no end in sight,' Coleman wrote to Deutsch. 'I suggest you ask the court to fund a trip for you to consult with your client, whom you have never met, since I am unable to consult with you in Chicago for health and financial reasons.'

Not unexpectedly, the court rejected the suggestion. On 16 July, Deutsch reported that his client was still unable to travel and produced medical certificates to that effect from Coleman's Swedish doctors. Chief Judge Moran then postponed the trial indefinitely and asked the assistant US attorney in charge of the case to arrange for an independent physician to examine Coleman to determine the nature and extent of his illness.

The responsibility for this, and also for bringing Coleman back within the orbit of the Justice Department, was assigned to the FBI, which seems to have concluded, rightly, that he was unlikely to return of his own accord. A pretext was therefore required to have him declared a fugitive. The Bureau could then ask Interpol to have him picked up when Coleman next presented his passport for inspection.

On 24 September, having been advised that a Dr Hakan Hallberg was prepared to examine Coleman in Sweden on the court's behalf, Chief Judge Moran ordered that unless Coleman submitted to an examination by Dr Hallberg within ten days, a bench warrant would be issued for his arrest.

Still ready to comply with the court's order (if not to surrender himself to its jurisdiction), Coleman duly telephoned Dr Hallberg for an appointment – and was astonished to learn that Dr Hallberg knew nothing whatever about the matter. He had never been approached by the American authorities, he said, and had certainly never agreed to carry out an independent examination for them.

At Coleman's request, Dr Hallberg provided a written statement to that effect. In English. Dated 27 September, it read simply: 'Coleman, Lester, has contacted this office, and we have no knowledge of any request from American authority to examine Mr Coleman.'

Guessing what lay behind the manoeuvre, Coleman immediately forwarded Dr Hallberg's letter to Micheal Deutsch in Chicago, but it was either too late or ignored. On 7 October 1991, a bench warrant was issued 'for failure to appear', and Coleman was duly reclassified as an international fugitive.

That meant he was no longer free to travel, if he wished to, beyond the frontiers of Sweden, whose government had taken the Colemans in as refugees while their petition for asylum was considered. To get him back, the US Justice Department was now in a position to sue for Coleman's extradition, if it was ready to risk a public hearing in Sweden, or, if it wasn't, either to press through diplomatic channels for his deportation, or to sanction his kidnapping and forcible return to the United States.

A further bonus from Washington's point of view was that the fugitive warrant dealt another body blow to Coleman's credibility as a witness. The assault on his character begun by Steven Emerson in the CNN newscast had become a priority after James Shaughnessy filed Coleman's affidavit in Pan Am's third-party suit.

On 30 May, a few days before the Colemans crossed into Sweden, John J. Connors, the attorney heading the government team, joined Colonel Bathen of the DIA and Micheal Hurley of the DEA in filing declarations directed, not so much at what Coleman had to say, but at the man himself. Most of it had to do with the phony passport charge. As in Pan Am's case, the government was in sole possession of the evidence Coleman needed to prove that he had been acting under orders when he applied for a Thomas Leavy passport, and, again as in Pan Am's case, the government had refused to produce that evidence, claiming the state secrets privilege.

Still following the Pan Am tactics, the Justice Department chose instead to make an *in camera, ex parte* showing of classified documents to Chief Judge Moran, who, on the strength of what he was shown, ruled that those documents did not support Coleman's defence and denied his motion for discovery. Exactly what he *did* see, however, is known only to the court and the government prosecutors. As they had charged Coleman in a criminal matter, they were unlikely to have produced documents that undermined their own case, so the value of the exercise was questionable. But it at least enabled Connors to imply in his declaration that Coleman's story was unsupported by the evidence.

'In an apparent attempt to bolster the credibility of Coleman and otherwise support their allegations against the DEA,' Connors went on, 'third-party plaintiffs requested . . . depositions of two German BKA agents, Bert Pinsdorf and Hartmut Mayer.'

Holding a watching brief for the government, Connors had attended those depositions in Germany and confirmed that both men had been instructed by their superiors not to discuss the Flight 103 investigation, although Pinsdorf did at one point deny that the BKA had received any advance warning of the bombing. Mayer, Connors went on, knew no more about it than he had read in the newspapers, but he confirmed that he had worked closely with DEA agents in Cyprus and that he knew Lester Coleman.

'The Coleman declaration specifically alleges that Mr Mayer was somehow involved in or knowledgeable about the DEA 'controlled delivery' which Pan Am alleges was subverted by the terrorists in order to put the bomb on the aircraft in Frankfurt,' declared Connors. 'However, he [Mayer] specifically confirmed [that] controlled deliveries are escorted through and do not bypass security, and specifically denied Coleman's allegation that the BKA or DEA train anyone to circumvent security at any airport.'

Connors evidently misread Coleman's affidavit, for nowhere did he 'specifically' allege that Mayer was involved in the particular controlled delivery that was subverted by the terrorists. What he *did* say was that Mayer was the BKA's liaison officer for the controlled deliveries mounted by the DEA through Frankfurt – a statement which Mayer confirmed, and that did little to support the DEA's contention that *no* controlled deliveries were being carried out in Europe at the time.

Nor did Coleman anywhere 'specifically' allege in his affidavit that the BKA or DEA trained anyone to circumvent airport security or, indeed, failed in this instance to 'escort' the controlled delivery through. What he *did* say was that 'baggage containing the narcotics used in the operation would be placed on flights to the United States *through agents* [author's italics], informants and/or sources . . . so as to avoid the possible interdiction of the shipments by airport and/or airline security.' In the Frankfurt context, this meant following the established routine of supervising a suitcase switch in the airport's baggage-handling area.

Contrary to Connors's suggestion, there is no discernible conflict between Coleman's statement and Mayer's – unless by 'escort' Mayer meant a group of DEA and BKA agents solemnly marching a courier through a crowded airport without allowing anyone to touch his bags. And when Mayer went on to say that Khalid Jafaar was not working for the DEA, as Connors reported in his declaration, what did he mean? On that particular occasion? That, as a subsource, he worked for a CI who was paid by the DEA? That he was working for some other agency? And in any case, how would Mayer know?

But for Coleman there were more important things to worry about. His first priority was to satisfy the Swedish authorities of the truth of his story and consequently of his need for their protection.

The family had entered the country legally, on valid American passports, making for Trollhattan, a small town of about 60,000 inhabitants, to which one of Mary-Claude's sisters and her husband had emigrated from Lebanon some five years earlier. Perhaps naively, Coleman had thought they might stay there on a temporary basis until the matter of the phony passport charge was cleared up, but he felt it wise to be frank with the Swedish authorities from the start, and a week after their arrival, he went with his brother-in-law to the local police station to explain his situation.

For one thing, they were broke and needed whatever help they could get.

The police were very nice to us [he recalled]. Very understanding. They passed us on for a second interview to an officer in charge of refugees, and in July, she arranged for us to move out of my brother-in-law's apartment into a refugee compound on the edge of town. There we found ourselves living with Lebanese, Syrians, Iraquis and, later on, Bulgarians, Albanians, Croatians, Serbians, gypsies – all manner of people seeking sanctuary. And still I told myself it was just temporary, while I got things cleared up. But then came the business with the fugitive warrant and I knew finally I could never go back.

In support of his formal petition for political asylum, Coleman supplied references from a number of witnesses prepared to testify on his behalf, including the Most Reverend Mother Teresa, of the Sisters of Charity; Conrad Martin, executive director of The Fund for Constitutional Government, Washington, D.C.; A. Ernest Fitzgerald, United States Department of Defense, and Elliot L. Richardson, former United States Attorney-General, who met over lunch with the Swedish ambassador to the United States on Coleman's behalf.

His connection with Richardson stemmed from an affidavit Coleman had sworn to about the bootleg PROMIS software he had seen at Cypriot Police headquarters and in the offices of the DEA's Eurame Trading Company in Nicosia. As attorney for William and Nancy Hamilton, the owners of Inslaw, Inc., Richardson had successfully sued the Justice Department in Federal Bankruptcy Court for forcing the company out of business and stealing its software, securing over $7 million in compensation for the department's 'trickery, fraud and deceit'.

This judgment was subsequently affirmed in Federal District Court, which found it just 'under any standard of review', and although the US Court of Appeals later set the decision aside on jurisdictional grounds, it did not disturb the conclusion that 'the government acted wilfully and fraudulently to obtain property it was not entitled to . . .'

On 3 August 1991, not long after the family had moved into the refugee compound on the outskirts of Trollhattan, Coleman took a telephone call from Danny Casolaro, an American freelance journalist in Washington, who had tracked him down after reading his affidavit in the Inslaw case.

He was working on a complex story about the octopus, Casolaro explained, linking the theft and unauthorized sale of PROMIS software to foreign governments with the BCCI scandal, the Iran/Contra affair and other questionable activities, including the so-called 'October Surprise'. Could Coleman perhaps help him with any of this? Did he know of anyone who might have further information?

Though disturbed that Casolaro should have traced him so easily, Coleman saw the chance of a trade-off. He had been trying to find James McCloskey, the quickie divorce lawyer who had recruited him into the DIA and who might again be prepared to speak up for him, but his amiable guru had apparently abandoned his practice and moved away from Timonium, Maryland, without leaving a forwarding address. When Coleman explained this to his caller, touching on McCloskey's links with the BCCI and the intelligence community, Casolaro thanked him for the tip and promised in return to let Coleman know as soon as he ran McCloskey to earth.

Nine days later, Ernest Fitzgerald, Coleman's friend at the Pentagon, called to say that Danny Casolaro had been found dead in a blood-boltered hotel bathroom in Martinsburg, West Virginia, both arms slashed open 12 times with a DIY knife blade. His briefcase was missing, and among other suspicious circumstances, the Martinsburg police, declaring Casolaro a suicide, had allowed the body to be embalmed before his family was even notified of his death. A firm of contract cleaners had also been called in to scour the room from top to bottom, so that any meaningful forensic investigation was impossible.

According to relatives and friends, Casolaro had gone to West Virginia, despite recent death threats, to see somebody he had met there who, he thought, could supply the missing links in the story he was working on. Everybody who knew Casolaro, including the Hamiltons and their counsel, Elliot Richardson, were convinced he had been murdered to shut him up.

Coleman was chilled by the news. If the person Casolaro had gone to see was McCloskey, then Coleman had sent Casolaro to his death. And if Casolaro *had* been killed because of what he knew, then Coleman's own chances of survival, if he fell into the same hands, looked slim. Thankful that he and Mary-Claude had decided to get out when they did, he prevailed on Fitzgerald to make further inquiries, although he found it hard to believe that the McCloskey he remembered could be involved in the murder.

The result was even more unsettling. The likelihood that Casolaro had gone to meet McCloskey increased when investigators established that, after leaving Timonium, McCloskey had bought a horse farm at Shepardstown, about fifteen minutes down the road from where Casolaro was murdered. As against that, McCloskey had not been seen in the area for two years, although there was a working telephone number listed in his name.

When Coleman dialled that number from Sweden, he got through to the Shenandoah Women's Center in Martinsburg, which claimed never to have heard of McCloskey. Efforts to trace him were then redoubled, but without result, and, as far as Coleman knows, McCloskey is still missing to this day.

On 16 October 1991, Coleman telephoned Elliot Richardson to pass on the results of these inquiries, but, as Richardson was out of the country, he spoke instead to William Hamilton, president of Inslaw, Inc., in Washington, D.C.

His revelations came as no great surprise. Hamilton himself had received 'threats of bodily harm from former US and Israeli covert intelligence operatives' embarrassed by his efforts to unmask the government's theft of Inslaw's software.

In a letter supporting Coleman's application for asylum in Sweden, Hamilton wrote:

We believe that Mr Casolaro was murdered to prevent the disclosure of evidence about this malfeasance. We also believe that some of the proceeds from the illegal sale of our PROMIS software to foreign governments have made their way into a political and intelligence slush fund in the United States and that this has seriously compromised the integrity of both our political system and our US Department of Justice . . .

I am inclined to credit as serious expressions of concern about personal safety by anyone such as Mr Coleman who may have pieces to the puzzle of this widely ramified criminal conspiracy that permeates US intelligence and law enforcement agencies.

Ernest Fitzgerald, doyen of Washington's whistle-blowers, went a good deal further in urging the Swedish government to act on Coleman's petition. Drawing on 25 years' experience of official persecution and harassment, much of it described in his book *The Pentagonists*, he wrote:

A live, talking and unfettered Lester Coleman represents an enormous potential embarrassment to powerful forces in our government and business establishment. Dead, silent or incarcerated, Les Coleman disappears as a problem. Other people in

Mr Coleman's situation have met untimely ends with distressing frequency.

Without being able to predict Mr Coleman's future in our country with certainty, I can tell you the views of other United States intelligence operatives I've dealt with in similar situations. Rightly or wrongly, these people believe that they cannot survive imprisonment in one of our penitentiaries. Conditions in these prisons are very harsh, and little inducement is required for long-term inmates to do deeds that would be unthinkable to the rest of us.

This fear is so real and pervasive among our intelligence operatives that they are often silenced without imprisonment. A tactic I have noted is to induce a guilty plea through plea bargaining, then impose suspended sentences for a list of offences which the charged agent claimed were perpetrated as official acts. Agents thus pled and sentenced are silenced out of fear that if they talk or write about government-sponsored misdeeds, the suspension of their sentences will be set aside and they will be forced to serve their sentences in prison with consequent exposure to violence, and perhaps subjected to further prosecution.

I should point out to you that it would not be necessary for Mr Coleman to be convicted of anything in order to subject him to a US prison environment. At this stage of his dispute with the federal government, our courts would be unlikely to approve bail for him, so he would most likely be incarcerated pending trial.

After his arrest by the FBI on so transparent a trumped-up charge, such fears had never been far from Coleman's mind, and certainly nothing had happened since then to dispel them, neither his deliberate exposure by Steven Emerson on Cable News Network nor the government's latest cynical ploy in having him declared a fugitive. Any lingering hope that he might one day clear his name through the courts had been snuffed out, as he explained in a further submission to the Swedish authorities.

Elements within the United States government, bizarre as this may seem, have both a motive and a capability to conduct covert 'sanctions', such as the death of Mr Casalaro and the disappearance of Mr McCloskey [he wrote]. I had first-hand knowledge of these capabilities in Lebanon, where I gathered intelligence that was used to target individuals perceived to be enemies of US interests.

I have no doubt that *I* am now a target, considering those former associates who are dead, and the death of Mr Casolaro. If I return to the United States, I will be jailed and almost certainly killed. The DEA has publicly labelled me a narcotics informant, and there are close on a million and a half people behind bars in the United States serving time for drug offences. I am therefore in genuine fear for my life. In 1990, 243 prisoners were murdered in American prisons.

With plenty of time to worry about such things, Coleman could not decide if he and the family were safer trying to keep out of sight or trying to keep in the public eye. No longer a moving target or, as Casolaro had demonstrated, particularly hard to find, he was inclined to favour a higher profile, if only because an 'accident' or unexplained disappearance would then be more noticeable, but against that, the Swedish police and immigration authorities were clearly not keen on his drawing attention to his situation. In the end, he tried to compromise by making himself available to the media but without encouraging their interest.

Not that the media needed much encouragement, particularly after an interview he had given to Michael Evans of *The Times* resulted in a pithy restatement of what he knew in its issue of 22 July 1991. Several journalists flew to Sweden to follow up on that story, including Roy Rowan of *Time* magazine, accompanied by Juval Aviv.

It was Coleman's first meeting with Aviv, and the first time he had seen the Interfor Report. Confining himself for the most part to what he had said in his affidavit, Coleman enjoyed talking to Rowan, a widely respected figure in his former profession, and tried to be as helpful as his circumstances would allow – without the faintest inkling of the furore that would follow *Time*'s cover article about Flight 103 a few months later.

Some warning of the depths to which the octopus would sink, however, came Coleman's way in December 1991. In the October/November issue of *Unclassified*, the bimonthly newspaper of the Association of National Security Alumni, its editor, David MacMichael, had run a piece about the spreading influence of the Defense Department over the US intelligence community, citing Coleman's experiences with the DIA.

This attracted the attention of Ron Martz, of the *Atlanta Journal-Constitution*, who, with Lloyd Burchette, had been placed in Coleman's charge by Micheal Hurley when they visited Cyprus in

1988 as guests of the DEA. Clearly not a subscriber to *Unclassified*'s credo that 'covert actions are counterproductive and damaging to the national interest of the United States ... corruptive of civil liberties ... and a free press', Martz addressed MacMichael as follows:

> Dear David,
> This letter is not for publication but please use the information in it as you see fit.

How Martz would have reacted if MacMichael had prefaced a letter to *him* in those terms is a matter for speculation, but he went on to claim that Coleman had contacted his (unnamed) 'primary assistant' in 1987 to offer his services 'for a relatively small amount of money' as a 'contact/fixer' on Cyprus during a visit they planned there to look into Lebanese drug trafficking.

As 'Les was living in Cyprus at the time' and 'passed himself off ... as a CI for DEA', Martz agreed to his proposition, but arriving in Cyprus found that 'Les Coleman was little more than a freelance journalist hustling money wherever and from whomever he could, including me. He had no connections with the Cypriot police or anti-drug squads, no connections with BKA and one minor connection with DEA as an 'unofficial consultant ... on non-secure communications.'

Several months later, Martz went on, he discovered Coleman had 'stolen some photographs I had taken of a terrorist car-bombing incident in Nicosia' and had sold them to *Soldier of Fortune* magazine under the name of Collin (sic) Knox. 'Then I learned the Cypriot police were looking for Les, who had departed Cyprus about the same time I did and left behind huge telephone bills and unpaid rent on his apartment in Nicosia.'

'Since then,' Martz continued, getting to the heart of the matter,

> Les has tried to put himself in the middle of several international events, most noticeably the Pan Am 103 bombing over Lockerbie. Les, who has had a long-running feud with DEA in Cyprus, managed to convince ABC News and Pierre Salinger that DEA in Cyprus was responsible for the Pan Am 103 bombing because it

was working a sting operation and allowed certain luggage to go on the plane unchecked. ABC went with the story, apparently largely on Les's information, but that story has since been thoroughly discredited.

I later checked out Les to see if he had any DIA connections as he claimed and found it had never heard of him or Collin Knox. This information comes from a high-ranking officer still on active duty who has served in a number of DIA positions in more than 25 years in the military, a man I trust implicitly and who gave me the information as an off-the-record favor . . .

The story he gave you concerning being in exile because of a DIA-DEA feud is a lot of crap. They may be feuding, but it's certainly not over Les Coleman. Les is in Sweden because the FBI was after him for filing a false passport application and impersonating a federal agent. If you're interested in more information about Les, I suggest you call Mike Hurley at DEA in Seattle (206–553–5443) . . .

From my experiences with him he very seldom, if ever, is what he claims to be.
Sincerely,
Ron Martz

Taking Martz at his word, MacMichael did not publish the letter, and all he saw fit to do with 'the information' it contained was pass it on to Coleman in Sweden.

Against his better judgement, although it turned out to be good practice for dealing with what was to come, Coleman took the time to prepare a point by point reply for MacMichael to forward to Martz. Though it seemed unlikely that Martz had gone to the trouble of writing a two-page, single-spaced letter simply out of a public-spirited desire to protect a fellow journalist, he had clearly not been very well briefed.

Hurley's own declaration, for instance, had established Coleman's DEA connection, describing him (incorrectly) as a CI, and Martz's 'high-ranking' source who told him the DIA had never heard of Coleman should perhaps have checked first with Colonel Bathen.

But the pattern of attack was clear, and soon to be repeated. First, the systematic reduction of his character to that of minor con man on the fringe of events, and then the accusations of petty dishonesty.

Coleman told MacMichael:

I don't know where to start. I didn't contact them. They came to me, looking for help with their Cyprus trip. I'd never met Martz before he came to see me in my private office at the University of Alabama. The DIA had parked me there for the winter as Director of Visiting International Scholars. So I certainly wasn't living in Cyprus at the time – I was living in Birmingham, Alabama.

The suggestion that he paid me is also a bit comical. The only money that changed hands was payment for the phone calls he made from my government apartment while they were out there in the spring of '88, and I turned this over to the DIA in accordance with standing orders. He didn't know that, of course, and I suppose I should take it as a compliment that he swallowed my cover so completely that he saw me as a hustling freelance journalist, although how he squares that with what I was doing for the DEA and with the Fulbright Commission as UA's Director of Visiting International Scholars, I don't know.

As for stealing his photographs, Lloyd Burchette *gave* me a set of five prints from a film he had developed in Larnaca while Martz was off on a cruise to Cairo with his wife. And Lloyd needn't have bothered because the lab he used handled all of DEA's film work on Cyprus and they always ran off an extra set of anything interesting for Mike Hurley anyway.

Nor did I sell them to *Soldier of Fortune*. The article that appeared with the Colin Knox byline was written by Mike Theodolus, a close friend of Hurley's and a writer for *Cyprus Life* magazine, which also ran the piece. The only contribution I made to *Soldier of Fortune* was in 1987, and that was a rehash I did on Hurley's instructions of an article called 'The Lebanese Connection' that appeared in the *Observer* in December 1986. Almost word for word, I'm ashamed to say.

And so it goes on. I left behind no unpaid telephone bills or unpaid rent. We were living in government accommodation, so the embassy picked up the tab. And if the Cypriot police *were* looking for me, I shouldn't have been hard to find because I was back in Nicosia, under my own name, in May 1991, en route to Sweden, and nobody bothered me. So I don't know where Martz got *that* from. And what's this about impersonating a Federal agent? That's a new one.

Before writing this, Martz obviously didn't read any of the court documents in the Pan Am case or in the passport frame-up, otherwise he would have known that the DEA had admitted I was a contract consultant and that the DIA had acknowledged I was working for them at the same time. If he honestly thinks I put myself in the middle of the Flight 103 case in the hope of gaining something by it then one of us belongs in a padded room.

No wonder his letter was not for publication. Like a few other reporters I know who make a business out of chasing dope stories around the world in their quiche-stained safari suits, Martz is no dope himself. If he wants a good scoop now and then, he knows he better play ball with the DEA.

It may just have been a coincidence that this attempt to discredit Coleman within the intelligence community came soon after Chief Judge Platt had declined to dismiss Pan Am's third-party suit in New York; soon after the government's deception of Chief Judge Moran in Chicago had resulted in the issue of a fugitive warrant, and soon after Danny Casolaro had been murdered while running down a Coleman lead, but there was no doubting the connection between *Time* magazine's cover article of 27 April 1992, and the vicious attack on Coleman launched as soon as the civil suit against Pan Am was over.

Christopher Byron teed off for the government in the 31 August issue of *New York* magazine.

A former employee of *Forbes* magazine, Byron found Roy Rowan's story about Flight 103 'a tangle of assertions and equivocations' based on Coleman's skill in 'conning the media'. Having bamboozled Brian Ross of NBC and Pierre Salinger of ABC, wrote Byron, 'Coleman finally found his loudest sounding board of all – the cover of *Time* magazine.'

One might have expected that anyone with such a phenomenal gift for deception would be living in luxury in the south of France rather than subsisting on the goodwill of the Swedish government, but Byron was clearly made of sterner stuff than his media colleagues.

'Beguiled by his astounding claim that the DEA was implicated in the Pan Am 103 disaster,' he went on, '*Time* made this the central thesis – with Coleman as the corroborating source – of its cover story entitled "The Untold Story of Pan Am 103".'

Byron did not feel it necessary to explain why *he* was not taken in as others were, nor did he suggest why, failing a financial motive, Coleman should have set out to deceive *anybody*, but it hardly mattered. Byron had already given most of the game away by describing him as a 'corroborating source', in effect accepting that the story had originated elsewhere as Ross, Salinger and Rowan had each insisted.

Byron next accused Coleman and Juval Aviv of collusion in selling Aviv's 'discredited' Interfor Report to *Time*, and, even more whimsically, of conspiring with Pan Am's lawyers to influence the civil liability trial. They 'all seem to have worked together – or at least in parallel – to get their story into *Time*,' is how he put it, falling just short of imputing libellous motives to an attorney of James Shaughnessy's calibre.

In fact, as Pan Am had dropped Aviv almost two years *before* the story appeared, and as Coleman had met Aviv for the first time some six months *after* he had sworn out his affidavit, their scope for collusion was limited. In any case, Coleman did not, and *does* not, accept Aviv's and Rowan's conclusion that a rogue CIA unit was instrumental in allowing a bomb aboard Flight 103.

'Just how badly did *Time* get snookered in all this?' asked Byron. 'For an answer, one need look no further than Michael Schafer, a young Christian Broadcasting Network cameraman who had worked for Coleman for six months in Beirut in 1985 and became the best man at his wedding.'

Schafer, known at the time as Michael Franks, had been sent to Beirut by Overseas Press Services Inc., a firm of 'consultants' with close ties to Oliver North, CIA director William Casey and the Nicaraguan Contras. The 'young cameraman' had spent most of his time in Beirut fighting with the right-wing Christian militias and, as best man, signed Coleman's marriage certificate as Michael Franks.

When Coleman later learned from Pan Am's lawyers that the mysterious David Lovejoy, who had told the Iranians about the American intelligence agents on Flight 103, was also known as Michael Franks, he gave Shaughnessy a photograph of his best man, and it was this picture that eventually appeared in *Time* magazine as a picture of David Lovejoy, 'a reported double agent for the US and Iran'.

(The same picture was also used on the forged CBN 'press credentials' that Schafer later produced in an attempt to cover up his lapse in signing Coleman's marriage certificate as Franks, the name he used in Lebanon in 1985 before it became generally known as a Lovejoy alias.)

'This whole thing is a disgrace,' Byron went on, quoting CNN investigative reporter Steven Emerson.

'I have reviewed the DEA file on Coleman,' Emerson had told him (perhaps unaware that this was not only prima facie evidence of a Federal crime but something which Coleman and the Pan Am legal team had conspicuously failed to accomplish by subpoena). 'The overwhelming evidence is that this man has invented his involvement in and knowledge of covert operations that never occurred.'

As the only 'evidence' this provided was of Emerson's inability to express himself clearly, Byron proceeded to enlarge on his remarks with a sceptical account of Coleman's career as an intelligence agent, ostensibly based on Coleman's own claims and assertions, but in reality cobbled together to fit the Byron/Emerson/DEA thesis that the *Time*/Aviv/Coleman story was a put-up job to get Pam Am off the hook.

'That's what Coleman says,' concluded Byron. 'Here's what others say about him.'

Eight loaded quotations followed from a list of 'character witnesses' headed by Lloyd Burchette Jr, a friend of Michael Franks/Schafer and 'primary assistant' to Ron Martz, who was apparently still too shy to come forward in person.

Billed now as a *reporter* for the *Atlanta Journal-Constitution*, Burchette declared: 'Les Coleman is the greatest bullshit artist I've ever met in my life. He ripped us off for $2000 and absolutely nothing he promised to do for us ever panned out. He also stole some photographs from me and my partner and sold them to *Soldier of Fortune* magazine. The man's a phony, and I wouldn't believe a word he says about anything.'

Burchette evidently has a forgiving nature, however. Later in his article, Byron says 'he [Burchette] stayed in touch with him [Coleman] thereafter' – and clearly on friendly terms, because in June 1990, according to Byron, Coleman called Burchette 'in hysterics' to say he had just been busted for a passport violation and that he was sure Hurley 'was behind the whole thing'. (Hardly the reaction of a guilty man, in any case.)

Next up in the firing line was Tom Slizewski, managing editor of *Soldier of Fortune* who said Coleman had written two stories for him under the pen name of Colin Knox and owed the magazine $1000 for a third, which he had failed to deliver.

Coleman had already answered this charge, and Burchette's, when it was first made by Martz, but his response had evidently failed to register. Coleman prepared the first article to appear, bylined Colin Knox, in 1987 and then surrendered the pen-name to a journalist friend of Hurley's.

Number three was Hurley himself, who departed from the text of his sworn declaration to describe Coleman as 'a part-time confidential informant' who 'stole $5500 from one of his own subinformants. Then he got in trouble with the Cypriot police for stealing from his landlord. He stole DEA files and sold them to *Soldier of Fortune*. Then Coleman talked about DEA informants in *Time* magazine, and he's blown their covers.'

These charges were particularly contemptible.

First, the $5500 was demanded by a cameraman in the full-time employ of a London television news company who shot some film for the DEA with his employers' equipment in the course of his official duties and thus wished to be paid twice. Coleman refused to give him the money.

Second, by 'stealing from his landlord', Hurley presumably meant the telephone bills which he had neglected to pay after Coleman left his government apartment and returned home.

Third, this was the first reference anywhere to the theft of DEA files, a more serious offence than a passport violation, particularly if they were then sold to *Soldier of Fortune*, a Federal crime on the part of both seller and buyer.

Fourth, as for blowing the covers of DEA informants in *Time* magazine, the only one mentioned by his real name was Ibrahim El-Jorr, an 'offence' of which Byron was also guilty, and who had long since dropped out of sight, no doubt because he knew too much about DEA-controlled deliveries from Cyprus.

Then came Peter Schweitzer of CBS News, who suggested that Coleman had conned the network's foreign desk in New York into having him tag along with Schweitzer and his team when they went out to Saudi Arabia 'to cover the hajj in September of 1985 . . . He was nice enough, it is true, but he was of no help and had no special expertise. He didn't speak Arabic or anything.'

Schweitzer's memory was evidently playing tricks. He had covered the hajj in 1984, not 1985, from his hotel room, keeping out of trouble while Coleman did battle – in Arabic – with Saudi

Ministry of Information officials to save the unit's video footage from censorship.

'My wife, her family, my many friends and my present employer who hired me as a part-time Arabic translator will be interested to know that I don't speak Arabic,' he wrote in a long letter of rebuttal to *New York* magazine (which neither acknowledged nor published it).

A spokesman for the University of Alabama came next. He claimed that Coleman had been hired as 'assistant director of international student affairs' but after a couple of months 'he just left, so we dismissed him.' They then discovered that some student visa forms had gone with him, and they 'wound up having to void every student visa he'd issued'.

Except one. Coleman's appointment had been a DIA set-up from the start, with the dual object of putting him on hold for the winter and importing Syrian George on a student visa. The DIA may not have confided this to the university's anonymous spokesman.

He was followed by an equally anonymous spokesman for Auburn University, Montgomery, Alabama, who declared, 'We've never had a Lester Coleman on the payroll.'

In Montgomery, no. But on the main campus at Auburn, Alabama, the DIA had arranged for him to take up a full teaching assistantship in the Department of Political Science. (The local newspaper ran a story about a lecture he gave there on Middle East politics, complete with Coleman's picture.) He was admitted to graduate school on 23 December 1986, and the records show – if they have not since been shredded – that when he arrived in Cyprus in February 1987, seconded to the DEA, he was enrolled for a course entitled Thesis Research. (The spokesman's confusion may have arisen because Coleman was paid by the DIA while on campus and not by the university.)

A similar problem afflicted the next anonymous spokesman, this one for the National Intelligence Academy, Fort Lauderdale. 'He [Coleman] worked here for eleven days in October of 1988. He was a videotape editor. That's all I know.'

In fact, it was 1987. Coleman was assigned to the Academy for six weeks, and he kept a souvenir – his official staff pass. It reads: 'Director, Video Operations'. Also, he does not know *how* to edit videotape.

Last but not least, Byron quoted yet another anonymous spokesman, this time for the Boy Scouts of America. 'He worked here in PR,' he said. 'Let's just say he's gone; things didn't work out.'

Just before his recall by the DIA for Operation Shakespeare, Coleman received his annual review as director of Marketing and Communications for the BSA, Chicago. In three areas of responsibility, his performance was rated: in one, 'Exceeded requirements'; in another, 'Far exceeded requirements', and in the last, 'Met requirements'.

If Byron's *New York* article had aspired to greater balance, he might have offset some of this with one or two more positive opinions.

If he had approached Msgr John A. Esseff, for example, who went out to the Middle East in 1984 to direct a Catholic church relief mission and later gave evidence to a Congressional committee inquiring into Lebanese drug trafficking, he would have heard that 'Les Coleman was the most respected, most knowledgeable source on the Middle East and the kinds of terrorist activities that had been engaged in by Syria, Iran and Libya that I had met . . .

'I find him trustworthy and courageous. He is not someone who has made these revelations to cater to sensationalism and journalistic playing to the crowd for material gain . . . Les may not see himself as a modern prophet, but I see him as a biblical prophet who is driven by a sense of justice, truth and honesty to reveal the truth.'

This and other testimonials from public figures in support of Coleman's plea for asylum in Sweden did not, however, fit well with Byron's *New York* thesis that 'Coleman's career underscores an important message about contemporary American life: how eager the media have become to charge the very worst about government, even when the evidence in a story points to the opposite conclusion.'

Though confusingly expressed, his meaning was clear. But equally it could be said that mistrust of government is enshrined in the American political process, and that, in the absence of evidence to the contrary, the media have a constitutional duty to assume the worst. In his eagerness to exonerate the government by blackguarding Coleman, Byron tortured the evidence in *his* story to the point of travesty.

In defence of Rowan's article, *Time* said it had obtained documents proving that Coleman had been, as he claimed, employed by both the DIA and the DEA.

'What *Time* didn't point out,' wrote Byron, 'was that two of these documents were affidavits of DIA and DEA officials that contradicted many of Coleman's claims.'

True. But they did *not* contradict the essential one, which was that Coleman had been employed by them. And that was the point *Time* had sought to verify.

Similarly with Coleman's pre-trial services report, from which *Time* had quoted this passage: 'Although Mr Coleman's employment history sounds quite improbable, information he gave has proven to be true.'

Uncomfortable with this official endorsement of Coleman's credibility, Byron wrote: 'What *Time* didn't tell its readers was that the information in the report came mainly from a court officer's interviews with Coleman himself, as well as from Brian Ross of NBC News: the very first sentence in the report says so.'

Really? The very first sentence of the report reads as follows: 'The information below was gathered through interview of the defendant and *through contact with DEA headquarters* [author's italics], NBC News and the subject's attorney.'

The reason for Byron's omission of DEA headquarters as a source for the report becomes clear in the text. This says plainly that Coleman 'worked as an undercover investigator for the Drug Enforcement Administration of the United States'. And it goes on: 'Ray Tripiccio, an agent with DEA in Washington, D.C., verifies that Coleman has formerly worked in a relationship with the Drug Enforcement Administration. The only information he could give on this secret activity is that Coleman was deactivated as a contract consultant as of 6–24–88.'

Not as a 'low level' informant, part-time or otherwise, but 'as a contract consultant'. Not 'fired' or 'terminated', but 'deactivated'.

Coleman's pre-trial services report gives the lie to all subsequent DEA statements about his status, starting with Steven Emerson's CNN newscast in December 1990, continuing with Micheal Hurley's sworn declaration 'under penalty of perjury', with Martz's 'not-for-publication' letter, Byron's systematic misrepresentation of his career, and Emerson's review of 'the DEA file on Coleman'.

Having failed to silence him, the DEA's motive in seeking to destroy Coleman's credibility was clear: he knew too much about the sequence of events that led up to the Flight 103 disaster, and it was imperative that no one should believe him.

Byron's motive in withholding information in order to assist the DEA in those efforts is a matter for speculation.

Still trying to attack his former colleagues at *Time* and denounce Coleman in the same breath, Byron accused Rowan of quoting selectively from the pre-trial services report in order to present Coleman as a credible source, 'ignoring those parts of it that clashed with that view [in the circumstances, a remarkable piece of hypocrisy].

'Thus, the story unquestioningly parroted Coleman's claim that he had been tricked into applying for a passport under a false name . . . Yet the pretrial services report states the truth of what actually happened: Coleman indicates that he is currently working on a book, and that he was attempting to make arrangements to return to the Middle East, in order to do more research . . . Coleman states that he needed a passport in a different name because his name is known to drug traffickers in the Middle East.'

This was indeed true, if not the whole truth – although how Byron could have known was not explained. At the time of his arrest, Coleman was certainly working on a book. His name was certainly known to drug traffickers in the Middle East. And he certainly needed a passport in a different name. What he did *not* reveal to the pre-trial services officer was his identity as a DIA agent who had been instructed to apply for another passport to use on a mission to Lebanon to investigate its military government's links with Iraq. Byron was either unaware of this or again chose to withhold the information.

The rest of his *New York* magazine article was a more or less standard rehash of the lies, half-truths and innuendo that had dogged Coleman from the day his cover was blown. But there were one or two ingenious twists. In order to get around the awkward problem of why other journalists of greater reputation should have asked Coleman to corroborate a story obtained from other, unconnected sources, Byron attempted to show that Coleman was also behind the other sources.

While it was clearly not safe to accuse Pierre Salinger of lying when the ABC newscast attributed its story about the DEA's involvement in the Flight 103 disaster to 'law enforcement officials', Byron *could* suggest, in language appropriate to someone tiptoeing around the edge of libel, that 'there is good reason to wonder whether Salinger properly understood the full picture of what they were telling him.'

Byron's theory was that when Coleman's attorney in Chicago subpoenaed the DEA and other agencies on 31 August 1990, he triggered an internal Justice Department inquiry into Coleman's story that lasted 'for many months' and resulted in the DEA giving itself a clean bill of health. While that was going on, 'the DEA began getting press inquiries from ABC itself regarding COREA – inquiries that it now seems evident were prompted by Coleman.' Evident to whom? Not, clearly, to Salinger, who had already said that he met Coleman in London shortly before the broadcast to corroborate material he had previously obtained from 'law enforcement officials'.

'Thus, without knowing each little fact of the matter,' Byron went on, 'we can begin to sketch the general outlines of what happened: ABC News, egged on by Coleman, called its law-enforcement sources on the COREA business, only to hear that the government was indeed looking into the question. In short, if ABC News thought it had "other sources" for its Pan Am story, it is equally possible that it had simply caught the scent of Lester Coleman disappearing around a corner.'

Unfortunately for Byron, 'each little fact of the matter' carries too much weight to be borne by so flimsy a piece of special pleading, despite his attempt to include readers in the conspiratorial 'we' and his disingenuous 'equally possible'.

It is not at all possible that Salinger, 'a journalist with a long and strong track record' who had told Byron there was 'no possible way' that his sources 'could have been in contact with Coleman or even have known him' was referring to sources within the government who had merely confirmed that the Justice Department was looking into 'the COREA business'. Who could reasonably assume from this that allegations of DEA involvement in the Lockerbie disaster were true? In any case, these government sources would certainly have known about Coleman even if they had not been in contact with him.

It is equally implausible to suggest that two months after inquiring if DEA agents in Nicosia had been running a controlled delivery operation at the time of the Flight 103 disaster their superiors in Washington still did not know the answer. And surely, if there *had* been an internal inquiry, it would have taken place a year earlier, in September 1989, when Pan Am attempted to subpoena the same documents?

In fact, the only 'good reason to wonder' Byron provides is whether he properly understands the nature of responsible journalism.

After a slanted synopsis of Bathen's DIA declaration and an embellished version of Hurley's, Byron turned again to Burchette for 'evidence' that Coleman was lying when he said he recognised a photograph of Khalid Jafaar.

'During the month he was on Cyprus, Lloyd Burchette says he met every informant working with or for Coleman and he maintains he never met anyone who even looked like Jafaar.' Burchette further claimed that Coleman called him after the ABC newscast, which had included a photograph of Jafaar, and *denied* that he recognized him.

This was conclusive enough for Byron.

'The fact that *Time* magazine was willing to put a charge of government complicity in the Pan Am bombing on its cover on the doubtful assertions of a private eye [Juval Aviv] and an international fugitive in a passport case, and against the strong protestations [later denied] of its own Washington-bureau experts,' he wrote, 'reveals more than sloppy journalism – it reveals something about the impulse to self-destruction that seems to be chipping away at America's faith in itself and its institutions.'

As an authority on American values, Byron's credentials are perhaps less impressive than they are in the matter of sloppy journalism – as witness the concluding paragraph of his article.

And what of Lester Coleman? As things turned out, he was never called as a witness in the Pan Am trial, and no affidavit, declaration or deposition from him was submitted at the trial, either. Apparently realizing they'd been snookered, Pan Am's lawyers seem to have concluded that if they put Coleman on the stand, the plaintiffs' lawyers would rip him apart. As a result, the only people who now need to be told the truth about the Pan Am bombing are the millions of TV viewers and magazine readers who weren't in the courtroom. Thanks in no small part to Lester Coleman and the American media, they no doubt continue to wonder whether the US government was, in fact, involved in the mass murder of American citizens.

Not knowing each little fact of the matter, Byron got most of this wrong as well. At no time had Coleman ever been considered as a possible witness in Pan Am's defence of the civil liability suit. His affidavit had been obtained in the course of Pan Am's third-party suit against the US government, and the only circumstances in which he might have been called as a witness in *that* action would have been if the government had produced the discovery material that Pan Am's counsel had asked for. As it did not, the third-party suit was dismissed on the eve of the liability trial.

The only issue that then remained was whether Pan Am's security lapses at Frankfurt amounted to wilful misconduct, and Coleman had never had anything to say about that. Even if Pan Am *had* wished to put him on the stand for some reason it could not have done so, not only in view of his circumstances but because the judge had already made it clear in advance that he would rule out any testimony suggesting government complicity in the bombing. The jury was there to try a claim against Pan Am, not the US government.

In fact, the only parties keen to 'rip him apart' were the Drug Enforcement Administration and, on this evidence, Christopher Byron (although he would shortly be joined by his colleague Steven Emerson). With that in mind, the last sentence of Byron's article takes on an unintended irony. Nor are the editors of *New York* magazine beyond reproach. When Coleman sent them a point-by-point rebuttal of the smear, they not only failed to publish it, thus denying the accused a chance to defend himself, but failed even to acknowledge his letter. (Or, if they did, he failed to received it.)

Hard on the heels of Byron's article, the September 1992 issue of the *Washington Journalism Review* fielded Steven Emerson on the same subject, using much the same material to arrive at much the same conclusion.

Leading off with the Franks/Schafer/Lovejoy business to demonstrate that '*Time* obviously screwed up,' Emerson was prepared to forgive the magazine for that but not for relying on Juval Aviv and Lester Coleman, whom he described as Pan Am's 'paid consultants'.

Aviv *had* been, of course, some two years earlier, but to describe Coleman in this way was about as accurate as Emerson's previous description of him on CNN as a disgruntled former DEA informant (and was no doubt attributable to the same source).

Coleman received nothing from Pan Am except travel passes and expenses incurred on Pan Am-related business. To assert, as Emerson did later in his article, that 'the two men have been paid tens of thousands of dollars by Pan Am's attorneys, according to officials close to the case', was presumably intended to suggest that Coleman had been a beneficiary of legitimate payments made to Aviv before he resigned as Pan Am's investigator, long before Coleman had even met him.

In its own interests, Pan Am had always been scrupulously careful to avoid compromising Coleman as a possible witness, preferring to leave the buying of testimony, as in the case of the Libyan defector, to the government.

After a brief synopsis of *Time*'s cover article, Emerson went on to note that the 'independent' President's Commission on Aviation Security and Terrorism had, in 1990, seen 'no foundation for speculation in press accounts that US government officials had participated tacitly or otherwise in any supposed operation at Frankfurt Airport having anything to do with the sabotage of Flight 103.'

What he, in common with most government spokesmen, failed to mention, however, was that the commission had been specifically excluded from any role in the investigation of the bombing and had thus never addressed the issue of government complicity.

Emerson did, however, concede that the indictment of two Libyans for the crime in November 1991 had 'generated some controversy, leading several critics to charge that the US government might be engaged in a cover-up.' *Time*, he felt, had 'exploited this controversy' by running a story derived from Aviv's original Interfor Report of 1989.

Without referring again to a possible cover-up, Emerson went over the government's now familiar dismissal of Aviv and his report, echoing the *Observer*'s 1989 charge that he 'had pieced together known events and facts in a wild conspiracy'. Things then died down, he wrote, until the NBC and ABC news reports in October 1990 revived the story of the DEA's involvement in the bombing.

Differing slightly from Byron's account of what happened then, Emerson claimed that 'within a week, the agency reviewed every file from the previous five years and sent inquiries to its agents overseas. The evidence collected by the DEA – and independently confirmed by the FBI – showed that the allegations reported by NBC and ABC were baseless . . .

'Still, some journalists were not convinced,' he wrote. 'In its 17 December 1990 issue, *Barron's* published a lengthy article reporting virtually everything in the Aviv report. The conspiracy theory would not die.'

The main reason for this, Byron suggested, was Lester Coleman, who had alleged that Khalid Jafaar was one of his informants and who had teamed up with Aviv in 1990.

Both statements were incorrect. Coleman had never claimed Jafaar as an informant and he met Aviv for the first time in late 1991.

Nevertheless, according to Emerson, the DEA had shown him 'an internal November 1990 DEA memo' which said Aviv had told a DEA agent that Coleman had contacted him several months earlier and that he (Coleman) was trying to sell information about the bombing. 'By the time NBC and ABC interviewed Coleman,' wrote Emerson, 'he had worked out his story with Aviv.'

Why Aviv should have reported Coleman to the DEA and then collaborated with him in concocting a story for NBC and ABC was not explained. Nor has Coleman been able to verify the existence or contents of the DEA internal memo for, unlike Emerson, he has never been able to obtain access to his DEA file, not even under Title 5, 552 (b) (6) of the Privacy Act.

Emerson's special relationship with the DEA was further demonstrated when he quoted from another internal DEA memo describing Coleman's association with DEA Cyprus. This, not unnaturally, echoed Hurley's sworn declaration on that subject, and led to 'corroborative' testimony from Ron Martz of the *Atlanta Journal-Constitution*, on the record this time, and Lloyd Burchette Jr., now described as 'a screenwriter'.

After that, Emerson drew his readers' attention to what he described as 'half-truths, misstatements and omissions' in the *Time* magazine story, displaying a measure of the same disregard for his own shortcomings in this respect as Byron had shown in *his* article, and, again like Byron, getting Coleman's status as a Pan Am witness completely wrong.

'According to sources familiar with the defence strategy,' wrote Emerson, 'Pan Am's attorneys began having doubts about Aviv and Coleman two years ago. Even so, they went along with the conspiracy story because it was their only hope of winning the case. But when the defence attorneys apparently realized that their prize witnesses and their story would be torn to shreds under cross-examination, they dropped the witnesses.'

It was clear from this that neither Byron nor Emerson had understood that there had been *two* lawsuits to be tried: the civil action against Pan Am brought by the families of the Flight 103 victims, and the action brought by Pan Am against the US government for third-party liability.

Coleman and Aviv *might* have been called as witnesses in the third-party suit if it had not been dismissed three days before the main trial began, but at no time – before, during or after – did Coleman have a role to play in the suit *against* Pan Am. On the issue of the airline's alleged 'wilful misconduct' in flouting FAA security regulations at Frankfurt, he had nothing whatever to contribute.

Although clear enough from the court records, the legal position was apparently too difficult for Byron and Emerson to grasp. In which case, their 'sources familiar with the defence strategy' might at least have spared them the humiliation of looking foolish in print.

On the other hand, perhaps they did not mind. For a parting shot at Coleman, Emerson turned again to reporter/screenwriter Lloyd Burchette Jr and the Franks/Schafer affair.

'Burchette recalls that one day in May 1988, in Cyprus, Coleman showed him a letter of identification stating that Michael Schafer "is a representative of CBN News assigned to the Beirut bureau",' he wrote. 'It included a photo of Schafer – the same photo *Time* said was David Lovejoy – and was signed by Coleman, who was then a CBN senior correspondent. A copy of this letter of identification shows that the photo of Schafer and that of Lovejoy are exactly the same. There is no evidence that Lovejoy exists.'

In fact, there *is* some evidence that Lovejoy exists, but aside from that, a less committed writer might just have paused here and asked Burchette these questions (or if he *did* ask them, to have favoured his readers with the answers):

Why would Franks/Schafer sign Coleman's marriage certificate as Franks if he was holding a letter of identification from Coleman in the name of Schafer?

If Coleman *had* given this letter of identification to Franks/Schafer in Beirut in 1985, what was Coleman doing with it in Cyprus in 1988?

How did he get it back from Franks/Schafer?

And how did Franks/Schafer then get it back from *him*?

For Coleman, safe for the moment in Sweden, these smears mattered only because they showed how far the US government was ready to go in suppressing the truth. And that was important because, having given up hope of a fair hearing in court or in the news media, he had sought to have the whole story of his career as an intelligence agent told in a book.

After the Byron and Emerson articles appeared, negotiations with a prospective publisher stalled, and when *New York* magazine and the *Washington Journalism Review* both failed to publish his rebuttal, they collapsed.

— XVIII —

Meanwhile, the families of the Flight 103 victims had won their suit against Pan Am.

On 11 July 1992, a New York jury found that the airline and two of its subsidiary companies, Pan American World Services and Alert Management, Inc., had been guilty of 'wilful misconduct' in failing to observe required security procedures at Frankfurt airport, thereby permitting the terrorists to smuggle a bomb aboard.

In Britain, the judgement was hailed by Peter Watson, lawyer for the British families, as 'a warning to the airline industry that, if their security is as lax, poor and haphazard as Pan Am's was on this occasion, then they face fearful damages. That is the only way a court can bring this home to an airline.'

As there is little doubt that Pan Am's security arrangements at Frankfurt on 21 December 1988, *were* as 'lax, poor and haphazard' as Watson maintained, his strictures were justified. But there remained a serious doubt that Pan Am's security arrangements were even *relevant* to the fate of Flight 103.

The plaintiffs' suit had rested squarely on the government's case against the Libyans. If the Libyans were guilty as charged, then so was Pan Am. If they were *not*, then the plaintiffs' suit was without foundation.

Lee Kreindler, lead counsel for the families, had been required to prove that the bomb, disguised as a Toshiba radio-cassette player, was packed in a suitcase and shipped from Malta to Frankfurt, where it slipped through Pan Am's security and was loaded aboard Flight 103. That could only have happened, he argued, because Pan Am had failed to observe the security rules which required unaccompanied baggage to be hand-searched.

In effect, Kreindler had been required to test part of the case against the Libyans before he could win the suit. If he failed to convince the jury that the bomb had originated in Malta, then Pan Am was off the hook. With no proof of how or where the bomb had been introduced into the baggage-handling system, how could anyone say the airline should have prevented the disaster?

For the defence, Pan Am's trial counsel, Clinton Coddington, admitted that as far as security at Frankfurt was concerned, 'there is no question we made slip-ups and goofs, but,' he insisted, 'they did not cause the tragedy.' Although he argued that the airline's security system had been approved by the FAA, the crux of his strategy was to show 'that the bomb could not have been from Malta'.

The task proved beyond him. Barred from suggesting that the bag had gone aboard at Frankfurt in a way that Pan Am could not have been expected to prevent and even from calling expert witnesses to challenge the validity of the plaintiffs' Libyan theory, he failed to persuade the jurors – but only just. After a trial lasting 11 weeks, they twice reported themselves deadlocked and twice Chief Judge Platt had to send them back to resume their discussions. In the end, it took the jury three days to arrive at a finding of wilful misconduct, which Pan Am immediately announced it would appeal.

'Much of what we do know with certainty about Lockerbie,' said Thomas G. Plaskett, the airline's former chairman, 'was not shared with this jury, and so today's verdict, much like the whole affair, remains clouded by uncertainty. We shall endeavour through the appeals process to shed some light on this uncertainty.'

This was not what the US government wished to hear. For one thing, it meant that the appeals court would review the Libyan theory, and if, as seemed likely, the judgement against Pan Am was reversed, the whole can of worms would be tipped over in full public view.

If the appeals court ordered a new trial, perhaps on the grounds that evidence for the plaintiffs had been improperly admitted while evidence for the defence had been improperly excluded, then Pan Am's counsel would be free to attack the plaintiffs' case with testimony they had not been allowed to present in the first trial – and it seemed unlikely that the Libyan theory could stand up to a battering by expert witnesses.

If Pan Am eventually succeeded in defending the liability suit, therefore, the government's case against Libya would be in shreds and its five-year cover-up left plain for all to see.

With Plaskett's announcement that Pan Am and its insurers intended to appeal, Washington went after James Shaughnessy with a vindictiveness without parallel in legal history. Whether as a last-ditch, all-out attempt to shake him off or simply to punish him for daring to challenge the official version of events, the Justice Department filed its long-threatened motion for punitive sanctions against him and his law firm in the amount of $6 million.

Referring to the civil action just ended, the preamble left the court in no doubt about the government's furious embarrassment:

> This litigation arose from the wilful misconduct of Pan American World Airways (Pan Am) which allowed a terrorist bomb to be placed aboard its Flight 103 which was destroyed over Lockerbie, Scotland, on December 21, 1988. Subsequently, this court, the families of the victims and the United States Government have been subjected to a calculated and callous litigation strategy intended to avoid liability for the carrier's misconduct.

> This strategy, initiated in mid-1989, has been followed to this very day by Pan Am's counsel and their client. Until the United States was finally dismissed in April 1992 [a reference to the dropping of the third-party suit on the eve of the civil action] these litigants, relying upon and wilfully implementing this strategy, successfully generated inflammatory but false allegations in the media and before this court which were intended, and did, in fact, divert attention from the legitimate focus of this litigation, Pan Am's own wilful misconduct.

> The resulting waste of time, effort and financial resources and, indeed, attempted misdirection of the criminal investigation itself, more than warrant the substantial sanctions sought by this motion.

More specifically, the government sought to punish Shaughnessy for:

(1) Pan Am's initial subpoenas to the intelligence, military and law enforcement agencies which were based upon the false allegations in the Aviv Report;

(2) the filing of the third-party complaint which was based upon those same false allegations and the equally false allegations directed against the Drug Enforcement Administration (DEA);

(3) the opposition to the motion of the United States to dismiss the third-party complaint which was based upon further false

representations that the Pan Am litigants possessed a basis for the claims in the third-party complaint;

(4) the post-filing discovery requests directed at the intelligence, military and law-enforcement agencies for classified and privileged information which is completely protected by statute and under existing precedent, as to which no legitimate argument for change could reasonably be made;

(5) the submission of Freedom of Information Act (FOIA) requests to various agencies which were identical to Pan Am's civil discovery requests, and

(6) the continuous opposition to all reasonable attempts to terminate the litigation activity against the United States which was based upon the false allegations which were repeatedly reasserted without any evidence to support them.

Taken at face value, the motion seemed to argue that nobody, not even in his own defence in a court of law, was entitled to question the government's good faith, its conduct, the truth of its assertions or its judgement in deciding matters of fact. It also seemed to insist that its files were sacrosanct, that they were not open to inspection even in matters as grave as determining who was responsible for the mass murder of 270 innocent people. Even the use of FOIA requests in this context was deemed an underhanded and therefore sanctionable act.

But the motion was not to be taken lightly. Unless the government's arguments were met and answered to the satisfaction of the court, Shaughnessy and his law firm faced bankruptcy and worse. Disciplinary proceedings, perhaps even disbarment and criminal charges, might follow if the government's position were upheld. The choice, therefore, was either to seek an accommodation with the Justice Department, which, as a minimum, would have meant abandoning the case, or to fight.

On 25 September 1992, Shaughnessy met the government head-on with a 73-page affidavit reviewing the entire sweep of his investigation from the moment it began ten days after the Flight 103 disaster.

On the 'false allegations in the Aviv report', Shaughnessy described what happened when he discussed its conclusions with his colleagues.

'Plaintiffs' case depended on their contention that the bomb had penetrated Pan Am's security,' he wrote. 'Mr Aviv's report indicated that the bomb had circumvented Pan Am's security. Thus, in order to properly defend our clients, we decided that we should serve subpoenas on a number of Federal agencies in an effort to determine whether the government had any documentation which would either confirm or dispute what Mr Aviv had reported.'

Partial corroboration of Aviv's thesis 'that a Turkish Pan Am baggage handler, following his usual practice with respect to narcotics shipments, switched the suitcase containing the bomb for an "innocent" suitcase' had been provided by two conversations between Michael Jones of Pan Am and Phillip Connelly of H.M. Customs and Excise in London. But when the subpoenas were served, 'it was obvious that there were very few sources of evidence . . . other than the governments allegedly involved and the terrorists themselves. The best, if not the only source of information that was accessible and was within the subpoena power of the United States courts was the government.'

After tracing the course of the government's stubborn refusal to disclose what it had on file, Shaughnessy reminded the court that his discovery subpoenas had finally been quashed on the strength of a briefing 'on undisclosed matters on unspecified dates by unidentified agents of the government'.

Whatever Chief Judge Platt was told, he later expressed the opinion that 'the key liability issue in this litigation was whether defendants [Pan Am] had met the applicable standard of care with respect to the security applied to interline baggage in Frankfurt.' (Given the determination with which the government had resisted producing the relevant documents, it is hardly likely that its agents would have told the court anything that pointed to a different conclusion.)

Shaughnessy then turned to the government's almost total lack of interest in the results of the polygraph tests he had arranged for the three Pan Am baggage handlers on duty in Frankfurt on the day of the disaster.

In the opinion of the examiner, James Keefe, who had conducted polygraph examinations for over 30 years for the US Army's Criminal Investigations Division, Tiling Kuzcu 'did not tell the truth when he stated that he did not know who switched the suitcases on Flight 103, and further when he stated that he did not switch those suitcases himself. Further, it was the opinion of the examiner that Tuzcu did not tell the truth when he stated that he was not told by Roland O'Neill, loadmaster, to switch the suitcases. Further, it was the opinion of the examiner that Tuzcu had a suspicion that the suitcase placed on Flight 103 contained a bomb.' (The significance of these results, like the significance of the Aviv report, had been largely obscured by the uproar that followed their leakage to the press. As with the report, the polygraph results were invariably described after that as 'discredited'.)

After running through a long list of sources tracked down *after* Aviv resigned as Pan Am's investigator in June 1990, Shaughnessy described his first meeting in London with Lester Coleman, who had gone there to meet Pierre Salinger of ABC News. Both NBC and ABC, he said, had told Gregory W. Buhler, deputy general counsel of Pan Am, who was also in London, that they 'had evidence that a DEA undercover operation was involved in the crash of Flight 103'. They had also assured Buhler 'that they had obtained their evidence from sources within the United States government and that they were merely using Mr Coleman to confirm certain details'.

At subsequent meetings in London, Coleman gave Shaughnessy 'detailed information concerning the DIA, the DEA and particularly the Cyprus office of the DEA. This information included code names of operations, file numbers of operations, names of confidential informants and names of subsources. Mr Coleman also provided me with copies of a number of documents, including an internal DEA memorandum and a passport of a man he said was a DEA confidential informant.' (This was the passport of Syrian George, for whom Coleman had organized a student visa, and who was as familiar with the DEA's couriers and its programme of controlled heroin deliveries from the Bekaa as Coleman himself. Syrian George was last heard of in the Seattle area, to which Micheal Hurley had been assigned after his recall from Cyprus.)

'Finally,' said Shaughnessy, 'he gave me a photograph which he said he had obtained from a contact in Athens which he said was a photograph of David Lovejoy who, at the time the photograph was taken in Beirut in 1985, was using the name Michael Franks.'

Besides newspaper reports about the interception of Lovejoy's calls to the Iranian Embassy in Beirut, Shaughnessy said that he 'had also been advised separately by four investigative journalists' that they had 'evidence' of these intercepts, one having claimed to have actually heard the tapes. 'Finally, I was told that Mr Lovejoy used a number of aliases, including Michael Franks.'

Turning next to the government's charge that there was no basis for the third-party complaint, Shaughnessy reminded the court that the government had been advised in advance of his intentions to file suit in order to protect the rights of Pan Am and their insurers before the two-year time period ran out. Plaintiffs in the civil suit against Pan Am had done the same thing, for the same reason.

However [he went on], the government claims that it was 'clear' even in December 1990 that there was nothing to defendants' claims. The government bases this claim on the following:

(i) the conclusions of the President's Commission, which was not tasked to investigate, and thus never addressed, the issue of government complicity, except in the broadest terms;

(ii) the determinations of Sheriff Principal Mowat at the [Scottish] Fatal Accident Inquiry, a proceeding which never investigated any facts in Frankfurt and never heard any evidence of, or addressed the issue of, government complicity; and those determinations were not issued until months after the filing of the third-party complaint;

(iii) a press release issued by the Department of Justice supposedly summarizing the results of an internal investigation following the NBC and ABC news reports which revealed that the FBI's investigation was continuing;

(iv) the declarations of government employees in response to government counsel's 'distillation' of Mr Aviv's 'accusations' . . .;

(v) Magistrate Judge Ross report . . . and

(vi) the testimony of Scottish Detective Constable Derrick Henderson at the Fatal Accident Inquiry [who] had no personal knowledge of any facts . . .

'I believed at the time we filed the third-party complaint, and still believe,' said Shaughnessy, 'that none of the sources cited by the government demonstrates that the allegations of the third-party complaint were not well grounded in fact.'

This brought him to the third charge, which was that he had opposed the government's motion to dismiss the third-party suit with 'further false representations', in particular the affidavit sworn out by Lester Coleman in Brussels on 17 April 1991. In reply, the government had filed declarations from Lt-Col. Terry Bathen of the DIA and Micheal Hurley of the DEA, and 'significantly', Shaughnessy went on, 'Colonel Bathen admitted that Mr Coleman had worked for the DIA and Mr Hurley admitted that Mr Coleman had worked in Cyprus for the DEA.

'Of even more significance, while Colonel Bathen and Mr Hurley went to some length to discredit Mr Coleman, neither of them, particularly Mr Hurley, attempted to address, much less rebut, the substantive statements made by Mr Coleman. This failure to deny the substance of Mr Coleman's statements sharpened our suspicions.' (As a footnote, he added: 'In light of certain allegations that have been made in the media, let me address one important point. Mr Coleman was never paid any amount except for his expenses in meeting first with me and then with [my colleague] Mr Prugh.')

Shaughnessy next described his attempts to secure depositions from Dalkamoni and Ghadanfar in Frankfurt, from Pinsdorf and Mayer of the BKA, from Talb and Moghrabi in Sweden, from the two principals of the Swiss firm that manufactured the batch of timers sold to the Libyans, and, in London, from Phillip Connelly, Dr Thomas Hayes, and David Leppard, to whom Dr Hayes had expressed the view that the bomb had most likely been triggered by a combined barometric switch and timer, rather than the simple timer supposedly employed under the Libyan theory. As the government had elected to have an attorney present on all these occasions, it was now trying to recover the costs it had incurred as a result.

Summing up, he declared that

what the government calls a 'callous litigation strategy intended to avoid liability' is what others call defending against unproven charges ... The initial subpoenas and the subsequent two discovery requests served upon the government, not to mention this court's July 19, 1991 order compelling the government to make discovery, were efforts to obtain information and evidence in this litigation. The third-party complaint was the result of information derived from our investigation ...

The government has fought strenuously and successfully for three years to prevent any discovery of it. Its success is the reason that defendants' third-party claims were dismissed, as a result of which those claims have never been adjudicated. Now, the government seeks millions of dollars of sanctions to punish and bankrupt my firm and me for having had the temerity not only to assert claims against the government but also for even seeking discovery from the government ...

The government condemns as sanctionable any view of the facts that differs from its own. In effect, what the government condemns is defendants' refusal to blindly adopt its version of the facts despite the government's refusal to produce the evidence from which defendants could have determined whether the government's version of the facts was correct . . .

The government expects this blind trust even though we had information from multiple sources that conflicted with the government's sweeping assertions and that suggested the government was responsible for the failure to prevent the bombing. I note that the government was never able to persuade the court, on the basis of [its] public statements and other facts that were publicly available, that the litigation against the government should cease . . .

Given the information in my possession, I believed that, in the exercise of my duties to my clients, I could not properly advise them simply to trust the government, to shut down discovery against the government, and to abandon the third-party claims without *convincing proof* that the government's self-serving statements of non-involvement and lack of knowledge were well-founded and our own information to the contrary was erroneous . . .

Not until the end of his long affidavit did Shaughnessy at last give vent to his anger at the attack on his character and professional conduct.

In closing, I want to say that I am outraged that the government . . . has accused me of deliberately making false allegations. This charge is wholly untrue and plainly unfair. The opening pages of government's memorandum graphically demonstrate that a major purpose of the motion is to smear me. The remainder of the memorandum, which ostensibly is offered to prove up the extraordinary allegations in the beginning, is based largely on innuendo and other unsworn speculation of government counsel; it misstates many facts, as I have shown in this affidavit, and it distorts legal precedents to such a degree as to make the memorandum unworthy of the Department of Justice.

Chief Judge Platt was inclined to agree.
In delivering a written judgement on 27 October 1992, he found that

. . . succinctly stated, this is an extraordinary motion in what has proved to be an extraordinary case.

In the first place ... the government's motion is unquestionably premature [and] quite apart from the prematurity of the motion, there are substantial questions whether any sanctions may properly be imposed ... for any of the alleged 'misconduct' on the part of Pan Am and/or its counsel ...

Viewing the case at bar as a whole ... this court may not say that there has been a clear showing of bad faith ... nor may it say that the persons sought to be sanctioned ... have served any papers with an improper purpose or without a reasonable belief that the paper was well grounded in fact ...

Parties and their attorneys, including those involved here, are entitled to base their complaints and their requests for discovery on statements of witnesses, reports of their investigators and hearsay reports and statements of others until such time, if ever, as they are satisfied that the statements and other evidence are not competent or are otherwise untrustworthy.

Thus, in the case at bar, the defendants and their attorneys were during most of the discovery period entitled to pursue their own discovery requests on the basis of the reports and testimony of Messrs. Juval Aviv and Lester Coleman and also to formulate and serve their third-party action against the United States of America in reliance on these two witnesses and the other related information which they had obtained from other sources.

By the admission of its own lawyers and other agents, the government has in its files substantial evidence which it claims proves the statements of Messrs. Aviv and Coleman to be false, but in order to protect its ongoing criminal investigations and cases, the government refused during all of the pre-trial period in question herein to disclose such evidence.

It ill behooves the government now to claim that defendants and their lawyers knew or should have known that the Aviv Report and Coleman affidavit were false when they have concededly withheld information from them which prove that their report and affidavit were in fact false ...

Nor is there truth to the government's assertion that defendants or that their lawyers fully conceded 'that there was no basis' for the third-party complaint or the allegations which were the purported basis for the discovery requests ... All that the defendants did concede at the outset of the trial, in this case, was that they had been unable to discover sufficient corroboration for the Aviv Report and the Coleman affidavit to withstand the government's motion for summary judgment dismissing their third-party complaint, particularly since the government was unwilling to disclose evidence in its own possession.

On the contrary, if anything, defense counsel James M. Shaughnessy should be commended for the concession which he did make at the start of the trial and for not attempting to espouse directly or indirectly during the trial the uncorroborated versions put forth by Messrs. Aviv and Coleman.

The government's motion for punitive sanctions was denied.

It was the last best shot of the Justice Department under President (and former CIA director) George Bush, who had gone to the White House a month after Flight 103 went down.

The stage was now set for the final act of the drama, in which a Democratic Administration will have to decide 'in the national interest' whether to open the Flight 103 files or, if its predecessor has not already done so, to shred them.

— XIX —

Sweden's idea of a refugee camp would not look out of place in any prosperous, middle-class suburb. Nor does its scale of support for refugees fall short of the minimum standard of life it underwrites for its own citizens. Indeed, the generosity with which the Swedish government treats the displaced and persecuted, and the numbers given asylum in relation to the country's population and economy, speak of a genuinely civilized society that, without setting out to do so, serves as both an example *and* a reproach to the rest of the world.

The Colemans' 'camp' was a modern apartment complex in a landscaped setting on the edge of town, with its own medical centre and children's nursery. While their claims for asylum are considered, newcomers are temporarily housed there in circumstances that, even by American standards, are little short of luxurious. Accustomed to a gulf between theory and practice in most Western professions of virtue, Coleman was astonished.

They put us up in a three-bedroom apartment with brand-new appliances, including a TV and a computerized refrigerator, and completely furnished, down to the bedsheets. It was summer, so we bought a used bicycle to go to the market, and every other Thursday, we'd stand in line outside the office to receive our stipend, which amounted to about £700 a month.

It was amazing. People arrive, exhausted and demoralized, expecting workhouse charity at best, and it's a shock, not to be greeted as a problem, as a bureaucratic nuisance. The Swedes never toot their horn about it, but they really *care*. They do all this for genuinely humane reasons. Outwardly, they may not seem a very emotional people, but they express their feelings in practical ways. They take everybody very slowly – you have to prove yourself. But once they accept you as a friend, you're a friend for life.

Even so, the Colemans were in exile. Despite the hospitality and protection of their hosts, there were endless adjustments to make in the business of day-to-day living, to differences in outlook, culture and language, and, not least for a Southerner like Coleman and his Mediterranean wife, to a change of climate as drastic as their change of status. Above all, there was an underlying sense of impermanence that nothing could dispel. The shabby pretext for issuing a fugitive warrant was proof enough that the octopus was still out there, waiting.

Having agreed to offer the Colemans sanctuary while their application for permanent asylum was considered, the Swedish government was clearly in no hurry to arrive at a decision. 'Refugees can wait for years, unable to work or live a normal life, the uncertainty gnawing away at you day by day,' says Coleman. 'They call it "living in splendid misery".

'After a year in the camp, when it became clear to everybody that the passport charge was a phony, the police moved us into a modern apartment in town for our own protection. The rent and utilities were paid for, and they gave us a grant of 50,000 kronor to furnish it. Not a loan – a *grant*. At that time, before the recession really hit, we also got 600 hours of free language tuition, bus tours all over the place, picnics, computer classes, and access to all the social services open to Swedish citizens. And that's remarkable, when you remember the cost was borne by a country of only eight million people with all kinds of economic problems of their own. But even so, we were still in limbo, still awaiting a decision.'

Meanwhile, the FBI had tried to get at him through his mother. On 26 March 1992, Special Agent Robert Sleigh (pronounced 'sly') of the FBI's CI-3 counter-intelligence section stopped by her house in Birmingham, Alabama, for a chat. After Syrian George had been debriefed by the DIA, Coleman had turned him over to Sleigh so that the FBI could determine his eligibility for a resident's visa.

Introducing himself politely, Sleigh proceeded to ask Margie Coleman a series of questions about her son.

Did she know where he was?

'Me?' she said. 'You're the FBI. Don't you *know* where he is?'

Well, they thought he was in Sweden. Did she know if he planned to come back?

'I don't know,' she said. 'Is there any reason why he shouldn't?'

Well, that was up to him. Did her son love America?

'A whole lot more than America loves *him*,' she said. 'After serving his country the way he has, he deserves better than this from you people.'

Well, would he renounce his American citizenship?

'Does he have a choice?' she asked. 'You better ask him yourself.'

Well, they certainly would like to talk this over with him. Could she give them his number?

'I don't think he wants to talk to *you*,' she said. 'Goodbye.'

Having shown Agent Sleigh the door, she went around to a neighbour's house and telephoned Coleman from there, just in case her line was tapped.

After thinking things over, Coleman informed the Swedish police, who advised him to report the incident in writing to the attorney who was helping him with his affairs.

> It is quite interesting [he wrote], that Agent Sleigh should appear at my mother's home within weeks after you and I were told by Swedish Immigration that the evidence I have presented in my claim for political asylum may be verified by the Swedish Foreign Office . . .
>
> I must conclude that the Swedish government is making inquiries in the USA about me, and this has alerted the FBI CI-3, whose job is to monitor foreign governments in the USA.
>
> I am sure the Swedish Foreign Office is aware that their secure cable and voice traffic is being monitored by the FBI. The bottom line is that the FBI now believes that I am in Sweden and is asking some very *political* questions about my patriotism.

Coleman's next disturbing call was from Joseph L. Boohaker, the Lebanese-American attorney who had arranged bail after his arrest on the passport charge. Somebody had contacted Boohaker to ask about him, and the circumstances were sinister enough for Boohaker to write this report on the incident while it was still fresh in his memory:

> On Thursday, 11 June 1992, at approximately 3:00 P.M. (CDT), I received an anonymous phone call from an individual who

identified himself only as a person calling from Washington, D.C. The individual had a message for me to convey to my 'friend living in the North country'. The message, roughly, was as follows:

'Mr Boohaker, tell your friend living in the North country that Monzer al-Kassar was arrested today in Barbados and that among his belongings was found a picture of your friend. Tell your friend to take extra security precautions.'

When I asked for the person's identity, he refused to give it. When I asked him, 'Should my friend from the North country ask where I got the information, what should I tell him?'

The anonymous caller said, 'Just tell him that it comes from a reliable source, and he will figure out who I am.' He continued, 'Also contact Sly [sic] and Strike 6 in Birmingham, and give him the same message.'

I asked, 'Who is Sly and Strike 6? Is it FBI?'

He replied, 'I can't tell you. You will have to find out for yourself.'

I contacted Mr Coleman, who gave me the identity of Sly. I contacted Sly and we met in my office on Friday, 12 June 1992. At that time, I gave Mr Bob Sly the same message related hereinabove. I also related to Mr Sly that my wife had indicated Thursday evening that the same anonymous caller had called my home looking for me and that his call was directed to my office.

Mr Sly was very gracious. He explained that the FBI was interested in my friend only as a fugitive from US justice. He also indicated that he wished to talk to my friend regarding Pan Am 103.

I provided Mr Sly with a copy of the *Time* magazine article written by Mr Rowan that featured an interview with my friend and that also referenced Mr al-Kassar. I told Mr Sly that the article would tie together the entire matter. Mr Sly asked for a copy of the article and I provided him with mine.

I expressed concern that an anonymous caller would call my home and asked Sly if he could tell me anything about what was going on. He did not know. However, he took a description of the caller from me and said that the telephone company may be able to trace the origin of the call. I gave him permission to find out. He called later and said that the phone company could not trace the call to the individual number that had placed it, but he did say that if I got another such call to notify him.

When he heard what had happened, Coleman asked Boohaker to do the same thing, because there was not enough there for him to 'figure out' who the 'reliable source' really was.

'Boohaker also told me that Sleigh wanted to talk about Flight 103,' he recalls, 'and did *I* want to talk to *him*? No, I said. "Well, he seems friendly enough," said Boohaker. "And he says he remembers you as being rather a nice fellow."

'"I'm sure he does," I said. "If he calls again, tell him I'm thinking about it."'

It was the first time that anybody, British *or* American, concerned with the official investigation had shown any interest in talking to him about the Flight 103 disaster. After thinking about it for almost a month, curiosity got the better of him.

I decided, well, what the hell . . . I had one of those USA direct number directories in my wallet, and one day I placed a call from here to the USA direct number in Austria and called Sleigh collect. So when the operator got on the line to the FBI, she offered a call from Mr Coleman in Austria.

'Well, hi,' he says. 'How'ya doing? Where are you? What's going on?'

'You tell me,' I said. I reminded him of the Syrian George episode and asked him if he'd realized I was working for the DIA at the time.

'Well, no,' he says, like it was big news. 'No, I didn't know that. But that's not what I want to talk to you about. I want to talk about the passport charge and this Flight 103 business.'

'Left it a bit late, haven't you?' I said. 'I'll call you back in five minutes.'

So I hung up and called him again, this time through the Swedish direct number operator.

'I can call you from Bangladesh next,' I said. 'In fact, we can play this game all day if you like.'

'No, come on,' he says. 'We know where you are. Let's talk about Flight 103. Let's see if we can't figure out some way to clear up this mess.'

'Sure,' I said. 'I'll talk about it. You get that US attorney up in Chicago to drop his phony charge against me and I'll talk all you want. But I guarantee you, he won't do it.'

'Well, it's not as easy as that,' he says. 'You know how it works. He's going to be looking for some kind of a deal here.'

'I already know what kind of a deal he's looking for. He wants a deal to *stop* me talking about Flight 103. Otherwise you guys are going to be tied up in hearings from now until Doomsday.'

'And what about you?' he says. 'You got a wife and kids. Are you being fair on *them*? Unless you cut some kind of a deal, you're going to be on the run for the rest of your lives. You can't just walk away from this, you know. They won't let you.'

'Then you better come and get me,' I said. 'If you know where I am, you can have me extradited. We'll have a public hearing in a neutral court, and talk about all the juicy little details, and we'll see what an impartial judge thinks about it.'

'Don't kid yourself, Les,' he says. 'This is the United States government you're talking about, and that you can't beat. Nobody can. If they want you bad enough, they're going to get you – we both know that. So why don't you make your peace? Now. While you still got the chance.'

'First drop the charge,' I said. 'Then pull the warrant. After that we can talk.'

And I guess that must have sounded pretty final because he just sighed and said, 'Okay. I'll run it up the flagpole. If anything comes back, we'll contact your attorney in Chicago.'

And that was it. I never heard from my attorney in Chicago.

Coleman knew in his bones that Sleigh was right. They would never leave him alone, although the chances that the FBI would resort to direct methods of the Fawaz Younis type seemed remote. It was one thing to snatch somebody in international waters, from Mexico or from a Central American banana republic and quite another to operate on Swedish soil. Besides being logistically difficult, the diplomatic fallout would be out of all proportion to the likely gain. But if force was ruled out, and probably extradition, there was still plenty of pressure that Washington could exert on the Swedish government to have him deported as an undesirable.

Trying hard to resist the claims of paranoia, and equally to avoid displeasing his hosts, Coleman signed up for his story to be told in a book.

There was no other way he could think of to defend himself against the octopus, against that ruthlessly powerful, self-protective oligarchy of senior intelligence, military and law-enforcement bureaucrats who were convinced they knew best, regardless of what the politicians had to say, and who cynically manipulated the machinery of government to cover their tracks.

As it lived away from the light and worked best in secret, Coleman felt he might be safer out in the open.

Stranded in Sweden, he also needed the money. If he restored his reputation, there was still an outside chance that he could pick up the threads of his former career, perhaps as a writer and journalist.

In the late summer of 1992, that prospect was all but extinguished by the flat-out assault on his character by Byron and Emerson in *New York* magazine and the *Washington Journalism Review*. Coleman was a soft target, as there was no risk of his responding with a libel suit, but it had an unexpected side effect. Until then, not a word about his application for asylum had appeared in Sweden, but now the country's national afternoon newspaper *iDAG* picked up the reference to his whereabouts in Byron's article and traced him through the immigration authorities.

He was interviewed in the conference room of his local police station. The superintendant served coffee and biscuits. And on 19 October 1992, the paper came out with this front-page banner headline:

USA AGENT SEEKS ASYLUM IN SWEDEN
Speaks Out on Murder Threat From His Hiding Place

Outlining how Coleman had been driven into exile, a two-page inside spread with pictures described him as 'The Man Who Knows the Truth About the Lockerbie Catastrophe'.

In a curious way, it made him feel less isolated, less like an object of no one's concern. Besides generating public awareness of his plight – Sweden had lost two of its citizens in the Flight 103 disaster – the *iDAG* interview also made it seem less likely that he would be targeted for covert action, authorized or not. To that extent, he felt more secure, particularly as the story carried the implicit endorsement of the Swedish police.

It also had the effect of dispelling his inhibitions about possibly embarrassing the Swedish government by drawing public attention to himself. Now that everybody knew he was there, the appearance of a book, with its attendant publicity, would serve only to underline his *need* for asylum.

And that seemed to be getting more acute. As Special Agent Sleigh had made plain, the octopus was still probing for him. From a contact in Washington, Coleman had learned that the American Embassy in London was inquiring through Interpol about his status in Sweden, to see if Swedish law provided for the possibility of deportation. Now, through another contact in the Justice Department, Coleman obtained a copy of a confidential FBI 'Investigative Summary', dated 30 March 1992, setting out the basis for the passport violation charge and the subsequent issue of a fugitive warrant.

It was the 'smoking gun' he had always hoped to find.

The charge had been rigged as a plea-bargaining counter for the government to exchange for his silence. No great care had been taken in framing it as there had never been any intention of going to trial. That would have defeated the object. But now Coleman had escaped from American jurisdiction, it was necessary to patch over some of the holes so that the charge held at least enough water to persuade the Swedish authorities that there was a real case for him to answer.

To do that, the Justice Department first had to get around the fact that Coleman had held a birth certificate in the name of Thomas Leavy since 1 March 1982, when it was given to him by the government itself. The other big obstacle it had to gloss over was that a copy of that birth certificate had already been misappropriated by the DEA, apparently to obtain a passport for one of its people in Egypt.

As no inkling of this could be revealed to Interpol or the Swedes without the frame-up becoming self-evident, there was only one thing to do, and that was to dissemble.

This investigation was instituted on February 7, 1990 [the FBI summary began], when New London, Connecticut Resident Agency, New Haven Division, reported that they had been notified by the New London Bureau of Vital Statistics that a person identifying himself as Thomas Leavy had requested a copy of his birth certificate. Leavy's date of birth (DOB) was listed July 4, 1948, his parents were listed as John and Mary Leavy, and Thomas Leavy's address was listed as 416 County Line Road, Barrington, Illinois. A computer check of the Bureau of Vital Statistics records revealed that the real Thomas Leavy had died in New London, Connecticut, two days after his 1948 birth.

On April 6, 1990, Richard Beckman, Chicago Passport Office . . . advised the Federal Bureau of Investigation (FBI) Chicago that he had a possible passport violation. An application submitted by a Thomas Leavy on March 26, 1990, at the Arlington Heights Post Office, had a number of indicators that pointed to a violation.

The first indication was the birth certificate for the dead baby. Other indicators were recently issued driver's license and Social Security Account numbers.

Though plausible on the surface, this raised or begged as many questions as it tried to answer.

If Coleman already *had* a Thomas Leavy birth certificate, issued 1 March 1982 (and still had photocopies), why would he need another one?

And why, if he did, would he apply to the New London Bureau of Vital Statistics when Connecticut's official authority for issuing birth certificates is located in the state capital of Hartford?

And why, if he did, would the New London Bureau go ahead and *give* Coleman, posing as Thomas Leavy, a copy of Thomas Leavy's birth certificate if a computer check revealed that he had been dead for 42 years?

And why, if it did, could Ms Gloria Hatfield, clerk of the Records Office in New London, later find no record of the alleged death of Thomas Leavy on 6 July 1948? (When asked about his alleged birth on 4 July she explained that a birth record required the presentation of documents which the researcher did not have.)

And how did Richard Beckman in the Chicago Passport Office *know* that the Thomas Leavy birth certificate was for a dead baby, and thus 'the first indication' of a 'possible passport violation'?

Thus committed to a piece of pure invention (reflecting no great credit on its author's imagination), the rest of the FBI's 'Investigative Summary' was concerned to ice the cake by putting a false construction on the admitted facts of the application, but even here it stumbled from one improbability to another.

'The home and work addresses on the application,' for instance, 'came back to two separate mail drop locations ... Another indicator was that the contact person listed on the application was a relative. The contact is Lestre Colman [sic] 416 West County Line Road, Barrington Illinois ... listed as a brother-in-law.

'Investigation at Chicago revealed that the owner of one mail drop and the office manager of the second identified the photo from the passport application as Lester Knox Coleman.'

But if Lester Coleman, or anybody but an imbecile, had wished to obtain a Thomas Leavy passport *for his own unauthorized use*, is it likely that he would have rented two mail drops in his *real* name?

Or, if the passport *was* for his own unauthorized use, is it even remotely probable that he would have given his own name and address as a reference?

Nor did the FBI or the prosecutor anywhere suggest a *motive* for the application. Why would Coleman want a Thomas Leavy passport for his own unauthorized use if he already had a perfectly good one in his own name?

The only motive ever proposed was the one he had himself suggested at the time of his arrest, when he was still concealing his identity as a DIA agent. He was returning to the Middle East to research a book, he had told the FBI, and needed a new passport because his real name was known to Arab drug dealers – but he had never seriously expected anyone to swallow *that*. Anybody proposing to visit an Arab country for such a purpose would normally be at pains to *avoid* using a Jewish-sounding name like Leavy. If Operation Shakespeare had gone ahead, the intention had been to travel on the Leavy passport only as far as Israel.

With the frame-up exposed in the FBI's own document, Coleman was not overly concerned that the Swedish authorities would take the charge at its face value or see it as grounds for deportation. But the octopus had long tentacles, and putting himself in the shoes of those who were probably now regretting that, out of deference to another agency, they had not gone for a Casolaro-type solution, Coleman approached the second anniversary of his arrival in Sweden with a growing apprehension that some new and more serious charge against him might be in the works.

If the risk of covert action had diminished, the possibility of perhaps some sort of treason-related case, properly constructed this time and backed by impeccably manufactured evidence of a kind the Swedes could not ignore, began to seem more likely. It was not a comfortable feeling for a family man, to know in his bones that Washington would prefer him to be dead.

His country had certainly not forgotten him. To mark the fourth anniversary of the Lockerbie disaster, Mike Wallace, for CBS in New York, returned to the attack by interviewing Juval Aviv in the 20 December edition of the network's flagship news programme '60 Minutes'.

CBS News had tried to inveigle Coleman into appearing also but, now wise in the ways of the octopus, he had prudently declined. Any programme produced with the help of Vincent Cannistraro, late of the CIA, Christopher Byron, fresh from setting out the government's stall in *New York* magazine, and Steven Emerson was hardly likely to deal objectively with anything he might have to say.

And he was right. Referring to the judgement against Pan Am in the civil liability suit a few months earlier, Wallace opened the proceedings by saying: 'It is not surprising that Pan Am and its lead insurer, US Aviation Underwriters, would appeal that verdict. What *is* surprising, perhaps, is that they would hire a private detective like Juval Aviv to help them avoid paying huge damage claims.'

Anyone who had not been following the case closely – that is, all but a handful of viewers – might have assumed from this that Pan Am and its insurers had hired Aviv *after* the judgement against them in an effort to avoid the consequences, that '60 Minutes' was about to report a new development. In fact, there was no connection at all between the verdict and the hiring of Juval Aviv. The juxtaposition of the two was simply to create the illusion of a news peg in order to justify a rerun of the charges already ventilated in *New York* magazine. Wallace well into the programme before he acknowledged that Aviv had resigned from the case on 31 May 1990 – two and a half years earlier.

After summarizing the always questionable construction that Aviv had placed on the intelligence data in his Interfor Report, Wallace invited Lee Kreindler, lead attorney for the victims' families, to comment on the 'brutal shock' his clients received when Aviv's findings were leaked to the media (in 1989!).

One of them, he said – 'I love her dearly, she'd lost her husband, a wonderful lady – and she said, "Lee," she said, "how do I renounce my American citizenship? The CIA killed my husband." All this is pure fabrication. Out of the mind of Juval Aviv.'

Vincent Cannistraro agreed.

As far as he was concerned, it was 'a transparent attempt to get Pan Am off the hook, which has, as its only purpose, to blame anyone else other than Pan Am for the crash of Pan Am 103'. There was never any CIA involvement with an undercover drug operation at Frankfurt airport, he said. 'No such element ever existed, no such "sting" operation existed at Frankfurt airport.' Nor was the plane targeted because of the five CIA agents aboard, returning home to blow the whistle on a rogue CIA operation.

'Completely false,' Cannistraro declared. 'First of all, there weren't five CIA agents on that plane. There were *two* CIA agents on that plane. And they made their travel arrangements at the absolute last minute, and therefore there was no way that they could have been targeted, or that flight could have been targeted in advance.' (He did not reveal that the agents had changed their plans on Cyprus, using the DEA's travel agents, RA Travel Masters. This had always suggested to Coleman the possibility that Hurley had told them it was all right to fly Pan Am 103 as it was a controlled delivery flight.)

Wallace then turned to Aviv's claim that he was a former member of the Mossad, a claim rejected by an Israeli source who had described him as 'a junior security officer for El Al'.

'You were fired in April, 1984, after less than eighteen months of work,' said Wallace, 'because you were, quote, "unreliable and dishonest", close quote. And [the statement] goes on to say that after that, you had been, quote, "involved during the years in various acts of fraud and impersonation". So they're lying about you?'

'I'm not saying anything,' replied Aviv. 'I do not discuss. They are free to say whatever they say. I know what I am, and I will not get into it.'

Wallace conceded that some law firms Aviv had worked for had praise for him, 'but others had charged him with everything from ripping off clients for tens of thousands of dollars for spurious investigations, to originally trying to sell his services to the families of those who were killed in the plane bombing . . .' (Two years earlier, Aviv's colleague and attorney, Daniel Aharoni, had explained to *Barron's* that 'our heart was with the families, but the problem was there were 270 victims, and families with all levels of sophistication. How do you report to 270 different clients? And Pan Am was very clear that they wanted the truth. They said, "Let the chips fall where they may".')

Kreindler's recollection was different. According to Wallace, 'he was appalled that Pan Am and the insurers would hire a man like Juval Aviv,' and Kreindler confirmed this on camera.

'They embraced this character, Juval Aviv,' he said. 'The slightest checking on their part would have shown that he was a fraud.' (In the same *Barron's* article, James Shaughnessy had stated that 'we asked him for references from other law firms . . . They checked out in glowing terms.')

At this point, Wallace set up Aviv for a face-to-face confrontation with Cannistraro.

'You've ever talked with him?' he asked Aviv.

'No.'

'Well, he says – Cannistraro told us – your theory is – is totally wrong. He says, a tissue of fabrication.'

'Well, that's his opinion. As ex-CIA, he has to do the party line. He's not going to simply come out and say, Now that I left, I was involved in maybe cover-up. He will not say that. He *can't* say that.'

'So you would like to talk to Cannistraro, let's say.'

'I would talk to – well, Cannistraro, I would like to talk to Cannistraro – '

'We're going to make that possible for you right now,' Wallace interrupted. 'Vince? Come on in.'

The results of this ambush, perhaps more appropriate to 'This Is Your Life' than a serious news programme, were not particularly illuminating.

'Almost everything you said is completely fabricated,' said Cannistraro. 'It's invented.'

'What you're doing right now – you don't discuss the issues,' Aviv replied. 'You're attacking me again.'

'Wait a minute,' said Wallace, intervening as they both started to talk at once. 'We're talking about Pan Am 103. What you have said, Juval Aviv, is that the United States government – that the United States *government* knew about that bag that was going aboard this particular flight, did nothing to stop it.'

'Yes.'

'Totally false,' said Cannistraro. 'Your report, which I have read very carefully, alleges the existence of a CIA element, which you call CIA-1, at Frankfurt airport. Totally false. Completely false. Today, Mr Aviv has only speculation, rumours and theory that has not been supported by one scintilla of material evidence. I would like to see it before we continue this discussion.'

Again, they both started to talk, and Wallace cut through to say: 'No, no, no – with all respect, Mr Cannistraro, you're ex-CIA.'

'Sure.'

'It has to be suggested that perhaps a former CIA man is not going to point the finger at his own government, at his own agency.'

'Well, I assure you, CIA is probably not very happy that I'm appearing on television, saying these kinds of things. But I had personal friends on that plane who died. And I assure you that I wanted to find the perpetrators of that disaster as much as anyone wanted to. And I really resent people like Juval Aviv and all the other shysters that were involved in constructing this government conspiracy theory blaming everyone else other than Pan Am for the negligence that resulted in that disaster.'

'And the fact is,' added Wallace, cutting away, 'that in a letter dated June 1990, the lead lawyer for Pan Am's insurers, James Shaughnessy, wrote to Juval Aviv that despite probably hundreds of thousands of dollars given him, Aviv had failed to come up with, quote, "a single piece of admissible evidence" for the Pan Am case. It was at that point that Aviv finally went off the insurers' payroll. (A moment's reflection on Wallace's part – or anybody's part – might have suggested that Shaughnessy's letter reflected, not 'a transparent attempt to get Pan Am off the hook', but a transparent conviction that Pan Am's case *could* be supported by admissible evidence.)

'Even after that, though,' Wallace went on, 'Pan Am kept pushing its case in the courts and in the press, kept pushing the idea of conspiracy, focusing now on the US Drug Enforcement Agency instead of the CIA, despite vehement denials from the US government.'

He sounded aggrieved, as if defending a lawsuit were somehow perverse.

Where did Pan Am's DEA evidence come from? [he asked]. One key source. This man – Lester Coleman, who claims to have been a key undercover agent for the US DEA. But according to the DEA, Coleman was little more than a low-level informant for a couple of years. He was ultimately fired for, quote, 'lack of integrity and a propensity for fabrication'– a description we heard repeated by many who have known Coleman over the years.

Currently, he is in Europe avoiding arrest on passport fraud charges in the United States. And who helped him get out of the US to Europe, from where he supplied an affidavit in support of Pan Am's charge?

Pan Am flew him there, free of charge.

It was a typical Byron-esque shot, right down to the sleazy implication that Pan Am had helped a wanted criminal escape.

At the end of the programme, Wallace would thank Christopher Byron for his help in sustaining the reputation that CBS had already earned in the trade as the Cheap Broadcasting System, but first he had a word with Tom Plaskett, board chairman of Pan Am at the time of the bombing.

'Aviv, who is charged with being an imposter; Coleman, fleeing the United States on passport fraud charges – these are two of the lead investigators for Pan Am?' Wallace suggested.

'I don't think it's proper to characterize them as "lead investigators",' Plaskett replied. 'In the first place, in intelligence and in the world in which some of these people operate, you simply don't have a diploma hanging on the wall which certifies their credibility.'

'Would you hire Aviv again?' asked Wallace.

'I don't think so,' said Plaskett. (And who could blame him, with media coverage like this?)

At this point, Wallace interpolated a comment from none other than Steven Emerson, who, he said, had written 'about the various parties who, he charges, knowingly bought into Aviv and Coleman's fabrication'.

'They knew they were being conned,' said Emerson, 'but they went along because they had a constellation of the same interests [sic]. The insurance companies wanted to avoid paying out. Pan Am wanted to avoid being accused of being negligent. And the media wanted a good story.'

Not unexpectedly, the principal culprits turned out to be ABC, NBC and *Time* magazine, who, if Emerson's remarks meant anything, must have been surprised to hear that they shared a common interest in helping the insurance companies to avoid paying out and Pan Am to avoid being accused of negligence.

Cutting back to Plaskett, Wallace quoted from a memo written by Bob Alford, former head of the claims department of the lead insurers, who was 'highly critical of the tactics used by his former employers to avoid paying those big damage claims to the families of Pan Am 103'.

'This man, Alford,' said Wallace, 'senior vice president of your own insurers, says, quote, "These families should have been compensated two years ago. The money that has been spent litigating this case is outrageous." And you acknowledge it's tens of millions.'

'Mike, it has been a very long and difficult process,' Plaskett replied, 'and I certainly have great empathy for the families in waiting so long. But no one has proven how the bomb got on the airplane. The act of wilful misconduct, on which the jury based its verdict, we do not believe will be sustained in a court of appeals.'

With this, Wallace returned to Cannistraro for his 'last word' on the conduct of Pan Am and the insurance companies.

It was 'reprehensible'. And 'despicable'.

'By the way,' added Wallace, in conclusion, 'we, like many in the media, were briefly taken in by Juval Aviv a few years back. We paid him no money but we did provide him with a letter indicating he was checking into certain stories for "60 Minutes". A mistake.'

This was a necessary admission, for Aviv had kept a copy of the letter. It had been written, not 'a few years back' but on 11 April 1991 – long after Aviv's 'fabrication' had been leaked to the media and 'discredited'; long after Pan Am's 'reprehensible' conduct had been denounced in the media; long after ABC and NBC had knowingly allowed themselves to be 'conned' by Lester Coleman, and months after Emerson had 'unmasked' Coleman on CNN television as a 'low-level DEA informant'.

With all this information at his disposal, Wallace had written:

Dear Juval Aviv,
    This letter will confirm that you will be working with myself and [producer] Barry Lando as a consultant on numerous assignments for '60 Minutes.'
    Sincerely,
    Mike Wallace,
    CBS News/60 Minutes

A mistake?

'. . . surprising, perhaps, that they would hire a private detective like Juval Aviv to help them . . .?'

'. . . when the slightest checking on their part would have shown that he was a fraud?'

It would be interesting to know what additional information had come Wallace's way between April 1991 and December 1992 to cause him to change his mind so completely about the competence and credibility of Aviv as an investigator. He certainly did not confide it to his viewers or, indeed, tell them anything new. In fact, with the families having already won their case against Pan Am, it was hard to see any point to the programme at all – except that, like Byron's *New York* magazine article, it served the government's purpose in helping to create a climate of opinion hostile to any further questioning of the official line on Flight 103.

So *who* was 'conned'?

ABC, NBC and *Time* by Pan Am, Aviv and Coleman?

Or Mike Wallace by the government, Cannistraro and Byron/Emerson?

In the days when CBS News enjoyed a reputation for independence and responsible reporting, '60 Minutes' might well have been more interested in examining the *substance* of Pan Am's appeal than questioning its *right* to appeal. For Coleman, watching the programme in Sweden and remembering the days of Ed Murrow and Walter Kronkite, it was a dispiriting experience, all too consistent with the standards of television journalism that had driven him into the coils of the octopus eight years earlier.

It was a bad time in any case.

On 6 January 1993, his father died. So far away, Coleman found that hard to grasp. He would have liked to have been there when his father's ashes were scattered on the lake. He would have liked to have felt, and to *be*, closer to his mother, and his children by his former marriage. His son was growing up and he had missed his daughter's marriage. There was something dream-like still in not really belonging anywhere, in waiting endlessly in exile for something to happen.

In February 1993, he heard on the grapevine that the Department of Justice had empanelled a Federal grand jury in the Eastern District of Virginia and was trawling through his record, calling witnesses who had known him in his six-year spell with the DIA.

Clearly, there was to be no forgiveness for anyone who had tried to bring out the truth about Flight 103 and the tragedy at Lockerbie. Among the grand jury's other targets were Juval Aviv and James M. Shaughnessy.

Then in March, just two months short of the second anniversary of the family's arrival in Sweden, Coleman heard that his application for permanent residence had been denied.

—— Epilogue ——

In May 1993, Pan Am's appeal was heard in the US Court of Appeals for the Second Circuit, and although a decision was not expected before the autumn, there seemed little doubt that the judgment against the airline in the 1992 liability trial would be set aside.

The issue had hinged on whether or not Pan Am had complied with FAA directives about the inspection of baggage. Counsel for the relatives had interpreted the regulations as requiring the airline physically to match all interline transfer bags with passengers, so that any bag not accompanied by a passenger would be identified and either hand-searched or left behind.

'To make out their liability theory,' Pan Am's attorneys argued, 'it was necessary for plaintiffs to prove that the bomb was in the suitcase, the suitcase was unaccompanied by any passenger, and the suitcase had been delivered into Pan Am's baggage system by interline transfer from another carrier, Air Malta.

'It was also neccessary to show not only that Pan Am's baggage security procedure violated FAA requirements, as construed by plaintiffs, but also that Pan Am had adopted the procedure with a mindset so indifferent to safety as to constitute wilful misconduct.' (On this point, plaintiffs contended that the airline had wilfully broken the rules in order to save money and improve on-time performance.)

In its defence, Pan Am had maintained that it had not only complied with FAA requirements by making an 'administrative match' between passengers and bags, as allowed by the rules, but had also used state-of-the-art X-ray machines to inspect *all* interline bags, accompanied or not. (A physical match would have required passengers to go out on the tarmac and identify their bags before they were loaded aboard the aircraft, a process so time-consuming that *no* airline routinely performed such a match, not even El Al.)

The airline's counsel went on:

Defendants attempted to show, but were precluded from showing, that because Pan Am believed the relevant FAA regulation to be unclear, it had obtained (or thought it had obtained) the FAA's concurrence with Pan Am's baggage security procedure. Defendants were also precluded from showing that Pan Am's X-ray inspection of interline bags was permitted by British aviation authorities, and defendants were precluded from rebutting the testimony of the plaintiffs' expert that unaccompanied bags posed such a unique risk as to make the use of X-ray inspection inappropriate.

In addition, Pan Am set out to show, but was precluded from showing, that plaintiffs' theory of how the bomb was planted on board the aircraft was implausible and that other possibilities for which Pan Am would not be responsible were more likely.

This last point was crucial.

While fully accepting the implications of the hard, forensic evidence, Pan Am's counsel insisted that the Libyan/Air Malta theory, advanced by government and plaintiffs alike, rested on circumstantial evidence alone: namely, that the bomb bag had contained items of clothing purchased in Malta, that baggage records from Frankfurt airport purported to show that an unaccompanied bag from Flight KM180 had been transferred to Flight 103, and that a schedule prepared by the Scottish police had matched every bag with a passenger except one, the unaccompanied bag containing the bomb.

With testimony and records from Air Malta showing that *no* unaccompanied bag had been loaded aboard Flight KM180, and with substantial questions still unanswered about the validity of both Frankfurt's baggage records *and* the bag-matching schedule, in Pan Am's view, the plaintiffs' circumstantial evidence was simply not enough to establish how the bomb got aboard.

Denied access to official sources of information on grounds of 'national security', the airline had attempted to offset its handicap by calling five expert witnesses who, between them, would have discounted the Air Malta theory as both implausible and insufficiently supported by the evidence. Four of the five were not permitted to testify, however, and the fifth only on a minor, peripheral matter.

(Two of the excluded experts were British: John Horne and Peter Gurney, both with wide experience of terrorist bombings and bomb disposal operations gained in service with the British Army and

Scotland Yard. Formerly in charge of the explosives section of the Yard's anti-terrorism branch, Gurney had personally disarmed a bomb intended for an El Al flight in 1986, and in 1991 had defused two IRA mortar bombs launched at 10 Downing Street.)

Worse still, at no point in the trial proceedings had Pan Am been allowed even to mention the possibility that a rogue bag might have been slipped into the system further down the line in order to bypass its security checks. Nor was it allowed to cross-examine one of the plaintiffs' own experts on the subject of 'rush-tag' bags, which, by definition, are unaccompanied by their owners.

This last turned out to be particularly damaging.

When Pan Am called Kurt Maier, operator of its baggage X-ray machine at Frankfurt on the day in question, he testified, first, that he had been told to call a supervisor if he saw a radio inside any bag, and second, that none of the 13 unaccompanied bags he screened for Flight 103 had contained a radio-cassette player. (When Maier's competence as an operator was challenged, Pan Am sought to demonstrate the X-ray machine to the jury in order to prove that anyone, trained or not, could identify a radio-cassette player from the image on its monitor, but once again, the airline was not permitted to do so.)

Maier's testimony was crucial because the plaintiffs (and the government) insisted that 12 of the 13 bags had been accounted for, and that the 13th was the one with the bomb.

Pan Am, on the other hand, contended that the 13th bag must have belonged to a Pan Am captain who had sent two suitcases home from Berlin via Frankfurt, rush-tagged to Seattle via New York, before piloting a flight to Karachi. One suitcase had unaccountably been left behind at Frankfurt. The other, containing Christmas presents for his family, was found at Lockerbie. As this was not among the 12 unaccompanied bags officially accounted for, and as all 13 had been X-rayed and cleared, the 13th bag could *not*, therefore, have contained the bomb.

On attempting to cross-examine one of the plaintiffs' own experts on the subject of rush-tag bags, however, Pan Am's counsel was specifically barred from asking if the 13th bag could not, in fact, have belonged to the pilot. They were also prevented from asking another of the plaintiffs' experts if it might not have been easier for a terrorist to have placed the bomb in a parcel of cargo rather than in an unaccompanied bag.

Having listed many instances where Pan Am's defence had been hampered, in counsel's opinion, by such rulings and by the improper *exclusion* of evidence, the airline's appeal documents then turned to those occasions when evidence for the plaintiffs had been improperly *admitted*. Depositions were allowed, for instance, alleging previous misconduct on Pan Am's part that had nothing to do with the plaintiffs' Libyan/Air Malta theory, and their experts were also permitted to give 'lengthy one-sided summaries of the evidence and to render expert opinions that [improperly] judged the credibility of witnesses'.

Closely reasoned, meticulously documented and including a catalogue of alleged procedural and technical errors, Pan Am's appeal brief, and the subsequent hearing in May 1993, left little doubt in anyone's mind that the original proceedings had been fatally flawed and that a new trial would be held before a different judge, probably in the spring of 1994.

Indeed, the only serious reservation expressed by legal observers about the outcome had less to do with the validity of Pan Am's appeal than with the integrity of the American judicial system under extreme government pressure. If a new trial *is* ordered, and *if* Pan Am is allowed to make its defence unhindered, the stage will be set for the final demolition of the plaintiffs' case against the airline, and with it, inevitably, the government's case against the two Libyans, al-Megrahi and Fhimah.

With a five-year cover-up to explain away, not to mention its cynical manipulation of the United Nations to engineer the imposition of international sanctions against Libya, the American government's commitment to the Libyan/Air Malta theory will subject the Federal judiciary to one of the most severe tests it has had to face since the separation of powers was written into the constitution.

If Lester Coleman's hopes are realized, the result of Pan Am's appeal may also persuade the octopus to leave him in peace at last, although, having gone to ground again in the face of Washington's vendetta, he now believes there is probably more to it than meets the eye. Since his story is now supported by no less an authority than Major Khalil Tunayb, a former chief of intelligence for the PFLP–GC, there would seem little point in continuing to harry him so relentlessly unless there *were* some wider reason.

(During the winter of 1992–1993, Tunayb surfaced in the media to confirm that Khalid Nazir Jafaar had been affiliated with Muslim fundamentalists in Lebanon and Detroit who knew he was working in drug operations for the DEA and CIA. According to Tunayb,

Jafaar was used by the PFLP-GC as an unwitting accomplice to get the bomb bag aboard Flight 103 and had been escorted from Beirut by two equally unwitting American agents. Significantly, Tunayb's story supports much of the intelligence data provided in Juval Aviv's original Interfor Report.)

So what else did he know, Coleman wondered, that might account for Washington's unabated intent to silence or discredit him?

Looking back over his career as an American agent in the Middle East, he realized that most of his work had been concerned with tracking Syria's involvement in terrorism, hostage-taking and narcotics. In the course of his duties, he had helped compile dossiers on the likes of Rifat Assad, Monzer al-Kassar and Ali Issa Dubah which, in any civilized country without a death penalty, would have put them behind bars for life.

All else being equal . . .

In fact, Rifat Assad, a vice president of Syria, returned home from exile in August 1992, and is thought to be undergoing a low-profile rehabilitation in Damascus with a view to succeeding his older brother, Hafez Assad, when the time comes. The President's health is poor, and his son, Basil, is generally regarded as too young and too lightweight for the job. As heir to the presidency, Rifat is clearly Washington's best bet in countering the threat of a militant fundamentalist take-over on his brother's death – and the fact that he was, or *is*, a CIA asset hardly undermines his qualifications!

Adding weight to the idea that the American government and its allies are lending a hand to clean up Rifat's act, the virtual disappearance of his partner Monzer al-Kassar after his arrest in Spain in the summer of 1992 neatly removed another awkward reminder of their controlling interest in America's heroin imports. (His conditional release a year later, on £10 million bail, was also a reminder of his enduring influence with the intelligence agencies of those governments.)

With Rifat's friend and colleague, General Ali Issa Dubah, promoted soon after to the post of Hafez Assad's deputy chief of staff for security affairs, and thus well clear of any further day-to-day involvement with the Syrian narcotics industry, Coleman was moved to wonder if, perhaps, he was now the last unmuzzled American witness who could testify directly as to Rifat Assad's unsuitability for *any* political role in the Middle East, most of all, that of America's key Arab ally.

Could it be, he asked himself, that what he knew about Lockerbie was just part of what he knew about Syria, and that what he knew about both left the whole of America's Syria-first policy open to question?

To see if a Democratic administration would take a more sympathetic view of his plight, Coleman addressed the following petition to President Bill Clinton, with a copy to the new Attorney-General, Janet Reno:

'Mr President,
I spent two years assigned to the White House as a radio correspondent during the Carter administration. My work has been recognized with two Emmys and several other national reporting honors.

In the mid-80's, I left journalism and became involved with two government agencies, the DIA and the DEA, affiliated with classified activities in Lebanon. My background in the Middle East was of interest to my government. I grew up in Iran and Libya, for example.

I witnessed conduct within the US DEA in particular that was not conducive to operational security. I still feel this lax security at DEA Country Office Nicosia may have contributed to the bombing of Pan Am 103. I gave an affidavit, April 1991, that I observed a Lebanese, later identified as Khalid Jafaar, at a DEA office where I was working in 1988, six months prior to the bombing. Jafaar was killed on 103. DEA has repeatedly denied Jafaar had any connection with them.

On May 2, 1990, I was arrested for making a false statement on a passport application, using a birth record provided to me by the US government. We now have conclusive evidence that this arrest was directly related to my knowledge of DEA's activities that may have been compromised by elements linked to the Pan Am bombing.

My wife, children and I were subsequently harassed. Death threats were made to us, and I was warned by a DEA agent directly not to get DEA involved in my case.

In 1991, in fear of our lives, we fled the USA and sought sanctuary in Sweden. I left the USA legally, with permission of the U.S. District Court in Chicago. After our arrival here, the FBI continued harassment by faking a doctor's appointment before the court. The doctor the FBI stated they had appointed declared that he was never contacted by the United States government. I complied with the terms of my bail release, reporting to pre-trial services biweekly up until the FBI's false doctor's appointment episode. Afterwards, I asked, and received, protection from the Swedish authorities for me, my wife and three children.

We have since obtained a copy of a FBI file which was leaked by closet patriots within the Bureau. This file contains false statements about me regarding the passport case pending in Chicago.

We have been waiting patiently, Mr President, for the appointment of a new Attorney General who will hopefully clean out the gross misconduct under the Bush administration, which includes persecuting this American citizen, forced to flee his homeland.

I request that Attorney General Janet Reno investigate this matter. We wish to return to America but will not do so until the United States government stops persecuting us, drops the charge in Chicago and shall look upon me as a witness, not a fugitive.

A book entitled 'Trail of the Octopus' documenting the events of the last three years shall be published this fall. I hope your administration will extend an olive branch and distance itself from the conduct of a morally corrupt Bush Justice Department and arrange for us to come home.

Coleman sent his petition by fax, the machine confirming that the transmission had been received, and provided a fax number to which the White House could reply.

That was on 15 March 1993.

By mid-June, having heard not a word, the Coleman family resigned itself to a life on the run.

Office of the Legal Attache
24 Grosvenor Square
London, England W1A 1AE

11 June, 1992

40-CG-76385

Sigvard Ronnback   Your File: IP1513/92/AC
Head of Interpol
Rikspolisstyralsen
Interpolsektionen
Box 12 256
S-102 26 Stockholm
Sweden

Subject: LESTER KNOX COLEMAN, III

    Reference is made to your communication dated 6 May,
1992 and a telephone call between Mr. Anders Claesson of your
office and myself.

    Enclosed per a request of Mr. Claesson is a report
detailing the background of Lester Knox Coleman.

    As Coleman is a fugitive, we would greatly appreciate
any information you may be able to provide on his current status
in Sweden and the possibility Swedish law would allow for his
deportation to the United States.

    As always, your assistance is greatly appreciated.

             Very truly yours,

             Susan A. Sprengel
             Assistant Legal Attache

        For: R. John Theriault, Jr.
              Legal Attache

Smoking gun I: Washington trys to persuade Stockholm to deport Coleman to the
United States.

U.S. Department of Justice

Federal Bureau of Investigation

In Reply, Please Refer to
File No.

Chicago, Illinois 60604
March 30, 1992

LESTER KNOX COLEMAN, III,
aka Thomas Leavy;
PASSPORT VIOLATION

Chicago
Investigative Summary prepared: March 30, 1992

Basis For Investigation:

This investigation was instituted on February 7, 1990, when New London, Connecticut Resident Agency, New Haven Division, reported they had been notified by the New London Bureau of Vital Statistics that a person identifying himself as THOMAS LEAVY, had requested a copy of his birth certificate. LEAVY's Date of Birth (DOB) was listed July 4, 1948, his parents were listed as JOHN and MARY LEAVY and THOMAS LEAVY's address was 416 County Line Road, Barrington, Illinois. A computer check of the Bureau of Vital Statistics Records revealed that the real THOMAS LEAVY had died in New London, Connecticut, two days after his 1948 birth.

On April 6, 1990, RICHARD BECKMAN, Chicago Passport Office, 230 South Dearborn Street, Chicago, advised the FEDERAL BUREAU OF INVESTIGATION (FBI) Chicago, that he had a possible passport violation. An application, submitted by a THOMAS LEAVY on March 26, 1990 at the Arlington Heights Post Office, had a number of indicators that pointed to a violation.

The first indication was the birth certificate for the dead baby. Other indicators were recently issued driver's license and Social Security Account Numbers. Also the home and work addresses on the applications came back to two separate mail drop locations. The home contact telephone number on the application is not a north suburban telephone exchange. The listing is for a cellular telephone.

This document contains neither
[illegible] and its content

LESTER KNOX COLEMAN, III

Another indicator was that the contact person listed on the application was a relative. The contact is LESTRE COLMAN, 415 West County Line Road, Barrington, Illinois, telephone number (708) 381-1056, listed as a brother-in-law. The telephone number, 381-1056, comes back to ARTHUR MCINTOSH, 416 West County Line Road, Barrington.

Investigation to date:

Investigation at Chicago revealed that the owner of one mail drop and the Office Manager of the second, identified the photo from the passport application as LESTER KNOX COLEMAN. The owner of a printing shop had advised that LESTER COLEMAN had ordered two sets of business cards. One was in the name LESTER COLEMAN, the other THOMAS LEAVY.

Numerous checks at the address listed for emergency contact, which was the same address the birth certificate was to be mailed to, failed to reveal any tenants. On April 16, 1990, the next door neighbor was approached for information. The neighbor advised that LESTER COLEMAN was house sitting for the owner of the home, ARTHUR T. MCINTOSH. The neighbor identified the photo from the application as LESTER COLEMAN. She advised that the COLEMAN family left on April 7, 1990 for California. COLEMAN was to go to Japan and on his return flight stop in Hawaii to meet the rest of the family. The neighbor stated that on April 11, 1990, KOLDEN MOVING AND STORAGE, 410 Telser Road, Lake Zurich, Illinois arrived to move COLEMAN's belongings to storage.

On April 17, 1990, Magistrate W. THOMAS ROSEMOND, Jr., Northern District of Illinois, issued a warrant for LESTER KNOX COLEMAN, III. This warrant was for willfully and knowingly making a false statement in an application for a passport, in violation of Title 18, United States Code, Section 1542.

On April 25, 1990, KOLDEN MOVING AND STORING advised that COLEMAN can be reached at telephone number (205) 540-2448. The telephone number was sent to the FBI Office in Mobile, Alabama. On May 1, 1990 LESTER KNOX COLEMAN, III, was arrested without incident at Townhouse Residence #E-14, 1616 Fort Morgan Road, Fort Morgan, Alabama.

After his arrest COLEMAN claimed to have petitioned to have his name changed to THOMAS LEAVY. A check with Jefferson County Probate Records Department, Birmingham, Alabama, revealed that COLEMAN did not petition the court until April 12, 1990 to change his name.

Smoking gun II: The FBI's so-called 'Investigative Summary' which accompanied the letter to Stockholm, setting out the basis for the passport charge.

To Whom it May Concern:

I am a journalist working on a book project which indirectly involves American foreign policy.

On January 18th, 1993, I called the Records Office in New London, Connecticut, and asked to speak to the Clerk, Gloria Hatfield. I asked Ms. Hatfield if the New London records showed that a Thomas Leavy had died on the 6th of July, 1948. Ms. Hatfield examined her files and informed me that she had looked under 1946, '47, '48 and '49, but could find no record of such a person. When I asked if she had information showing the birth of a Thomas Leavy as being July 4, 1948, she replied that obtaining a birth record required the presentation of documents, which I did not have.

Sincerely,

~Diana Holdsworth   date   Jan 25, 1993

EVELYN F. NABBAH
NOTARY PUBLIC
MY COMMISSION EXPIRES MARCH 31, 1995
Notary Public, State of Connecticut   date   1/25/93

Smoking gun III: The sworn statement of Diana Holdsworth contradicting the FBI's assertion that the 'real' Thomas Leavy died on 6 July 1948.

coleman.ord

UNITED STATES DISTRICT COURT
FOR THE NORTHERN DISTRICT OF ILLINOIS
EASTERN DIVISION

UNITED STATES OF AMERICA,   )
        Plaintiff,   )
)   No. 90 CR 365
        v.   )   Judge Moran
)
LESTER K. COLEMAN III,   )
        Defendant.   )
                        ORDER

        It is hereby ordered that within ten (10) days of the date of
this order, Lester Coleman is required to provide his medical
records to Dr. Hallberg, Tröllhatton Sweden and to submit to a
medical examination before Dr. Hallberg   Failure to comply with
this order will result in the issuance of a bench warrant for
defendant's arrest.

Dated: 9/24/91   _James B. Moran_____
                                The Honorable James B. Moran
                                United States District Judge

Fugitive warrant ploy:
Ordered by the Federal cc
to report to Dr Hakan
Hallberg in Trollhättan f
a medical examination,
Coleman discovers that
Dr Hallberg knows
nothing about the
arrangement. Although
Coleman submits a
written statement
from the doctor to
that effect, a bench
warrant is issued for
Coleman's arrest
on grounds of
'failure to appear'.

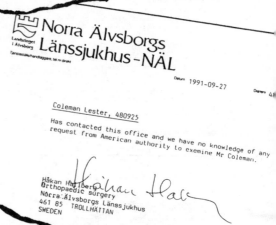

Norra Älvsborgs
Länssjukhus-NÄL
Landstinget i Älvsborg
Tjänsteställe/handläggare, tel nr direkt

Datum 1991-09-27

Coleman Lester, 480925

Has contacted this office and we have no knowledge of any
request from American authority to examine Mr Coleman.

Håkan Hallberg
Orthopaedic surgery
Norra Älvsborgs Länssjukhus
461 85 TROLLHÄTTAN
SWEDEN

Minute Order Form   (rev. 12/90)
UNITED ST...ES DISTRICT COURT, NORTHERN DIS...ICT OF ILLINOIS

Name of Assigned Judge or Magistrate Judge	JAMES B. MORAN	Sitting Judge if Other Than Assigned Judge	
Case Number	90 CR 365-1	Date	Oct 7, 1991
Case Title	U.S.A. VS LESTER COLEMAN III		

[In the following box (a) indicate the party filing the motion, e.g., plaintiff, defendant, 3rd-party plaintiff,
... state briefly the nature of ... ...ented.]

... ...ure to ...

(10) [X] [Other docket entry]
          Order bench warrant issued as to Lester Coleman III for failure
          to appear.   Issued BW to USA
                                10/9/91

(11) [ ]   [For further detail see   [ ] order on the reverse of   [ ] order attached to   the original minute order form.]

No notices required, advised in open court.		number of notices	
No notices required.		OCT 30 1991	date docketed
Notices mailed by judge's staff.	ED-5		docketing dpty. initials
Notified counsel by telephone.	RECEIVED FOR DOCKETING		date mailed notice
[X] Docketing to mail notices.	91 OCT-7 AM II: 31	OCT 8 1991	
Mail AO 450 form.			mailing dpty. initials
Copy to judge/magistrate Judge.		Document # 47	
courtroom deputy's initials	Date/time received in central Clerk's Office		

PRETRIAL SERVICES REPORT

District/Office SOUTHERN/ALABAMA	Charge(s) (Title, Section, and Description) FALSE STATEMENT ON A PASSPORT APPLICATION
Judicial Officer Magistrate William H. Steele	
Docket Number (Year-Sequence No.-Deft. No.)	

DEFENDANT

Name LESTER KNOX COLEMAN, III	Employment/School Self-emp: Journalist
Address No permanent address in U.S.	Address

Time at Address	Time in Community 2 weeks	Monthly Income $3500	Time in Empl./School Over 10 yrs.

DEFENDANT HISTORY

1. DEFENDANT HISTORY/RESIDENCE/FAMILY TIES 2.EMPLOYMENT HISTORY/FINANCIAL RESOURCES 3. HEALTH 4. PRIOR RECORD 5. ASSESSMENT OF FLIGHT/DANGER

The information below was gathered through interview of the defendant and through contact with DEA Headquarters, NBC News, and the subject's attorney.

I. Lester Coleman was born in Pensacola, FL on September 25, 1943.

II. Although Mr. Coleman's employment history sounds quite improbable, information he gave to the Pretrial Services Officer has proven to be true. Coleman is a free-lance journalist, specializing in the Middle East, who has also worked as an undercover investigator for the Drug Enforcement Administration of the United States. NBC News Foreign Correspondent Brian Ross contacted this office on May 3, 1990 to verify Coleman's relationship with NBC News. He also indicated Coleman has worked with other news agencies, as well. Ross indicated Coleman has contributed stories regarding Middle East terrorism and drug trafficking to NBC News numerous times throughout the 1980's. They have interviewed him on the air, on NBC nightly news, as an

expert in terrorism and drug production in the Middle East. Ross also verified that Coleman has testified before Senate committees on these same subjects.

Ray Tripiccio, an agent with DEA in Washington, D.C., verifies that Coleman has formerly worked in a relationship with the Drug Enforcement Administration. The only information he could give on this secret activity is that Coleman was deactivated as a contract consultant as of 6-24-88.

Joseph Boohaker of the Counsel of Lebanese-American Organizations, verifies that Coleman has been employed with that group in the past, for about a year. His contract ended 3-31-90, and it appears likely that Coleman has not had a regular pay check, since that time. Coleman indicates that he is currently working on a book, and that he was attempting to make arrangements to return to the Middle East, in order to do more research. (It is noted that Coleman has gone to Jefferson County Probate Court in Birmingham, to have his name legally changed to, "Thomas Leavy.") Joseph Boohaker, the subject's attorney, verifies that this was accomplished sometime in April. (The present charge from Chicago apparently pre-dates the legal name change.) Coleman states that he needed a passport in a different name, because his name is known to drug traffickers in the Middle East.

IV. I have no information indicating that Mr. Coleman has ever been arrested.

Coleman's Pretrial Services Report, in which the Drug Enforcement Administration describes him, correctly, as a 'contract consultant' engaged in 'secret activity'.

UNITED STATES DISTRICT COURT
NORTHERN DISTRICT OF ILLINOIS
EASTERN DIVISION

UNITED STATES OF AMERICA,   )
)
        Plaintiff,   )
)   90 CR 365
    vs.   )
)
LES COLEMAN,   )
)
        Defendant.   )

MOTION FOR PRODUCTION OF DOCUMENTS
UNDER RULE 16(a)(I)(C)

Now comes the defendant Les, Coleman by his undersigned
counsel and respectfully requests the following government
documents which are material to the preparation of defendant's
defense:

1. All records by the Drug Enforcement Administration
(DEA), the Defense Intelligence Agency (DIA) and any other
United States Intelligence or Law Enforcement Agency reflecting
their employment and/or working relationship with the
defendant, Les Coleman, including all DEA records referring to
DEA Informant ID #SX9860002, all records of DIA MC 10
pertaining to the defendant, as well as all files from the CIA
and DEA related to an operation named "COREA" from December
1987 to January 1989.

Included in the document request are all documents or
other writings reflecting payment, work assignments,
evaluations, travel authorizations, equipment requisitions or
any other reference to a Les Coleman, Benjamin B, Thomas Leavy,

1

Jr., Stevens Mantra Corp., Middle East Television, Condor
Television Ltd., AMA Industries, and Wildwood Video. All of
these names are code names and front companies under which
defendant worked for the government.

In support of this request defendant states that his
defense to the charge in making a false statement in
application for a passport, is that he was working for the
government at the time he made such false statements and that
the alleged false birth certificate upon which the false
statement is based was supplied to him by the government and
was used to obtain a passport to conduct a secret intelligence
operation for the government. Consequently, all documents
showing the defendants working relationship with government
intelligence agencies would be corroborative of his claim and
material and necessary for his defense.

Respectfully submitted,

Dated: August 30, 1990

Michael E Deutsch
MICHAEL E. DEUTSCH
Attorney for Defendant

343 S. Dearborn
Suite 1607
Chicago, IL   60604
(312) 663-5046
      235-0070

Defending himself against the passport charge, Coleman seeks a court order on 30 August 1990, requiring the DEA, the DIA and other agencies to produce his government employment records. Washington refused to comply on grounds of 'national security'.

Coleman's affidavit in Pan Am vs USA, to which was appended a transcript of his conversation with Micheal T. Hurley in which, seven months before Lockerbie, he warned the DEA attaché about 'a disaster waiting to happen'.

Sworn to before me this 17th day of April, 1991

LESTER K. COLEMAN

UNITED STATES DISTRICT COURT
EASTERN DISTRICT OF NEW YORK

IN RE AIR DISASTER AT LOCKERBIE,)
SCOTLAND, ON DECEMBER 21, 1988)
------------------------------)   M.D.L. 799 (PLATT, CH. J.)
PAN AMERICAN WORLD AIRWAYS, INC.,)   (ALL CASES)
PAN AMERICAN WORLD SERVICES, INC.,)
and ALERT MANAGEMENT SYSTEMS, INC.,)
      Defendants/Third-Party)
            Plaintiffs,)
)
      - against -)
)
UNITED STATES OF AMERICA,)
)
      Third-Party Defendant)
)
)
)

DECLARATION OF LIEUTENANT COLONEL TERRY E. BATHEN

I, Terry E. Bathen, Lieutenant Colonel, United States Army,
Assistant General Counsel, Defense Intelligence Agency, do hereby
declare the following to be true and correct:

1. I am an attorney in the office of Defense Intelligence

3. Through the exercise of my official duties, I have become
familiar with the contents of an affidavit dated April 17, 1991,
submitted by Mr. Lester K. Coleman in connection with lawsuits
arising from the crash of Pan American Flight 103 at Lockerbie,
Scotland.

5. My review of Department of Defense HUMINT records reveals
that Mr. Coleman was formerly associated with a Department of
Defense intelligence activity. On or about October 25, 1985
Coleman contacted Defense Intelligence Agency personnel

4. In response to personally reviewed the automated and documentary
Coleman, I personally reviewed the automated and documentary
files of the Defense Intelligence Agency and associated
Department of Defense intelligence activities which contain
information about Mr. Coleman. The statements made herein are
based upon my personal knowledge, upon information made
available to me in my official capacity, and upon determinations
made in accordance therewith.

5. My review of Department of Defense HUMINT records reveals
that Mr. Coleman was formerly associated with a department of
Defense intelligence activity. On or about October 25, 1985, Mr.
Coleman contacted Defense Intelligence Agency personnel by
telephone and volunteered to provide information concerning the
Middle East. Mr. Coleman's offer to provide video tapes
associated with his travels in that part of the world was
favorably evaluated, and he became affiliated with a classified
Department of Defense intelligence activity during November 1985.

6. Mr. Coleman's activities on behalf of this classified
organization require use of sources and methods that are
not involved

I certify under penalty of perjury that the foregoing is
true and correct to the best of my knowledge and belief.

                            Terry E. Bathen
                            Terry E. Bathen
                            Lieutenant Colonel, U.S. Army
                            Assistant General Counsel
                            Defense Intelligence Agency

Executed this 29th day of May 1991.

Limited hang-out I: The declaration by DIA counsel in Pan Am vs USA which
unexpectedly admits that Coleman worked for the Defense Intelligence Agency, although
it plays down the extent and nature of his employment as a HUMINT agent.

UNITED STATES DISTRICT COURT
EASTERN DISTRICT OF NEW YORK
- - - - - - - - - - - - - - - - - - X
IN RE AIR DISASTER AT LOCKERBIE,   : M.D.L. (TCP)
SCOTLAND ON DECEMBER 21, 1988   : (All Cases)
- - - - - - - - - - - - - - - - - - X
PAN AMERICAN WORLD AIRWAYS, INC.,   :
PAN AM WORLD SERVICES, INC. and   :
ALERT MANAGEMENT SYSTEMS, INC.,   :
                                     :
            Defendants/   :
            Third-Party Plaintiffs, :
                                     :
    - against -   : (JS-7190)
                                     :
UNITED STATES OF AMERICA,   :
                                     :
            Third-Party Defendant.   :
- - - - - - - - - - - - - - - - - - X

DECLARATION OF MICHEAL T. HURLEY

I, MICHEAL T. HURLEY, declare and say:

1. I am a Special Agent (criminal investigator) of the Drug
Enforcement Administration (DEA), a component of the United
States Department of Justice. I have been employed by DEA and
its predecessor agencies since September 1968.

2. I submit this declaration in connection with the
allegations against the United States Drug Enforcement
Administration regarding the terrorist bombing of Pan Am Flight
103 over Lockerbie, Scotland, on December 21, 1988.

6. Coleman was established as a DEA cooperating individual
("CI") on January 31, 1986, partially because of his technical
capabilities and he said that he could establish a CI network in
Lebanon. He was to recruit sub-sources to collect data regarding
opium production in Lebanon. The data would enable DEA to
develop strategic information on opium production in that region,
including crop estimates, crop eradication, and major trafficking
routes.

I hereby declare under penalty of perjury that the foregoing
is true and correct.

Signed this 31st day
of May, 1991.

_____
MICHEAL T. HURLEY
Special Agent
Drug Enforcement Administration

Limited hang-out II: The declaration by Micheal Hurley in Pan Am vs USA in which
he concedes that Coleman worked for the DEA in Cyprus, while playing down the
nature of his assignment, and from which it is clear that Coleman was working for
the Defense Intelligence Agency *at the same time* .

92-9251

REDACTED VERSION

UNITED STATES COURT OF APPEALS
FOR THE SECOND CIRCUIT

Docket Nos. 92-9251, 92-9253 and 92-9255

IN RE: AIR DISASTER AT LOCKERBIE, SCOTLAND
ON DECEMBER 21, 1988

JUDITH A. PAGNUCCO, Individually and as Executrix of the Estate of
Robert I. Pagnucco, deceased; MOLENA A. PORTER, Individually and as Administratrix
of the Estate of Walter L. Porter, deceased; and DONA BARDELLI BAINBRIDGE,
Individually and as Administratrix of the Estate of Harry M. Bainbridge,

Plaintiffs-Appellees,

v.

PAN AMERICAN WORLD AIRWAYS, INC., and
ALERT MANAGEMENT SYSTEMS, INC.,

Defendants-Appellants.

On Appeals from the United States District Court
for the Eastern District of New York

BRIEF FOR APPELLANTS PAN AMERICAN WORLD AIRWAYS, INC.
AND ALERT MANAGEMENT SYSTEMS, INC.

Clinton H. Coddington
Coddington, Hicks & Danforth
Suite 300
555 Twin Dolphin Drive
Paragon Center, Redwood Shores
Redwood City, California 94065
(415) 592-5400

James M. Shaughnessy
Windels, Marx, Davies & Ives
156 West 56th Street
New York, New York 10019
(212) 237-1000

Richard M. Sharp
Frederick C. Schafrick
Eric C. Jeffrey
Lisa A. Landsman
Shea & Gardner
1800 Massachusetts Ave., N.W.
Washington, D.C. 20036
(202) 828-2000

*Attorneys for Pan American World Airways, Inc. and
Alert Management Systems, Inc.*

Under Seal Version Dated: January 28, 1993
Redacted Version Dated: February 9, 1993

Extracts from Pan Am's appeal brief against the finding 'wilful misconduct' by a New York jury in the 1992 compensation suit brought by the families of the victims of the Lockerbie disaster.

---

though he would not go so far as to [...]
jurors to opine on causation (J.A. 2700-01).

2. **Defendants' Contention: The Method of Bombing Was Not Established**

Defendants contended that it could not be determined from the evidence developed by the parties how the terrorists had planted the bomb on Flight 103.[6/] Defendants were precluded from presenting the opinions of three experts (Ariel Merari, Noel Koch, and Peter Gurney)[7/] that the plaintiffs' theory as to how the bomb got on board was implausible and the evidence was insufficient to permit an expert to conclude that the bomb bag had been transferred in Frankfurt from Air Malta (e.g., J.A. 3465-68). In consequence, the jury heard only one expert for the defense (Dr. Lee Grodzins), and his testimony, as truncated by another ruling (see pp. 8-9 below), related to technical aspects of x-ray that were not in dispute by the parties (Tr. 5728-57).

Defendants were permitted to adduce testimony and records from Air Malta to show that no unaccompanied bag had been loaded onto Flight KM 180.[8/] Plaintiffs' supposedly contradictory baggage records from varying sources in the FAG, defendants contended,

---

6/ In a series of discovery rulings, defendants were prevented from obtaining discovery from the United States as to information that it might have regarding how the bombing was committed.

7/ See J.A. 4435-38 (Gurney); J.A. 3498-502 (Merari); Offer of Proof for Noel Koch, J.A. 448.

8/ On Air Malta, the head loader must physically count the number of bags loaded in a plane's cargo hold to ensure that it equals the number on the baggage manifest (J.A. 3358 (Agius)). Moreover, no baggage of any kind from Flight KM 180 had been designated on the passenger transfer message (J.A. 1151) for transfer to Pan Am Flight 103 (J.A. 3367 (Borg)).

contained so many demonstrable errors and omissions that no reliable conclusion could be based on them (J.A. 3603-12).

Defendants also adduced testimony that plaintiffs' theory of the bombing (the "Air Malta theory") was wrong because a bag containing a radio-cassette player had not been seen by the operator who x-rayed the interline bags that were loaded on to Pan Am Flight 103 in Frankfurt. Kurt Maier, who performed that inspection on December 21, 1988, testified that his duty report (J.A. 1099-1100) showed that he had x-rayed 13 bags for Flight 103, that he had been told to call a supervisor if he saw a radio inside any bag, and that none of the 13 bags x-rayed for Flight 103 contained a radio-cassette player (J.A. 3382-83, 3388-89, 3392-93).[9] Plaintiffs contended that Mr. Maier had not been properly trained as an x-ray operator and that he had not been wearing his eyeglasses (J.A. 2967 (Vincent)). Mr. Maier rejoined that his eyeglasses were only reading glasses that he did not need or use to perform his job (J.A. 3379-80).

Pan Am was precluded from presenting a demonstration of the x-ray equipment that would have supported Mr. Maier's testimony and would have shown the freeze-frame image produced on the monitor by a Toshiba radio-cassette player inside a Samsonite suitcase. The demonstration would have been presented by Dr. Lee Grodzins of M.I.T. The court ruled that the demonstration was irrelevant on the ground that plaintiffs, in effect, stip-

_____

[9] Maier was intensely cross-examined on, among other subjects, earlier deposition testimony that appeared to say that he stopped bags with radio-cassette players only if they appeared "suspicious." Maier explained that he would have stopped any radio-cassette player as being suspicious (J.A. 3394-96, 3408-09). Some of the difficulties with Maier's deposition appear to have been caused by the poor quality of the translation between English and German. (Maier does not speak English.) See, e.g., J.A. 3411 (in-court trans-lator notes video deposition translation is "poor German, and ambiguous").

ulated that radio-cassette players would be visible on the x-ray's monitor (J.A. 3331-34), even though plaintiffs contended that Maier himself had been incapable of detecting such a radio.

Twelve of the 13 bags x-rayed by Maier for Flight 103 could be traced to passengers. Plaintiffs asked the jury to infer that the thirteenth bag was the alleged unaccompanied bomb bag from Air Malta. Defendants introduced evidence that the thirteenth bag was not the bomb bag, but rather was the unaccompanied "rush-tag" bag[10] of a Pan Am pilot, Captain Hubbard, who had sent two bags home, one of which was found at Lockerbie.[11]

B.   The Parties' Contentions On Wilful Misconduct Relating To Plaintiffs' Air Malta Theory

1. The Alleged Violation of the ACSSP. Plaintiffs contended that Pan Am's x-ray procedure violated the aviation security requirements contained in the FAA's Air Carrier Standard Security Program ("ACSSP"). At the time of the Lockerbie disaster, ACSSP § XV.C.1(a) required that carriers at "extraordinary security" airports, such as Frankfurt, Heathrow, and other major European airports:

_____

A "rush-tag bag" is a bag that has become separated from its owner/passenger. This common, some would say routine, occurrence on every airline. The general practice of the airlines is to specially ticket the bags ("rush-tag") and send them on their way. At Frankfurt, Pan Am x-rayed such bags before carrying them. See note 11 infra.

Captain Hubbard tagged two bags for carriage from Berlin to his home in Seattle, and he piloted an aircraft to Karachi (Tr. 5420-43). One of his bags arrived at Seattle; the other was found at Lockerbie. Pan Am introduced evidence to show that because it required rush-tag bags to be x-rayed, one could infer that the Hubbard bag found at Lockerbie had been x-rayed by Maier before being placed on board Flight 103. (J.A. 1120-... Tr. 5241 (Wunderlich).) Plaintiffs contended either that Hubbard's bag was put on Flight 103 in London (J.A. 762 (memo. of Jones)) or that it was not x-rayed in Frankfurt ... 5263-66 (Wunderlich)).

SUBCOMMITTEE STAFF REPORT

Syria, President Bush and Drugs

-- the Administration's Next Iraqgate --

November 23, 1992[1]

---

[1]Chairman Charles E. Schumer of the House Judiciary Committee's Subcommittee on Crime and Criminal Justice directed the Subcommittee majority staff to prepare this report. This report has not been reviewed or approved by other Members of the Subcommittee.

Extracts from a congressional report prepared by the House Judiciary Committee's Subcommittee on Crime and Criminal Justice documenting Syria's involvement in Lebanese narcotics trafficking.

...atory is affiliated with an armed Palestini... ...te Syrian officials and makes the necessa...

...tains throughout the Bekaa Valley, it ... ...d exist without the active collusion of the ... ...body or nothing gets into, or out of, the ... ...thout the cooperation of the entire Syrian ... ...me in Lebanon -- cultivation, production

...ome military units or Syrian officials, Syrian Government involvement and the that they are not in a position to substantiate such charges. U.S. Government officials publicly claim with former government officials who confirmed the existence of satellite photos showing Syrian military units, including tanks, artillery, and infantry encampments, strategically placed in, and adjacent to, recognized fields and known heroin laboratories.

Another source with intimate knowledge of the U.S. Government's files on Lebanese drug traffickers informed Subcommittee staff that the U.S. Government now possesses extensive intelligence information implicating many Syrian Government officials in the Lebanese drug trade. Much of this information is raw intelligence in the form of reports from confidential informants, intercepted wire and telephone communications, and other intelligence information received from foreign governments.

1. Monser al-Kassar -- "The Drug Prince of Marbella" and "The Godfather of Terrorists"

To better understand why the U.S. Government is apparently hesitant to act on such information, consider our Government's response, or lack thereof, to the infamous Monser al-Kassar.

The al-Kassar family has been part of the present Damascus regime since Hafez Assad took power in 1970. Monser's father, Mohammad al-Kassar, served in the Syrian diplomatic corps. The al-Kassars have been characterized as "the largest drug and arms dealing family in Syria."

2. Rifaat Assad

From about 1976 until about 1984, President Assad's younger brother, ... leading baron of the Lebanese drug trade. He used Syrian military trucks ....raft and diplomatic pouches as tools of his international drug network which he based out o: ... northern Bekaa. The 569th Syrian Army division which he commanded was reportedly little more than "muscle" for his drug trafficking organization.

Specializing in opium and heroin, Rifaat amassed an illicit fortune. After an unsuccessful attempt to depose his brother, Hafez, he was effectively exiled and now leads a life of luxury in his heavily-guarded villa on the French Riviera. He reportedly continues to play a substantial role in Bekaa Valley drug trafficking with the tacit approval of some Western governments. Two of Rifaat's sons, Darid and Firas, are also reportedly based in France and involved in smuggling arms and drugs throughout the Mediterranean.

3. Mustafa Tlass, Syrian Minister of Defense

Syrian Defense Minister Mustafa Tlass is associated with at least three known drug traffickers including Hamad Ali al-Kis from Baalbak. Tlass was recently involved in procuring an exit visa for a very high-profile trafficker who had to leave Syria quickly, presumably to avoid "problems." This is consistent with other reports of his obtaining visas for traffickers traveling to Argentina, Spain and Germany.

During August 1989, the Syrian Defense Ministry reportedly distributed more than 1,000 "laissez passer" or travel permits at $10,000 each to "friends" of the Defense Ministry. This report is consistent with news accounts that drug smugglers from Lebanon were intercepted on their way to Israel and Egypt with special travel passes signed by "M. Tlass." At least one government source has told the Subcommittee staff that the U.S. Government presently possesses sufficient information to indict Tlass for drug trafficking.

4. General Ali Dubah, Commander of Syrian Military Intelligence

Dubah, related to Monser al-Kassar by marriage, is one of President Assad's closest friends and confidantes. He is connected with many major Lebanese traffickers including the Jaffar clan.

He also coordinates Syrian extortion efforts to ensure that sufficient drug profits are left over from the "personal corruption" so that the Syrian military intelligence service is not deprived of its institutional share. Dubah's role in the drug trade has been characterized as "having his hand in everyone's cookie jar."

12

5. General Ghazi Kenaan, Commander of Syrian Military

Kenaan has often been called "the godfather ...ary intelligence in Lebanon, he is in a unique ...coddle known drug traffickers. If the "price ...will intervene on behalf of major traffickers.

Information provided to the Subcommittee ...following Lebanese traffickers: Ali and Husse... Saikali, Abdul Halim Karakalla, Khalil Naba...

Kenaan has also been known to arbitrate disputes between... ...own drug trafficking clans, presumably for a fee.

Tlass, Dubah, and Kenaan have all *personally* issued travel passes to known drug ...affickers. Such passes allow the dealer to move freely in Lebanon and/or Syria "with his car, ...s personal weapon and cargo, without being, searched or detained."

Working together with the Lebanese clans who have traditionally controlled the drug ...ade, these and other lesser officers are heavily involved with the Lebanese trafficking networks ...o serve essentially their own purposes:

(1) They rake off whatever immediate drug profits they can for personal enrichment;

(2) They use the drug money for other purposes related to their military/intelligence activities (i.e. they buy informers); and

(3) They use their ability to manage the drug trade of any of the organized groups by either threatening to seize that group's drugs, or more subtly, by allowing one group to move its product to market more quickly and cheaply.

VI. Syrian Military and Diplomatic Officials Have Been Repeatedly Linked to Drug Trafficking During the Last Ten Years.

Syrian military and intelligence officials in occupied Lebanon are involved in the drug trade at all levels: cultivation, production and transportation. *Such connections between high-level Syrian Government officials and drug traffickers are not coincidental. These bonds are merely a representative sample of the Syrian Government's widespread pattern and practice of associating itself with those who peddle poison around the world.*

13

INTERFOR, INC.

575 MADISON AVENUE · NEW YORK, N.Y. 10022 · SUITE 1006 · TEL. 212-605-0375 · TLX: 237699 WWBUS · FAX: 212-308-9834

INVESTIGATIVE REPORT

I. ASSIGNMENT:

As the overall assignment, Defense trial counsel retained us to
investigate the facts of the disaster, gather intelligence, develop leads, locate and obtain physical evi-
dence, and to locate expert witnesses and advise and consult
with counsel as it may direct. The first stage assignment was
to determine the facts and then to identify the sources, nature, extent, form and quality of available evidence; and then
to recommend the action to obtain such evidence in court-admis-
sible form, and to estimate the likelihood of obtaining same
and the costs.

II. REPORTED RESULTS OF LAW ENFORCEMENT INVESTIGATIONS:

The assignment commenced some six months after the disaster
during which time law enforcement agencies of Great Britain,
Federal Republic of Germany and the United States have investigated the matter. Reports of their results and theories have
been published in various journals via direct quotes attributed
and unattributed from official investigative sources. Review
of same shows that many key facts have been established while
others remain in dispute. Therefore, it is useful to summarize
same before we state our independent findings.

A. Facts Generally Agreed By Law Enforcement:

The flight originated in Frankfurt on a Boeing 727 on December
21, 1988. The flight landed in London's Heathrow airport. A
second plane, a Boeing 747, was then used for the continuation
leg to New York JFK under Number 103. All continuing passengers deplaned in Heathrow and then boarded the 747 with the
London passengers. The flight crashed over Lockerbie, Scotland, due to a bomb explosion, with all lives lost.

Law enforcement investigators have determined that the bomb was
made of Semtex explosive and concealed in a suitcase which was
in a cargo hold, that it weighed approx. 1.25 pounds (568
grams), that it exploded over Lockerbie, and that it was sufficient in explosive power to cause the plane to crash.

3/27

Extracts from a confidential
report on the Flight 103
disaster commissioned from
Juval Aviv, of Interfor Inc.,
by James M. Shaughnessy
in the course of Pan Am's
own investigation.

A. SOURCES.

Source 1 is comprised of six persons working in different
of the intelligence community of a Western government.
bility of this information is very good. Generally this
of agencies is only fair to good among the various person
porting based on our prior experience and its past record
ever, the very number of separate sources in these agenci
(not necessarily sympathetic to each other), all sharing t
conclusion, as well as the depth of the intelligence gathe
and the agencies' considerable resources and special inter
in the matter, justifies rating this information as very g

Source 2 is comprised of three persons working in different
units of the intelligence agency of a second Western govern
ment. Reliability of this information is very good, not so
much due to prior experience with the sources, which is goo
very good, but because of their position to know the partic
facts.

Source 3 is one person working for the intelligence agency o
third Western oriented government. Reliability of this info
ation is excellent based on our prior experience with both t
agency and the particular person, its and his prior record
its position to know first hand these matters.

Source 4 is one person working for the intelligence agency o
fourth Western government. Good. It is normally rated very
good but is conservatively downgraded as to this matter becau
its information seems in some aspects to be derivative, i.e.
great part based on information received from other agencies.

[It must be emphasized that these sources did not have as the
objective the acquisition of evidence for the apprehension an
trial of the perpetrators; rather, their objective is to moni
tor terrorist acts, draw conclusions based on their expertise,
and then use what they learn so as to defend their countries i
the future.]

Source 5 is an experienced Director of airport security for th
most security conscious airline. He was in a position to receive the inside consensus of various security officers at
Frankfurt Airport, which he reported to us. He also receives
daily terrorism intelligence from his company's liaison with
its host country's highly regarded intelligence service, and

7/27

The subject disaster resulted from planning and eve...
ning a couple of years earlier.

Libya's Qadaffi is a major funder of terrorism. He tired of
the ineffectiveness and costs of the internal jealousies among
terrorist factions, wanted more effective terrorism against
America, yet did not want to suffer further American retaliation. He demanded that the more skilled terrorist groups co-
ordinate better, and do it so as to preserve his deniability.

At the same time, Syrian intelligence, which had been exposed
as planning the Hindawi bomb attempt against El Al in London
out of its embassy there, sought deeper cover and backed Ahmed
Jibril's PFLP as its front team.

Meetings were then held among leaders of various factions:
Ahmed Jibril of PLFP, Abu Nidal, George Habash, Ali Issa Duba
of Syrian intelligence, and Iranian radicals, (named by us
hereafter for convenience as the "Interterror Group"). They
agreed to cooperate and seek secure routes for smuggling contraband and people for terrorism while raising additional funds.
(Some of these groups had been doing so individually for some
time). They never trusted each other, kept secrets from each
other, and never worked together in full cooperation, but there
were frequent although wary joint contacts and operations.

They set up a complex drug and arms smuggling operation via
various European cities. Eventually Abu Nidal ran the drugs-
arms operations, while Ahmed Jibril concentrated on arms and
terrorist planning.

Monzer Al-Kassar, born 7/1/47, in Nabek, Syria, is married to
Raghda Duba, the sister of Syrian intelligence chief Ali Issa
Duba, (sometimes spelled Douba). Al-Kassar is a major arms and
drug smuggler who has played a key role in terrorism banking
and "diplomacy" among terrorist groups, and has acquaintance
with certain Western leaders. For example, he is known to have
had friendly contacts with former Austrian Chancellor Bruno
Kraisky.

Al-Kassar has had long term romantic affairs with Raja
Al-Assad, the daughter of Rifat Assad, who is the brother of
Syrian President Hafez Assad, spending time with her at her

...e Frankfurt smuggling operation worked as follows: an
...ce boarded flights with checked luggage containing in
...tems. An accomplice Turkish baggage handler for PanAm
...sed to identify the suitcase, then switched it with an
...al piece holding contraband, which he had brought into
...port or otherwise received there from another accomp-
...The passenger accomplice then picked up the baggage on
... It is not known how this method passed through arri-
...stoms where such existed, but this route and method
...steadily and smoothly for a long time.

...rkish baggage handlers attended mosques in Cologne and
...which were fundamentalist Islamic sects. It was there
...they were recruited.

...d Jafar was a regular "passenger" accomplice for the drug
...

...BKA/DEA/CIA surveillance operation continued to monitor the
...e without interfering with it, apparently seeking intelli-
...to identify the extent of the operation they deci-
...ce. As they realized the operation into less numerous areas so
...t they could concentrate their surveillance focus. So BKA
...an a combination of arrests and visible police presence at
...er drug operation locales in West Germany, which eventually
...duced the operators, at Frankfurt airport, PanAm.
...sible presence to concentrate where there was no such

...KA had another motive to channel the operation to PanAm's bag-
...age area. It had for some time been surveilling separate acti-
...ties there involving shipments (contents unspecified) to and
...rom the East Bloc via PanAm through Frankfurt, Berlin and
...oscow. This would enable them to more efficiently monitor
...both operations now.

The CIA unit involved in this Frankfurt airport surveillance
works in West Germany with BKA and has a control at an unknown
location in the Washington area. We cannot say with certainty
that the activities of this unit were fully reported if at all
up the channels to CIA HQ; it appears that it eventually operated to some or a large extent as an internal covert operation
without consistent oversight, a la Oliver North or Edwin
Wilson. To distinguish what it knew as opposed to what CIA HQ
definitely knew, we refer to that unit as CIA-1.

CONCLUSIONS.

...contradictions among the sources as to the essent-
...f various persons comprising the intelligence
... have too many diverse interests and turf to pro-
...d in a disinformation effort. The most telling
...our terrorist underground intelligence is the
...clusion and opinion that our sources is the
...w, where, when, by whom and what act was com-
...c. ...ad what prior warnings and when and what they

From this perspective the apparent contradictions in the reports of the official investigations might be explained as follows: (1) Jafar checked a suitcase, possibly in a manner which
was not recorded or noticed, and we stand by our sources as to
this; (2) The signs of an explosion in the CIA luggage was
likely an anti-entry small explosive often used by them, and
was likely triggered by the first explosion or a hurtling
object; (3) the nervous CIA presence and strange behavior at
the crash site indicates the sensitivity of the contents of the
CIA passengers' luggage.

It is pointless to try to pin down further the exact motives
and identities and roles of the terrorists. All had the same
goal: to strike at America. They are known to work together,
albeit in duplicity. Confusion of funders, planners, perpetrators and motive is a mark of Syrian intelligence planning.

We are also persuaded by the intelligence as to the BKA-CIA-1
surveillance, videotape and possession of key evidence by the
U.S. Government, as well as the communications codename. The
persons so reporting spoke from what appears to be detailed
knowledge. It was our impression that more than one of these
persons prefers to keep the truth hidden (and assumes that it
will remain so) while others prefer that it emerge, although
not in a position to do so.

From the perspective of intelligence analysis our findings are
conclusive. From the perspective of journalists it is publishable speculation. From the perspective of trial lawyers it
probably remains inadmissible speculation or hearsay.

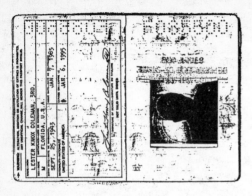

The police authority of Trollhättan, Sweden, hereby merely certifies that this is a copy of a page in a passport, which has been presented before the police authority by a gentleman, who states that his name is Lester Knox Coleman and who has applied for asylum in Sweden on political grounds. The police authority does not certify the authenticity of the passport in question.

POLISMYNDIGHETEN

Ulrica Ericsson
Deputy Police Superintendent

The police authority of Trollhättan, Sweden, hereby merely certifies that this is a copy of a page in a passport, which has been presented before the police authority by a gentleman, who states that his name is Lester Knox Coleman and who has applied for asylum in Sweden on political grounds. The police authority does not certify the authenticity of the passport in question.

POLISMYNDIGHETEN

Ulrica Ericsson
Deputy Police Superintendent

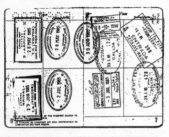
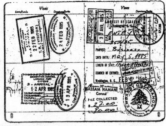
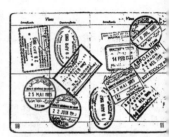

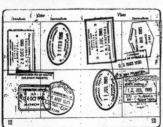
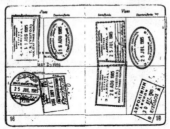
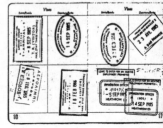

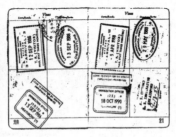
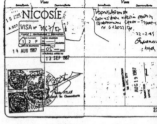

Specimen pages from Coleman's still valid American passport with some of the visas and entry and exit stamps that support his account of his movements as a DIA secret agent.

— Index —

Abbas, Abu 82, 86
ABC Network 49, 103, 146, 180–1,
    186, 217–18, 223, 252–3, 262, 266–7,
    275, 295
Aharoni, Daniel 292
Air Jordan 152, 156
Air Malta 73, 75, 113, 177–8, 183, 236,
    238, 298–9
al-Assad, Raja 82
al-Kassar, Monzer 16–19, 50, 80, 82–6,
    107–8, 119, 142, 166–7, 169–71, 197,
    201, 235–6, 284
al-Megrahi, Abdel 183–4, 186, 301
al-Moghrabi, Mahmoud 112, 233, 277
Al Shiraa 136
al-Zawi, Ahmed 187
Alabama, University of 191–2, 200,
    205, 259
Alert Management Inc. 270
Alford, Bob 295
AMA Industries 130
Amal militia 108–9, 152–3
American Victims of Flight 103 52
Ammerman, Bert 52
Anderson, Jack 50
Anderson, Terry 130
Antoine 102
Aoun, Gen. Michel 4, 208–10
APEXCO 190
Arlington Hall 7, 21, 25, 28, 91–2
Arnett, Peter 4, 211
Asmar, Tony 3, 101–4, 109–10, 121,
    128–30, 132–5, 189, 194, 198, 203–6
Assad, Pres. Hafez 50, 86, 132, 167–8,
    172, 208, 302
Assad, Rifat 16–18, 30, 82, 119, 151, 153,
    166–7, 302
Auburn University 132, 136, 149, 259
Aviv, Juval 42, 78–88, 90, 138–42, 181,

219, 224, 235–9, 241, 251, 256, 265–8,
    272–6, 290–7, 302, 318

Baabda 4, 210–11
Bahamas 57, 61–4
Baker, James 139
Baltimore 65
Bank of Credit & Commerce International
    (BCCI) 107, 121, 247
Barber, Alden 38, 40
Barr, William 182
Barron's 181–2, 266, 292
Bathen, Lt-Col. Terry E. 228, 230–2, 244,
    263, 276–7
Beaini, Fohad 154
Bechari, Ibrahim 186
Beckman, Richard 288–9
Behrens, Lesley 5–9, 23
Beirut 4, 19, 50, 83, 96, 98–110, 129–32,
    142, 161, 168, 192, 203, 209, 256
Bekaa Valley 17–19, 29, 119, 122, 152–3,
    163–5, 167, 170, 226
Bell, Ian 179, 182
Bern 169–70
Bernard, Laurie 66
Berri, Nabi 108–9, 152, 156
Bitar, Victor 210
Black September 41–2, 44
Boohaker, Joseph L. 8, 21–4, 26, 208–10,
    283–5
Boutros, Marcel 210
Boy Scouts of America 37–40, 45, 57,
    205, 208–9, 259–60
Boyce, William D. 37
Boy's Life 57
Broadcasting 95
Brokaw, Tom 20, 45, 206
Bufkins, Russ 38
Buhler, Gregory W. 139, 146–7, 275

Bundeskriminalamt (BKA) 14–19, 42, 46, 49, 56, 71–2, 74–7, 82–6, 117, 142, 166, 221, 245–6
Burchette, Lloyd 200, 251, 254, 257–8, 263–4, 267
Bush, George 49–51, 70, 114, 117, 119, 172, 184, 186, 209, 280, 304
Byron, Christopher 255–65, 268, 287, 291, 294, 296

Cable News Network (CNN) 66, 129–30, 175, 211, 218–19, 228, 250, 261
Calero, Adolfo 102
Calero, Mario 102, 106
Cannistraro, Vincent 175–6, 181, 291–3, 295
Casey, William 96, 101, 103, 108, 122, 130, 149, 256
Casolaro, Danny 247–51, 255
CBN 95–8, 101–2, 105–10, 121
CBS News 67–8, 258, 290, 294, 296–7
Cetera, Mario 190
Channon, Paul 49, 186
Christian Broadcasting Network 95, 101, 159, 231, 256
Christian Lebanese Forces 102, 106, 142, 205–8, 211–12
CIA 7, 15–19, 30, 45–6, 57, 61, 64, 66, 79–89, 92, 116, 139, 149, 153, 156, 165–6, 169, 172–6, 181, 190, 193, 197, 214, 217, 230, 236–7, 256, 293
Clayton, Mark 37, 41
Clinton, Bill 303
Coddington, Clinton 271
Colby, William 27
Coleman, Jocelyn 36, 58, 60
Coleman, Lester Knox 31–2
Coleman Jr, Lester Knox 31, 34, 297
Coleman III, Lester Knox 2–10, 13, 20–45, 47–8, 56–69, 87–8, 91–110, 120–36, 146–70, 173, 175–6, 189–221, 226–31, 235–7, 239–41, 243–69, 275–7, 281–90, 294, 297, 301–2, 305–6, 308–13, 320
    Squeal 61, 64, 159
Coleman, Margie 213, 282
Coleman, Mary-Claude 4, 6–9, 24, 26, 100, 104–5, 108–10, 126, 129, 148, 189, 203, 205–7, 212, 220–1, 229
Commission on Aviation Security & Terrorism 114–17, 266, 276
Condor Television Ltd 121–2, 124–5, 133, 231

Connelly, Phillip 46–7, 138, 226, 233, 274, 277
Connors, John J. 244–5
Contras 16, 83, 101–3, 106, 108, 110, 149, 166, 201, 207, 247, 256
COREA see Operation Corea
Council of Lebanese-American Organizations 210
Crane, David 66–7
Cronkite, Walter 38–9, 57
Cypriot Police Force Narcotics Squad (CPFNS) 153–5, 193, 195, 197
Cyprus 3, 17–18, 29–30, 42, 50, 56, 107, 109–10, 121, 124, 126, 138, 142, 146, 148–66, 188, 192–204, 218, 225–6, 229, 252, 292, 313

Daily Mail 78
Daily Telegraph 78, 185
Dakar 172, 175–6
Dalkamoni, Hafez Kassem 14–16, 47–9, 71, 187, 233, 277
Damascus 50, 142, 302
Daod, Abou 155–6
DeCesare, Don 67–8
Defense Intelligence Agency (DIA) 2, 19, 24–8, 45, 48, 56, 65, 91–4, 97–8, 101–2, 105–8, 121, 129–30, 142–4, 149, 192, 194, 197, 200, 206, 209, 213–17, 227–8, 230–2, 253, 260, 310, 312–13, 320
Deutsch, Michael 214, 243–4
Dhyer, Pierre 106
Donaghue, Ethel 60
Donleavy, Bill 93–5, 97–100, 105, 107–8, 110, 121–9, 132–5, 148–50, 160, 164, 166–8, 189–92, 194, 196, 205–6, 232
Drug Enforcement Administration (DEA) 1–2, 6–7, 17–19, 22–3, 25, 27–30, 42, 48, 50, 81–3, 87, 122, 138–9, 145–6, 148–9, 153, 160, 163–5, 169, 175–6, 180, 182, 188–90, 192–7, 204, 207, 213–20, 225–32, 235, 245–6, 255, 261–3, 265–7, 272, 294, 303, 309–11, 313
Dubah, Gen. Ali Issah 82, 86, 167, 171, 302
Dumfries & Galloway Constabulary 45, 111–12

Eddi, Raymond 210
El Al 14, 55
El-Jorr, Ibrahim 42, 151–2, 189, 192–6, 198–9, 202–3, 258

Elias, Abu 187
Emerson, Steven 158, 175, 218, 250, 257, 261, 265–8, 287, 291, 295
Esseff, John A. 210, 220, 260
Esseff, Joseph 210
Esson, George 111–12
Eurame Trading Company 29, 146, 193–8, 202, 204
Evans, Michael 251
Express, L' 172–3

Fadellah, Sheik Mohammed Hussein 102
Fatal Accident Inquiry 111, 114, 179, 276
FBI 4–5, 7, 9, 28, 47, 61, 89, 139, 141, 157, 174, 176–7, 180, 182, 214, 216, 235, 238–9, 243, 282, 288–90, 303–4, 306–7
Federal Aviation Administration (FAA) 28, 52–4, 114–16, 225, 271, 298–9
Federal Tort Claims Act 145, 180
Fenton, Tom 67
Fhimah, Lamen Khalifa 183–4, 186, 301
Fitzgerald, A. Ernest 247–50
Fitzwater, Marvin 184
Flint, Julie 174-5
Foster, Tom 223
Frankfurt 16, 80, 84, 88, 119, 125
    Airport 14, 17, 19, 46–7, 49, 51–5, 71–8, 82–3, 113, 115–16, 119, 137, 145–6, 224–5, 270–1, 299
Franks, Michael 102–3, 108, 110, 200–1, 256, 268, 275
Fraser, Lord 49, 111, 113, 184, 186
Freedom of Information Act 223–4, 273
Frezeli, Charles 209
Fulbright Commission 192, 254
Gaddafi, Col. Muammar 16, 82, 126–8, 173–4, 176, 186–7
Gallagher, Neil 47
Ganem, Fred 164, 195, 199
Gannon, Matthew Kevin 83, 85, 143, 206
Gauci, Tony 183
Gavzer, Bernie 26
Gazarik, Richard 237
Geagea, Shamir 211–12
Geohagen, Tom 40–1, 43
George (Syrian) 151, 155, 162, 170, 190–1, 194, 205, 259, 275, 282, 285
George (Taxi) 151, 155
Gerardo, Frank 107
Germany 46, 183, 185, 233
Ghadanfar, Abdel Fattah 14–16, 47, 49, 71, 233, 277
Gilbey, Emma 223

Goben, Mobdi ('the Professor') 15, 84
Graham, Gen. Danny 40, 43–4, 62
Greene, Stephen H. 180, 225
Grissom, Gregory 88–9
Guardian 78
Gurney, Peter 299–300

Habib, Dany 125, 150–1, 164, 196, 216
Haddad, Khaisar 187
Hadjiloizu, Penikos 155
Hallberg, Dr Hakan 244, 308
Hamadan, Jamal 153–4, 156–8
Hamilton, Adrian 186
Hamilton, William 247–9
Haser, Arman Jirayer 169–71
Hashim, Gushan 102, 106, 108–10
Hatfield, Gloria 289
Hayes, Dr Thomas 178, 233, 239, 277
Helms, Richard 93
Helsinki 19, 53, 175
Henderson, DC Derrick 276
Hershow, Sheila 28–9, 50
Hezbollah 17, 109, 122, 129, 131
H.M. Customs & Excise 18–19, 46–7, 54, 138, 226
Holdsworth, Diana 307
Hoobaka, Eli 106–7, 205
Horne, John 299
hostages (Beirut) 129–32, 168, 192, 204
House Government Operations Sub-committee 28, 180
House Judiciary Committee, Subcommittee on Crime & Criminal Justice 316
Hudson, Paul 182
Hurd, Douglas 186
Hurley, Michael T. 1–3, 7, 18, 25–9, 110, 122–5, 148–56, 158–66, 168–70, 189–92, 194–204, 215–16, 218, 227–32, 244, 253–4, 257–8, 261, 267, 275–7, 311, 313
Hussein, Saddam 4, 50, 119, 169, 172, 181, 209

iDAG 287
Imandi, Marten 112, 117
Independent 74, 78, 172–5, 181
Inslaw Inc. 198, 247, 249
Intelligence & Security Command 95
Interfor Report 78–89, 139, 141, 181–2, 219, 224, 237–8, 251, 256, 266, 291, 302, 318
Iran 13, 17, 20, 32, 34, 70, 83, 102, 112, 117, 135–7, 142, 166, 174, 184–6, 188, 197, 236, 241

Iranian Airbus 1, 11, 13, 17, 20, 143
Iraq 4, 181, 190, 209, 262
Israel 4, 19, 106, 183, 185
Israeli Defence Forces 143, 225

Jafaar, Khalid Nazir 29–30, 47–8, 83–6, 146, 170, 180, 196, 229, 239–40, 246, 263, 267, 301–3
Jafaar, Sami 152–4, 156–8, 169–71, 190
Jafaar clan 17–19, 29–30, 152–3, 189–90, 195–6
Jeffries, Jan 58
Jiacha, Abdu Maged 183–4
Jibril, Ahmed 13–14, 16–17, 19, 47, 82, 84–5, 119, 175–6, 181, 185, 187, 235, 242
Johnston, David 46
Jones, Michael F. 46–7, 138, 226, 274

Kabbara, Zouher & Nadim 152, 189–90
Kappler, Lt Gen. James 92
Kasikopu, Andreous 154
Keefe, James 88–9
Keenan, Brian 130
Kenaan, Gen. Ghazi 130, 132, 167–8
Khomeini, Ayatollah 13
Khreesat, Marwan Abdel 14–16, 71, 74, 82, 118, 179
Kimbrough, Walton 33–4
King, David 200–1
Kohn, Aaron 58
KPI Report 53–4, 56
Kreindler, Lee 235, 238, 270, 291–2
Kurz, Anat 185

Langotsky, Yossi 53
Larnaca 121, 151, 190, 195
Lasser, Stanley 169–70
LBC 106
Leavy, Thomas J. 3, 7, 22, 63–4, 94, 149, 210–12, 216–17, 221, 231, 245, 288–90, 307
Lebanese Army 209
Lebanon 3, 17–19, 102, 121, 196, 204, 208–11, 262
Leppard, David 74, 81, 112–13, 116, 178, 238–42, 277
Lester, Jocelyn see Coleman, Jocelyn
Levin, Jerry 129–30
Libya 16, 20, 34, 44, 70, 73–4, 76, 82, 113, 117, 119, 125–8, 168, 172–9, 182–8, 239, 241, 270–1, 299, 301
Libyan Arab Airlines 183–4
Lindsey, John 139

Lockerbie 1, 12, 20, 45–6, 48, 116, 172–3, 186
  Incident Centre 48, 112
Lovejoy, David 19, 143, 201, 225, 236, 256–8, 275
Luqa Airport 72–4, 178, 183–4, 236

McAteer, Det. Insp. Watson 178, 241
McCarthy, John 130–1
McCloskey, James B. 65–6, 68, 91–2, 94, 110, 121, 231, 248–9
McDermott, Martin 192
McFarlane, Robert 102, 135–6
Mack, Linda 218
McKee, Major Charles 45, 83, 85, 143, 204, 206, 235–7
McLaughlin, Ann 114
MacMichael, David 251–4
MacQuarrie, James 11
Magharian, Berkev & Jean 169–71
Mahan, Danny 60–1
Maier, Kurt 300
Major, John 186
Malta 73–4, 76, 89, 112–13, 173, 176, 178, 181, 183, 236, 239, 270–1, 299
Marchetti, Victor 181
Maroni, Walid 210
Martin, Conrad 247
Martz, Ron 200, 251–5, 257–8, 261, 267
Mayer, Hartmut 42, 44, 166, 220–1, 233, 245–6, 277
Megrahi, Abdel see al-Megrahi
Merritt, John 77, 81, 118–19, 141, 237–8
MI6 95, 98, 106
Middle East Media Operations 161
Middle East Television (MET) 95–7, 102, 105
Mikalis, Sgt 155–6
Miller, Marshall Lee 26–8, 120, 147, 213
Miller, Neal 192, 205–6
Mills, David 159–60, 218
Mims, Lambert 37
Mobile 5, 21, 23–4, 35–7
Mogamarat 167, 170–1
Moghrabi, Mahmoud see al-Moghrabi
Mohtashemi, Ali Akbar 13, 187, 241
Moran, James B. 214, 216, 243–5, 255
Mossad 15, 17, 19, 42, 84–5, 102, 194, 292
Mowat, Sheriff Principal 276
Mueller, Robert 182, 184
Mugraby, Dr Muhamad 210
Munich Olympics 41–2, 152, 166
Mutual Radio 126–7, 159

Nader, Pierre Abu 107
NARCOG 149, 151–3, 155, 159, 161, 163–4, 166, 168, 170, 192, 198, 201, 204, 207, 220
National Alliance of Lebanese Americans (NALA) 208, 210
National Intelligence Academy 191–2, 259
National Security Agency 92, 139, 223, 224
NBC News 20, 22, 45, 145–6, 159, 180–1, 206–7, 217–18, 266–7, 275, 295
Neuss 14–16, 112–13, 117
New York 255, 259–60, 262, 265, 269, 287, 291
New York Post 53
New York Times 172, 186
Newsday 184
Newsweek 159, 218
Newton, Wayne 159
Nicosia 18, 25, 29, 50, 121, 146, 149, 154, 161, 164, 192–3, 195
Nidal, Abu 82, 84, 167
Niknam, Hussein 143
North, Lt-Col. Oliver 16, 48, 101–2, 107–8, 110, 130, 135–6, 159, 166, 200, 256

Observer 71–2, 77–81, 84, 88–9, 113–14, 118, 141, 174, 179, 186–7, 237–8, 254, 266
O'Connor, Bonnie 184
Olmert, Yossi 185
O'Neill, Roland 88–90, 140, 274
Operation Blessing 108
Operation Corea (Courier) 80, 86, 88, 146, 180, 236, 263
Operation Dome 193
Operation El Dorado Canyon 126, 159
Operatoin Goldenrod 152–3, 158, 169
Operation Polar Cap 169, 190
Operation Shakespeare 3, 23, 56, 192, 211, 216, 260, 290
Operation Steeplechase 101, 105–6
Operations Sub-Group on Terrorism 152
Orr, DCS John 48–9, 51, 71–2, 74, 112
Overseas Press Services Inc. 102–3
Owens, Richard 169

Palestine Liberation Organization (PLO) 163, 183, 187, 194
Pan Am 2, 19, 46, 50–6, 71–6, 82–5, 89–90, 114–16, 138–41, 207, 215, 217–18, 220, 239–40, 311–14, 318

Flight 103 1, 12, 19, 30, 48, 53, 80, 85, 88, 118–19, 143, 145, 206
lawsuits 78, 81, 137–8, 145, 180–1, 222–6, 233–5, 255–6, 264–8, 270–80, 291, 294, 298–301, 311–15
Pan American World Services 270
Parkinson, Cecil 50–1
Passic, Gregory 169
Pavlick, Michael 152, 170
Pedemonti, Richie 60–1
Pentagon 7, 26, 94, 209, 216
Phillippo, Ron 38
Philps, Alan 185
Pindling, Lyndon O. 63–4
Pindsorf, Bert 221, 233, 245, 277
Plaskett, Thomas G. 114–15, 139, 271, 294–5
Platt, Judge Thomas C. 140–2, 144, 233–5, 240, 242, 255, 271, 274, 278
Popular Front for the Liberation of Palestine–General Command (PFLP–GC) 13–17, 19, 47, 49–50, 70–5, 82, 84, 112, 117, 119, 142–3, 167, 174–5, 177–9, 185, 187–8, 198, 235–6, 302
Private Eye 51, 185–6
PROMIS Ltd 197–8, 247, 249

Racep, Ali 84
Rath, Volker 185
Rather, Dan 67
Reagan, Ronald 152, 157–8, 184
Rebmann, Kurt 80
Reefe, James 274
Reich, Rocky 36
Reno, Janet 303–4
Richardson, Elliot L. 247–9
RKO Radio Network 59
Robertson, Pat 48, 95–7, 101–3, 109–10, 159, 231
Robertson, Tim 96–7, 106, 109
Rockwell, Norman 57
Rogers III, Capt. Will 13
Romeo 95–6
Rosenthal, A.M. 186
Ross, Judge Allyne 141, 224, 238
Ross, Brian 22, 29, 146, 159, 218, 255–6, 261, 276
Rowan, Roy 235–8, 240, 251, 255–6, 260–1, 284

Salazar, Raymond 114–15
Salinger, Pierre 49, 146, 186–7, 218, 252, 255–6, 262–3, 275
Sands, Jim 35

Sarnoff, Robert W. 38
Sasser, Col. John 110, 121–2, 124, 158
Saudi Arabia 67–8, 258
Schafer, Michael *see* Franks, M.
Schreiber, Manfred 42
Schweitzer, Peter 67–8, 258
Shaughnessy, James M. 81, 87–9, 138–45,
    147, 222–7, 230–1, 233–4, 236–7, 244,
    256, 271–80, 292–4, 297, 318
Shaw, Connor 32
Silverman, Ira 159
Singlaub, Gen. John K. 101–2, 110
Skunk Kilo 154–5, 157
Sleigh (Sly), Robert 205, 282–7
Slizewski, Tom 257
Smith, Raymond 114
Soldier of Fortune 228–9, 252, 254, 257–8
Starnes, Evelyn 126–7
Steele, William H. 23–4
Stephen, Andrew 114
Stetham, Robert 152
Stringer, Howard 67
Suit, W. Dennis 102–3, 159–60
Sunday Correspondent 111
Sunday Telegraph 53
Sunday Times 49, 74, 81, 112–13
Sweden 112, 117–18, 221, 233, 243–4,
    246, 251, 281–3, 287–8, 290,
    297, 305–6
Swire, Dr James 184–5
Syracuse Post Standard 223
Syria 14, 16–20, 50, 70, 82, 102, 115,
    117–19, 131–2, 153, 165, 168, 172,
    174, 181, 184–6, 188, 208–9, 241,
    302–3, 316

Talar, Abou 154
Talb, Mohammed Abu 16, 73, 112, 117,
    183, 233, 277
Teresa, Mother 221, 247
Terrell, Jack 200
Thatcher, Margaret 49–51, 70
Theodolus, Mike 254
Thompson, Charlie 28
Time 235–41, 251, 256, 258, 260–1,
    264–7, 284, 295
Times 47, 78, 185, 251
Traficant, James 78–9, 81, 139
Trelford, Donald 187
Tribune-Review 237

Tripiccio, Ray 22, 261
Tripoli 113, 125–7, 173, 175, 184, 186
Tunayb, Major Khalil 301
Turner, Ed 130
Tuzcu, Kilin Caslan 88–90, 140, 274
TWA 747 hijack 152, 156

Unclassified 251–2
United States
    Department of Defense 94, 97, 251
    Justice Department 23, 81, 183, 198,
        214, 222, 244–5, 247, 249, 262,
        272–3, 276, 278, 280, 288, 297, 304
    State Department 18–20, 53, 85, 88,
        139, 209
US Aviation Underwriters 291

Van Atta, Dale 50
Vincennes, USS 1, 11, 13, 20

Waite, Terry 130–1, 185
Wallace, Mike 290–6
WAPI-TV 57
Washington Journalism Review 265,
    269, 287
Washington Post 50, 238–9, 241
Watson, Peter 270
WBZ-TV 58
Webster, William 139
Wehbe, Nabile 84
Werbell III, Lt Gen. Mitchell 103
Westinghouse 58–9
WFSB-TV 60–1
Whelen, James 101
Whitaker, Lawrence G. 178, 241
White House press corps 59–60
Wilkinson, Paul 174–5, 185
Williams, Hollis 226
Wilson, Edmund 20
Windels, Marx, Davies & Ives 81, 138
WMAR-TV 65–6
Woonie Radio 36–7
WSGN 58, 126, 129
WTN 131

Yeffet, Isaac 53–4
Younis, Fawaz 152–4, 156–7, 169,
    190, 218

Zurich 126, 128, 170